POEMS FROM BL MS HARLEY 913
'THE KILDARE MANUSCRIPT'

EARLY ENGLISH TEXT SOCIETY
O.S. 345
2015

Womā man þe man if wille. Whar þo wol pilt hir to:
þis þe resun a' skille. þ ye deuil cō hir furst to,
Gete þe seid of þis appil. if þ þou wolt with be.
þe worþ alwiati of unizt a' wille: al god hī silf i cinre
hi mad wit þ appil i zecte. þ þe sin nas i do:
glad was þe deuil wol ze wirt. for þe sorolk þ he sold to.
of padis hi wer ute pilt. whip fuail har luieledo to wiue:
a' ure flemid for har gilt. a' neu efte padis to cō mue.
In þe ude of ebir-hil luieladd he moft slymk sore:
Wiþ sorolk a' care a' drere. Won he luied. iii. zer a' more.
Afur if lif þ he þad þei: neois he moft wend to helle:
for þe þat þ he did her: þ he moft bite a' dlkelle.
God makid makiu more. ok to helle þe deuil ha lize:
i eū hā tid pro i lore. nō fin hi fcapid nozt.
god if þþitus to hā fend. a' feid hob hi fold be filuid:
as bi moifel þ am wend. a' ze þe þþitea ite i fiuid.
god wift wel bi pillt fay. þ bi no man þ was þ cor:
Whan bi þþis no bi lai. þ cōmuetich hine wer for lor.
þot wkif fort fulfil. god is Angle aud forþ fend:
as bi angle gabiel. þ to þe maid was wend.
fleef he wolt of maid i narr. god a' man if fund to gadir:
a' þ was a gr ma tß. þ þe darur ber þe fader.
ajaid bet heuen kig. þ if al ure caruire:
maid ber þe siber ying. þ for flo ne let nozt hir flur:
god hi zed au erp here. xxx. witer a' fo mdel auo:
af holi wrir vf gan lere. he fuffrid lope pine a' wo.
ajan a zenl god fo gilt. to heuen nō foille ne mizte:
fort god if fone i rore was pilt. a' wan us heuen lizt.

BL MS Harley 913, fol. 30ʳ, 'Fall and Passion', lines 57–112.
Reproduced with the permission of the British Library Board

POEMS FROM BL MS HARLEY 913

'THE KILDARE MANUSCRIPT'

EDITED BY

THORLAC TURVILLE-PETRE

Published for
THE EARLY ENGLISH TEXT SOCIETY
by the
OXFORD UNIVERSITY PRESS
2015

OXFORD

UNIVERSITY PRESS

Great Clarendon Street, Oxford, OX2 6DP,
United Kingdom

Oxford University Press is a department of the University of Oxford.
It furthers the University's objective of excellence in research, scholarship,
and education by publishing worldwide. Oxford is a registered trade mark of
Oxford University Press in the UK and in certain other countries

First edition published in 2015
Impression: 1

British Library Cataloguing in Publication Data

Data available

ISBN 978-0-19-873916-6

Typeset by Anne Joshua, Oxford
Printed in Great Britain
on acid-free paper by
TJ International Ltd, Padstow, Cornwall

ACKNOWLEDGEMENTS

I am grateful to John Burrow for his wise comments on literary aspects; to Robin Frame for advice on the historical context of the manuscript; to Judith Jesch for information on Icelandic texts; to Mike Rodman Jones for his knowledge of Cistercian misbehaviour; and to Ian Short for his generous help with the editions of the Anglo-Norman poems. Helen Spencer, Bonnie Blackburn, and Anne Joshua steered the volume through all stages of its production. Most particularly I must thank Ralph Hanna who, while writing several books of his own, somehow found the time to read this edition for EETS and to make a multitude of suggestions for improvement.

T.T.-P.

CONTENTS

LIST OF ILLUSTRATIONS

LIST OF EDITED POEMS

ABBREVIATIONS

AN	Anglo-Norman
AND	*Anglo-Norman Dictionary*, ed. William Rothwell, Louise W. Stone, and T. B. W. Reid (London, 1992); online at www.anglo-norman.net/
BL	British Library
Chaucer	*The Riverside Chaucer*, ed. Larry D. Benson (Boston, 1987)
CT	Chaucer's *Canterbury Tales*
CUL	Cambridge University Library
Dean	Ruth Dean and M. Boulton, *Anglo-Norman Literature: A Guide to Texts and Manuscripts*, ANTS (London, 1999)
DIMEV	Digital Edition of the *Index of Middle English Verse*, ed. Linne R. Mooney, Daniel W. Mosser, and Elizabeth Solopova, at www.dimev.net
DOE	*Dictionary of Old English A to G online*, ed. Antonette diPaolo Healey, at www.doe.utoronto.ca
DOST	*Dictionary of the Older Scottish Tongue*, online at www.dsl.ac.uk
EETS	Early English Text Society (OS Original Series, ES Extra Series, SS Supplementary Series)
LAEME	*The Linguistic Atlas of Early Middle English 1150–1325*, ed. Margaret Laing, version 3.2 (2013), at www.lel.ed.ac.uk/ihd/laeme2/laeme2.html
LALME	A. McIntosh, M. L. Samuels, and M. Benskin, *A Linguistic Atlas of Late Mediaeval English*, 4 vols. (Aberdeen, 1986)
Langland	*William Langland: Piers Plowman: A Parallel-Text Edition of the A, B, C and Z Versions*, ed. A. V. C. Schmidt, i (London, 1995), ii (Kalamazoo, 2008)
ME	Middle English
MED	*Middle English Dictionary*
MedL	Medieval Latin
MLG	Middle Low German
ODNB	*Oxford Dictionary of National Biography*, online at www.oxforddnb.com

OED	*Oxford English Dictionary*, 3rd edn., online at www.oed.com
OF	Old French
ON	Old Norse
PL	*Patrologia Latina*
RS	Rolls Series
TNA	The National Archives
V&A	Victoria and Albert Museum
Walther, *Initia*	Hans Walther, *Initia carminum ac versuum medii aevi posterioris Latinorum* (Göttingen, 1959)
Walther, *Proverbia*	Hans Walther, *Proverbia sententiaeque Latinitatis medii aevi* (Göttingen, 1963–9)
Whiting	Bartlett J. Whiting, *Proverbs, Sentences, and Proverbial Phrases from English Writings mainly before 1500* (Cambridge, Mass., 1968)

INTRODUCTION

British Library, MS Harley 913 is a small miscellany containing Latin prose and verse, and English and French poems. It has traditionally been known as 'the Kildare Manuscript' because the author of one of the English poems names himself 'Frere Michel Kyldare', though the volume was in Waterford at the Reformation, and may have been written there. Its main scribe was probably a member of the Anglo-Irish Franciscan community; certainly its contents show it to have been a Franciscan production.

I. DESCRIPTION OF THE MANUSCRIPT

s. xiv$^{2/4}$. Vellum. Ff. 64. 140 × 95 mm; writing space very variable, typically c.112 × 66 mm. The hand responsible for the bulk of the texts is a textura semi quadrata with some anglicana forms (see Frontispiece). Size of writing varies from small to very small, and lines per leaf vary correspondingly, e.g. item 2 has twenty-four to twenty-five lines to the page, item 16 has as many as thirty-six. Colour of ink ranges from black to brown, some faded. The conclusion may be that the scribe compiled the manuscript over quite a long period of time. All margins have been cut down, removing all original catchwords and signatures and most pricking. Some pricking is still visible, especially very roughly made on ff. 57 and 60. Parts of the manuscript are very dirty and stained, with some texts difficult to read.

Decoration. Lombards at heads of texts, usually of three or four lines, often quite elaborately infilled, usually red, a few blue. A particularly large and elaborate seven-line blue 'þ' with tail extended to the foot is on f. 20^r, at the head of 'Fifteen Signs'. On f. 48^v, at the start of a new section of 'Seven Sins' (15.60), the 'F' is green infilled with red, the tail extending eight lines.

Binding. Before 1877 (dated note on rear binding leaf), stamped with Harley arms on front cover.

Hands. These have been described in meticulous detail by Michael Benskin, correcting previous accounts.[1] This account follows his.

[1] Michael Benskin, 'The Hands of the Kildare Poems Manuscript', *Irish University Review*, 20 (1990), 163–93.

A: The main scribe. Very variable in size and aspect.

B: Anglicana, perhaps contemporary with A. Latin proverbs on f. 15^r (item 10), continued in top margins of ff. 15^v and 16^r.

C: Secretary, xv$^{2/2}$. On lower half of f. 15^v (item 12), copies B's proverb from the top of f. 16^r, as well as a recipe; titles on f. 25^{r-v} (within item 16) and elsewhere; prophetic verses at foot of f. 53^v (item 38).

D: Anglicana; small and faint. On ff. 23^r–27^v (items 16–18). (The first 16 lines on f. 24^v, originally the start of this section, are A's textura). The hand is perhaps to be identified with hand A writing anglicana.

E: Anglicana, similar to B. On f. 39^r (item 25).

Marginal Hands. Several hands added notes in the margins and at the top of the page. The most persistent of these annotators, a s. xvi hand here designated F, supplied subject guides ('Agaynst pride', etc.) to 'Sarmun' (on ff. 16^r–19^v), 'Fifteen Signs' (ff. 20^v–21^v), 'Fall and Passion' (f. 30^r), 'Ten Commandments' (f. 31^v), 'Song on the Times' (ff. 44^v, 45^v), and the title 'Age' on f. 54^v.

Abbreviations. A good range of abbreviations and suspensions is illustrated in the Frontispiece. One is distinctive, the use of *a'* for 'and' (Frontispiece, ll. 2, 4, etc.), used throughout the English texts, and also appearing for *-an*: 'wo(m)ma(n)' (Frontispiece, l. 1). The tironian nota (l. 14) is rarely used for 'and'. Very common but not illustrated here is *i^c* for 'ich'; the full form is used only nine times (4.94, 112; 13.5, 87, 127, 177; 14.85, 132; 19.42).

Other abbreviations are those standard for English texts. A tilde represents the nasal, *m* or *n*, as ll. 2 'co(m)', 4 'i(n)'. A curl after *u* represents *er*, as in ll. 8 'neu(er)', 14 'eu(er)'. An upward loop after final *-r* represents *e*, as ll. 12 'her(e)', 23 'ber(e)'. The same loop represents *er* after *þ* in l. 12; 'þer' is also written as *þ* with superscript *e*. Rarely *h'* (not illustrated here) represents *her*, as 'h(er)ring 4.10, 'h(er)inne' 5.6, but sometimes it is merely a flourish as in 'mich'el' 4.1, 'betach't' 22.36. A superscript vowel is commonly used to represent *r* + vowel, as here in ll. 4 't(ri)nite', 7 't(ra)uail', 9 'eb(ro)n', 12 't(re)pas', 13 'b(ro)ʒt', 14 'f(ra)m'. A line through the foot of *þ* is for *ar*, as in l. 7 'þ(ar)adis'; *þ* with a loop stands for *pro*, as l. 15 'p(ro)phetis'. 'That' is always *þ^t* (l. 2). Numerals are most commonly roman, so l. 10 *ix* with superscript *c* is for '900'.

Layout and Punctuation. The layout of the poems is remarkably varied. 'The Land of Cokaygne' (ff. 3ʳ–6ᵛ) is set out elegantly in single lines with about twenty-five lines a side. Punctuation is by punctus at the end of the line and in lists within the line (e.g. 2.58, 'cherch . cloister . boure and halle'); the paragraphing (by '//') is not rubricated. 'Satire' (on ff. 7ʳ–8ᵛ) with its longer lines is set out at thirty lines a side; it is unpunctuated, but the rhymes are linked by lines in the right margin, even though the third and fourth lines of the stanza are unrhymed. 'The Song of Michael Kildare' (ff. 9ᵛ–10ʳ) is much more cramped, at sixty lines a leaf, the first stanza set out as prose with line-divisions indicated by punctus, otherwise the first eight lines of each stanza set out side by side, divided by a vertical line, the last two lines running across the page divided by a punctus.

In general, paragraphing of the poems is very variable; often there is none, but 'Lullaby' on f. 32ʳ⁻ᵛ has a rubricated paraph at the head of each stanza and an unrubricated 'Þ' before the fifth line of each stanza (beginning 'Lollai').

In the middle of f. 48ᵛ 'Seven Sins' switches from six-line tail-rhyme stanzas to short couplets; the scribe sets out the tail rhymes to the right, then, following a rubricated lombard 'F', writes each couplet on one line with a mid-line punctus elevatus and a final punctus.

In the rhyme-beginning poem 'Repentance of Love' on f. 58ʳ the scribe has left space for rubricated letters at the beginning of each stanza to highlight the rhyme, but uniquely omitted to fill them in.

The title 'XV signa ante iudicium' is written in red at the head of 'Fifteen Signs', perhaps by Hand B. Otherwise the English poems do not have original titles, though Hand F has added 'Age' at the start of 'Elde' (item 39). The second of the alliterating French verses (item 11) is headed 'Proverbia comitis Desmonie', and the 'Walling of New Ross' (item 40) has the rubric 'Rithmus facture ville de Rosse'. A number of the Latin texts have descriptive titles or rubrics, as noted.

Blank Pages. The following pages are, or were originally, blank: ff. 1ʳ, 2ᵛ, 15ʳ (now hand B), 24ʳ, 39ᵛ, 54ʳ. It looks as though 24ʳ has been washed to erase scribbles. Scribe A has left considerable space unfilled on 15ᵛ, 22ᵛ, 23ᵛ, 29ʳ, 39ʳ (now with hand E), 44ʳ, 58ʳ.

Structure. The binding is tight and catchwords and quire signatures have been cropped, so that the structure is difficult to determine. Sewing is visible between ff. 7–8, 16–17, 24–5, 33–4, 43–4, 51–2, 58–9 and 62–3.

The manuscript now begins with a bifolium blank on one side (1^r and 2^v). The present collation is thus:

1^2 (ff. 1–2); 2^{10} (ff. 3–12); 3^8 (ff.13–20); 4^8 (ff. 21–8); 5^{10} (ff. 29–38); 6^{10} (ff. 39–48); 7^6 (ff. 49–54); $8^{8 \text{ (lacks 7, 8)}}$ (ff. 55–60); 9^4 (ff. 61–4).[2] See Fig. 1.

It is evident from examining the disposition of individual texts that this is very different from the original order and that some leaves are now missing. First, the disarrangement. In the fourth quire the Portiuncula Indulgence material begins with 'The *Tractatus* of Francesco della Rossa Bartholi' (item 16) in the middle of f. 25^r, continuing on the verso, and ending on f. 23^{r-v}, leaving the lower half of f. 23^v and the whole of f. 24^r blank. 'The Letter of Theobald' (item 17) begins on f. 24^v and is completed on f. 26^{r-v}, followed by 'The Testimony of Friar Michael Bernardi' (item 18) beginning five lines down on f. 26^v, continuing on f. 27^{r-v} and completed in the middle of f. 25^r. The original order indicated by the contents is 24, 26, 27, 25, 23. Thus in the modern quire 4 the central two bifolia have become separated into single leaves and subsequently misbound.

'Seven Sins' (item 15) begins on f. 48^{r-v} (the end of quire 6) and is continued in quire 4 on f. 22^{r-v}, breaking off to leave most of f. 22^v blank. This implies that f. 48 is a misplaced single leaf .'Song on the Times' (item 33) begins at the top of f. 44^v and runs through to f. 47^v, after which it is interrupted by the beginning of 'Seven Sins', followed by three short texts on f. 49, then 'Pers of Bermingham' (item 36) on ff. 50–1, before 'Song on the Times' concludes on f. 52^{r-v}, with 'Recipes' and 'Prophetic Verses' (items 37–8) following on ff. 52^v–53^v. 'Song of the Times' and 'Pers' would run from beginning to end if the two bifolia 50/53 and 51/52 were reversed in the order 52, 53, 50, 51 and followed f. 47. Thus the inner leaves of quire 6 (ff. 40–7) followed by the inner leaves of quire 7 (ff. 50–3) would once have formed a sequence, beginning with short Latin pieces (items 26–32).

In the seventh quire f. 54^r is blank, and 'Elde', beginning on f. 54^v, is completed on f. 62^r, now in the ninth quire. Two bifolia, beginning with the blank recto, in the order ff. 54, 62, 63, 49, would make sense of the series of texts there. 'Walling of New Ross' begins in the ninth

---

[2] For a detailed examination see Angela M. Lucas and Peter J. Lucas, 'Reconstructing a Disarranged Manuscript: The Case of MS Harley 913, a Medieval Hiberno-English Miscellany', *Scriptorium*, 14 (1990), 286–99.

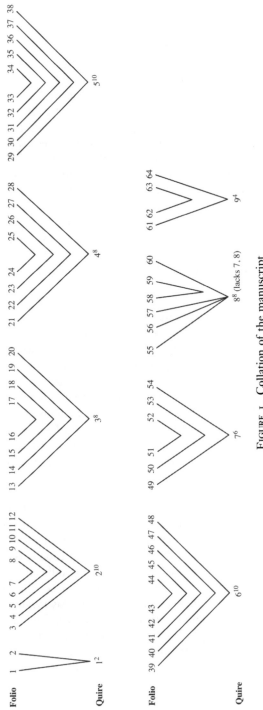

FIGURE 1. Collation of the manuscript

quire, following the order ff. 64, 61, continuing onto ff. 55 and 56 now in quire 8. The bifolium has been reversed, and ff. 55 and 56 consist of two separate leaves pasted onto a stub.

Quires 2–5 and the outer leaves of quire 6 formed a major booklet with texts continuing across quire boundaries, beginning with 'Cokaygne' and ending with 'Song on the Times' and the first lines of 'Seven Sins' (items 2–33). This booklet was apparently followed by what is now the last quire, since next to the beginning of 'Lullaby' on f. 32^r the scribe notes that the Latin version, now on f. 63^v, may be found twelve folios ahead: 'Require ista in latino xii folio'. We may say, therefore, that a booklet consisting of ff. 3–38 + 39 was originally followed by a quire in the order ff. 54, 62–3, 49.

To sum up, insofar as the original order of the surviving leaves can be ascertained, it would have run as follows: ff. 3–21 [loss] 48, 22, 24, 26, 27, 25, 23, 28–38, 39, 54, 62–3, 49, 40–7, 52–3, 50–1, 64, 61, 55–60.

At some date a few folios were numbered in the bottom right corner, and more numbers may have been cropped: f. 28 is '13' and f. 48 is perhaps '9' (both the last leaves of quires), f. 50 is '12', f. 54 is '14', and f. 56 is perhaps '15' (the last leaf of a reconstructed quire). Fifteenth- and sixteenth-century marginal notes imply that by that stage the texts were disarranged. At the foot of f. 3^v is the s. xv catchword 'þ^r is a wel &c' with the puzzling instruction to 'turn ouer i leaf' in a post-medieval hand, indicating that a leaf intervened, though the text continues on the recto, while on f. 5^v is a faint note 'turn back 3' [pages?]. The earlier folio numbers also suggest confusion: 2 is now 2, but 3 was earlier 2, 4 was 3, 5 was 4, 6 was 2 (?), and after that the current numeration is two ahead of the old.

Now the losses. Sir James Ware and his amanuenses copied eleven texts from the manuscript into BL MS Lansdowne 418 (on which see Appendix), five of which are now lost, which suggests that losses from Harley 913 may have been considerable. 'Fifteen Signs' ends incomplete at the foot of f. 21^v with 'Sine reliquid operis facto' written in a s. xvi/xvii hand. On f. 4^v, in the middle of 'Cokaygne', a later hand has written 'hic aliqua videntur deesse', smudged onto f. 5^r, though it is not obvious that 'Cokaygne' has lost text.

Lucas and Lucas observe that the major part of the surviving manuscript (ff. 3–53) is a booklet containing material associated with Kildare: the 'Song of Michael of Kildare' and the English poems stylistically associated with it, as well as the account of Pers of

Bermingham, who was buried in the Kildare friary. The later parts of the manuscript contain two of the four poems, 'Elde' and 'Earth', from outside Ireland, as well as a poem about New Ross. This may indicate that material from different sources was assembled and copied at different times, perhaps in Waterford, where the manuscript was preserved at the Dissolution.

Contents. Latin prose and verse texts occupy half the manuscript.[3] Most of the Latin compositions are found elsewhere in manuscripts from England and the Continent, though one, 'The Abbot of Gloucester's Feast' (item 6), appears to have been composed or at least adapted in Ireland. There are seventeen poems in English, and three in Anglo-Norman.

The evidence for an Irish provenance is quite clear. Two poems deal specifically with events in Ireland: one in Anglo-Norman describes the building of the town wall in New Ross in 1265 (item 40), the other in English celebrates the slaughter of the O'Conors by Pers of Bermingham in 1305 and laments his death in 1308 (item 36). One of the two short Anglo-Norman lyrics (item 11) is ascribed to the earl of Desmond. Furthermore, two items now lost but recorded by Ware refer to the political situation in the town of Waterford and the events of the Bruces' invasion of Ireland, the first text in English and the second in Latin.

Nor is there reason to doubt that the manuscript is a Franciscan production. Of Franciscan interest are a number of the Latin texts: in particular an enumeration of Franciscan custodies and houses across the world, beginning with Irish houses and ending with a boast about their comparative number in Ireland (item 28), a brief extract from Bonaventure's Life of St Francis (31), longer extracts from texts supporting the authenticity of the Portiuncula Indulgence granted to the saint (16–18), as well as a meditation on the body of Christ: 'Hanc meditacionem de corpore Christi composuit Frater Johannes Pecham de ordine Fratrum Minorum' (42).

Christ's sufferings on the cross are also the subject of an English poem embedded in Latin devotions (19), as well as a Latin hymn added by Hand E (25). The English 'Fall and Passion' describes Christ's sufferings as a consequence of man's sin (20). It is one of a

---

[3] These are listed by Neil Cartlidge, 'Festivity, Order, and Community in Fourteenth-Century Ireland: The Composition and Contexts of BL MS Harley 913', *Yearbook of English Studies*, 33 (2003), 33–52, Appendix, pp. 49–52.

group of English verse sermons: one on the subject of the seven sins calls itself 'þis predicacioune' (15.9), another on the vanity of life is 'þis sarmun' (13.238), others are on the ten commandments (21) and the signs before doomsday (14). Friar Michael of Kildare names himself as author of a reflection on the brevity of life and the certainty of death (5.144), and may well be the author of some of the other homiletic poems.

Four other poems in English, 'Christ on the Cross' (19), 'Lullaby' (22), Elde (39), and 'Earth' (48), have linguistic features that distinguish them from the poems composed in Ireland, and versions of 'Lullaby' and 'Earth', together with the brief 'Five Evil Things' (3), are recorded in England and are evidently of English rather than Irish origin.

A broad vein of satire runs through the manuscript. Two of the most striking English poems merrily describe the worldliness of monks ('The Land of Cokaygne', 2) and the shortcomings of towns-people ('Satire', 4), while 'Nego' (44) mocks students of dialectics. In 'Song on the Times' (33) homiletic material about the burdens of life encloses a bitter fable about the corruption of power, while in Latin 'Beati qui esuriunt' (45) is a forthright attack on judicial corruption. Rather more genial are other satires in Latin mocking the misbehaviour of the religious orders in general and monks in particular: their drunkenness and gluttony (6, 41), and their lechery (46). A letter from the Devil (23) ironically praises the religious orders for following his example, while a papal letter in reply deplores their lechery and greed (24), all except for the Dominicans. Evidently this text is a Dominican production in which the Franciscans are censured as much as the other orders, greatly affronting a later reader, who has erased the words 'minores fratres' from the description of Franciscan self-indulgence. There are two Latin liturgical parodies, one an office in praise of sleep (7) and the other a drinkers' Mass (8).

Short Latin items provide useful information, historical notes about the Trojan war (26–7), about the chronology between Adam and Christ (30), some notes from Orosius (32), a list of biblical exemplars of the sins and virtues (34), and recipes for the scribe mixing colours (37). Finally there are a number of proverbs (10, 12) and riddles (35).

Many of the Latin pieces are extracts from much longer works. The impression given is that the compiler jotted down information that he thought interesting or useful as it came into his hands. His interests extended quite widely, and it may be misleading to try to pick out particular agendas. For example, the contents have sometimes been described as anti-monastic, and it is true that monks come in for a fair amount of ribbing in several texts including 'Cokaygne', 'The Abbot of Gloucester's Feast', and others. It cannot be maintained, however, that there is a sustained attack on the monastic orders. It is more satisfactory to see the variety of the texts in Harley 913 as reflecting a range of interests and concerns of Anglo-Irish Franciscans in the early fourteenth century.

Date and Place. The enumeration of Franciscan custodies and houses (item 28) matches a list taken from a record drawn up at the General Chapter of Perpignan in 1331 (see pp. 60–1). Alan Fletcher dates the list *post* 1338 and *ante* 1342, but it reflects the situation *before* the foundation of the English house of Ware in 1338.[4] Other *post quem* dates in hand A are provided by the death of Pers of Bermingham in 1308 (item 36) and the rubric attributing the two French lyrics (11) to 'comitis Desmonie': Maurice fitz Thomas Fitzgerald was created first earl of Desmond in 1329. A date for the manuscript during the 1330s would fit these facts, though, given the variability of hand and layout, it is probable that the manuscript was compiled over quite a long period. This is also suggested by the work of Hand D, the Portiuncula Indulgence material. The extract from Bartholi's *Tractatus* (item 15) describes an episode that took place on 20 February 1328, and later in the work (ch. 40) Bartholi gives 1334 as the year he was given information about another event.[5] Sabatier suggests the work was completed in 1335.[6] The extract in Harley 913 is corrupt and abbreviated, and it seems unlikely that it was copied as early as the 1330s.

In 1904 Wilhelm Heuser entitled his edition of the collection *Die Kildare-Gedichte* mainly on the basis of the attribution of one of the poems to Michael of Kildare. He speculated that the manuscript was written at the Grey Abbey, the Franciscan friary at Kildare, where, he noted, Pers of Bermingham, whose castle was at Carbury in County Kildare, was buried, and he proposed to identify this with the 'þe

[4] Alan J. Fletcher, 'The Date of London, British Library, Harley MS 913 (The "Kildare Poems")', *Medium Ævum*, 79 (2010), 306–10.

[5] *Fratris Francisci Bartholi de Assisio Tractatus de Indulgentia S. Mariae de Portiuncula*, ed. Paul Sabatier, Collection d'études et de documents sur l'histoire religieuse et littéraire du Moyen Âge, ii (Paris, 1900), 86, l. 31.

[6] Ibid., p. c.

mochil grei abbei' in 'Cokaygne' (2.164; see note there). However, on the basis of rhyme evidence, in particular the spelling *chirch* in rhyme (texts 13, 20, 33) against in-line *cherch* and *church*, Michael Benskin has argued that the scribal language is not identical with the authorial language. In his opinion 'there is sufficient evidence to link the non-rhyming language of the Kildare poems fairly firmly with Waterford'.[7] This accords well with the later ownership of the manuscript and its title as reported by Sir James Ware in 1609 (see below). If it is indeed from Waterford, it is contemporary with Cambridge, Corpus Christi College MS 405, a collection important especially for its Anglo-Norman texts including the *Hospitallers' Riwle*, with three English scraps; it is a much larger composite manuscript compiled at the house of the Knights of St John of Jerusalem in Waterford.[8]

History of the Manuscript. On fol. 2[v], otherwise blank, is written 'Iste liber pertinet ad me Georgium Wyse' in a sixteenth-century hand. The Wyse family were early settlers in Waterford.[9] In an account of Harley 913 in *The Popular Songs of Ireland* published in 1839, Crofton Croker identified George Wyse as bailiff of Waterford in 1566 and mayor in 1571, having compared a specimen of his signature in 'the State Paper Office'.[10] Even though profiting at the Dissolution, the family remained Catholic through the Reformation, and probably George Wyse rescued the manuscript from a dissolved friary, perhaps at Waterford or New Ross, or nearby. Another ownership inscription on the blank lower half of f. 29[r] is mainly illegible, but Bliss and Long read it as 'Iste liber pertinet ad Iohannem lambard . . . Waterfordie . . .'.[11] The Lumbards or Lombards served frequently as mayors and bailiffs throughout the century, e.g. James Lombard following George Wyse as bailiff in 1567, and Nicholas serving as mayor in 1568.[12] Peter Lombard (*c.*1554–1625) became Catholic archbishop of

---

[7] Michael Benskin, 'The Style and Authorship of the Kildare Poems—(I) *Pers of Bermingham*', in J. Lachlan Mackenzie and Richard Todd (eds.), *In Other Words: Transcultural Studies in Philology, Translation and Lexicology* (Dordrecht, 1989), 57–75 at 59 and n. 4.

[8] Images and full description available on Parker Library on the Web, http://parkerweb.stanford.edu.

[9] See D. G. Paz, 'Wyse, Sir Thomas (1791–1862)',*ODNB*.

[10] Thomas Crofton Croker, *The Popular Songs of Ireland* (London, 1939), 284. For the Wyses see R. Lincoln, 'A List of the Mayors and Bailiffs of Waterford from 1365 to 1649', *Journal of the Royal Society of Antiquaries of Ireland*, 7th ser. 5 (1935), 313–19 at 317.

[11] Alan Bliss and Joseph Long, 'Literature in Norman French and English to 1534', in Art Cosgrove (ed.), *A New History of Ireland*, ii: *Medieval Ireland 1169–1534* (Oxford 1987), 708–36 at 721. Also legible under ultra-violet light is 'in villa De Suell (?)'.

[12] See Lincoln, 'A List', 317; Cartlidge, 'Festivity', 45.

Armagh, and his *De regno Hiberniae* argued strongly in support of Irish Christianity.[13] On f. 39ᵛ the s. xv inscription 'Sum Richarde Rouse' is just visible.

In 1608 Harley 913 came into the hands of Sir James Ware, auditor-general in Ireland (father of Sir James the Irish antiquary), who transcribed eleven items from Harley 913, five now lost from there, into a miscellany which is now BL MS Lansdowne 418, taken 'out of a smale olde booke in parchment, called the booke of Rosse or of Waterford'.[14] One of these items was the first verse of a poem beginning 'Yung men of Waterford'.

In 1697 Bernard's *Catalogi librorum manuscriptorum Angliae et Hiberniae* listed Harley 913 as no. 784 in the library of John Moore, bishop of Norwich. In 1705 George Hickes obtained the manuscript from Thomas Tanner, later bishop of St Asaph, and transcribed 'Cokaygne' and 'Five Evil Things' into his *Linguarum vett. septentrionalium thesaurus* (i. 231–3). From there it passed to the library of Robert Harley (1661–1724), where it was excellently catalogued by Humphrey Wanley between 1708 and his death in 1726. Wanley certainly found it engaging; he described 'Hore Sompnolentium' ('The Sleepers' Hours', item 7) as 'the Divine Service villainously altered', and called the 'Missa de potatoribus' (item 8) 'even much more villainous (or rather blasphemous)'. With the rest of Harley's library the manuscript passed to the British Museum in 1754.

2. LANGUAGE

In his detailed description of the language, Wilhelm Heuser lists a great many forms from the manuscript, and sets out rhyme words.[15] The seminal analysis of the dialect is by Angus McIntosh and M. L. Samuels.[16] Norman Davis gives an account of the language of another early Hiberno-English text, *Pride of Life*.[17] Forms significant for establishing the dialect are listed below.

---

[13] Terry Clavin, 'Lombard, Peter (*c.*1554–1625)', *ODNB*.

[14] See Appendix.

[15] *Die Kildare-Gedichte*, ed. Wilhelm Heuser (Bonn, 1904), 20–55.

[16] 'Prolegomena to a Study of Mediæval Anglo-Irish', *Medium Ævum*, 37 (1968), 1–11.

[17] *The Pride of Life*, ed. Norman Davis, in *Non-Cycle Plays and Fragments*, EETS ss 1 (1970), pp. xci–xcvii.

Phonology

A. Vowels

The reflex of OE *a* before a nasal is written *a*: *can, gan, man* (but *mon* 48.5), *mani, name, wan* (*LALME*, dot maps 90, 94); 'upon' is usually *apan* (rhyming with *man*), except for *opon* 4.110, 20.144, and *vppon* 33.190, *uppon* 48.63. Before lengthening groups the spelling is *o*: *hond, lond, stond, dronk* pa. sg., *þonk, wome* (OE *wamb*). However, before *ng* the spelling is generally *a*: *lang, sang* (rhyming with *þeramang*), *strang* 19.33 (rhyming with *hond*), apart from *long* 4.115, 48.64, and *song* 4.119.

The reflex of OE *ā* is written *o*: *go, more* (but *mare* 19.29), *sore, wo*.

The reflex of OE *ǣ*[1] is written *e*: *lere* rhyming with *here* 'here' 20.107, *lede* 'lead' with *hede* 'heed' 14.163, *teche*. When shortened it is written *a* in *radde* p.p., and *adradde* p.p., *spradde* pa., which rhyme with *ladde* p.p., *madde, gladde* 5.121–9 (dot map 975).

'There' is *þer*, generally abbreviated, with *þar(e)* in rhyme only.[18] 'Each' (OE *ǣʒhwylc, ǣlc*) is *euch*, apart from *vch* 39.32, *uch* 39.68, *uche* 5.81 (*LALME*, iv. 24, dot maps 88, 89).

The reflex of OE *y* is mostly written *i*: *fille* 'fill', *hil* (dot map 994), *sin(ne)* often confirmed by rhyme, but *sunne* rhyming with *munne* 39.20, *chirch* (always in rhyme), but *cherche* 2.58, *church(is)* 4.34, 5.124 (dot maps 384–6), *gilt(e), biriid* (dot map 973), *miri* (but *meri* 20.212). Before a lengthening group: *bild, ding* 'dung', *mund* 'mind'; *kund* 'kindred', is usual, though 'Song on the Times' has *kind : behind* 33.91, *kund : munde* 33.108, and *kund : bind* imp. 'bind' 33.118 (dot map 1042). The verb 'trust' is *trist* 15.147, but *trusteþ* 39.26 (OE **trystan?*). So also *stinteþ* 'stop' 2.99, *stunt* 39.51 (dot map 1044). OE *ȳ* is usually *i*: *fire* (dot map 409), *fist, hire, litil* (but *lutil* 48.50), *liþer* (but *luþer* 39.19). 'Pride' is *prude* (9×) and *pride* (3×).

OE *e* in closed syllables is written *e* in: *brest, prest, wreche*; *i* in *gist, ʒit* (but *ʒete* 39.17) (dot maps 242–3), *silf* (dot map 520), *sigge* 'say' (dot map 507), *wille* 'well' n.; 'length' and 'strength' are *leinþ* and *streinþ* (dot map 264).

OE *ege*, 'fear', is *eie*; OE *seh*, pa. 3 sg. 'saw' is *sei* (dot map 511), 'die' is *dei* (ON) (dot map 394). *ei* 'eye' (OE *ēge*) rhymes with *hei* (OE *hēh*) 13.90 (dot map 439).

The descendant of OE *feala, fela*, 'many', is written *fale*, rhyming with *niʒtingale* 2.95, *smale* 4.92, *tale* 13.209. For the restricted distribution of this spelling, see dot map 984.

---

[18] See Benskin, 'Hands', 191, and *LALME*, iv. 90–2.

OE *full* appears as *ful(le)* except for *fol(le)* in 'Elde' and 'Earth'.

The reflex of OE *ēo* is written *e*: *lede*, 'land' rhymes with *hede*, 'heed' and *dede*, 'dead'; also infin. *be(n)*; *tre*, *þef*, *lef*, *fend*, *frend*.

OE *īe* (out of *ēa* + *i*-mutation) is written *i* in *hire*, *hird* pa. *ihird* p.p. 'hear' (dot map 1014); *ʒime* 'protect' 13.74 beside *ʒem(e)*.

B. Consonants

Final *-d* is occasionally unvoiced: *fent* 'fiend' 5.57; see Jordan, para. 200. It may be lost altogether after consonants, especially *n* and *l*: *chil* 22.35, *Engelon* 36.15, *nol* 'would not', 20.145, *wol* 20.164, *schef* 'creature' (OE *sceaft*) 22.8, *towar* 14.77. So *beheld* rhymes with *del* 'sorrow' 20.173. The reverse spelling, with addition of *-d*, is found in rhymes: *prisund* 'prison' rhyming with *ibund* 33.131, *nond* 'none' rhyming with *stond* 36.35, *hold* 'whole' rhyming with *gold* 15.138.[19] This is characteristic of Anglo-Irish, according to McIntosh and Samuels.[20]

In the non-Irish poems 'Elde' and 'Earth' final *-þ* may be spelt *-d* (dot map 1177); see 39.7 note.

OE initial *f* spelt *v/u* in *ivette*, *uadir*, *velle*, *uerisse* 'fresh', *verþ(ing)*, *uo*, *vode*, *uorbisen*, *uoxe*. There is the reverse spelling *file* for *vile*. See Jordan, para. 215; dot map 1180.

OE *hw-* is generally spelt *wh-*, but occasionally *w-* (dot map 274): *wan*, *war*, *wat(e)*, *wy*, *wil(e)*, *wo* (dot map 1104). 'Which' is *woch* in 'Seven Sins', *whoch* in 'Song on the Times' (dot map 80).

OE *sc* usually as *sch-* initially, but quite often as *ss*, both initially and after i: *sso* 'she', *ssamles* 'shameless', *ssow* 'show' (also *schow*), *bissop*, *fleisse* 'flesh' (dot map 421) rhyming with *meisse* 'food' (OF *mes*), *fissis*, *neisse*, 'weak', *uerisse*, *þruisse* 'thrush', *waiissing* 'washing', *wirssiþ*. Also as *s*: *anguis* and *angus*, *yrismen*, *sadde*, pa. 'shed' (cf. *schaddist*), *sild* v. 'shield', *worsiþ*. See glossary for forms of 'shall', including *ssal(t)*, *ssul*, *ssold*, as well as *sal*, *sold*, *schal*, *schul*, etc. (dot maps 147–8, 160).

'through' is *proʒ*; 'though' is usually *þoʒ* (dot map 202), but *þeʒ* 5.50, 109, and *þeiʒ* 13.93, 109 twice each, and *þouw* once 48.50 (dot map 197).

Doubling of medial and final consonants, for example: *hoppe*, *clippeþ*, *wrekke*, *ette*, *bitte*, *didde*, *gladde*, *iss*, *wasse*, *hosse*, *nosse*,

---

[19] See Richard Jordan, *Handbook of Middle English Grammar: Phonology*, trans. and rev. Eugene J. Crook (The Hague, 1974), para. 200, n. 3.
[20] 'Prolegomena', 5.

commiþ, berriþ, alles 'awls', *welle*, is characteristic of Anglo-Irish, according to McIntosh and Samuels.[21]

Accidence

A. Nouns

Pl. in *-(e)s, -(i)s,* and once *-eʒ (princez* 2.60), with quite frequent pl. in *-(e)n* from various OE sources: *axen* ∼ *axin,* 'ashes', *breþerin, been, children, ein, eldren, knen, lendin* 'limbs', *meden, schennen* 'shins', *schone, schuldren* (also *schuldres*), *weden.* 'Day' has pl. *daies* and *dawes.* Mutated plurals are *geet, men, ted* 'teeth', etc. Unchanged plurals without ending are OE neuters: *þing, word, wound*; OE fem. *hond*; nouns ending /s/: *fax, spouse*; *hille* (in rhyme) 14.86, *ʒer(e)* and *winter* (after numeral).

Gen. sg.: *-is: deuilis, Goddis,* apart from *Goddes* 4.50, *kinnes* 19.29. Often the ending is written separately, especially after proper names, *Benet is, god is, sowle is, swine is,* etc. For development of this practice see *OED* (3rd edn., 2013), *his* adj. 5. Here the spelling is always *is,* never *his,* suggesting that the scribe did not identify the ending with the adjective. Some genitives without ending: *helle, heuen, sinne.* Gen. pl.: *lordingen, schepen, worme is.*

B. Adjectives

Final *-e* has already lost all significance as a grammatical marker, much earlier than the English south-western dialects.[22] Thus adjectives may have *-e* but are generally without it; in pl.: 'Al is commune to ʒung and old' (2.63), 'riuers gret and fine' (2.45), 'wiþ ʒur gret packes' (4.62); definite adjectives in the sg.: 'þe brod lake' (4.8) 'þe brode crune' (33.62); sg. indefinite adjectives: 'þi felle . . . þat stinkiþ lolich and is blakke' (13.30–2). The form *al* is both sg. and pl.; *alle* is generally, but not always, pl. However, it should be noted that the option of etymological and grammatical final *-e* was still available to careful poets; in the regular metre of 'Song of Michael Kildare' the scribe spoils the rhythm of the first line by dropping *-e* from the first word: 'Swet Iesus hend and fre' (5.1), and again from 'rich men' (5.21), etc.

C. Verbs

Infinitive usually without *-n,* confirmed by rhyme: *go : wo* 14.168, *wend : end* 33.161, *bring : king* 36.104. With *-n* are *spekin* 15.6, and in

---

[21] 'Prolegomena', 5.   [22] Ibid. 8–9.

'Elde' and 'Earth' *hien* 39.6, *feden* 48.14 (confirmed by rhyme), *wroten* 48.18. OE *-ian* verbs may end *-i*: *amonsi* 33.25, *forroti* 15.23, *nemeni* 15.57, *witi* 15.120, *woni* 5.115, *worþi* 'honour' 21.36; and a few verbs from French: *amendie* 15.35, *honuri* 20.152, *robbi* 33.27, *saui* 14.4 (dot map 1193).

Pr. 2 sg. *-ist*, rarely *-est*: *findest*, *wandrest*; also *seiist / seest / sest* 'see'; *worþe* 'become'; *wost*, 'know'.

3 sg. usually *-iþ*, and *-þ* after vowel, as *deþ* 'does', *seeþ*; occasionally *-eþ*: *anueþ*, *benimeþ*, *pisseþ*. A few endings *-it*: *fallit*, *þenchit*, *wexit*. 'Elde' and 'Earth' have (sometimes confusingly) the spelling *-d* for *-þ* (dot map 1177): *answerid* 'answers' 48.25, *blowid* 'blooms' 39.7, *verrid* 'uses' 48.26, *fordede* 'destroys' 39.27 rhyming with *ted* 'teeth' (see above, 'Consonants'). Without ending *bischrew* 'curses' rhyming with *on rewe* 39.32. Syncopated forms are quite common: *bilt*, *bint*, *bit*, *get* and *gette*, *halt* and *holt*, *sent*, *sit* and *sitte*, *trust*, *went*, *wet*, *worþ*.

Pl. forms are the same as 3 sg., usually *-iþ* and *-þ* after vowel, less often *-eþ*, occasionally *-it*: *clippeþ*, *commiþ*, *liuiþ*, *leuith*, *louiþ*, *stiuiþ*, *stinkeþ*, *goþ*, *seeþ*, *wringit*. With syncope: *fint*, *sit*. No ending with pron. immediately following: *ȝiue ȝe* 4.64.

Imp. pl. usually *-iþ* and *-eþ*, but *bind*, *do*, *ȝiue*, *lok(e)*, *ren*, *tak*, *todraw* without ending.

The present participle generally has *-end*, also *-ind* (dot maps 348–9): *ernend*, *roilend*, *wrikkend*, *stinkind*; 'going' is *gond* 15.18; *-ing* in *fleing* 2.124. 'Christ on the Cross' has a variety of forms in rhyme: *glisniing : bleding* 19.17–18; *gredind : deiend* 19.31–2.

Weak pa. and p.p. usually *-id*, occasionally *-ed* (dot map 1196).

Past participles usually have prefix *i-* if there is no other prefix: *iblessid*, *iboȝt*, *ibund*, *icharged*, *icloþed*, *iclung*, *icom*, *ycor*. In strong verbs p.p. is usually without ending, as *iloke*, *ilor*, *ispoke*, though monosyllables ending in a vowel may have *-n*: *gon*, *sene*. Forms of p.p. 'come' are *com*, *come*, *icom*, *icommen*, *icommin*.

For forms of anomalous verbs see the glossary, s.v. *be*, *hab*, *mai*, *sal*, *wol*.

D. Personal Pronouns

1 sg.: nom. most commonly *i^c* (here expanded to *ich*), *ich* (8×), *ihc* 13.54, *y* 33.104, 39.30, *i* (2×);[23] acc. dat. *me*, *mei* (rhyming with *belami* 33.107); gen. *mi(ne)*.

2 sg.: nom. *þou*; acc. dat. *þe*; gen. *þi(ne)*.

<hr>

[23] See *LALME* iv. 203–4; Benskin, 'Hands', 190.

3 sg. m.: nom. *he*; acc. dat. *him*; gen. *(h)is*.

f.: nom. *ʒo, ʒho, sso* (dot maps 13, 20; instances in 'Fall and Passion' only); acc. dat. gen. *hir*.

n.: nom. acc. dat. *(h)it*; gen. *is*.

1 pl.: nom. *we*; acc. dat. *us, vs(e), ous*; gen. *ur(e), oure*.

2 pl.: nom. *ʒe, ʒow* 4.57; acc. dat. *ʒow, ʒou, ʒeu* 5.39 (or nom.); gen. *ʒour(e), ʒur(e)*.

3 pl.: nom. *hi, i, þai* (dot maps 31, 36); acc. dat. *(h)am* (dot map 45); gen. *(h)ar, her* (dot map 57).

þai is also used as an indeclinable demonstrative pron. 'those': contrast *þai* and *hi* in 33.26: 'Al þai, whate hi euir be'; see Glossary.

Vocabulary

A very few words are of Irish origin. Two are in 'Satire': *tromcheri* (4.106) is from Irish *tromchroí*, 'liver'; *corrin*, 'drinking vessel' (4.43), also found three times in the Latin 'The Abbot of Gloucester's Feast' (text 6) as *currinum*, is of Celtic origin (cf. Irish *cuirin*). 'Land of Cokaygne' has *russin*: 'snack' (2.20), Irish *ruisín*. 'Pers' uses *keþerin*, 'footsoldiers, kern' (36.104) of the O'Conor contingent invited to the dinner. It is noteworthy that these words occur only in the satirical and political pieces.

Dialect

The verb inflexions are sufficient to associate the dialect with the language of the south west and south-west Midlands, with infinitive *-i* for OE *-ian, -þ* as the ending of pr. 3 sg. and pl., and the p.p. prefix *y-*. The 3 pl. personal pronouns *hi, ham*, and *har* have similar distribution. Some other words and forms are more restricted, and McIntosh and Samuels, 'Prolegomena', demonstrate that they point to no one area, but that a number of south-western dialects are involved. This is confirmed by *LALME*'s County Dictionary. So *hab* 'have' (infinitive) is Gl as is *ssold* 'should'; *ssal* 'shall' sg. is Ex, Gl, Som, Wlt; *euch* is Gl, Hrf; *ʒo* 'she' is Gl, Wor, Wlt, and *ʒho* Wlt, with *sso* only recorded as a minority Gl form; *woch* for 'which' is recorded in Gl, Ha; *streinþ* is Gl, Hrf, Sal; *hire* 'hear' is Dvn, Gl, Hrf; *fale* 'many' is Gl, Som; *togadir* is Hrf; *proʒ* is Hrf, Sal. Yet *stid* is recorded further north, Chs, La. Medieval Hiberno-English is an amalgam of features from various south-western dialects, reflecting the origins of the majority of settlers.

Four poems, 'Christ on the Cross', 'Lullaby', 'Elde', and 'Earth', betray their non-Irish origins in a few forms and rhymes. In the first of these the scribe corrects his usual form *more* to *mare* to rhyme with *þare* (19.29). In 'Lullaby' *wore* 22.4, generally an EMidl. form, is needed for rhyme in place of scribal *were* (dot map 133), *iborn*, etc. in place of scribal *ibore* etc. 22.25–8 (see note); *gest*, *ikest* instead of scribal *gist*, *icast* 22.31–2; the form *betacht* is written for *betoght* rhyming with *wroȝt* 22.36. In 'Elde' infinitive *-en* is retained in *done* : *shone* 39.38–9; 'each' is *vch* 39.32, *uch* 39.68, 'yet' in rhyme has been altered from *ȝite* to *ȝete*, and OE *y* is rounded so that 'trust' is *trusteþ* 39.26 rather than *trist*, 'sin' is *sunne*, 'stint' is *stunt* 39.51. So, too, in 'Earth', 'little' is *lutil* 48.50, 'man' is *mon* 48.5, 'though' is *þouw* 48.50, infinitive *-en* is retained in *wroten* 'writhe' 48.18, infinitive *feden* rhymes with pl. *meden* 'rewards' 48.14. 'How' is *wouw* 39.64; *MED* records the spelling *wou* in Cambridge, Trinity 323 (B.14.39), which *LALME* locates in west Wor. (LP 7721).

3. THE HISTORICAL CONTEXT

In 1169 Dermot Mac Murrough, dispossessed king of Leinster, came to England to solicit help to defeat his Irish enemies. He returned to Ireland with his new army, many from the March of south Wales.[24] When he died in 1171, the English lords and their followers stayed on, among them Maurice fitz Gerald, ancestor of the Geraldines, and hero of *The Conquest of Ireland* by his kinsman, Gerald of Wales. Henry II, alarmed by the lack of royal authority, sailed to Ireland in 1171, and ensured the submission of both the English lords and the Irish kings to the English Crown. However, this did nothing to end conflict. A pattern was established in which Irish and English leaders engaged in temporary alliances to defeat enemies both within and outside their own communities. The new settlers were quick to exploit conflict between the Irish leaders, who in their turn took advantage of rivalry between English nobles.

The period to which these texts relate, a century later, was an especially turbulent time.[25] (See Map for places mentioned.) In 1254 Henry III granted Ireland to his son Edward, though both were

[24] Robin Frame, *Colonial Ireland 1169–1369* (2nd edn., Dublin, 2012), 8–30.
[25] The activities of many of the main players are analysed by Robin Frame, 'Power and Society in the Lordship of Ireland 1272–1377', *Past and Present*, 76 (1977), 3–33, repr. in *Ireland and Britain, 1170–1450* (London, 1998), 191–220.

MAP 1. Map of Ireland

preoccupied with concerns elsewhere, not least with the Barons' War which broke out in 1264.[26] Henry and Edward exercised a measure of control over the colony by promoting factions between the barons in Ireland. There had been discord for some time between the two most powerful English factions, the Geraldines and Walter de Burgh, who had just been created earl of Ulster, and it appears likely that the rebels in England were attempting to use the Geraldines as proxies in

[26] See James Lydon, 'The Years of Crisis 1254–1315', in Art Cosgrove (ed.), *A New History of Ireland* (Oxford, 1987), ii. 179–204.

securing power in Ireland.[27] The *Annals of Connacht* for 1264 record
that 'great war broke out between Macwilliam Burke, earl of Ulster,
and Mac Gerailt [Fitzgerald] this year, and a great part of Ireland was
ruined between them. In this war the earl took all Mac Gerailt's
castles in Connacht, burned his manors and plundered his people'.[28]
On 6 December 1264 the Geraldines, led by Maurice Fitzgerald and
his uncle, Maurice fitz Maurice Fitzgerald, seized Richard de la
Rochelle, the royal justiciar of Ireland, and others at Castledermot
(Co. Kildare) and imprisoned them. In reply Walter de Burgh seized
Geraldine castles and manors in Connacht. The widespread dis-
turbances that followed were 'tantamount to a civil war'.[29]

This dangerous situation was the incentive for the citizens of New
Ross, Co. Wexford, to set about building a defensive wall to encircle
their town, as described here in 'The Walling of New Ross': 'They
were fearful of a war taking place between two lords . . . Sir Maurice
and Sir Walter' (40.10–13). But the wall served equally to protect the
townspeople from another danger, as the poet comments: 'There is
not an Irishman in Ireland so bold as to dare attack it' (40.200–1).
That the warmongering of both the settlers and the indigenous Irish
posed a constant threat to the community is amply borne out by the
events of the years that followed.

By 1289 John fitz Thomas Fitzgerald, nephew of Maurice fitz
Maurice, and later to be created earl of Kildare, had established
himself as lord of Offaly, and indentured a local magnate, Pers (Peter)
de Bermingham, lord of Tethmoy, as a member of his household,
partly to support him in his battles with the Irish of Offaly and
elsewhere, but equally to help him in faction fighting.[30] An obstacle to
fitz Thomas's rise to power was the justiciar, William de Vescy, lord
of neighbouring Kildare. In 1294 fitz Thomas joined Calvagh
O'Conor of Offaly to raid de Vescy's castle of Kildare and destroyed
the county records, and in 1297 he and a group of O'Conors attacked
and robbed the town and castle of Kildare.[31] In the same year, fitz

---

[27] Peter Crooks, ' "Divide and Rule": Factionalism as Royal Policy in the Lordship of
Ireland, 1171–1265', *Peritia*, 19 (2005), 263–307.

[28] Ed. A. M. Freeman (Dublin, 1944), 144.

[29] Lydon, 'Years of Crisis', 183. See Robin Frame, 'Burgh, Walter de, first earl of
Ulster (d. 1271)', and 'Fitzgerald, Maurice fitz Thomas, first earl of Desmond (c.1293–
1356)', *ODNB*.

[30] On his career see Cormac Ó Cléirigh, 'Fitzgerald, John fitz Thomas, first earl of
Kildare (d. 1316)', *ODNB*; Lydon, 'The Years of Crisis', 185–8.

[31] *Calendar of the Justiciary Rolls*, ed. James Mills (Dublin, 1905–14), ii. 190.

Thomas, having long cast envious eyes upon Connacht in the west, rode with Pers of Bermingham and defeated the king of Connacht, Aedh O'Conor, who had raided as far east as Offaly. But fitz Thomas's claims to lands in Connacht and Ulster, both areas where de Burgh was dominant, inevitably brought to a head his simmering quarrel with Richard de Burgh, earl of Ulster, son of his uncle's great rival. Fitz Thomas imprisoned the earl in Lea Castle for three months, an act that led to widespread disturbance. Their dispute was formally settled in 1298, when fitz Thomas agreed to surrender lands in Connacht and Ulster in return for lands belonging to the earl in Leinster and Munster.

Meanwhile Bermingham was still being financed for his battles against the Irish. In 1299, for example, he was funded 'to maintain his war which the Irish felons of the parts of Offaly raise against him'.[32] The lengths to which he took his duties are described in the elegy on his death in 1308, 'Pers of Bermingham'.[33] The poem relates that the Irish of Offaly plotted to kill Bermingham, as well as fitz Thomas and his son-in-law Edmund Butler, the deputy justiciar, and Richard de Burgh, who, once the plot was revealed, all vowed to exact retribution. In the event it was de Bermingham alone who took action. Having, so it appears, reached a settlement with the O'Conors of Offaly, standing sponsor to Calvagh O'Conor's child, he invited them all to a feast on Trinity Sunday 1305. The *Annals of Inisfallen* gives the following account:

Muirchertach Ó Conchobuir Fhailgi [Murtagh O'Conor of Offaly] and In Calbach [Calvagh] his brother, were slain by Sir Piers Bermingham, after he had deceitfully and shamefully invited them and acted as godfather to [the child of] the latter and as co-sponsor with the other. Masir, the little child who was a son of the latter, and whom Piers himself had sponsored at confirmation, was thrown over [the battlements of] the castle, and it was thus it died. And twenty-three or twenty-four of the followers of those men mentioned above, were slain, for In Gaillsech Shacsanach [i.e. 'Saxon foreigner'] (she was the wife of the same Piers)[34] used to give warning from the top of the castle of any who went into hiding, so that many were slain as a result of those warnings. And woe to the Gaedel who puts trust in

---

[32] *Calendar of the Justiciary Rolls*, ii. 286.

[33] For the historical context see John Scattergood, 'Elegy for a Dangerous Man: *Piers of Bermingham*', in *Occasions for Writing: Essays on Medieval and Renaissance Literature, Politics and Society* (Dublin, 2010), 85–106.

[34] She was a daughter of William d'Oddingseles, one of the king's household knights (ex info. Robin Frame).

a king's peace or in foreigners after that! For, although they had [the assurance of] their king's peace, their heads were brought to Áth Cliath [Dublin], and much wealth was obtained for them from the foreigners.[35]

For *The Remonstrance of the Irish Princes* of 1317, this slaughter was the prime example of the brutality of the settlers, who regarded it as a perfectly acceptable action:

For from antiquity they had this wicked and perverted habit which has not yet died out among them but every day becomes stronger and more powerful: when they invite nobles of our nation to a banquet, either at the actual feast or at the time of resting, they mercilessly shed the blood of the unsuspecting invited guests, in this way bringing their abominable feast to an end. After this deadly deed the heads of those whom they have killed are cut off and have been sold to their enemies for money, as did the baron Peter Bermingham, a notorious and well-known double-dealer, in the case of his godfather Maurice [O'Conor] and his brother Calvagh, men of noble birth and renown among us, after inviting them to a banquet on the feast of the most Holy Trinity. On that day after the feast was over, as they rose from the table with twenty-four older men of their retinue, he cruelly killed them and sold their heads at a high price to their enemies. And when he was afterwards accused of this crime before the king of England (that is the father of the present king), the king imposed no punishment on this nefarious double-dealer.[36]

Indeed, the *Remonstrance* continues, this was far from an isolated instance of savagery, and Bermingham was not alone in being rewarded for the heads of the Irish:

Likewise Geoffrey de Pencoyt of the same nation, after giving a feast for Maurice king of Leinster and Arthur his father, men of great nobility and authority, killed them on the same night, as they slept in their beds in his house.

Fitz Thomas himself was another offender:

Furthermore three days after an Irish nobleman, his godfather, had been accidentally killed, not by him but by others, John fitz Thomas earl of Kildare had his head cut off in order to sell it shamefully. . . . Let these few cases, notorious to everyone, suffice on this occasion by way of example from the innumerable vices of that people.

---

[35] Ed. S. Mac Airt (Dublin, 1951), 396.
[36] These three extracts quoted from *Remonstrance of the Irish Princes*, in Walter Bower, *Scotichronicon*, ed. D. E. R. Watt et al. (Aberdeen, 1991), vi. 393–5.

The *Remonstrance* was right to complain that the settlers warmly endorsed such actions, and indeed Bermingham was handsomely rewarded by the justiciar. An entry in the Close Rolls of 2 June 1305 records an order to pay Peter Bermingham £100 'to subdue Irish felons of Offaly of the kindred of the Oconoghors and to decapitate the chiefs of the said lineages. Peter has now sent to Dublin the heads of Moriardagh and Malmorthe Oconoghors, chieftains of those lineages, and also 16 heads of others of the same lineages and their accomplices'.[37] A year later, on 9 June 1306, he was paid another £23 'for beheading of divers felons'.[38] At his death in 1308 he was lauded as 'nobilis debellator Hibernicorum'.[39] The last lines of the poem record that it was commissioned by a supporter of Pers who travelled far to bring back an indulgence. This perhaps suggests that the poet's patron was an official at the Franciscan friary at Kildare where Pers was buried.[40]

The settlers of the succeeding generation were no more peaceable than their elders, and the situation was further inflamed by the invasion of the Scots under Edward Bruce in 1315, later supported by his brother, Robert king of Scotland, as described in Ware's copy of the 'Litera Domini Ade de Briton militis' (see Appendix). The leading Geraldine of the time was Maurice fitz Thomas Fitzgerald, who in 1309 inherited lands in Munster in the south of Ireland.[41] He became embroiled in conflict over his expropriation of de Clare lands in Thomond and Cork after the death of Richard de Clare's infant son Thomas in 1321 and the division of the lands between absentee heiresses. In this Maurice came up against other lords in southern Ireland, including the le Poers, who were established in Waterford, where Maurice also held lands.[42] In 1326 Maurice invaded Waterford and Arnold le Poer, the leading member of the family, fled to Dublin.

[37] TNA (PRO), E 101/233/23, online in *A Calendar of Irish Chancery Letters c. 1244–1509* at http://chancery.tcd.ie/.

[38] *Calendar of the Justiciary Rolls*, ii. 270.

[39] *Annals of Ireland*, in *Chartularies of St Mary's Abbey Dublin*, ii, ed. John T. Gilbert, RS 80 (London, 1884), 336.

[40] *Chartularies of St Mary's Abbey*, ii. 281; *Materials for the History of the Franciscan Province of Ireland, A.D. 1230–1450*, ed. E. B. Fitzmaurice and A. G. Little (Manchester, 1920), 88.

[41] His early career is described by Robin Frame, *English Lordship in Ireland 1318–1361* (Oxford, 1982), 172–220; and idem, 'Fitzgerald, Maurice fitz Thomas'. See also Beth Hartland, 'English Lords in Late Thirteenth and Early Fourteenth Century Ireland: Roger Bigod and the de Clare Lords of Thomond', *English Historical Review*, 122 (2007), 318-48.

[42] See Ciarán Parker, 'Paterfamilias and Parentela: The le Poer Lineage in Fourteenth-Century Waterford', *Proceedings of the Royal Irish Academy*, 95C (1995), 93–117.

In 1327 it was reported that because Arnold gave support to the de Burghs, and 'because of the monstrous words used by Arnold in calling him a "rhymer"' Maurice and William, son of Pers of Bermingham, attacked the le Poers and the de Burghs, 'et multos Poerinorum occiderunt, et fere omnes eorum terras combusserunt et destruxerunt'.[43] Arnold le Poer took refuge in Waterford before fleeing to England, but since Isabella and Mortimer, having just murdered Edward II, were attempting to establish the new regime, they were in no position to offer support. In 1329 Maurice was bought off with the earldom of Desmond, a grant of lands, and a pardon. However, he was very soon in conflict again with William de Burgh, earl of Ulster, and in 1331 he was arrested. It was claimed that he had been involved in a conspiracy with Thomas fitz John, earl of Kildare, and John Bermingham, earl of Louth, and others to declare himself king of Ireland. Whatever the truth of the matter, he was released in 1333. The two Anglo-Norman lyrics ascribed to him in the manuscript complain about the sorrows of being alone and reflect on the foolishness of relying on force. It may be that these lyrics (whether or not by Maurice himself) relate to his situation in 1331, with his imprisonment coupled with the death of his wife, a daughter of Richard de Burgh, but they are primarily exercises in poetic elaboration rather than expressions of personal feelings.

The fragment of 'Young men of Waterford' that survives in Ware's transcript in the Lansdowne manuscript is another indication of a pro-Geraldine orientation of the texts of Harley 913. No doubt its warning to beware of the le Poers reflects the violence between Maurice and his enemies in 1326–7, but it may also reveal local concerns. The le Poers exercised tight control over Waterford, regularly acting as sheriffs of Co. Waterford from at least 1305, when it was agreed that John le Poer 'who is able to chastise to the full all such malefactors of his race and their accomplices, be made sheriff'.[44] Any young man would be well advised to burnish his anvil and prepare to defend his life, as the opening verse recommends.

The destruction and disorder that resulted from the Bruce invasion of 1315–18, coupled with the effects of the disastrous famine of those

---

[43] John Clyn, *The Annals of Ireland by Friar John Clyn*, ed. Bernadette Williams (Dublin, 2007), 189. For the *rymoure* gibe see *Chartularies of St Mary's Abbey, Dublin*, ii. 364; James Lydon, 'The Impact of the Bruce Invasion 1315–27', in Art Cosgrove (ed.), *A New History of Ireland* (Oxford, 1987), ii. 275–302 at 299.

[44] *Calendar of the Justiciary Rolls*, ii. 118.

years and the economic collapse, are reflected in the statutes of the Dublin parliament of 1320.[45] These describe how the rule of law has collapsed to such an extent that the common people are robbed by the rich, who travel round the country with *hobelours*, extorting money and goods and demanding bribes from those who can least afford it:

And inasmuch as the common people of Ireland are greatly distressed and well nigh destroyed, and the lands of Holy Church and of the people are wasted and destroyed by divers evildoers, . . . and others there are also, who are or pretend to be men of birth, and they collect to themselves a great company of hobelers [*hobelours*], idle men and other evil persons against the peace, and other men on foot, who go from town to town, from man to man, demanding presents [*curtoisies*] of money, corn and other kinds of victuals, and if one gives them not at their will, they threaten people with loss of life and limb, and further, they take the goods of honest people, by way of pledge [*en noun de gage*], and hold them until they have their demand.[46]

This is exactly the situation described in 'Song on the Times'. The poet complains bitterly that all love and justice have departed, and that the most powerful are the most evil. Holy Church and the law of the land should exercise their authority to dispel avarice and injustice. Law-abiding men are robbed by 'þos hoblurs' (33.29) who steal their property and silver and demand bribes; they are thrown into prison and held there until they pay up. Instead of upholding the law, the ministers of the King take bribes from these thieves and criminals.

At the centre of the poem is the fable of the fox, the wolf, and the ass, who are summoned for judgement at the court of the lion, the king of beasts. The first two send presents, but the ass gives nothing on the grounds that he is innocent. The fox is accused of stealing geese and hens, the wolf, who comes 'of grete kind', of taking sheep. The king pardons both of them on the grounds that their action was in their nature. But the ass, who admits he has taken a few sage leaves, is sentenced to be dismembered and eaten. Unlike other versions of this fable, this is explicitly political and refers to the corruption and misuse of power by royal officials.

Inevitably there was corruption at all levels of officialdom; indeed some of the most powerful of the King's ministers were convicted of it. In 1325 Alexander Bicknor, archbishop of Dublin, former Treasurer of Ireland and in 1318–19 Justiciar and head of the Irish

[45] Lydon, 'Impact of the Bruce Invasion', 296–7.
[46] *Statutes and Ordinances, and Acts of the Parliament of Ireland, King John to Henry V*, ed. Henry F. Berry (Dublin, 1907), 282–3.

government, admitted he had forged his accounts and defrauded the King of the staggering sum of £1,168. Because of the 'heinousness and enormity of the aforesaid offence', Bicknor was imprisoned and his assets confiscated, yet 'because of devotion to Holy Church and reverence for the episcopal dignity' Edward II ordered that he should be released from prison.[47] As in the poet's fable, the most powerful are treated with most leniency.

Such corruption of power was not, of course, confined to ministers in Ireland, and complaints against crooked officials, particularly in their conduct of purveyance, were commonplace and general, both in the legal record and in literary texts.[48] There is no specific detail in 'Song on the Times' to tie the poem to Ireland in the 1320s, and yet it would certainly fit comfortably with conditions at that time.

As it happens, another complaint poem in the manuscript, 'Beati qui esuriunt', makes the point that these contemporary satires are not necessarily to be seen as commentaries on Irish conditions, even if they resonated with an Irish readership. 'Beati qui esuriunt' describes in detail the corruption of court officials, from judges to sheriffs, none of whom will do anything without a bribe, and who build up vast landed wealth out of their peculation. However, it was probably not composed in Ireland, since it is also extant in two manuscripts of English origin, and reflects anxieties about the judicial system expressed in England as well as Ireland.[49]

4. THE FRANCISCANS IN IRELAND

The Franciscan Order, which arrived in Ireland by 1231, expanded rapidly and within a century was established throughout the south and east of the country.[50] The friary at Waterford was founded before

[47] James F. Lydon, 'The Case Against Alexander Bicknor, Archbishop and Peculator', in Brendan Smith (ed.), *Ireland and the English World in the Late Middle Ages* (Houndmills, 2009), 103–11.

[48] See Michael Prestwich, *Plantagenet England 1225–1360* (Oxford, 2005), 72–6; for a literary parallel see the Harley lyric 'Ich herd men vpo molde' (DIMEV 2198) in *Alliterative Poetry of the Later Middle Ages*, ed. Thorlac Turville-Petre (London, 1989), 17–20.

[49] For the historical context see Anthony Musson, 'Rehabilitation and Reconstruction? Legal Professionals in the 1290s', in Michael Prestwich, R. H. Britnell, and Robin Frame (eds.), *Thirteenth Century England IX* (Woodbridge, 2003), 71–87.

[50] See Niav Gallagher, 'The Irish Franciscan Province', in Michael Robson and Jens Röhrkasten (eds.), *Franciscan Organisation in the Mendicant Context* (Berlin, 2010), 19–42. There is a map of houses in J. A. Watt, *The Church and the Two Nations in Medieval Ireland* (Cambridge, 1970), 179.

1250, and that at Kildare a few years later by William de Vescy and
Gerald Fitzmaurice, ancestor of the earls of Kildare, many of whom
were buried there, as was Pers of Bermingham.[51] Though most
friaries were established in the towns of the English colony, quite a
number were in Irish areas, and at the same time native Irish friars
lived in English houses.[52] Friar John Clyn of Kilkenny, citing a list of
custodies and houses drawn up at the General Chapter at Perpignan
in 1331, named thirty-two Franciscan houses in five Irish custodies,[53]
and Harley 913 (item 28, ff. 41^r–43^r), evidently using the same
source, gives the same number, as well as enumerating the custodies
and houses throughout the world. The list in Harley ends with the
boast that 'Prouincia Hybernie excedit 9 prouincias ordinis in
conuentuum numero et in numero fratrum multo plures'. Notwith-
standing such insular loyalty, interest in the wider world of the Order
was strong. The Franciscans had set up a mission as far away as
China,[54] and Harley's list includes the vicariates of 'Tartarie Aqui-
lonaris' and 'Tartarie Oriental'. Odoric of Pordenone travelled to
China in 1318 in the company of friar James of Ireland, and gave
detailed accounts of cities such as Hangzhou and Beijing.[55] A
thirteenth-century Franciscan manuscript from Ireland, Dublin,
Trinity College MS 347, includes the introductory section of
Descriptiones Terrarum, with references to the author's preaching in
Bohemia, though the copyist stops short of a description of Tartary.[56]
Two Irish friars, Simon Semeonis and Hugh the Illuminator, under-
took a pilgrimage to the Holy Land in 1322–4, of which Simon wrote
a lively account.[57] The Harley scribe's interest in Franciscan activities
abroad is shown by texts 16–18 concerning the validity of the
Portiuncula Indulgence granted to Francis in Assisi, which can
have had little direct application in Ireland.[58]

  At the same time there were many conflicts among the Franciscans,
some throughout the Order and others particular to Ireland. St

---

[51] See Colmán Ó Clabaigh, *The Friars in Ireland 1224–1540* (Dublin, 2012), 12–13.

[52] Watt, *Church and Two Nations*, 177.

[53] Printed in John Clyn, *Friar John Clyn, The Annals of Ireland*, ed. R. Butler (Dublin,
1849), 38–9. Williams gives details of the manuscript copies in *Annals of Ireland*, 21 and 25
nn. 28, 31.

[54] Michael Robson, *The Franciscans in the Middle Ages* (Woodbridge, 2006), 108–18.

[55] Ibid. 115–18.

[56] Ed. in Marvin L. Colker, 'America Rediscovered in the Thirteenth Century?',
Speculum, 54 (1979), 712–26.

[57] The *Itinerarium* is summarized by Ó Clabaigh, *Friars in Ireland*, 194–8.

[58] For details see Headnote on p. 41.

Francis's insistence on absolute poverty needed to be interpreted in the light of the day-to-day running of the Order.[59] An early copy of his deathbed Testament, in which he reaffirmed the importance of holy poverty, begging where necessary to support life, is preserved in Dublin, Trinity College MS 347, mentioned already.[60] Almost immediately after the saint's death, disputes arose between two groups of his followers, the Observants, who insisted on adhering to the strict rigor of absolute poverty, and the Conventuals, who argued that the needs of the apostolate required some relaxation. In his first letter as Minister General written in 1257, St Bonaventure, Francis's biographer, complained of laxity in following the rule which Francis had declared to be the very foundation of the Order, resulting in idleness and unnecessary begging.[61] In 1269, near the end of his life, Bonaventure wrote the *Apologia pauperum*, the classic theological argument in favour of the perfection of absolute poverty as practised by Christ and his disciples.[62] In the brief extract from Bonaventure's biography, the *Legenda maior*, in Harley 913 (item 31), Francis, concerned about the bad behaviour of some of his followers, is assured by God that he will protect the Order. After Bonaventura's death the Conventuals reasserted their position, arguing that the rule was impossibly strict, and in 1311 they set out their arguments before the Pope in open consistory. Neither side ended up satisfied with Clement's arrangements.[63] That the dispute was an issue in Ireland is shown by the denunciation in the *Annals of Inisfallen* for 1311 of a 'dangerous sect . . . They desired (they claimed) to sweat under the rigours of sterner life.'[64] In the 1320s Pope John XXII attempted to settle the issue by decreeing that the rule should be relaxed.[65] The fiercest critic of the Franciscans was to be one of the Anglo-Irish, Richard FitzRalph, archbishop of Armagh, who argued in his *defensio curatorum* of 1357 that it was illogical to have an order founded on the evil of poverty.[66] The 'Satire' makes light-hearted reference to an

---

[59] The classic account is M. D. Lambert, *Franciscan Poverty* (London, 1961); also Gordon Leff, *Heresy in the Later Middle Ages* (new edn., Manchester, 1999), 51–166.

[60] Ó Clabaigh, *Friars in Ireland*, pp. xiv–xv; Marvin L. Colker, *Trinity College Library Dublin: Descriptive Catalogue of the Medieval and Renaissance Latin Manuscripts* (Aldershot, 1991), i. 714–26.

[61] Robson, *Franciscans*, 85–8; Lambert, *Franciscan Poverty*, 124.

[62] Lambert, *Franciscan Poverty*, 127.   [63] Ibid. 195.

[64] Quoted by Ó Clabaigh, *Friars in Ireland*, 149.

[65] Lambert, *Franciscan Poverty*, 208–46. Robson, *Franciscans*, 130–40.

[66] Cited by T. P. Dolan, 'Langland and FitzRalph: Two Solutions to the Mendicant Problem', *Yearbook of Langland Studies*, 2 (1988), 35–45. See Katherine Walsh, *A*

abuse which was to be treated much more savagely by writers such as Langland, that the followers of St Francis included many beggars who had no need to beg. The phrase 'bold begger' used in the 'Satire' (4.28) is that also used by Langland to refer to the able-bodied who ought to earn a living: 'Bolde beggares and bygge that mowe here breed byswynke' (C.8.223). Langland, like others at the time, held that friars should have secure provision, 'a fyndynge' (C.22.383), so that they could have 'bred withouten beggynge' (C.5.174).

There was also discord on quite another front. The first hints of this are expressed by Nicholas Cusack, the Franciscan bishop of Kildare, who warned Edward I that 'certain religious of the Irish tongue (*lingue hibernice*)' were disturbing the peace.[67] In 1291 it was reported that at the general chapter of the Franciscans at Cork the Irish brothers squabbled with their English confreres and killed many of them.[68] Such ethnic tensions lie behind and help to explain the conflicts between the Franciscans during the Bruce invasion, when the Scots appealed for support from their fellow Gaels. Robert Bruce wrote to the inhabitants of Ireland that 'we and you, and our people and your people, free since ancient times, share the same national ancestry and are urged to come together more eagerly and joyfully in friendship'.[69] Many native Irish Franciscans responded eagerly, but solidly English friaries such as that at Dundalk in the north east were attacked and burnt, their libraries destroyed. John Clyn reported that in June 1315 'Scoti cum Hibernicis combusserunt Dondalk et locum Fratrum spoliarunt libris, pannis, calicibus, vestimentis, et multos occiderunt'.[70] In September of that year Edward II instituted an enquiry into the loyalty of the Franciscans, complaining that native Irish friars were in league with the Scots and were preaching sedition, and asked the minister general to discipline those who were supporting Bruce.[71] In 1317 Pope John XXII threatened to excommunicate those who preached against the king, in the same year as the Irish

---

Fourteenth-Century Scholar and Primate: Richard FitzRalph in Oxford, Avignon and Armagh (Oxford, 1981), 349–451.

[67] Ó Clabaigh, *Friars in Ireland*, 31.

[68] For discussion of the incident see Niav Gallagher, 'The Franciscans and the Scottish Wars of Independence: An Irish Perspective', *Journal of Medieval History*, 32 (2006), 3–17.

[69] Quoted by G. W. S. Barrow, *Robert Bruce and the Community of the Realm of Scotland* (4th edn., Edinburgh, 2005), 408.

[70] Clyn, *Annals of Ireland*, ed. Williams, 163.

[71] Ó Clabaigh, *Friars in Ireland*, 36; Gallagher, 'The Franciscans and the Scottish Wars', 7–8.

princes sent him their *Remonstrance*, complaining about the brutality
of the colonists, and singling out a certain Friar Simon of the order of
Friars Minor for 'claiming that it is no sin to kill an Irishman of Irish
birth and if he himself were to commit such a deed he would
nonetheless celebrate mass'.[72] It is within this setting of racial
hatred that we can understand the vitriol of 'Pers of Bermingham'.

After Edward Bruce's death in 1318, measures were taken to
reduce the danger of seditious friars. In 1324 a papal investigation
led by William Rudyard, dean of St Patrick's, Dublin, was set up, and
found that the loyalty of the houses of Cork, Limerick, Buttevant,
Ardfert, Nenagh, Claregalway, and Athlone was unreliable, and that
their native Irish friars should be dispersed to other houses and
'should live communally and mixed throughout all the houses of their
Order in Ireland'.[73]

The contents of Harley 913 need to be seen in the context of the
society in which Anglo-Irish Franciscans were so deeply enmeshed,
the tensions both religious and ethnic within the Order itself, the
conflicts between Anglo-Irish lords and between the settlers and the
native Irish, and beyond all that the political and religious develop-
ments in the wider world. There is a further element to the contents
of the manuscript: their practical value in the day-to-day preaching
mission of the friars, and this is most directly represented by the
English poems.

5. THE LITERARY CONTEXT OF THE ENGLISH POEMS

MS Harley 913 gives us a glimpse, the only glimpse we have, of the
range of English lyric verse circulating in Ireland in the early
fourteenth century.[74] The one lyric genre missing from the collection

---

[72] Bower, *Scotichronicon*, vi. 397.

[73] Watt, *Church and Two Nations*, 193.

[74] There are isolated scraps of English verse in some other early manuscripts of probable
Irish provenance: from about 1300 are BL Harley 3724 (see below); Cambridge, Corpus
Christi College 405 with its important Anglo-Norman texts (see above, 'Manuscript', p. xxii);
and two manuscripts of Latin sermons, Lambeth Palace Library 557 and Dublin, Trinity
College Library 347 (Franciscan, perhaps from Multyfarnham; see below, pp. 83–4). Slightly
later, CUL Gg.1.1, containing mainly Anglo-Norman verse, also has copies of *The Northern
Passion* and *The Proverbs of Hendyng*. On these manuscripts and their English texts see John J.
Thompson, 'Mapping Points West of West Midlands Manuscripts and Texts: Irishness(es)
and Middle English Literary Culture', in Wendy Scase (ed.), *Essays in Manuscript Geography*
(Turnhout, 2007), 113–28; and Margaret Laing, *Catalogue of Sources for a Linguistic Atlas of
Early Medieval English* (Cambridge, 1993), 51, 112.

is love poetry, unless 'Repentance of Love' can be counted as such. The majority of its seventeen poems in English were composed in Ireland, though the compiler has included at least five from England, 'Five Evil Things', 'Christ on the Cross', 'Lullaby', 'Elde', and 'Earth' (see 'Language', pp. xxviii–xxix above). The most celebrated of its poems is the witty satire 'Cokaygne', and no less accomplished is the mordant 'Lullaby', reminding the little baby that it is facing a life of misery. Even more savage is the celebration of mass murder in 'Pers of Bermingham', its tone in sharp contrast to the genial mockery of 'Satire'. At the heart of the collection, however, are the verse-sermons and preaching materials. These vary considerably in quality and sophistication, from the accomplished dexterity of 'Song of Michael Kildare' to the dreary recitation of basic tenets of faith in 'Seven Sins' and 'Ten Commandments'. We can sympathize with the scribe who abandoned his copying of 'Seven Sins' in the middle of a line, and we do not wish he might have persevered.

One function of the manuscript is as a sermon notebook, and the poems themselves draw attention to their practical use.[75] 'Seven Sins' calls itself 'þis predicacioune' (15.8), addressing 'Mi leue frendis . . . Ʒung, old, pouer and reche' (15.31–2); 'Sarmun' reminds its congregation that 'freris prech of heuen and helle' (13.109), and ends by offering seven years' pardon to 'Alle þat beþ icommin here / Fortto hire þis sarmun' (13.237–40). Several of the sermon-poems were composed as a set, presumably by one author: the first lines of 'Sarmun', 'Fifteen Signs', and 'Fall and Passion', are strikingly similar, and passages from 'Sarmun' are repeated in 'Ten Commandments' (13.233–5 = 21.77–80), and 'Song on the Times' (13.161–72 = 33.157–68, 13.185–8 = 33.193–6). This may imply that the poems of the manuscript are more narrowly focused than in fact they are. It is significant that lines from the wholly secular 'Lullaby' are recorded elsewhere in a Latin sermon, and two related lullaby poems are written down in Friar John of Grimestone's preaching notebook. So, too, versions of the brief 'Five Evil Things' are common in sermon collections.[76] Themes characteristic of the sermon-poems also feature in other texts in this collection: the argument of 'Earth' is that all men are dust, and 'Song on the Times' plays with the same conceit, 'Whan

---

[75] See Alan J. Fletcher, *Late Medieval Popular Preaching in Britain and Ireland* (Turnhout, 2009), 241–71.

[76] For both see Siegfried Wenzel, *Preachers, Poets, and the Early English Lyric* (Princeton, 1986), 165–6, 176–82.

erþ haþ erþe igette' (33.153); 'Elde', with its bleak picture of old age, not offering the consolation of the resurrection, is a reminder of the inevitable horrors that await us all, expressed also in the opening stanza of 'Song on the Times':

> Whose þenchiþ vp þis carful lif
> Niȝte and dai þat we beþ inne,
> So moch we seeþ of sorow and strif,
> And lite þer is of worldis winne. (33.1–4)

The expression of such monitory sentiments is ubiquitous in lyric poetry of this period and later. Satire and social and political commentary, though not without contemporary examples in English, are more characteristic of Latin and Anglo-Norman verse, and indeed the satirical lyrics find parallels in the Latin satires in the manuscript, though these are more explicitly and narrowly anti-clerical, and indeed anti-monastic, than the English poems. The short poem 'Nego', deriding the convolutions in the study of dialectics, may be compared to a contemporary Latin satire on the chop-logic of scholars,[77] though 'Nego' has the advantage in drawing the contrast between the plain, straightforward English and the Latin quiddities. There are analogues to 'Cokaygne' in French and Dutch, and probably all are ultimately derived from a Latin story.[78] Only in the Irish poem is this happy land peopled by monks and nuns, and here it shares details with the Anglo-Norman 'Ordre de bel eyse' (Dean, no. 96) in which, for example, the double houses of the Gilbertines have no walls so that the brothers may resort to the sisters 'a lur pleysyr' (ll. 44–9).[79] The Anglo-Norman poem in turn relates to the donkey's search for the ideal religious order in *Speculum Stultorum*. The portraits of town tradesmen in 'Satire', the stench made by the skinners, the flies swarming round the butchers, the tripe, cows' feet, and sheep's heads of the hucksters, owe something to the tradition of estates satire, but I know of nothing really similar in English. It is true that 'The Simonie' (DIMEV 6677) in the contemporary Auchinleck manuscript surveys the estates, including urban officials and merchants, but its tone of bitter indignation is more akin to that of 'Song on the Times' with its central exemplum of

[77] In *Political Songs of England*, ed. Thomas Wright (new edn., Cambridge, 1996), 206–10.
[78] See Herman Pleij, *Dreaming of Cockaigne* (New York, 2001).
[79] *Anglo-Norman Political Songs*, ed. Isabel S. T. Aspin, Anglo-Norman Text Society (Oxford,1953), 130–42.

the lion's judgement. This fable is found in Latin and Anglo-Norman; nowhere else is it given a political dimension, but that aspect of the poem can be paralleled in a number of Latin and French complaints on the corruption of the age, including in this manuscript 'Beati qui esuriunt' on judicial corruption, and in BL MS Harley 746 'Vulneratur karitas' (Dean, no. 101), in alternating stanzas of Latin and French, complaining of the depredations of the nobles, 'li bers ravisanz, / Ore perissent de pes et de la ley li sustenanz' (ll. 53–4).[80] Furthermore, 'Song on the Times' shows that there is no necessary divide between the sermon-poems and the political poems, since the poet concludes that in the face of injustice and oppression we will do best to honour God and Holy Church.

The variety of subject is matched by the metrical variety, and it is evident that the compiler had a keen appreciation of the range of poetic forms.[81] Indeed, as well as supplying the usual braces and brackets to indicate the rhyme-schemes, the scribe writes 'at one rime' in the margin of f. 46[r] to point out that the b-rhymes of three quatrains (33.69–80) are all the same two words. One text, 'Repentance of Love', is a poetic exercise: its form is what is arresting. The last word of the line is repeated as the first of the next, playing on polysemy (*þoȝt*, 'distress, and 'intention', ll. 1–2) and homonymy (*ar*, 'mercy' and 'before', ll. 11–12) with the first eight lines on two rhymes, the last four on another two. In early Irish the form is called *aicill*, and a similar device is found in skaldic verse: Snorri cites a stanza (47) in *Háttatal*, calling it *iðurmælt*.[82] In all cases the ultimate models are probably early Latin hymns, and the form is also found in twelfth-century Latin poets.[83] The two alliterating French stanzas each running on one letter are similar tours de force; a contemporary manuscript of Irish provenance, Harley 3724, has another such exercise, a couplet describing the sad sight of a naked fledgling attempting to fly:

> Silly sicht i seich, unsembly forte se,
> A fwil ar it was fetherid fundid forte fle.[84]

---

[80] *Anglo-Norman Political Songs*, 149–56.

[81] Some account is given by Bliss and Long, 'Literature in Norman French and English', 722–31.

[82] See Gerard Murphy, *Early Irish Metrics* (Dublin, 1961), p. 83; Snorri Sturluson, *Edda: Háttatal*, ed. Anthony Faulkes (2nd edn., London, 2007).

[83] See A. G. Rigg, *A History of Anglo-Latin Literature* (Cambridge, 1992), 29 and 197.

[84] DIMEV 4804, transcribed in Laing, *Catalogue of Sources*, 97. Harley 3724 also has an English Creed and Pater Noster (DIMEV 4300), as well as versions of items 7 ('Hore

Coincidentally, this couplet runs on the same two alliterating letters as the two French stanzas in Harley 913.

Poems written in standard four-stress couplets are 'Cokaygne', 'Seven Sins' (ll. 61–180), 'Christ on the Cross' (ll. 19–42), and 'Nego', as well as the Anglo-Norman 'Walling of New Ross'. Most of the verse-sermons are composed in four-line stanzas with alternating rhymes. To speak charitably, the verse is unsophisticated. Rhymes are repeated on identical words or are lacking altogether, a feature more probably to be attributed to authorial laziness than to scribal error. In blessed contrast is the competence of 'Song of Michael Kildare'. This is in tail-rhyme stanzas of ten lines, rhyming : aaa^{4}b^{3}a^{4}b^{3}a^{4}b^{3}a^{4}b^3, in which the seventh and ninth lines of every stanza have internal rhyme. The rhythm is very regular, though scribal spellings disguise the fact. At the end of his poem Michael claims his authorship with justified pride.[85]

The first sixty lines of 'Seven Sins' are in six-line tail-rhyme stanzas, aa^{4}b^{3}aa^{4}b^3; 'Pers' is also in six-line stanzas, but of three stresses, aabccb. 'Lullaby' is composed in aaaabb septenaries, and 'Earth', with the same rhyme scheme, has four-stress lines in rough triple rhythm. The message of 'Earth' is expressed by playing on and extending the use of the word:

> Erþ askiþ erþ, and erþ hir answerid,
> Whi erþ hatid erþ, and erþ erþ verrid.
> Erþ haþ erþ, and erþ erþ teriþ. (25–7)

'The world asks man (and he answers her) why he hates earth and yet makes use of the fruits of the earth. Man has possessions and earth covers him.' The translation, of course, entirely misses the point expressed by the puns: that human beings are born and are buried, having spent the intervening period on Earth consuming and consumed by dust and ashes.

The six-line stanzas of 'Satire' begin with four-stress lines in triple rhythm, reminiscent of the nursery rhyme:

Sompnolentium') and 46 ('Passio unius Monachi laciuii') in Harley 913. For an account of the manuscript see John J. Thompson, 'Books beyond England', in Alexandra Gillespie and Daniel Wakelin (eds.), *The Production of Books in England 1350–1500* (Cambridge, 2011), 259–75.

[85] 'Young Men of Waterford', of which only the first verse remains in Ware's transcript, begins with a nine-line bob and wheel stanza, aaaa^{4}b^{1}ccc^{3}b^2.

> Ride a cock horse to Banbury Cross
> To see a fine lady upon a white horse;
> Rings on her fingers and bells on her toes,
> She shall have music wherever she goes.

But the striking difference is that in 'Satire' the second pair of lines is unrhymed. The jingling rhythm coupled with this apparent incompetence undermines the poet's complacent assertions of technical brilliance in the last couplet of each stanza, a skill, he claims, fitting for a scholar-poet such as himself: 'Sikirlich he was a clerk / þat wrochte þis craftilich werk' (4.59–60). His delight is focused on his art rather than on content, so that, supported by its metrical form, the poem is gaily light-hearted and its satire is directed as much at the poet himself as at the scenes he describes.

Finally there is 'Elde', a remarkable poem that has not been given the attention it merits. Its power lies in its metrical structure and lexical extravagance. The stanzas vary in arrangement, and the lines have heavy, sometimes very heavy, alliteration. The opening words, 'Elde makiþ me geld and growen al grai', establish the form of the first eight-line stanza in which the half-lines are generally linked by alliteration, and the word 'elde' is insistently repeated as the first stress of every line except the last, where it is the penultimate stress; 'wy is elde ihatid' (39.8). Rhyme with 'elde' at the end of the half-line is carried through six lines, as is the line-end rhyme with 'grai'; there is the same pattern in the last two lines of this stanza with the new half-line rhyme on 'old', maintaining an obsessive focus on age. The rest of the poem is in tail-rhyme stanzas of six and twelve lines, including a tour de force in the stanza ll. 39–50, where the lines are three and four stress, with every stress alliterating, the unstressed syllable almost always occupied by the pronoun *I*, throwing great weight on the stressed syllables: 'I grunt, I grone, I grenne, I gruche'. The result is a rhythm that cruelly mimics the shuffling movements of the old man. Many of the words in this stanza are onomatopoeic, several recorded nowhere else, some of them presumably drawn from the spoken vocabulary.

Of Harley 913's vernacular texts, only two extracts are recorded elsewhere. The first fourteen lines of 'Christ on the Cross' are a marginal addition in a separate quire in Cambridge, St John's College, MS A.15. A few lines from 'Lullaby' are quoted in a Latin sermon in Worcester Cathedral Library MS F.10. Nevertheless, cognate material is preserved in a group of three other trilingual miscellanies of the period.[86] The earliest of these is Oxford, Bodleian Library MS Digby 86, copied after 1282; Cambridge, Trinity College MS B.14.39 (323) may be dated *c*.1300; and BL MS Harley 2253 was completed in about 1340.

The closest links are with Harley 2253.[87] The famous lyrics of Harley 2253 have as wide a range of metrical forms and an awareness of their expressive possibilities as those of Harley 913. There is a short and punchy text of 'Earth' (printed on p. 87 below), as well as the old man's lament, 'Maximion' (DIMEV 1769), less angry and more regretful than 'Elde', but equally as bereft of hope. The Body and Soul dialogue, 'In a þestri stude y stod' (DIMEV 2462), is a lament for the evil and luxurious life that has brought the body to the grave and the soul to judgement, and it incorporates a seven-version scheme of the signs before Doomsday; the poem has many correspondences to several of the homiletic poems of Harley 913, especially the 'Song of Michael Kildare'. The gentle mockery of religious orders, as in 'Cokaygne', is represented in Harley 2253 by the French 'Ordre de bel eyse', while the French complaint about contemporary injustice, 'Trailbaston' (Dean, no. 93), begins with the same words as 'Walling of New Ross': 'Talent me prent de rymer e de geste fere'.[88] English complaints about injustice are 'Ich herd men vpo molde' (DIMEV 2198) and 'Ne mai no lewed lued' (DIMEV 3683), which may be compared with 'Song on the Times'. A set of recipes for colours in English (f. 52^v) bears some comparison with Latin recipes in Harley 913 (ff. 52^v–53^v): in one is 'Vorte tempren Asure', and in the other 'De temperatura azorii'. There are no texts in common here, but the scribe of Harley 2253 copied the complaint about judicial practices, 'Beati qui esuriunt', into a sister manuscript, BL Royal 12.C.xii.

Digby 86 shares eight texts with Harley 2253, including 'In a þestri stude' and 'Le regret de Maximian'.[89] Its 'XIV singnes de domesday'

---

[86] See John Scahill, 'Trilingualism in Early Middle English Miscellanies', *Yearbook of English Studies*, 33 (2003), 18–32.

[87] Reproduced in *Facsimile of B.M. MS. Harley 2253*, introd. N. R. Ker, EETS os 255 (1965). Edited as *The Complete Harley 2253 Manuscript*, ed. and trans. Susanna Fein, with David Raybin and Jan Ziolkowski, TEAMS (Kalamazoo, 2014).

[88] *Anglo-Norman Political Songs*, 67–78.

[89] Reproduced in *Facsimile of Oxford, Bodleian Library, MS Digby 86*, introd. Judith Tschann and M. B. Parkes, EETS ss 16 (1996). Texts in *Codicem manu scriptum Digby 86 in Bibliotheca Bodleiana asservatum*, ed. E. Stengel (Halle, 1871).

(DIMEV 1309) is a translation of the same French poem as 'Fifteen Signs' in Harley 913. Despite the half-century that separates them, Digby's closest connections are with Harley 2253.[90] Yet both share with the Irish manuscript a wide variety of similar devotional and satiric material in all three languages.

Trinity MS B.14.39 (323) is a trilingual handbook for preachers of the same small dimensions as Harley 913, but its contents of 140 items are more narrowly focused, with none of the satirical playfulness and metrical experimentation that enlivens the Irish collection.[91] With Harley it shares sermons (both prose and verse), short rhyming pieces in English and French which could be used in sermons, and longer poems on the same kinds of topics as the homiletic poems in Harley 913. Entirely typical of the texts in Trinity is the verse-sermon beginning 'þene latemeste dai, wenne we sulen farren / Vt of þisse worlde wid pine ant wid care / Also we hideir comen naket and bare' (DIMEV 5640), a poem also in Digby 86. There are also many useful Latin proverbs, indeed one that is shared with Harley 913, describing the 'Three Sorrowful Things' (Trinity f. 84^v; Harley f. 15^r), beginning : 'Sunt tria, we, que mestificant me nocte dieque' (Walther, *Proverbia* 30850), but the text then varies. Among Trinity's English poems that share particular themes with texts in Harley 913 are six lines on the signs of death, beginning 'Wenne þin eyen beit ihut' (DIMEV 6460), a sixteen-line rhyming list of the Ten Commandments (DIMEV 1814), and, once again, 'In a þestri stude'. The long poem 'Louerd ass þu ard on God' (DIMEV 3187) is an account of salvation history from Adam to the Resurrection, similar in scope, but more accomplished, than Harley's 'Fall and Passion'. Three short poems describing Christ's agonies on the cross, 'On leome is in þis world ilist' (DIMEV 493), 'þu þad madist alle þinc', and 'Wose seþe on rode' (DIMEV 5859 and 6627), are prefaced respectively by the texts 'Candet nudatum pectus' and 'Respice in faciem Christi tui', as is Harley's 'Christ on the Cross'.

These three trilingual manuscripts are all from a fairly small area of the south-west Midlands, within a radius of some 15 miles, just the area which shares so many features of dialect with Hiberno-English.

---

[90] See Marilyn Corrie, 'Harley 2253, Digby 86, and the Circulation of Literature in Pre-Chaucerian England', in Susanna Fein (ed.), *Studies in the Harley Manuscript* (Kalamazoo, 2000), 427–43.

[91] Its texts are edited in *Religiöse Dichtung im englischen Hochmittelalter*, ed. Karl Reichl (Munich, 1973).

Harley 2253 was written by a scribe working in Ludlow in south Shropshire; Digby was written for a gentry household near Worcester;[92] Trinity is a collaborative production by some twelve scribes, probably working in Worcester.[93] A fifteenth-century manuscript from Worcester, Worcester Cathedral MS F.10, has sermons in Latin and English, and the writer of a Latin sermon quotes lines from 'Lullaby', saying that it 'used to be a popular song'.[94] All of this reveals the common literary heritage of the Anglo-Irish and their cousins in the south-west Midlands. Harley 2253 has a flyleaf containing accounts from Ardmulghan, Co. Meath, relating to the Mortimers who held property in both Co. Meath and Ludlow, thus underscoring the constant traffic between Ireland and the south-west Midlands.[95]

A number of trilingual manuscripts used to be classed as 'friars' miscellanies', but this view has now been revised.[96] Wherever the scribe of Harley 2253 obtained his exemplars, it is likely that he copied the manuscript for his gentry employers, such as the Talbots of Richard's Castle, just south of Ludlow.[97] Digby 86 was pretty certainly prepared for the Worcestershire household of Richard de Grimhill, who was perhaps also the main scribe.[98] The editor of Trinity suggests the manuscript had an institutional function and was compiled by the Franciscans of Worcester to support their teaching role, and while this seems likely enough, there is no clear evidence to support Franciscan origin.[99] One trilingual manuscript from this

[92] See B. D. H. Miller, 'The Early History of Bodleian MS. Digby 86', *Annuale medievale*, 4 (1963), 23–56.

[93] *Religiöse Dichtung*, ed. Reichl, 49–58. *LALME* placed the combined scribal language in west Worcs, though *LAEME* now suggests various parts of Herefords as the language of the scribes.

[94] See 'Lullaby', headnote. On the manuscript see Siegfried Wenzel, *Latin Sermon Collections from Later Medieval England* (Cambridge, 2005), 151–8.

[95] On the scribe see Carter Revard, 'Scribe and Provenance', in Susanna Fein (ed.), *Studies in the Harley Manuscript* (Kalamazoo, 2000), 21–109; on the significance of the flyleaf see David L. Jeffrey, 'Authors, Anthologists, and Franciscan Spirituality', in the same volume, pp. 261–70 (at p. 269); and Thompson, 'Mapping', 126. Karl Reichl makes pertinent comparisons between Harley 2252 and 913 in 'Satirische und politische Lyrik in der anglo-irischen Kildare-Handschrift (HS. BL Harley 913)', in Christoph Cormeau (ed.), *Zeitgeschehen und seine Darstelling im Mittelalter* (Bonn, 1995), 173–99.

[96] See in particular John Frankis, 'The Social Context of Vernacular Writing in Thirteenth-Century England: The Evidence of the Manuscripts', in P. R. Coss and S. D. Lloyd (eds.), *Thirteenth-Century England* (Woodbridge, 1986), 175–84; Scahill, 'Trilingualism'.   [97] Revard, 'Scribe and Provenance', 22.

[98] *Facsimile*, introd. Tschann and Parkes, p. lvii.

[99] *Religiöse Dichtung*, ed. Reichl, 15–38; Frankis, 'Social Context', 182.

same restricted area that is undoubtedly Franciscan is William
Herebert's preaching notebook. BL Additional MS 46919 was
written partly by Herebert himself at the Hereford friary sometime
about 1330.[100] The Anglo-Norman works are mainly by the prolific
Franciscan poet Nicholas Bozon, probably based at Nottingham (cf.
item 33, note to l. 45); Herebert's sermons are in Latin, as is the
Tractatus de Veneno, a treatise on the seven sins by the Irish
Franciscan Malachy; the nineteen English lyrics Herebert himself
composed are for the most part translations from Latin and from
Bozon.

Some forty years later, in 1372, a Norfolk Franciscan, John of
Grimestone, completed his collection in Advocates MS 18.7.21, of
English verse-pieces for use in sermons.[101] He drew on texts
circulating among the Franciscans, as is evident from two lyrics
beginning 'Lullay, Lullay, little child' that are closely associated with
Harley's 'Lullaby'. Both Grimestone lyrics address the Christ-child
lamenting the sufferings he must undergo. One of the Grimestone
lyrics, 'Lullay, lullay litel child, child reste þe a þrowe' (DIMEV
3300), is in the same stanza, and was presumably written as a pair to
'Lullaby', in which it is the child born in wickedness that must suffer
the punishments incurred by sin. The other (DIMEV 3301) takes the
first line of 'Lullaby', 'Lullay, lullay, litel child, qui wepest þu so
sore?' as its refrain. Elsewhere Grimestone used the same Latin
meditations as the basis for English reflections as Harley's 'Christ on
the Cross' and Trinity B.14.39.[102] 'Candet nudatum pectus' is
translated by Grimestone as 'Wit was his nakede brest' (DIMEV
6540.5), and 'O homo vide' as 'Senful man beþing & se' (DIMEV
4849). Though Harley 913 took its non-Irish material from a small
area of the south-west Midlands, testifying to a localized literary
culture, some of this material escaped via the Franciscan network and
was distributed in other parts of the country.

Unlike the Latin texts, none of the vernacular poems in the
manuscript directly addresses specifically Franciscan concerns; but
there again, unlike the Latin texts, several of the vernacular poems
deal with issues relating to Ireland, some directly, such as 'Pers of

---

[100] For discussion see *The Works of William Herebert, OFM*, ed. Stephen R. Reimer
(Toronto, 1987); Thorlac Turville-Petre, *England the Nation* (Oxford, 1996), 185–92.

[101] See Edward Wilson, *A Descriptive Index of the English Lyrics in John of Grimestone's
Preaching Book*, Medium Ævum Monographs, NS 2 (Oxford, 1973).

[102] See 'Lullaby', headnote.

Bermingham', 'Walling of New Ross', 'Song on the Times', and 'Young Men of Waterford', some more tangentially, such as 'Cokaygne' and 'Satire'.[103] These poems provide a unique expression of the concerns and preoccupations of an English Franciscan community in Ireland during the early fourteenth century.

6. PREVIOUS EDITIONS

The standard edition of the English poems is by Wilhelm Heuser, *Die Kildare-Gedichte* (Bonn, 1904). This has extensive treatment of the language, discursive headnotes, and includes an appendix of related poems, but it has no annotations or glossary, so that many details of the texts are not elucidated. More recently, Angela M. Lucas, *Anglo-Irish Poems of the Middle Ages* (Dublin, 1995) provided a facing translation. F. J. Furnivall printed texts of twelve of the poems as early as 1858 as part 2 of *Transactions of the London Philological Society*, reissued as *Early English Poems and Lives of Saints* (Berlin, 1862), and shortly afterwards Eduard Mätzner supplied useful editions of five of the poems in *Altenglische Sprachproben*, i: *Poesie* (Berlin, 1867). There are valuable editions of 'Land of Cokaygne' in *Early Middle English Verse and Prose*, ed. J. A. W. Bennett and G. V. Smithers, with a glossary by Norman Davis (Oxford, 1966), and of 'Pers of Bermingham' by Michael Benskin, 'The Style and Authorship of the Kildare Poems—(I) *Pers of Bermingham*', in J. Lachlan Mackenzie and Richard Todd (eds.), *In Other Words: Transcultural Studies in Philology, Translation and Lexicology* (Dordrecht, 1989), 57–75. 'Walling of New Ross' was first printed by Frederick Madden in *Archaeologia*, 22 (1829), 307–22; subsequently it was edited and translated by Hugh Shields, 'The Walling of New Ross: A Thirteenth-Century Poem in French', *Long Room* (Dublin), 12–13 (1975–6), 24–33.

7. TREATMENT OF THE TEXTS

Word-division, capitalization, and punctuation are altered to conform to modern conventions. That includes the joining of genitive *is* to the noun, as in *Benetis, Godis, sowleis* (see p. xxvi). Abbreviations (as listed on p. xi) are expanded without notice. I have chosen to expand *a'* to

---

[103] This aspect of the poems is discussed in Turville-Petre, *England the Nation*, 155–75.

and, though it would be equally appropriate to expand to *an*; the only full forms of 'and' are *and* 5.4 and 33.57, and *an* 20.137; one might add that the indef. art. *an* is never abbreviated, though 'on' appears once as *a'* 4.110. *i^c* is expanded to *ich*. Roman numerals are represented by the Middle English or French forms used elsewhere in the texts, *s'* expanded to *seint*, *ihc̄* to *Iesus* and *ihū* to *Iesu*. Flourishes on final consonants may sometimes represent -*e*: so the distinct loop after -*r* has been expanded; but probably final -*h'* and the small transverse bar on the leg of final -*k* are meaningless and they have been ignored. The scribe's usage of *u/v* has been followed, and long and short forms of *i/j* are printed *I* and *i*. Final -ȝ has been printed as -*z* in the French texts where it represents a sibilant. The scribe's paraphs have been followed. Line-division has been guided by rhyme, as in the case of 'Song of Michael Kildare', where the scribe sets out the first stanza as prose with line-divisions indicated by punctus, with the first eight lines of the remaining stanzas set out side by side, divided by a vertical line, the last two lines running across the page divided by a punctus. The couplets of the last section of 'Christ on the Cross' similarly run across the page and have here been divided according to convention. Titles of Latin texts that are given in the manuscript are within inverted commas. Scribal corrections and additions have not been noted unless there seemed good reason to do so. Emendations are marked in the text within square brackets and are listed in the variant apparatus.

CONTENTS OF THE MANUSCRIPT

BIBLIOGRAPHY

PRIMARY SOURCES

Acta Sanctorum, ed. J. Bollandus and others (Antwerp, 1643–1940).

[Ælfric, *De octo vitiis*] *Two Ælfric Texts: The Twelve Abuses and The Vices and Virtues*, ed. Mary Clayton (Woodbridge, 2013).

Alliterative Poetry of the Later Middle Ages, ed. Thorlac Turville-Petre (London, 1989).

Altenglische Dichtungen, ed. K. Böddeker (Berlin, 1878).

Altenglische Legenden: Neue Folge, ed. Carl Horstmann (Heilbronn, 1881).

Altenglische Sprachproben, i: *Poesie*, ed. Eduard Mätzner (Berlin, 1867).

Analecta Hymnica Medii Aevi, ed. Clemens Blume and Guido M. Dreves, 55 vols. (Leipzig, 1886–1922).

Ancrene Wisse, ed. Bella Millett and Richard Dance, EETS os 325–6 (2005–6).

Anglo-Irish Poems of the Middle Ages, ed. Angela M. Lucas (Dublin, 1995).

Anglo-Norman Political Songs, ed. Isabel S. T. Aspin, Anglo-Norman Text Society (Oxford, 1953).

Annals of Connacht, ed. A. M. Freeman (Dublin, 1944).

Annals of Inisfallen, ed. S. Mac Airt (Dublin, 1951).

Annals of the Kingdom of Ireland by the Four Masters, ed. John O'Donovan (Dublin, 1856).

Apocalypse of Paul (*Visio Sancti Pauli*), trans. M. R. James, *The Apocryphal New Testament* (Oxford, 1924), 525–55.

Arthurian Romances, trans. D. D. R. Owen (2nd edn., London, 1993).

[Audelay, John] *The Poems of John Audelay*, ed. Ella Keats Whiting, EETS os 184 (1931).

Awntyrs off Arthure, ed. Ralph Hanna (Manchester, 1974).

Bonaventure, St, *Legenda Maior Sancti Francisci*, ed. Michael Bihl, OFM, in *Legendae S. Francisci Assisiensis saeculis XIII et XIV conscriptae*, Analecta Franciscana, 10 (Quaracchi, 1926–41), 555–652.

Bower, Walter, *Scotichronicon*, ed. D. E. R. Watt et al., vi (Aberdeen, 1991).

[Bozon, Nicolas] *Les Contes moralisés de Nicole Bozon*, ed. Lucy Toulmin Smith and Paul Meyer, Société des anciens textes français (Paris, 1889).

Calendar of the Justiciary Rolls, ed. James Mills (Dublin, 1905–14).

Chartularies of St Mary's Abbey Dublin, ii, ed. John T. Gilbert, RS 80 (London, 1884).

Cleanness, ed. J. J. Anderson (Manchester, 1977).

[Clyn, John] *Friar John Clyn, The Annals of Ireland*, ed. R. Butler (Dublin, 1849).

[Clyn, John] *The Annals of Ireland by Friar John Clyn*, ed. Bernadette Williams (Dublin, 2007).

Codicem manu scriptum Digby 86 in Bibliotheca Bodleiana asservatum, ed. E. Stengel (Halle, 1871).

The Complete Harley 2253 Manuscript, ed. and trans. Susanna Fein, with David Raybin and Jan Ziolkowski, TEAMS, 3 vols (Kalamazoo, 2014).

Cursor Mundi, ed. R. Morris, EETS OS 57, 59, 62, 66, 99, 101 (1874–93).

Daretis Phrygii De Excidio Troiae Historia, ed. Ferdinand Meister (Leipzig, 1873).

[Dunbar] *The Poems of William Dunbar*, ed. James Kinsley (Oxford, 1979).

Early English Poems and Lives of Saints, ed. F. J. Furnivall (Berlin, 1862).

Early Middle English Verse and Prose, ed. J. A. W. Bennett and G. V. Smithers, with a glossary by Norman Davis (Oxford, 1966).

The Early South-English Legendary, ed. Carl Horstmann, EETS OS 87 (1887).

English Lyrics of the XIIIth Century, ed. Carleton Brown (Oxford, 1932).

Everyman, ed. A. C. Cawley (Manchester, 1961).

Facsimile of B.M. MS. Harley 2253, introd. N. R. Ker, EETS OS 255 (1965).

Facsimile of Oxford, Bodleian Library, MS Digby 86, introd. Judith Tschann and M. B. Parkes, EETS SS 16 (1996).

Fratris Francisci Bartholi de Assisio Tractatus de Indulgentia S. Mariae de Portiuncula, ed. Paul Sabatier, Collection d'études et de documents sur l'histoire religieuse et littéraire du Moyen Âge (Paris, 1900).

[Gower, John] *The Complete Works of John Gower*, ed. G. C. Macaulay, 4 vols. (Oxford, 1899–1902).

Hali Meiðhad, in *Medieval English Prose for Women*, ed. Bella Millett and Jocelyn Wogan-Browne (Oxford, 1990).

The Harley Lyrics, ed. G. L. Brook (4th edn., Manchester, 1968).

Havelok, ed. G. V. Smithers (Oxford, 1987).

[Herebert, William] *The Works of William Herebert, OFM*, ed. Stephen R. Reimer (Toronto, 1987).

Hoccleve's Minor Poems, ed. I. Gollancz, EETS ES 73 (London, 1897).

Hymns to the Virgin and Christ, ed. Frederick J. Furnivall, EETS OS 24 (1867).

Innocent III, *De miseria conditionis humane*, ed. Robert E. Lewis (Athens, Ga., 1978).

Isidori Hispalensis Episcopi Etymologiarum sive Originum libri XX, ed. W. M. Lindsay (Oxford, 1911).

Die Kildare-Gedichte, ed. Wilhelm Heuser (Bonn, 1904).

Kyng Alisaunder, ed. G. V. Smithers, EETS OS 227, 237 (1952, 1957).

Laȝamon: *Brut*, ed. G. L. Brook and R. F. Leslie, EETS OS 250, 277 (1963, 1978).

[Mannyng, Robert] *Robert of Brunne's Handlyng Synne*, ed. Frederick J. Furnivall, EETS OS 119, 123 (1901, 1903).

[Mannyng, Robert] *Robert Mannyng of Brunne, The Chronicle*, ed. Idelle Sullens (Binghamton, NY, 1996).

[Map, Walter] *The Latin Poems Commonly Attributed to Walter Mapes*, ed. Thomas Wright, Camden Soc. 16 (London, 1841).

[Map, Walter] *De Nugis Curialium*, ed. M. R. James, rev. C. N. L. Brooke and R. A. B. Mynors (Oxford, 1983).

Materials for the History of the Franciscan Province of Ireland, A.D. 1230– 1450, ed. E. B. Fitzmaurice and A. G. Little (Manchester, 1920).

Medieval English Political Writings, ed. James M. Dean (Kalamazoo, 1996).

Meditationes piissimae, in *Sancti Bernardi Opera omnia*, ed. Jean Mabillon (Paris, 1839), ii, part i, cols. 661–91.

Middle English Debate Poetry, ed. John W. Conlee (East Lansing, Mich., 1991).

Middle English Legends of Women Saints, ed. Sherry L. Reames (Kalamazoo, 2003).

The Middle English Poem Erthe upon Erthe, ed. Hilda M. R. Murray, EETS OS 141 (1911).

The Minor Poems of the Vernon Manuscript, Part 2, ed. Frederick J. Furnivall, EETS OS 117 (1901).

The N-Town Play, ed. Stephen Spector, EETS SS 11–12 (1991).

[Odo of Cheriton] *Les Fabulistes latins depuis le siècle d'Auguste jusqu'à la fin du moyen âge*, ed. Léopold Hervieux (2nd edn., Paris, 1893–9).

Owayne Miles, in *St Patrick's Purgatory*, ed. Robert Easting, EETS OS 298 (1991).

The Owl and the Nightingale, ed. Neil Cartlidge (Exeter, 2001).

[Paris, Matthew] *Matthæi Parisiensis Chronica Majora*, ed. Henry Richards Luard (1872–80, repr. Cambridge, 2012).

The Peterborough Chronicle, ed. Cecily Clark (2nd edn., Oxford, 1970).

Pierce the Ploughmans Crede, ed. Walter W. Skeat, EETS OS 30 (1867).

Piers Plowman, see Langland in Abbreviations.

Political Songs of England, ed. Thomas Wright (London, 1839), repr. with introduction by Peter Coss (Cambridge, 1996).

[*Prick of Conscience*] *Richard Morris's Prick of Conscience*, ed. Ralph Hanna and Sarah Wood, EETS OS 342 (Oxford, 2013).

The Pride of Life, ed. Norman Davis, in *Non-Cycle Plays and Fragments*, EETS SS 1 (1970).

Promptuarium exemplorum, in *Die Fabeln der Marie de France*, ed. Karl Warnke (Halle, 1898).

[pseudo-Bede] *Collectanea pseudo-Bedae*, ed. Martha Bayless and Michael Lapidge, Scriptores Latini Hiberniae, 14 (Dublin, 1998).

Les Quinze signes du jugement dernier, ed. Erik von Kræmer, Commentationes Humanarum Litterarum, 38/2 (Helsinki, 1966).

The Red Book of the Earls of Kildare, ed. G. Mac Niocaill (Dublin, 1964).

Religiöse Dichtung im englischen Hochmittelalter, ed. Karl Reichl (Munich, 1973).

Religious Lyrics of the XIVth Century, ed. Carleton Brown (2nd edn., Oxford, 1957).

Reliquiæ Antiquæ, ed. Thomas Wright and James Orchard Halliwell, 2 vols. (London, 1845).

Remonstrance of the Irish Princes, in Bower, *Scotichronicon*, ed. Watt et al., vi.

Saga of Olaf Tryggvason, trans. Theodore M. Andersson (Ithaca, 2003).

St Patrick's Purgatory, ed. Robert Easting, EETS os 298 (1991).

Sammlung altenglischer Legenden, ed. Carl Horstmann (Heilbronn, 1878).

Seinte Marherete, ed. Frances M. Mack, EETS os 193 (1934).

A Selection of Religious Lyrics, ed. Douglas Gray (Oxford, 1975).

['The Simonie'] *Medieval English Political Writings*, ed. James M. Dean (Kalamazoo, 1996).

Sir Gawain and the Green Knight, ed. J. R. R. Tolkien and E. V. Gordon, rev. Norman Davis (2nd edn., Oxford, 1967).

Sir Orfeo, ed. A. J. Bliss (Oxford, 1954).

The South English Legendary, ed. Charlotte d'Evelyn and Anna J. Mill, EETS os 235, 236, 244 (1956, 1959).

Speculum Vitae, ed. Ralph Hanna, EETS os 331–2 (2008).

Statutes and Ordinances, and Acts of the Parliament of Ireland, King John to Henry V, ed. Henry F. Berry (Dublin, 1907).

Sturluson, Snorri, *Edda: Háttatal*, ed. Anthony Faulkes (2nd edn., London, 2007).

The Towneley Plays, ed. Martin Stevens and A. C. Cawley, EETS ss 13–14 (1994).

Tractatus de Purgatorio Sancti Patricii, in *St Patrick's Purgatory*, ed. Robert Easting, EETS os 298 (1991).

[Trevisa, John] *On the Properties of Things*, gen. ed. M. C. Seymour (Oxford, 1975).

Visio Sancti Pauli, see *Apocalypse of Paul*.

The York Plays, ed. Richard Beadle, EETS ss 23–4 (2009–13).

Ywain and Gawain, ed. Albert B. Friedman and Norman T. Harrington, EETS os 254 (1964).

SECONDARY SOURCES

Alford, John A., *Piers Plowman: A Glossary of Legal Diction* (Cambridge, 1988).

Angelelli, Ignacio, 'The Techniques of Disputation in the History of Logic', *Journal of Philosophy*, 67 (1970), 800–15.

Barrow, G. W. S., *Robert Bruce and the Community of the Realm of Scotland* (4th edn., Edinburgh, 2005).

Bayless, Martha, *Parody in the Middle Ages: The Latin Tradition* (Ann Arbor, Mich., 1996).

Bennett, Judith M., *Ale, Beer and Brewsters in England: Women's Work in a Changing World 1300–1600* (Oxford, 1996).

Benskin, Michael, 'The Hands of the Kildare Poems Manuscript', *Irish University Review*, 20 (1990), 163–93.

—— 'The Style and Authorship of the Kildare Poems—(I) *Pers of Bermingham*', in J. Lachlan Mackenzie and Richard Todd (eds.), *In Other Words: Transcultural Studies in Philology, Translation and Lexicology* (Dordrecht, 1989), 57–75.

Bliss, Alan, and Joseph Long, 'Literature in Norman French and English to 1534', in Art Cosgrove (ed.), *A New History of Ireland*, ii: *Medieval Ireland 1169–1534* (Oxford 1987), 708–36.

Bloomfield, Morton W., *The Seven Deadly Sins* (East Lansing, Mich., 1952).

The Booke of Meery Riddles (London, 1629).

Bradley, J., 'The Topography and Layout of Medieval Drogheda', *Co. Louth Archaeological and Historical Journal*, 19 (1978), 98–127.

Breeze, Andrew, 'Middle English *tromcheri* and Irish *tromchroí* "Liver" ', *Notes and Queries*, 238 (1993), 16.

—— 'The Virgin's Tears of Blood', *Celtica*, 20 (1988), 110–22.

Bühler, Curt F., 'Astrological Prognostications in MS. 775 of the Pierpont Morgan Library', *Modern Language Notes*, 56 (1941), 351–5.

Cartlidge, Neil, 'Festivity, Order, and Community in Fourteenth-Century Ireland: The Composition and Contexts of BL MS Harley 913', *Yearbook of English Studies*, 33 (2003), 33–52.

Cheney, C. R., *Handbook of Dates* (repr. Cambridge, 1996).

Clavin, Terry, 'Lombard, Peter (*c.*1554–1625)',*ODNB*, accessed 12 December 2014.

Colker, Marvin L., 'America Rediscovered in the Thirteenth Century?', *Speculum*, 54 (1979), 712–26.

—— *Trinity College Library Dublin: Descriptive Catalogue of the Medieval and Renaissance Latin Manuscripts*, 2 vols. (Aldershot, 1991).

Coote, Lesley A., *Prophecy and Public Affairs in Later Medieval England* (Woodbridge, 2000).

Copeland, Rita, 'The Middle English *Candet Nudatum Pectus* and Norms of Early Vernacular Translation Practice', *Leeds Studies in English*, NS 15 (1984), 57–81.

Corrie, Marilyn, 'Harley 2253, Digby 86, and the Circulation of Literature in Pre-Chaucerian England', in Fein (ed.), *Studies in the Harley Manuscript*, 427–43.

Croker, Thomas Crofton, *The Popular Songs of Ireland* (London, 1839).

Crooks, Peter, '"Divide and Rule": Factionalism as Royal Policy in the Lordship of Ireland, 1171–1265', *Peritia*, 19 (2005), 263–307.

Dolan, T. P., 'Langland and FitzRalph: Two Solutions to the Mendicant Problem', *Yearbook of Langland Studies*, 2 (1988), 35–45.

Dronke, Peter, '*The Land of Cokaygne*: Three Notes on the Latin Background', in Christopher Cannon and Maura Nolan (eds.), *Medieval Latin and Middle English Literature* (Cambridge, 2011), 65–75.

Duffy, Seán, 'Burgh, Richard de, second earl of Ulster (b. in or after 1259, d. 1326)',*ODNB*, accessed 12 December 2014.

Easting, Robert, *Visions of the Other World in Middle English*, Annotated Bibliographies of Old and Middle English Literature, 3 (Woodbridge, 1997).

Feifalik, Julius, 'Studien zur Geschichte der altböhmischen Literatur V', *Sitzungsberichte der Kaiserlichen Akademie der Wissenschaften: Philosophisch-Historische Classe*, 36 (1861), 119–91.

Fein, Susanna (ed.), *Studies in the Harley Manuscript* (Kalamazoo, 2000).

Fletcher, Alan J., 'The Date of London, British Library, Harley MS 913 (The "Kildare Poems")', *Medium Ævum*, 79 (2010), 306–10.

—— 'God's Jesters and the Festive Culture of Medieval Ireland', in *Medieval Dublin* V, ed. Seán Duffy (Dublin, 2004), 277–90.

—— *Late Medieval Popular Preaching in Britain and Ireland* (Turnhout, 2009).

Frame, Robin, 'Burgh, Walter de, first earl of Ulster (d. 1271)',*ODNB*, accessed 12 December 2014.

—— 'Butler, Edmund, earl of Carrick (d. 1321)',*ODNB*, accessed 12 December 2014.

—— *Colonial Ireland 1169–1369* (2nd edn., Dublin, 2012).

—— *English Lordship in Ireland 1318–1361* (Oxford, 1982).

—— 'Fitzgerald, Maurice fitz Thomas, first earl of Desmond (*c.*1293–1356)',*ODNB*, accessed 12 December 2014.

—— 'Power and Society in the Lordship of Ireland 1272–1377', *Past and Present*, 76 (1977), 3–33, repr. in his *Ireland and Britain, 1170–1450* (London, 1998).

Frankis, John, 'The Social Context of Vernacular Writing in Thirteenth-Century England: The Evidence of the Manuscripts', in P. R. Coss and S. D. Lloyd (eds.), *Thirteenth-Century England* (Woodbridge, 1986), 175–84.

Gallagher, Niav, 'The Franciscans and the Scottish Wars of Independence: An Irish Perspective', *Journal of Medieval History*, 32 (2006), 3–17.

—— 'The Irish Franciscan Province', in Michael Robson and Jens Röhrkasten (eds.), *Franciscan Organisation in the Mendicant Context* (Berlin, 2010), 19–42.

Galloway, Andrew, *The Penn Commentary on Piers Plowman*, i (Philadephia, 2006).

—— 'The Rhetoric of Riddling in Late Medieval England', *Speculum*, 70 (1995), 68–105.

Garbáty, T. J., 'Studies in the Franciscan "The Land of Cokaygne" in the Kildare MS', *Franziskanische Studien*, 45 (1963), 139–63.

Given-Wilson, Chris, *Chronicles: The Writing of History in Medieval England* (London, 2004).

Golubovich, P. Girolamo, *Biblioteca bio-bibliografica della Terra Santa e dell'Oriente Francescano*, ii (Florence, 1913).

Gwynn, A., and R. N. Hadcock, *Medieval Religious Houses: Ireland* (London, 1970).

Hanna, Ralph, '*The Bridges at Abingdon*: An Unnoticed Alliterative Poem', in Michael Calabrese and Stephen H. A. Shepherd (eds.), *Yee? Baw for Bokes* (Los Angeles, 2013), 31–44.

—— 'Editing "Middle English Lyrics": The Case of *Candet Nudatum Pectus*', *Medium Ævum*, 80 (2011),189–200.

Hartland, Beth, 'English Lords in Late Thirteenth and Early Fourteenth Century Ireland: Roger Bigod and the de Clare Lords of Thomond', *English Historical Review*, 122 (2007), 318–48.

Heist, William W., *The Fifteen Signs before Doomsday* (East Lansing, Mich., 1952).

Henry, P. L., 'The Land of Cokaygne: Cultures in Contact in Medieval Ireland', *Studia Hibernica*, 12 (1972), 120–41.

Hill, Thomas D., 'Parody and Theme in the Middle English "Land of Cokaygne"', *Notes & Queries*, 220 (1975), 55–9.

Hore, P. H., *History of the Town and County of Wexford*, 6 vols. (London, 1900–2).

Jansen, Katherine Ludwig, *The Making of the Magdalen: Preaching and Popular Devotion in the Later Middle Ages* (Princeton, 2000).

Jeffrey, David L., 'Authors, Anthologists, and Franciscan Spirituality', in Fein (ed.), *Studies in the Harley Manuscript*, 261–70.

Jordan, Richard, *Handbook of Middle English Grammar: Phonology*, trans. and rev. Eugene J. Crook (The Hague, 1974).

Kitson, P. R., 'Old English Bird-Names (I)', *English Studies*, 78 (1997), 481–505.

Kölbing, Eugen, 'Kleine Publicationen aus der Auchinleck-HS: V. Ueber die sieben Todsünden', *Englische Studien*, 9 (1886), 42–6.

Laing, Margaret, *Catalogue of Sources for a Linguistic Atlas of Early Medieval English* (Cambridge, 1993).

Lambert, M. D., *Franciscan Poverty* (London, 1961).

Lascelles, Mary, 'Alexander and the Earthly Paradise in Mediaeval English Writings', *Medium Ævum*, 5 (1936), 31–47.

Leff, Gordon, *Heresy in the Later Middle Ages* (new edn., Manchester, 1999).

Lehmann, Paul, *Die Parodie im Mittelalter*, 2nd edn. (Stuttgart, 1963).

Lincoln, R., 'A List of the Mayors and Bailiffs of Waterford from 1365 to 1649', *Journal of the Royal Society of Antiquaries of Ireland*, 7th ser. 5 (1935), 313–19.

Little, A. G., 'The Administrative Divisions of the Mendicant Orders in England', *English Historical Review*, 34 (1919), 205–9.

—— *Studies in English Franciscan History* (Manchester, 1917).

Lucas, Angela M., and Peter J. Lucas, 'Reconstructing a Disarranged Manuscript: The Case of MS Harley 913, a Medieval Hiberno-English Miscellany', *Scriptorium*, 14 (1990), 286–99.

Lydon, James, 'The Case against Alexander Bicknor, Archbishop and Peculator', in Brendan Smith (ed.), *Ireland and the English World in the Late Middle Ages* (Houndmills, 2009), 103–11.

—— 'The Impact of the Bruce Invasion 1315–27', in Art Cosgrove (ed.), *A New History of Ireland* (Oxford, 1987), ii. 275–302.

—— 'The Years of Crisis, 1254–1315', ibid. ii. 179–204.

McIntosh, Angus, and M. L. Samuels, 'Prolegomena to a Study of Mediæval Anglo-Irish', *Medium Ævum*, 37 (1968), 1–11.

McNamara, Martin, 'The (Fifteen) Signs before Doomsday in Irish Tradition', *Warszawskie Studia Teologiczne*, 20 (2007), 223–54.

Mann, Jill, *From Aesop to Reynard: Beast Literature in Medieval Britain* (Oxford, 2009).

Massing, Ann (ed.), *The Thornham Parva Retable* (Turnhout, 2003).

Meyer, Wilhelm, 'Quondam fuit factus festus: Ein Gedicht in Spottlatein', in *Nachrichten von der königlichen Gesellschaft der Wissenschaften zu Göttingen*, Philologisch-Historische Klasse (Göttingen, 1908), 406–29.

Miller, B. D. H., 'The Early History of Bodleian MS. Digby 86', *Annuale medievale*, 4 (1963), 23–56.

Mitchell, Bruce, *Old English Syntax* (Oxford, 1985).

Murphy, Gerard, *Early Irish Metrics* (Dublin, 1961).

Muscat, Noel, *In Defence of the Portiuncula Indulgence* (Malta, 2012), at http://i-tau.com/franstudies/texts/portiuncula_indul.pdf.

Musson, Anthony, 'Rehabilitation and Reconstruction? Legal Professionals in the 1290s', in *Thirteenth Century England IX*, ed. Michael Prestwich, R. H. Britnell, and Robin Frame (Woodbridge, 2003), 71–87.

Mustanoja, Tauno F., *A Middle English Syntax* (Helsinki, 1955).

Ó Clabaigh, Colmán, *The Friars in Ireland 1224–1540* (Dublin, 2012).

Ó Cléirigh, Cormac, 'Fitzgerald, John fitz Thomas, first earl of Kildare (d. 1316)', *ODNB*, accessed 12 December 2014.

Orpen, G. H., *Ireland under the Normans*, 4 vols. (Oxford, 1911–20).

Parker, Ciarán, 'Paterfamilias and Parentela: The le Poer Lineage in

Fourteenth-Century Waterford', *Proceedings of the Royal Irish Academy*, 95C (1995), 93–117.

Patch, Howard R., *The Other World* (Cambridge, Mass., 1950).

Paz, D. G., 'Wyse, Sir Thomas (1791–1862)',*ODNB*, accessed 12 December 2014.

Pleij, Herman, *Dreaming of Cockaigne* (New York, 2001).

Prestwich, Michael, *Plantagenet England 1225–1360* (Oxford, 2005).

Reallexikon der germanischen Altertumskunde, ed. Heinrich Beck et al. (Berlin, 1973–).

Reichl, Karl, 'Satirische und politische Lyrik in der anglo-irischen Kildare-Handschrift (HS. BL Harley 913)', in Christoph Cormeau (ed.), *Zeitgeschehen und seine Darstelling im Mittelalter* (Bonn, 1995), 173–99.

Revard, Carter, 'Scribe and Provenance', in Fein (ed.), *Studies in the Harley Manuscript*, 21–109.

Rigg, A. G., *A Glastonbury Miscellany of the Fifteenth Century* (Oxford, 1968).

—— *A History of Anglo-Latin Literature* (Cambridge, 1992).

—— 'Medieval Latin Poetic Anthologies (II)', *Mediaeval Studies*, 40 (1978), 387–407.

—— 'Medieval Latin Poetic Anthologies (III)', *Mediaeval Studies*, 41 (1979), 468–505.

—— ' "Metra de Monachis Carnalibus": The Three Versions', *Mittellateinisches Jahrbuch*, 15 (1980), 134–42.

Riley, Henry Thomas, *Memorials of London and London Life* (London, 1868).

Robbins, Rossell Hope, 'Signs of Death in Middle English', *Mediaeval Studies*, 32 (1970), 282–98.

Robson, Michael, *The Franciscans in the Middle Ages* (Woodbridge, 2006).

Roth, Francis, *The English Austin Friars 1249–1538* (New York, 1966).

Scahill, John, 'Trilingualism in Early Middle English Miscellanies', *Yearbook of English Studies*, 33 (2003), 18–32.

Scase, Wendy, *Literature and Complaint in England, 1272–1553* (Oxford, 2007).

Scattergood, John, 'Elegy for a Dangerous Man: *Piers of Bermingham*', in his *Occasions for Writing: Essays on Medieval and Renaissance Literature, Politics and Society* (Dublin, 2010), 85–106.

Seymour, St John D., *Anglo-Irish Literature 1200–1582* (Cambridge, 1929).

Shields, Hugh, 'The Walling of New Ross: A Thirteenth-Century Poem in French', *Long Room* (Dublin), 12–13 (1975–6), 24–33.

Sinclair, Keith V., 'On the Text of the Anglo-Norman Poem *The Walling of New Ross*', *Romanische Forschungen*, 106 (1994), 225–35.

—— '*The Walling of New Ross*: An Anglo-Norman Satirical *Dit*', *Zeitschrift für französische Sprache und Literatur*, 105 (1995), 240–80.

Suto, Taki, *Boethius on Mind, Grammar and Logic* (Leiden, 2012).

Thompson, John J., 'Books beyond England', in Alexandra Gillespie and Daniel Wakelin (eds.), *The Production of Books in England 1350–1500* (Cambridge, 2011), 259–75.

—— *The Cursor Mundi: Poem, Texts and Contexts*, Medium Ævum Monographs, NS 19 (Oxford, 1998).

—— 'Mapping Points West of West Midlands Manuscripts and Texts: Irishness(es) and Middle English Literary Culture', in Wendy Scase (ed.), *Essays in Manuscript Geography* (Turnhout, 2007), 113–28.

Turville-Petre, Thorlac, 'Alliterative Horses', *Journal of English and Germanic Philology*, 112 (2013), 154–68.

—— *England the Nation* (Oxford, 1996).

Väänänen, Veikko, 'Le "Fabliau" de Cocagne: Le motif du pays d'abondance dans le folklore occidental', *Neuphilologische Mitteilungen*, 48 (1947), 3–36.

Vos, Antonie, *The Philosophy of John Duns Scotus* (Edinburgh, 2006).

Walsh, Katherine, *A Fourteenth-Century Scholar and Primate: Richard FitzRalph in Oxford, Avignon and Armagh* (Oxford, 1981).

Walther, Hans, 'Zur lateinischen Parodie des Mittelalters', *Zeitschrift für deutsches Altertum und Literatur*, 84 (1952–3), 265–73.

Watt, J. A., *The Church and the Two Nations in Medieval Ireland* (Cambridge, 1970).

Wattenbach, W., 'Beschreibung einer Handschrift der Stadtbibliothek zu Reims', *Neues Archiv der Gesellschaft für ältere deutsche Geschichtskunde*, 18 (1893), 491–526.

—— 'Über erfundene Briefe in Handschriften des Mittelalters, besonders Teufelsbriefe', *Sitzungsberichte der Königlich Preussischen Akademie der Wissenschaften zu Berlin* (Berlin, 1892), 91–123.

Wenzel, Siegfried, *Latin Sermon Collections from Later Medieval England* (Cambridge, 2005).

—— *Preachers, Poets, and the Early English Lyric* (Princeton, 1986).

Wilson, Edward, *A Descriptive Index of the English Lyrics in John of Grimestone's Preaching Book*, Medium Ævum Monographs, NS 2 (Oxford, 1973).

Woolf, Rosemary, *The English Religious Lyric in the Middle Ages* (Oxford, 1968).

Wright, Charles D., 'The Lion Standard in *Exodus*: Jewish Legend, Germanic Tradition, and Christian Typology', in R. M. Liuzza (ed.), *The Poems of MS Junius 11* (London, 2002), 188–202.

Zippel, Gianni, 'La lettera del Diavolo al clero dal sec. XII alla Riforma', *Bullettino dell'Istituto storico italiano per il medio evo*, 70 (1958), 125–79.

THE TEXTS OF BL MS HARLEY 913

Nota quod secundum theologos quaelibet littera aliud significat . . . boni et mali operis quam vinee cultores acceperunt.

Two sets of theological interpretations of the alphabet. For example, A is the first of the letters and signifies the Trinity because it contains three angles ('habet tres angulos in se qui significant trinitatem'). In BL Add. MS 32622 (s. xiv¹) is a section explaining significations of letters, beginning 'A triangula, B apis . . .'. See Andrew Galloway, 'The Rhetoric of Riddling in Late Medieval England', *Speculum*, 70 (1995), 68–105 at 76–7. See also text 35d below.

2. THE LAND OF COKAYGNE ff. 3ʳ–6ᵛ

DIMEV 1259

The motif of the land of sensual bliss is widespread. There are medieval analogues to 'The Land of Cokaygne' in French and Dutch, the former edited by Veikko Väänänen, 'Le "Fabliau" de Cocagne: Le motif du pays d'abondance dans le folklore occidental', *Neuphilologische Mitteilungen*, 48 (1947), 3–36, the latter edited and discussed by Pleij, *Dreaming of Cockaigne*, 431–42. Both French and Dutch versions concentrate on food and drink. Neither is a source of the English poem, and Pleij, pp. 3–4, 59, supposes that the features of Cokaygne derive from oral tradition. Some details recur as standard in this blissful land—buildings made of food, geese that fly into the mouth ready-cooked—to be supplemented in the twentieth century by the cigarette trees of 'The Big Rock Candy Mountain'. The author of the poem in English has extended and deepened the theme by incorporating religious satire. The inhabitants of Cokaygne are monks and nuns, and many features of the country are drawn from accounts of the Earthly Paradise. Various classical sources have been proposed, in particular Lucian's *True Story* describing a journey to the Island of the Blest, a parody of travellers tales. Peter Dronke, '*The Land of Cokaygne*', in Christopher Cannon and Maura Nolan (eds.), *Medieval Latin and Middle English Literature* (Cambridge, 2011), 65–75, points out that Lucian was unknown at the time, and instead suggests as a source the account of the Camarini in an anonymous *Totius orbis descriptio*. A much more obvious source, however, is the extremely influential

Apocalypse of Paul (*Visio Sancti Pauli*), translated by M. R. James, in *The Apocryphal New Testament* (Oxford, 1924), 525–53; for its influence in Middle English see Robert Easting, *Visions of the Other World in Middle English*, Annotated Bibliographies of Old and Middle English Literature, 3 (Woodbridge, 1997). This in turn was the inspiration for another very popular work the Irish poet clearly knew, the *Tractatus de Purgatorio Sancti Patricii*, ed. Robert Easting, in *St Patrick's Purgatory*, EETS os 298 (1991), 121–54. These, together with passages from the Old and New Testaments, provided the poet with the information he needed to describe this Earthly Paradise. For satire against the religious orders, see especially texts 23 and 24 below, the 'Letter from the Prince of Hell' and the 'Reply by Pope Dositheus', as well as the Anglo-Norman *Ordre de bel eyse* in Harley 2253, in *Anglo-Norman Political Songs*, ed. Aspin, 130–42.

f. 3ʳ

Fur in see bi west Spayngne
Is a lond ihote Cokaygne;
þer nis lond vnder heuenriche
Of wel, of godnis, hit iliche.
þoȝ Paradis be miri and briȝt,   5
Cokaygn is of fairir siȝt.
What is þer in Paradis
Bot grasse and flure and grene ris?
þoȝ þer be ioi and gret dute,
þer nis met bote frute;   10
þer nis halle, bure no bench,
Bot watir manis þurst [t]o quench.
Beþ þer no men bot two,
Hely and Enok also;
Elinglich mai hi go   15
Whar þer woniþ men no mo.
   In Cokaigne is met and drink
Wiþvte care, how and swink;
þe met is trie, þe drink is clere
To none, russin and sopper.   20
I sigge for soþ, boute were,
þer nis lond on erþe is pere,
Vnder heuen nis lond iwisse
Of so mochil ioi and blisse.

þer is mani swete siʒte,   25 f. 3ᵛ
Al is dai, nis þer no niʒte.
þer nis baret noþer strif,
Nis þer no deþ, ac euer lif,
þer nis lac of met no cloþ,
þer nis man no womman wroþ,   30
þer nis serpent, wolf no fox,
Hors no capil, kowe no ox,
þer nis schepe no swine no gote
No non horwʒ, la, God it wote!
Noþer harace, noþer stode,   35
þe lond is ful of oþer gode.
Nis þer flei, fle no lowse
In cloþ, in toune, bed no house;
þer nis dunnir, slete no hawle,
No non vile worme no snawile,   40
No non storme, rein no winde.
þer nis man no womman blinde
Ok al is game, ioi and gle,
Wel is him þat þer mai be.
þer beþ riuers gret and fine   45
Of oile, melk, honi and wine,
Watir seruiþ þer to noþing,
Bot to siʒt and to waiissing,
þer is [euerich] maner frute,
Al is solas and dedute.   50
    þer is a wel fair abbei
Of white monkes and of grei.   f. 4ʳ
þer beþ bowris and halles,
Al of pasteiis beþ þe walles,
Of fleis, of fisse and rich met,   55
þe likfullist þat man mai et.
Fluren cakes beþ þe schingles alle
Of cherch, cloister, boure and halle,
þe pinnes beþ fat podinges,
Rich met to princez and kinges.   60
Man mai þerof et inoʒ,
Al wiþ riʒt and noʒt wiþ woʒ.
Al is commune to ʒung and old,
To stoute and sterne, mek and bold.

þer is a cloister fair and liȝt,   65
Brod and lang, of sembli siȝt.
þe pilers of þat cloister alle
Beþ iturned of cristale,
Wiþ har [b]as and capitale
Of grene iaspe and rede corale.   70
In þe praer is a tre
Swiþe likful forto se:
þe rote is gingeuir and galingale,
þe siouns beþ al sedwale,
Trie maces beþ þe flure,   75
þe rind canel of swet odur,

f. 4ᵛ   þe frute gilofre of gode smakke,
Of cucubes þer nis no lakke;
þer beþ rosis of rede ble
And lilie likful forto se;   80
þai faloweþ neuer dai no niȝt,
þis aȝt be a swet siȝt.
þer beþ fure willis in þe abbei
Of triacle and halwei,
Of baum and ek piement,   85
Euer ernend to riȝt rent:
Of þai stremis al þe molde
Stonis preciuse and golde.
þer is saphir and vniune,
Carbuncle and ast[r]iune,   90
Smaragde, lugre and prassiune,
Beril, onix, topasiune,
Ametist and crisolite,
Calcedun and epetite.
þer beþ briddes mani and fale: 95
þrostil, þruisse and niȝtingale.
Chalandre and wodwale,
And oþer briddes wiþout tale,
þat stinteþ neuer bi har miȝt
Miri to sing dai and niȝt.   100

f. 5ʳ   Ȝite I do ȝow mo to witte:
þe gees irostid on þe spitte
Flee[þ] to þat abbai, God hit wot,
And grediþ 'Gees, al hote, al hot!'

Hi bringeþ garlek gret plente,   105
þe best idiȝt þat man mai se.
þe leuerokes þat beþ cuþ
Liȝtiþ adun to manis muþ,
Idiȝt in stu ful swiþe wel,
Pudrid wiþ gilofre and canel.   110
Nis no spech of no drink,
Ak take inoȝ wiþvte swink.
    Whan þe monkes geeþ to Masse,
Al þe fenestres þat beþ of glasse
Turneþ into cristal briȝt   115
To ȝiue monkes more liȝt.
Whan þe Masses beþ iseiid
And þe bokes up ileiid,
þe cristal turniþ into glasse,
In state þat hit raþer wasse.   120
    þe ȝung monkes euch dai
Aftir met goþ to plai.
Nis þer hauk no fule so swifte
Bettir fleing bi þe lifte
þan þe monkes heiȝ of mode   125 f. 5ᵛ
Wiþ har sleuis and har hode.
    Whan þe abbot seeþ ham flee,
þat he holt for moch glee;
Ak naþeles al þeramang
He biddiþ ham liȝt to euesang.   130
þe monkes liȝtiþ noȝt adun,
Ac furre fleeþ in o randun.
    Whan þe abbot him iseeþ
þat is monkes fram him fleeþ,
He takeþ [a] maidin of þe route   135
And turniþ vp h[i]r white toute,
And betiþ þe taburs wiþ is hond,
To make is monkes liȝt to lond.
    Whan is monkes þat iseeþ,
To þe maid dun hi fleeþ   140
And geþ þe wench al abute
And þakkeþ al hir white toute
And siþ aftir her swinke
Wendiþ meklich hom to drink

And geþ to har collacione,   145
A wel fair processione.
   Anoþer abbei is þerbi,
For soþ a gret fair nunnerie,

f. 6ʳ

Vp a riuer of swet milke,
Whar is plente gret of silk.   150
Whan þe someris dai is hote,
þe ȝung nunnes takiþ a bote
And doþ ham forþ in þat riuer,
Boþe wiþ oris and wiþ stere.
Whan hi beþ fur fram þe abbei,   155
Hi makiþ ham nakid forto plei
And lepiþ dune into þe brimme
And doþ ham sleilich forto swimme.
þe ȝung monke[s] þat hi seeþ;
Hi doþ ham vp, and forþ hi fleeþ   160
And commiþ to þe nunnes anon,
And euch monke him takeþ on,
And snellich berriþ forþ har prei
To þe mochil grei abbei,
And techiþ þe nunnes an oreisun   165
Wiþ iambleue vp and dun.
   þe monke þat wol be stalun gode
And kan set ariȝt is hode,
He schal hab wiþoute danger
Twelue wiues euch ȝere,   170
Al þroȝ riȝt and noȝt þroȝ grace,
Forto do himsilf solace.

f. 6ᵛ

And þilk monke þat slepiþ best
And doþ is likam al to rest,
Of him is hoppe, God hit wote,   175
To be sone uadir abbot.
Whose wl com þat lond to,
Ful grete penance he mot do:
Seue ȝere in swineis dritte
He mote wade, wol ȝe iwitte,   180
Al anon vp to þe chynne,
So he schal þe lond winne.
Lordinges gode and hend,
Mot ȝe neuer of world wend,

Fort ȝe stond to ȝure cheance   185
And fulfille þat penance,
þat ȝe mote þat lond ise
And neuermore turne aȝe.
Prey we God, so mote hit be,
Amen, par seint charite.   190

Finit

12 þurst to] þursto   49 euerich] *om.*   69 bas] las   83 fure] iiij
90 astriune] astiune   103 Fleeþ] Fleeȝ   135 a maidin] amaidin *with first
letter subpuncted and erased*   136 hir] *altered to* har   159 monkes] monkeþ
170 Twelue] xij

3. FIVE EVIL THINGS   f. 6ᵛ

DIMEV 2994

The list of five abuses is widespread in various forms, including
sermon collections. Sixteen versions are assembled as DIMEV 2994.
See Wenzel, *Preachers, Poets*, 176–82. An Old English prose version
appears in Aelfric's homily *De Octo Viciis*, ed. Mary Clayton, in *Two
Ælfric Texts: The Twelve Abuses and The Vices and Virtues* (Wood-
bridge, 2013).

Bissop lorles,
Kyng redeles,
Ȝung man rechles,
Old man witles,
Womman ssamles: 5
I swer bi heuen kyng
þos beþ fiue liþer þing.

4. SATIRE   ff. 7ʳ–8ᵛ

DIMEV 1750

The poem has twenty stanzas, the first five addressing saints, the
second five clerics, followed by nine trades and an address to the
audience in the last stanza. The first eighteen stanzas begin 'Hail!'
except for the second. Poems beginning 'Hail' are common. John
Audelay has a set of salutation poems, to the Virgin and saints
Bridget and Winifred, in which most lines begin 'Hayle!' (*The Poems*

of John Audelay, ed. Ella Keats Whiting, EETS os 184 (1931), nos.
19, 20, 23, 25), and another to St Anne, in which every line begins
'Gaude!' (no. 26).

Though efforts to identify the town are pointless, the earlier title
'Satire on the Townsfolk' captures one aspect of the poem, but
ignores the last stanza, revealing that this is a humorous version of the
widespread practice of *minnis-drykkja* or *minnetrinken*, toasting the
saints. For example, the *Saga of Olaf Tryggvason*, trans. Theodore M.
Andersson (Ithaca, 2003), 75, describes how St Martin appeared to
Olaf urging him to desist from toasting Thor and Odin, and drink to
him instead. See Christiane Zimmermann, 'Minne und Minnetrin-
ken', in *Reallexikon der germanischen Altertumskunde*, ed. Heinrich
Beck et al., xx (Berlin, 2002), 49–56, for a full account and
bibliography. The life of St Wenceslaus describes drinking a toast
'in nomine Beati Archangeli Michaelis' (*Acta Sanctorum*, 46.829): cf.
the first stanza here. After nineteen such toasts, the company may be
in no condition to obey the poet's final instruction. The poem is very
much in the goliard tradition, with the narrator repeatedly referring
to himself as a *clerk*.

f. 7ʳ

Hail, Seint Michel wiþ þe lange sper!
Fair beþ þi winges vp þi scholder.
þou hast a rede kirtil anon to þi fote,
þou ert best angle þat euer God makid.
   þis uers is ful wel iwroȝt;   5
   Hit is of wel furre ybroȝt.

Hail, Seint Cristofre wiþ þi lang stake!
þou ber ur louerd Iesus Crist ouer þe brod lake.
Mani grete kunger swimmeþ abute þi fete.
Hou mani hering to peni at West Chep in London?   10
   þis uers is of Holi Writte;
   Hit com of noble witte.

Seint Mari bastard, þe Maudleinis sone,
To be wel icloþed wel was þi wone.
þou berrist a box on þi hond ipeintid al of gold.   15
Woned þou wer to be hend, ȝiue us sum of þi spicis.
   þis uers is imakid wel
   Of consonans and wowel.

Hail, Seint Domnik with þi lang staffe!
Hit is at þe ouir end crokid as a gaffe.   20
þou berrist a bok on þi bak, ich wen hit is a bible.
þoȝ þou be a gode clerk, be þou noȝt to heiȝ.
    Trie rime, la, God hit wote!
    Soch anoþir an erþe I note.

Hail, Seint Franceis wiþ þi mani foulis,   25
Kites and crowis, reuenes and oules,
Fure and tuenti wild ges and a poucok!
Mani bold begger siwiþ þi route.
    þis uers is ful wel isette;
    Swiþe furre hit was ivette.   30

Hail be ȝe freris wiþ þe white copis!   f. 7ᵛ
ȝe habbiþ a hus at Drochda war men makiþ ropis.
Euir ȝe beþ roilend þe londis al aboute;
Of þe watir-daissers ȝe robbiþ þe churchis.
    Maister he was swiþe gode   35
    þat þis sentence vnderstode.

Hail be ȝe Gilmins wiþ ȝur blake gunes!
ȝe leuith þe wildirnis and filleþ þe tunis.
Menur wiþoute and prechur wiþinne,
ȝur abite is of gadering; þat is mochil schame.   40
    Sleilich is þis uers iseid;
    Hit wer harme adun ileiid.

Hail, ȝe holi monkes wiþ ȝur corrin,
Late and raþe ifillid of ale and wine!
Depe cun ȝe bouse, þat is al ȝure care.   45
Wiþ Seint Benetis scurge lome ȝe disciplineþ.
    Takeþ hed al to me!
    þat þis is slech, ȝe mow wel se.

Hail be ȝe nonnes of Seint Mari house,
Goddes bourmaidnes and his owen spouse!   50
Ofte mistrediþ ȝe ȝur schone, ȝur fet beþ ful tendre;
Daþeit þe sotter þat tawiþ ȝure leþir!
    Swiþe wel ȝe vnderstode
    þat makid þis ditee so gode.

Hail be ȝe prestis wiþ ȝur brode bokes!   55
þoȝ ȝur crune be ischaue, fair beþ ȝur crokes.
Ȝow and oþer lewid men deleþ bot ahouue,
Whan ȝe deliþ holibrede, ȝiue me botte a litil.
   Sikirlich he was a clerk
   þat wrochte þis craftilich werk.   60

Hail be ȝe marchans wiþ ȝur gret packes
Of draperie, auoir-depeise, and ȝur wol-sackes,
Gold, siluer, stones riche, markes and ek pundes!
Litil ȝiue ȝe þerof to þe wrech pouer.
   Sleiȝ he was and ful of witte   65
   þat þis lore put in writte.

Hail be ȝe tailurs wiþ ȝur scharpe shores!
To mak wronge hodes ȝe kittiþ lome gores.
Aȝens midwinter hote beþ ȝur neldes;
þoȝ ȝur semes semiþ fair, hi lestiþ litil while.   70
   þe clerk þat þis baston wrowȝte,
   Wel he woke and slepe riȝte nowȝte.

Hail be ȝe sutters wiþ ȝour mani lestes,
Wiþ ȝour blote hides of selcuþ bestis,
And trobles and treisuses, bochevampe and alles!   75
Blak and loþlich beþ ȝur teþ, hori was þat route.
   Nis þis bastun wel ipiȝte?
   Euch word him sitte ariȝte.

Hail be ȝe skinners wiþ ȝure drench-kiue!
Whoso smilliþ þerto, wo is him aliue,   80
Whan þat hit þonneriþ, ȝe mote þerin schite.
Daþeit ȝur curteisie, ȝe stinkeþ al þe strete!
   Worþ hit wer þat he wer king
   þat ditid þis trie þing.

Hail be ȝe [b]o[ch]ers wiþ ȝur bole-ax!   85
Fair beþ ȝur barmhatres, ȝolow beþ ȝur fax.
Ȝe stondiþ at þe schamil, brod ferlich bernes,
Fleiis ȝow folowith, ȝe swolowiþ ynow.
   þe best clerk of al þis tun
   Craftfullich makid þis bastun.   90

f. 8ᵛ

Hail be ʒe bakers wiþ ʒur louis smale
Of white bred and of blake, ful mani and fale!
Ʒe pincheþ on þe riʒt white aʒens G[o]ddes law;
To þe fair pillori ich rede ʒe tak hede!
   þis uers is iwrowʒte so welle   95
   þat no tung iwis mai telle.

Hail be ʒe brewesters wiþ ʒur galuns,
Potels and quartes ouer al þe tounes!
Ʒur þowmes berriþ moch awai, schame hab þe gyle,
Beþ iwar of þe coking-stole, þe lak is dep and hori.   100
   Sikerlich he was a clerk
   þat so sleilich wroʒte þis werk.

Hail be ʒe hokesters dun bi þe lake,
Wiþ candles and golokes and þe pottes blak,
Tripis and kine fete and schepen heuedes!   105
Wiþ þe hori tromcheri hori is ʒure inne.
   He is sori of his lif
   þat is fast to such a wif.

Fi a debles, kaite[f]s, þat kemiþ þe wolle,
Al þe schindes of þe tronn an heiʒ opon ʒur sculle!   110
Ʒe makid me sech a goshorne ouer al þe wowes,
þerfor ich makid on of ʒou sit opon a hechil.
   He was noble clerk and gode
   þat þis dep lore vnderstode.

Makiþ glad mi frendis, ʒe sitteþ to long stille,   115
Spekiþ now and gladieþ and drinkeþ al ʒur fille!
Ʒe habbeþ ihird of men lif þat woniþ in lond;
Drinkiþ dep and makiþ glade, ne hab ʒe non oþer nede.
   þis song is yseid of me;
   Euer iblessid mot ʒe be.   120

Explicit.

27 tuenti] xxᵗⁱ   85 bochers] potters   93 Goddes] Gddes   109 kaitefs]
kaites

ff. 9ʳ–10ʳ

5. SONG OF MICHAEL KILDARE

DIMEV 5073

The author, who names himself as 'Frere Michel Kyldare' in l. 144, exhorts the audience to turn aside from earthy treasures, to care for the poor, and repent. The 'song' thus takes up many of the themes of the other verse-sermons, but does so more competently and confidently. In *The English Religious Lyric in the Middle Ages* (Oxford, 1968), 107, Rosemary Woolf justly remarks on 'the power of the style'. The poem is written in rather complex ten-line stanzas on just two rhymes, rhyming aaabab* abab, with internal rhyme in lines 7 and 9. So line 7 of the second stanza can be emended with confidence. A-rhyme lines are of four stress, b-rhymes generally of three. The first stanza is written out as prose, the remainder set out in double columns with the ninth and tenth lines as one line across the page. Paraphs mark each stanza.

f. 9ʳ

Swet Iesus, hend and fre,
þat was istraw3t on rode-tre,
Nowþe and euer mid vs be
 And vs schild fram sinne;
Let þou no3t to helle te   5
 þai þat beþ herinne!
So bri3te of ble, þou hire me,
 Hoppe of alle mankynne,
Do us ise þe Trinite
 And heueneriche to winne!   10

þis worldis loue is gon awai,
So dew on grasse in someris dai,
Few þer beþ, weilawai,
 þat louiþ Goddis lore.
Al we beþ iclung so clai,   15
 We schold rew þat sore;
Prince and [rai], what weniþ þai
 To libbe euirmore?
Leueþ 3ur plai and crieþ ai
 'Iesu Crist, þin ore!'   20

Alas, alas, [3]e rich men,
Of muk whi wol 3e fille 3ur denne?

Wende 3e to ber hit henne?
   Nai, so mote I þriue!
3e sulle se þat al is fenne,   25
   þe catel of þis liue.
To Criste 3e ren and falleþ o knen
   þat wondis þoliid fiue;
For 3e beþ trenne worþi to brenne
   In bittir helle kiue.   30

Godde 3ow hauiþ to erþe isent,
Litil dwel 3ov hauiþ ilent,
He schal wit how hit is spent,
   I rede 3ou tak hede.
If hit be hidde, 3e beþ ischent,   35
   For helle worþ 3ur mede.
þe bow is bend, þe fire itend
   To 3ow, if 3e beþ gnede;
Bot 3eu amend, 3e sul be wend
   In euer-glowind glede.   40

Pouir was þin incomming,
So ssal be þin outegoing,
þou ne ssalt of al þi þing
   A peni ber to molde.
þat is a rewful tiþing,   45
   Whose hit hire wold.
Louerd King, to hori ding
   What makiþ man so hold?
In pining 3iue a ferþing
   He ne sal, þe3 he wold.   50

Riche man beþench þe,
Tak gode hede wat þou be!
þou ne art bot a brotil tre
   Of schorte seuen fote,
Ischrid wiþvte wiþ gold and fe: 55
   þe ax is at þe rote;
þe fent vnfre halt al to gle
   þis tre adun to rote.
So mote ich þe, ich rede þe fle,
   And do þi sowleis bote.   60

Now þou art in ro and rest,
Of al þe lond þou art þe mest,
þou doist no streinþ of Godis hest;
    Of deþ whi neltov þenche?
Whan þou wenist libbe best,   65
    þi bodi deþ sal qwench;
þe pouer chest ssal be þi nest,
    þat sittist bold a bench;
Est and west schal be þi qwest,
    Ne miȝt þou noþing blench.   70

Be þou barun oþer kniȝte,
þou salt be a sorful wiȝte,
Whan þou liste in bere itiȝte
    In fulle pouer wede;
Nastou noþer main no miȝte.   75
    Whil þou no man drede,
Wiþ sorwȝful siȝt—and þat is riȝte —
    To erþe me sul þe lede,
þan ssal þi liȝt turn into niȝte:
    Beþench, man, þis I red.   80

þe pouer man bit uche dai
Gode of þe, and þou seiist ai:
'Begger, wend a deuil wai!
    þou deuist al min ere.'
Hungir-bitte he goþ awai   85
    Wiþ mani sorful tere.
A wailowai! þou clotte of clai!
    Whan þou list on bere,
Of fow no grai, no rede no rai
    Nastov bot a here.   90

Crist telliþ in holi writte
þat a man of wiþir witte
Ibiriid was in helle pitte,
    þat in þis lif was riche;
Ssal he neuer þan flitte   95
    Fram þe sorful diche.
He sal sitte in helle flitte
    Wiþoute wyn and miche;

þe fent sal sitte is knot to knitte;
  Sore mai he skriche.   100

þe pouer man goþ bifor þe,
Al idriid als a tre,
And grediþ: 'louerd, help me,
  Hungre me hauiþ ibund.
Let me dei, par charite,   105
  Ibroȝt ich am to grund.'
So mot I þe, and Crist ise,
  If he dei þat stund
His lif sal be icrauid of þe,
  þeȝ þou ȝif him no wonde.   110

I þe rede, rise and wake
Of þe hori sinne lake;
If þou be þerin itake,
  Iwisse þou schalt to helle,
To woni wiþ þe fentis blake   115
  In þat sorful wille.
þi wei þou mak, þou dri þe stak,
  To prest þi sinnes telle;
So wo and wrake sal fram þe rake
  Wiþ fendis grimme and felle.   120

If in sinne þi liue is ladde,
To do penance ne be noȝt sadde:
Who so doþ, he nis noȝt madde,
  As Holi Church vs techith.
þerof be þou noȝt adradde,   125
  Crist sal be þi lech,
þus Crist us radde, þat [on] rode spradde,
  Wiþ a blisful spech.
Whan he so bad, þou miȝt be gladde,
  Ne louiþ he no wreche.   130

Iesu, king of heuen fre,   f. 10ʳ
Euer iblessid mot þou be!
Louerd, I besech þe,
  To me þou tak hede;
Fram dedlich sinne þou ȝem me,   135
  While I libbe on lede!

þe maid fre þat bere þe
  So swetlich vnder wede,
Do vs to se þe Trinite;
  Al we habbeþ nede!   140

þis sang wroȝt a frere [menur],
Iesus Crist be is socure,
Louerd, bring him to þe toure,
  Frere Michel Kyldare;
Schild him fram helle boure,   145
  Whan he sal hen fare!
Leuedi, flur of al honur,
  Cast awei is care;
Fram þe schoure of pinis sure
  þou sild him her and þare! Amen.   150

17 rai] king   21 ȝe] þe   127 on] *om.*   141 frere menur] frere *with erasure*

6. THE ABBOT OF GLOUCESTER'S FEAST

Walther, *Initia* 16347

Quondam fuit factus festus / et uocatus ad commestus . . . Prelatores non spernebis / contra tuum regula.

The abbot and prior of Gloucester get drunk together at a feast. The abbot orders the wine to be passed round the monks, but the prior says they have had enough, and both vomit. The authorities hear of the behaviour and, in order to hush it up, decide to impose a small fine rather than send them to the pillory. One of the monks prays that they will choke on their drink. The prior, in fury, sentences him to a period of fasting, after which he must prostrate himself before prior and abbot. The poem, in deliberately execrable Latin, is written in forty-three four-line aaab stanzas, with the b-rhyme on -(*i*)*a*. The poet makes humorous use of a number of English words, as in 'Vomis cadit super floris' (on the flower/floor). The Irish word *corrin*, 'tankard' (Ir *cuirin*), elsewhere recorded only in 'Satire' 4.43, occurs three times as *currino*, *currinum*, but only in this version. The text in Cambridge, Trinity College MS O.9.38 (from Glastonbury abbey) reads *Leycestris* for *Glowcestrus*, but the latter is perhaps the original, since Continental manuscripts corrupt it to *clocestum* and *cocletestus*. It is relevant that Glastonbury, like Gloucester, was a Benedictine abbey, whereas Leicester was a house of Augustinian canons. In stanza 34 on f. 11^v 'canone' has been erased and replaced by non-rhyming 'monache' in a later hand.

This is much the earliest of at least twelve manuscripts and its text varies considerably from the four others edited by Wilhelm Meyer, 'Quondam fuit factus festus: ein Gedicht in Spottlatein', in *Nachrichten von der königlichen Gesellschaft der Wissenschaften zu Göttingen*, Philologisch-Historische Klasse (Göttingen, 1908), 406–29. This copy is printed in *Reliquiæ Antiquæ*, ed. Thomas Wright and James Orchard Halliwell, 2 vols. (London, 1845), i. 140–4. See A. G. Rigg, *A Glastonbury Miscellany of the Fifteenth Century* (Oxford, 1968), 46–7, for notice of the Trinity copy.

7. 'HORE SOMPNOLENTIUM'   ff. 12^r–13^r

Rubric: 'Incipiunt [Hore Sompnolentium adversus Capitulum]' according to the Harley catalogue. Now mainly illegible.

Fratres nolumus uos ignorare de dormientibus . . . Ex tunc vigilabis. Oratio ut supra.

An office in celebration of sleep, citing seven famous Old Testament sleepers (Adam, Noah, Jacob, Sampson, Samuel, Ezechiel, and Jonah) rather than the Seven Sleepers of Ephesus whose feast was on 27 June. The opening words are from 1 Thess. 4: 12, used in Masses for the dead, and the text parodies both the Bible and some well-known hymns, such as 'Somno refectis artibus', of which an English version is 'Owr wery lymes refreschyd now with rest' (DIMEV 4330). One antiphon is a parody of a well-known sequence for St Francis, 'O stupor et gaudium':

> O stupor et tedium
> o sopor sompnolentium
> tu nostre milicie
> currus et auriga
> egros sopore desides
> pone in quadriga
> et ad chorum psallencium
> pigritantes stiga.

(O stupor and weariness, o sleep of sleepers, may you, chariot and charioteer of our army, set in your chariot the sick ones immersed in sleep, and lift up the sluggish ones to the singers' choir.)

Ed. by Hans Walther, 'Zur lateinischen Parodie des Mittelalters', *Zeitschrift für deutsches Altertum und Literatur*, 84 (1952–3), 265–73, who cites no other copies.

ff. 13^v–14^v

8. 'MISSA DE POTATORIBUS'

Rubric: 'Incipit M[issa de Potatoribus]' according to the Harley catalogue. Now largely illegible.

V. Introibo ad altare Bachi. *R.* Ad uinum qui letificat cor hominis. . . . Dolus uobiscum etc. Ite bursa uacua. Reo gratias.

A parody of parts of the Mass, including this version of the Lord's Prayer:

Pater noster, qui es in ciphis, sanctificetur uinum istud. Adueniat Bachi potus, fiat tempestas tua sicut in uino et in taberna. Panem nostrum ad deuorandum da nobis hodie, et dimitte nobis pocula magna sicut et nos dimittimus potatoribus nostris, et ne nos inducas in uini temptacionem, sed libera nos a uestimento.

Ed. and translated by Alan J. Fletcher, 'God's Jesters and the Festive Culture of Medieval Ireland', in *Medieval Dublin* V, ed. Sean Duffy (Dublin, 2004), 277–90. There is an earlier edition by Paul Lehmann, *Die Parodie im Mittelalter*, 2nd edn. (Stuttgart, 1963), 233–41, with readings from six manuscripts, including the slightly earlier BL MS Harley 2851, on which see Rigg, *A History of Anglo-Latin Literature*, 238. See also Martha Bayless, *Parody in the Middle Ages: The Latin Tradition* (Ann Arbor, 1996), 93–128 and 114–15, for parodies of the Lord's Prayer.

f. 14^v

9. QUOTATION FROM 'BEDE'

Sacerdos qui est sine mortali peccato et in bono proposito si non celebrat, et habeat copiam celebrandi, quantum in ipso est celestem trinitatem priuat gloria, et angelos in celesti Jerusalem manentes leticia et gaudio, homines in terra laborantes beneficio et gracia, animas in purgatorio degentes patrocinio et uenia. Huc usque Beda.

Followed by brief commentary.

   This censure of priests who do not celebrate is found frequently, usually ascribed to Bede. It is also in Trinity College Cambridge MS

O.9.38, f. 58^v, printed in Rigg, *Glastonbury Miscellany*, 79, and in CUL MS Ll.1.18, f. 81^v.

10. METRICAL PROVERBS

Heading: 'Secundina et Maceria id est boyn'.

Nunc lege, nunc hora, nunc cum feruore labora; Sic erit labor leuis, et hora ipsa breuis. . . . Si vis potare, chiphis moueatur ab are; Gambiit sit amotum, ne polluat wunga po[tum].

Metrical proverbs in Latin, mostly widely recorded. They include Walther, *Proverbia* 8819, 18772a, 19348, 19717, 24381, 28381, 28408, 30850, and a distich from a poem attributed to Walter Map (*The Latin Poems Commonly Attributed to Walter Mapes*, ed. Thomas Wright, Camden Soc. 16 (London, 1841), 86). In Hand B.

11. TWO ALLITERATING FRENCH VERSES

f. 15^v

Dean no. 271

Written as prose with rubricated initials. Both poems printed in *Reliquiæ Antiquæ*, ii. 256; also printed and translated by St John D. Seymour, *Anglo-Irish Literature 1200–1582* (Cambridge, 1929), 91–2. According to the rubric, the second is a lament by the 1st earl of Desmond (cr. 1329, d. 1356). Desmond may indeed be the author of one or both: he was insultingly derided by Arnold le Poer as a 'rymoure'; see Introduction, p. xxxv. The poem reflects on the remedy for being alone: Desmond was imprisoned in 1331, and it is perhaps also relevant to note that his first wife, Katharine Burgh, died in the same year. On his turbulent career see Frame, 'Fitzgerald, Maurice fitz Thomas'.

(1)

Folie fet qe en force sa fie,   f. 15^v
 Fortune fet force failire.
Fiaux funt fort folie,
 Fere en fauelons flatire.
Fere force fest fiaux fuir,   5
 Faux fiers fount feble fameler.
Fausyne fest feble fremir,
 Feie ferme fra fausyn fundre.

(2) 'Proverbia comitis Desmonie'

Soule su, simple e saunz solas,
    Seignury me somount soiorner;
Si suppris sei de moune solas,
    Sagesse deit soul solacer.
Soule ne solai soiorner,   5
    Ne solein estre de petit solas;
Souereyn se est de se solacer,
    Qe se sent soule e saunz solas.

12. LATIN PROVERB AND RECIPE

Later additions filling a blank half page. Proverb: 'Si quis centiret,
quo tendit & vnde veniret; / Numquam gauderet, sed in omni
tempore fleret' (Walther, *Proverbia* 29074). Copied by Hand C from
Hand B's heading to item 13 at the top of f. 16ʳ. Below the proverb,
in the same hand, are directions for desalinating water: 'Ad
extrahendum salem de potagio'.

13. SARMUN

DIMEV 5306

This 'sarmun' (l. 228) is based on *Meditationes piissimae* once
ascribed to St Bernard (ed. *Sancti Bernardi Opera omnia*, ed. Jean
Mabillon (Paris, 1839), ii, part i, cols. 661–91; also *PL* 184, cols.
485–508). Another Middle English rendering of the *Meditationes*, the
'Sayings of St Bernard', was frequently copied with various incipits
(DIMEV 4564, 5215), all ed. F. J. Furnivall, in *The Minor Poems of
the Vernon Manuscript*, Part 2, EETS os 117 (1901), 511–20. For
discussion of these texts see Woolf, *English Religious Lyrics*, 107–13.
Like the other verse-sermons, this poem is written in four-stress
quatrains rhyming abab. The a-rhymes fail at ll. 123 and 127, but no
obvious emendations suggest themselves. Headings are added by
Hand F at the top of most leaves (see commentary).

    There are particular correspondences with the other verse-sermons
in the manuscript, suggesting that they were composed as a group: see
notes to ll. 1, 121–36, 140, 161–72, 185–8, and 233–5.

þe grace of Godde and Holi Chirche,   f. 16ʳ
þroȝ uertu of þe Trinite,
Ȝif ous grace soch workes to wirche
þat helplich to ure sowles be.

þes wordes þat ich speke nou last,   5
In Latin hit is iwritte in boke:
'Wel mow we drede and be agast,
þe dede beþ so lolich to loke.'

þerfor he seiiþ 'A, man, hab munde
þat of þis lif þer commiþ ende!   10
Of erþe and axen is ure kunde
And into duste we schulliþ wende'.

So seiþ seint Bernard in his boke
And techiþ vs ofte and lome
To be hend; if we wold loke,   15
Wel file hit is þat of us come.

Man, loke þin ein and þi nosse,
þi mouþ, þin eris al aboute!
Fram þi girdil to þi hosse,
Hit is wel vile þat commiþ vte.   20

Man, of þi schuldres and of þi side
þou miȝte hunti luse and flee;
Of such a park I ne hold no pride,
þe dere nis nauȝte þat þou miȝte sle.

If þou ert prute, man, of þi fleisse   25
Oþir of þi velle þat is wiþoute,
þi fleisse nis naȝte bot wormeis meisse;
Of such a þing whi ert þou prute?

Wormis of þi fleisse schul spring,   f. 16ᵛ
þi felle wiþoute nis bot a sakke   30
Ipudrid ful wiþ drit and ding
þat stinkiþ lolich and is blakke.

Sire, wharof is þe gentilman
Of eni oþer þan of þis?
Himsilf mei se, if gode he can,   35
For he sal find þat so hit is.

þat hit be soþ and noȝt les,
þou loke þi neȝbor: whare and how?
þou loke in his biriles;
He was prute as ert þou.   40

Whate prude saltou se þar
Bot stench and wormis icrop in dritte?
Of such a siȝt we aȝt be ware
And in vre hert hit hab iwritte.

Silk no sendale nis þer none   45
No bise no no meniuer,
þer nis no þing aboute þe bone
To ȝeme þat was ihuddid here.

þe wiked wede þat was abute,
þe wormis hit habbiþ al forsoȝt.   50
Alas! wharof is man so prute,
Whan al is pride sal turne to noȝte?

If man is prute of worldis welle,
Ihc hold a fole þat he be;
Hit commiþ, hit goþ, hit nis bot dwelle,   55
Bot dritte, gile and wanite.

f. 17ʳ Lo, þat catel nis bot gile,
Trewlich ȝe mov isee
He nel be felaw bot a while,
þou salt him leue, oþer he sal þe.   60

Hit is mi rede, while þou him hast,
þou spen it wel þat helplich be
For god; but þou nelt at þe last,
Oþer men sulle aftir þe.

Nouþe oþer mister-men þer beþ,   65
þroȝ coueitise hi beþ iblend,
þat wer leuer wend to þe deþ
þan spene þe gode þat God ham send.

þoȝ man hit hab, hit nis noȝt his,
Hit nis ilend him bot a lone   70
Fortto libbe is lif iwisse
And help þe nedful þat naþ non.

Nou mani wrecch becommiþ þralle,
Hi nul noȝt spene, bot ȝime in store;
Becom hi beþ þe deuilis þralle,   75
Niȝt and dai hi libbeþ in sore.

For niȝt and dai is al har þoȝte
How hi hit mow hab and winne,
Fast to hold and spene riȝt noȝte,
And lediþ euer har lif in pinne.   80

þe wrechis wringit þe mok so fast,
Up hamsilf hi nul noȝt spened,
Ȝit hi sul dei at þe last,
And to þe deuil hi sul wend.

Siþ such a wringer goþ to helle   85   f. 17ᵛ
For litil gode þat nis noȝt his,
Whate mai ich bi þe riche man telle
þat lediþ al is lif in blisse?

Hit is as eþe forto bring
A camel into þe neldis ei   90
As a rich man to bring
Into þe blisse þat is an hei.

þeiȝ man be rich of lond and lede
And holdiþ festis ofte and lome,
Hit nis no doute he sal be dede   95
To ȝeld recning at þe Dome.

Ȝet sulle we ȝiue acuntis
Of al þat we habbiþ ibe here,
Ȝe, of a verþing, soþ iwisse,
Of al þi time fram ȝer to ȝere.   100

And bot þou hit hab ispend ariȝte,
þe gode þat God þe haþ ilend,
Of Iesus Criste þou lesist þe siȝt,
To helle pine þou worþe isend.

Of helle pine we aȝt be ware   105
And euermore hit hab in þoȝt,
Ac non nel be oþer iware
For[t] hamsilf be in ibroȝt.

þeiȝ freris prech of heuen and helle,
Of ioi and pine to mani man,   110
Al þat him þenchit bot dwelle,
As men telliþ of Wlonchargan.

f. 18ʳ
Ak ȝite þat ilk dai sal be,
þer nis non þat nold him hide,
So sore we sul drede to se   115
þe wondis of Iesus Cristis side.

His hondes, is fete sul ren of blode,
þou woldist fle, þou ne miȝt noȝ[t] þan,
þe sper, þe nailes and þe rode
Sal crie: 'tak wrech of sinful man.'   120

þe erþe þe watir þan sal sprede,
Route and driue al for wode:
'Nov Iesus Crist, we sul þe wrekke
Of sinful man þat sadde þi blode.'

Boþe fire and wind lude sal crie: 125
'Louerd nov let vs go to,
For ich wl blow, þe fire sal berne
Vp sinful man þat haþ misdo.'

Heuen and erþe sal crie and grede,
And helle sal berne, þou salt ise.   130
O! sinful man, wo worþ þi rede,
Whan al þis wrech sal be for þe.

Hit is so grisful forto loke
And forto hir þe bittir dome;
Angles sul quake, so seiþ þe bok,   135
And þat þou hirist of[t] and lome.

Sei, sinful man, whi neltou leue
þat al þing sal com to hepe?
Wel aȝt þi hert þroȝute cleue,
þin eiine blodi teris wepe.   140

f. 18ᵛ
Hit is to late whan þou ert þare
To crie 'Iesu þin ore!'
While þou ert here, be wel iware,
Vndo þin hert and liue is lore.

Vndo þin hert þat is iloke   145
Wiþ couetise and prvde þeran,
And þench þos wordis her ispoke,
Forȝite ham noȝt, ac þench apan.

And bot þou nelt þench herapan
Fort vnderfong gode lore,   150
Iwis for soþ, as þou ert man,
þou salt hit rew bitter and sore.

Manis lif nis bot a schade,
Nov he is and nov he nis;
Loke hou he mei be glade,   155
þoȝ al þis world miȝt be his.

Wold he þench, þe vnseli man,
Into þis world whate he broȝte—
A stinkind felle ilappid þeran,
Wel litil bettir þan riȝt noȝt.   160

What is þe gode þat he sal hab,
Oute of þis world whan he sal go?
A wikid wede, whi sold I gab?
For he ne broȝt wiþ him no mo.

Riȝt as he com, he sal wend   165
In wo and pine and pouerte;
Takiþ gode hede, men, to ȝur end,
For as I sigge, so hit sal be.

I note wharof is man so prute   f. 19ʳ
Of erþe, axin, fel and bone,   170
For be þe soule enis oute,
A uilir caraing nis þer non.

Mani man þenchit on is þoȝt,
He nel noȝt leue his eir al bare,
His eir sal fail and ber riȝt noȝte   175
And wast þe gode wel widewhare.

Ich warne þe, for isold hit sal
Al þat þou wan here wiþ pine,
A broþin eir sal wast it al
And be al oþeris þat was þine.   180

Nouþ siþ þat þe world nis noȝt
And catel nis bot vanite,
Haue God in ur þoȝt
And of þe catel be we fre.

Anouriþ God and Holi Chirch　　　　　　　185
And helpiþ þai þat habiþ nede,
So Godis wil we sul wirch,
þe ioi of heuen hab to mede.

What is þe ioi þat man sal hab,
If his lif he speniþ wel?　　　　　　　　190
Soþ to sigge, and noȝt to gab,
þer nis no tunge þat hit mai tel.

If I sal tel al þat I can,
In holi boke as we can rede,
Hit is a ioi þat fallit to man,　　　　　　195
Of hel pine he ne dar drede.

f. 19ᵛ　þe man þat mai to heuen com
þe swete solas forto se,
Seue siþis briȝtir þan þe sun
In heuen sal manis soule be.　　　　　　200

His bodi sal þer be also
So fair and strang, ȝe mou wel leue,
Iuil is euer fur him fro,
þer nis no þing þat him sal greue.

To met no drink þer nis no nede,　　　　　205
No for no hungir he ne sal kar;
þe siȝte of God him sal fede,
Hit is wel miri to woni þar.

þer beþ woningis mani and fale,
Gode and betir, tak god hede;　　　　　　210
þe last word bint þe tale:
Wo best mai do, best is his mede.

Heuen is heiȝ, boþe lange and wide,
Mani angles þer beþ an,
Boþe ioi and blis in euch side,　　　　　215
þerin sal woni gode Cristin man.

þe lest ioi þat þer is in:
A man sal know is owin frend,
Is wif, is fader and al is kin,
Of al þis ioi þer nis non end.   220

We sul se Oure Leuedi briȝte
So fulle of loue, ioi and blisse,
þat of hir neb sal spring þe liȝte,
Into oure hert þat ioi iwisse.

þe siȝte of þe Trinite,   225   f. 20ʳ
þe mest ioi þat mai befalle,
Boþe God and man in mageste,
þe Heiȝ King aboue vs alle.

þe siȝt of him is ure vode,
þe siȝt of him is ure [fe]st,   230
Al ure iois beþ ful gode,
þe siȝt of him is alir best.

Besech we him mek of mode,
þat soke þe milk of maidis brest,
þat boȝt us wiþ is der blode,   235
Ȝiue us þe ioi þat euer sal lest.

Alle þat beþ icommin here
Fortto hire þis sarmun,
Loke þat ȝe nab no were,
For seue ȝer ȝe habbiþ to pardoun.   240

50 hit] þat hit   108 Fort] For   118 noȝt] noȝ   136 oft] of   181 noȝt]
0 *written above* a   199 Seue] S *unclear*   230 fest] virst

14. FIFTEEN SIGNS: 'XV SIGNA ANTE IUDICIUM'   ff. 20ʳ–21ᵛ

DIMEV 5308

The enumeration of the Fifteen Signs before Doomsday was widely
popular throughout the Middle Ages, falsely attributed to Jerome. In
English the Signs are described in lyrics, sermons, biblical history,
and drama. William W. Heist, *The Fifteen Signs before Doomsday*
(East Lansing, Mich., 1952) argued for an Irish origin of the topos,
but his views have been questioned; see Martin McNamara, 'The

(Fifteen) Signs before Doomsday in Irish Tradition', *Warszawskie Studia Teologiczne*, 20 (2007), 223–54. The direct source of the poem here, as shown by Heist, pp. 180–1, and amply demonstrated by more detailed comparison, is *Les quinze signes du jugement dernier (QSJD)*, ed. Erik von Kræmer, Commentationes Humanarum Litterarum, 38/2 (Helsinki, 1966) from twenty-two Anglo-Norman and Continental manuscripts, including a copy in CUL MS Gg.1.1, an early four-teenth-century manuscript of probable Irish provenance. For analysis of this source see Heist, *Fifteen Signs*, 24, 28–9. The same poem lies behind the Signs in *Cursor Mundi*, ll. 21885–920 and ll. 22427–719 (see John J. Thompson, *The Cursor Mundi: Poem, Texts and Contexts*, Medium Ævum Monographs, NS 19 (Oxford, 1998), 168–70), as well as the fragmentary 'Les xv singnes de domesday' in MS Digby 86 (DIMEV 1309), ed. Stengel, in *Codicem manu scriptum Digby 86*, 53–7, and its later version in Cambridge, Trinity College B.11.24 (263) (DIMEV 3000), ed. Frederick J. Furnivall, in *Hymns to the Virgin and Christ*, EETS OS 24 (1867), 118–25. A forty-line prologue, omitted in some MSS of *QSJD*, is translated in *Cursor Mundi*, ll. 21885–920, but not in the poem here. Another tradition of the Signs is derived from a brief enumeration in pseudo-Bede (ed. and trans. in *Collectanea pseudo-Bedae*, ed. Martha Bayless and Michael Lapidge, Scriptores Latini Hiberniae, 14 (Dublin, 1998), 178–9; also in *PL* 94, col. 555), and thence in Peter Comestor. The only English version of this tradition is in *Prick of Conscience*, ed. Ralph Hanna and Sarah Wood, EETS OS 342 (2013), ll. 4738–817. Elements of this tradition are included in the poem here; see notes to ll. 53–4, 101–4. The title 'XV signa ante iudicium' is written in red at the head of the poem. This is repeated by Hand F at the top of ff. 20^v and 21^v, and the 'tokens' are numbered at ll. 33 ('The first tokyn', wrongly, see note to 33–5), 45 ('2', wrongly again), 57 ('3', etc.), 69, 73, 85, 97, 113, 129, 145 (see note), 169, and 177. The poem breaks off at the foot of f. 21^v after the beginning of the twelfth sign. A hand of s. xvi (Hand F?) has written 'sine aliquid operis facto', with 'desunt nonnulla' in a modern hand. Probably leaves have been lost, although there is now no physical evidence of loss.

f. 20^r þe grace of Iesu fulle of miȝte,
                þroȝ prier of ure swete Leuedi,
                Mote amang vs nuþe aliȝte
                And euer vs ȝem and saui.

Man and woman, þou aȝtist tak gome   5
þis worldis ending how hit ssal be,
þe wondres þat sal com befor þe Dome,
þat ȝung and old hit sal ise.

þe fiftene tokingis ichul ȝou telle,
As us techiþ Ysaie;   10
þe Holi Gost him taȝt ful welle,
And he hit prechid for profecie.

Hit is iwrit in holi boke,   f. 20ᵛ
As clerkis hit mow se and rede,
þat no þing no man mai loke   15
þat is so grisful forto drede.

þer nis aliue so sinful man,
If he þerof wold tak kepe,
And he wold þench apan,
þat nold wel sore in hert wepe.   20

Godmen, takiþ nou gome
Of tokninges þat commiþ bifor,
þe children wiþin þe moder wome
Wel sore sul dute and drede þerfor.

Wiþin þe moder wom hi sul grede   25
Vp Iesu Criste euer to crie:
'Louerde Crist, þou red vs rede,
And of vs þou hab mercie.

'We wold, Louerd, þat we ner
In world icom forto bene   30
And vnbeȝet of ure fader wer,
þat al þing nou sal suffri tene.'

þe first tokning sal be þusse,
Al for soþ we sul hit see,
And þat oþer sal be wors,   35
For soþ ȝe mou wel liue me.

þe sterris þat þou sest so briȝte,
In heuen aboue þat sit so fast,
For manis sin sal ȝiue no liȝt,
Ac sal adun to erþe be cast.   40

As fair and briʒte as þou seest ham,
Hi worþ becom as blak as cole
And be of hiwe durke and wan,
For manis sin þat hi sul þole.

þer nis aliue so stidfast man   45
þat þerof ne sal agrise
Him to hide he ne can,
No whoder to fle, in none wise;

Bot as bestis þat wer wode
Aʒe oþir to erne, her and þare;   50
Forþi hi ne sul can no gode,
See no lond hi ne sul spare.

þan þe dede up sal arise,
Up har biriles forto sitte,
Of þilk dai hi sul agrise   55
And lok as bestis þat cun no witte.

þe þrid dai þan amorow
Grisful hit sal be to loke,
Of moch weping and of sorow,
As we fint in holi boke.   60

þe sone þat nov schiniþ so briʒt,
þilk dai þou salt ise
Wel grene and wan sal be is liʒt,
And þat for dred so hit sal be.

Abute þe time of middai   65
He worþ as blak as þe cole,
We mov sigge wailawai,
Moch is þe pine þat we sul þole.

þe ferþ dai þat silf son
Worþ as rede as hit wer fire,   70
For ferd of Dome, þat he sold come
Bifor Iesus, þe heiʒ sire.

þe fifte tokning þat sal befal,
þat allirkin maner beste
Wel sore hi sul quak wiþal,   75
Wil þat ilk dai sal lest.

Towar heuen behold sul hi
Wiþ har mund and wiþ har þoȝt,
Of Iesu Crist merci to cri,
þoȝ þat hi ne mou spek riȝt noȝt.   80

Alas, Louerd, wat sul we tak,
We þat abbiþ sin iwroȝt?
Niȝt and dai we aȝt sore quake,
Whan we it sold þench in ure þoȝt.

þe sixte dai ne lef ich noȝt,   85
Wan þes montis and þes hille
Al for soþ hit wurþ ibroȝt
þes depe dalis forto fille.

þer nis castel no ture none
þat euer was, no be salle,   90
Imakid was of lime and ston
þat ne sal adun tofalle.

No no tre in erþ so fast
Mid al har rotis so fast [ipiȝt],
þat ne sal adun toberst   95
þilk silue dai er hit be niȝt.

þe sefþe dai hit sal grow aȝe,
Har crop adun, har rote an hei.
Such wondris we sul ise,
For Godis wreþ þat sit an hei.   100

þe tren sul blede, a wonder þing,
þe þing þat bodi no flesse naþ non,
For dred of þe heuen king
Vnkundlich þing ded sal don.

þan sal dei boþe pouer and rich,   105
Ne sal þan þer wiþstond no þing,
Al we sul ben ilich,
Boþe kniȝt and barun, erl and king.

Ne sal þer help castel no ture,   f. 21ᵛ
Palfrei, chasur no no stede,   110
No for al is moch honur,
þat he ne worþ wel sone dede.

þe eiȝt dai so is dotus,
And þat ful wel þou salt se,
Ful of tene and angus   115
Al þis dai so sal be.

Al þe see sel draw ifere,
As a walle to stond upriȝt,
And al þos watris þat beþ here
Sal cri merci up God almiȝt.   120

þe fissis þat beþ þerin iwroȝt,
þe see so hard sal ham todriue
þat hi wol wene in her þoȝt
þat God of heuen nis noȝt aliue.

þan þe see sal draw aȝe   125
Into þe stid þer hit was,
And euch uerisse watir þan sal he
Becom to is owin plas.

þe ninþe tokin sal be þus,
þe wonderis þat worþ þilk dai   130
Ouer al þat oþer sal deuers;
Wate hit is ich ȝow tel mai.

þe holi man telliþ, seint Austin,
þat þe skeis so sal spec þan,
Wan al þing so sal hab fine,   135
In steuen, as hit wer man.

Hi sul grede lude wiþal
In uois of man up God to cri,
As heuen and erþe sold tofal:
'God and man, nouþ merci.   140

'Louerd, merci of miȝt,
Nouþ is al ur time ispend;
For sinful manis ein-siȝt
Ne let us neuer ben ischend!'

þer nis no seint in heuen abow   145
In al Godis ferred,
þat þerof ne sal amoue
And of þilk tokin be aferd.

þus vs telliþ seint Ieronime
And seint Gregori also   150
þat þan sal quake seraphin
And cherubin, þat beþ angles two.

þer nis in heuen angil iwis
þat to oþer sal hab spech,
So sore iworþ adrad iwis   155
Of Iesus Cristis gremful wreche.

Al þe fendis þat beþ in hel,
Wiþ grete din hi wol com þan,
Har mone þou salt hire ful wel,
Hou hi sul cri to God and man.   160

O, man and womman, þou take hede,
Hou þe fentis sul men har mone,
Wel aʒtist þe fair to lede,
Wile þou art in þis wrech wone.

Vp Iesus Crist hi sul cri   165
Wiþ such a steuen of pine and wo
'Louerd, ʒif vs ur herbe[r]gi,
Aʒe to helle let us neuer go.'

þe endlefte dai fure windis sul rise,
And þe reinbow þan sal fal,   170
þat al þe fentis sal of agris
And be ifesid into helle.

For, wolny nulni, hi sul fle
And þat into þe pine of helle,
Maugrei ham þer hi mot be   175
Wiþ duble pine þerin to dwel.

þe twelfte dai þe fure elemens sul cri
Al in one heiʒ steuene:
'Merci Iesus, fiz Mari,
As þou ert God and king of heuene!'   180

9 fiftene] xv   94 so fast ipiʒt] ipiʒt so fast (*last two words possibly marked for insertion*)   129 ninþe] ix   149 seint] seint seint   167 herbergi] herbegi
169 endlefte] xi   177 twelfte] xij

ff. 48^{r–v},
22^{r–v}

15. SEVEN SINS

DIMEV 5355

The first 108 lines are written on f. 48^{r–v}, and the remainder on f. 22^r, ending incomplete with just eight and a half lines on f. 22^v. The poem begins in ten six-line tail-rhyme stanzas marked with paraphs, with tail-rhyme lines written to the right, then switches to couplets each written as one line with medial punctus elevatus. There are forty lines on pride, sixty-two on avarice, and nineteen lines on envy, with decorated capitals at ll. 1, 61, 101, and 164, and breaking off mid-line at the top of the page, leaving the rest blank. It is presumably coincidental that these three sins are the focus of 'Song on the Times' (item 33); see esp. ll. 13–15, 149–50.

On the many treatments of the topic see Morton W. Bloomfield, *The Seven Deadly Sins* (East Lansing, Mich., 1952), who says this poem 'shows features unusual in the English tradition' (p. 160), without specifying what these features are.

f. 48^r

þe king of heuen mid vs be,
þe fend of helle fram vs te,
  Todai and euir more.
Todai me ȝiue gode beginninge
þe king of h[e]uen to worþing   5
  And spekin of is lore;

And þat ȝe hit mote vnderstonde
(þe fend to mochil schame and schonde)
  þis predicacioune;
And þat ȝe hit hold mote,   10
Bodi and soule to mochil bote
  And to saluacioune.

Alle we beþ meiis and mowe
And of one foule erþe isowe,
  Whoso hit wold vnderstond.   15
þis worldis wel nis bot wowe,
þis wrecche lif nis bot a þrow,
  Al dai hit is gond.

Man, ne be þou neuer so riche,
Behold whom þou art iliche   20

Whan þou ert al nakid.
Beþench þat þou salt iworþe
And forroti to axin and erþe,
   Wharof þou ert imakid.

Clansi þe of þi misdede   25
And lerne welle þi lif to lede,
   þe while þou art aliue;
To none frend þou nab triste,
Bot to one Iesus Criste,
   To child no to wiue.   30

Mi leue frendis, ich ȝou biseche,
Ȝung, old, pouer and reche,
   Herkniþ to Godis speche!
In þe name of God and seint Marie,
Ȝoure sinful lif to amendie
   Todai ich wol ȝow teche;   35

And þat he me let so wel to spek,
Todai þe Deuilis staf to brek
   And wiþ him so to fiȝte,
þerto, par charite, ich ȝou crie   40
A Pater Noster and Aue Marie
   In þe name of God almiȝte.

þat pees þat is in Godis huse
Todai be amangis vse
   þroȝ is holi grace,   45
þat me ȝiue lif and gode ending,
And to ȝou ȝiue gode lusting
   In þis silue place!

God himsilf seiiþ in his gospel,   f. 48ᵛ
Mi leue frendis, ich wol ȝou tel,
   Nimiþ to me gome!   50
O worde ich ȝou lie nelle
Of heuen blis no pine of helle
   No of riche Dome.

And of þe heuid-sinnes seuene,   55
Wharfor men lesiþ heuene,
   Ich wol ȝou nemeni alle;

And har namis ich wol ȝou teche,
And hou hi wol men bipeche
   And make ham to falle. 60

First at prude ich wol begin,
For hit is heuid of al sinne.
Ich hit wol ȝou do to wit,
In holi boke hit is iwrit:
Lucifer þat was so briȝte, 65
þat fairist was of al wiȝte,
Wiþoute God in heuen nas
Non so fair als he was;
Nas neuer non so fule ifund
As he in helle liþ ibund. 70
Nad he no more gilte,
Wharfor he was of heuen ipilte:
A litil prude him was incom,
þerfor God him hauiþ benome
Heuen blisse þat euer sal last, 75
And into helle he is cast,
þer he sal woni euermore
And is prude abigge wel sore.
Alas, man, whi artou prute?
Whannin commiþ þi fair schrute 80
Mid whate þou art ischrid aboute?
Noȝte of þe, man, boute doute!
þine owen schond þou werist on,
þat heliþ þi fleis and þi bone.
Ich wol þat þou iwit wel, 85
Hit nis bote a hori felle,
þat is þine owen riȝt wede;
Beþenche þe, man, and hab drede!
Man and womman, vnderstond þis:
Betak euch beste his, 90
þat ert so fair mid bigon,
Linnin, wollin, glouis and schone,
þat þou art in hit so prute,
Ne sal þe leue neuer a cloute.
þerfor, man, ich þe forbede 95
Worldlich prude in hert and dede,

And lede þi lif bi Godis rede
To loui God, and hab drede
þat þou be Godis sone,
And him to queme at þe Dome.   100

Coueitise is þat oþer;
Herkne nov, leue broþer!
þer is mani man bipeiȝte,
So þe fend him hauiþ iteiȝte.
þe man þat is coueituse,   105
Ne commiþ he neuer to Godis huse.
Suche þer beþ al to fele
þat louiþ more þis worldis welle
þan God þat haþ ham of erþe iwroȝte   f. 22ʳ
And so swiþe dere ham boȝte.   110
He nel is catel spen in wast,
Ac euer he hit witiþ fast.
He nold þat aliue nere
None so riche as he were,
And euer so he hauiþ more,   115
þe faster he gaderiþ to store;
And euer he wol is lif so lede
In mochel sorow and in drede;
Nel he neuer hab rest
Is mochil mukke to witi fast,   120
þat ne mai in him slepe cum,
Lest is muk be him benome.
Leuer him wer ȝiue of is blode
þan ani man of is gode!
Nel he of oþir þing hede,   125
But is fule bodi fede
Mid is siluir and is gold,
Noȝt is soule þat he schold.
Apan is muk he sit abrode;
He þat þus doþ mid is gode   130
He ne þenchith noȝt in is end
þat he sal of þis world wend;
And vnderstonde noȝt he nelle,
What he is, no whoder he schel.
His catel he weniþ witi wel,   135

Oc in is soule þenche he nelle;
Wiþ is siluir and is gold
He weniþ euer is lif hold.
Whan he weniþ liuie wel,
Mid deþ adun fal he schel;   140
þe deuil benimiþ him is breþ,
Moch sorow þan he him deþ.
For is gode þe fend him deriiþ,
And is soul to helle he feriiþ;
þe deuil is his executur   145
Of is gold and is tresure
þat he so moch trist to;
Loke nou hou he is ago!
þerfor, man, in alle wise
Ich þe forbede coueitise.   150
To worldis wel nab þou no triste.
Hit went awei so doþ þe miste;
Her it is and her hit nis,
Al so fariþ þe worldis blis.
Ne be he neuer so riche,   155
Whan he liþ a cold liche,
If he hauiþ an old clute
He mai be swiþe prute,
Wharmid ihelid he sal be
þat no man nakid him ise.   160
Of what he gadred and is was,
Nis þis rewþ? alas, alas!

þe þrid sin so is onde
þat mochil nuþe is in lond,
And euir hi quemiþ þe fend of helle;   165
In woch maner ich wol ʒou tel.
Leue breþerin, herkniþ now,
And ich wol ʒou tel how.
Worldis wel falliþ vnliche,
And noʒt euch man ilich.   170
Sum þer beþ þat cun noʒt libbe,
Sum þat hauiþ frendis sibbe;
f. 22ᵛ   And sum þer beþ þat swinkiþ sore,
Winne catel to hab more,

Hamsilf fair to susteni,   175
And euer more hi beþ nedi;
And sum þer beþ, leue broþer,
þat more haþ þan anoþer
And more loue of gode man.
Anoþer wol after þan   180
Areri cuntake

5 heuen] houen   83 on] *altered from* an   93 hit] *altered from* his

16–18. PORTIUNCULA INDULGENCE MATERIALS   ff. 23^r–27^v

Three texts relating to the indulgence obtained by St Francis. In
1216 Francis is supposed to have persuaded Pope Honorius III to
grant a perpetual indulgence to all who visited the Portiuncula chapel
near Assisi between Vespers on 1 August and Vespers on the
following day. The various testimonies were assembled by Francesco
della Rossa Bartholi in *c*.1335. There is disorder in the sequence of
the texts here, indicating disarrangement of the leaves, but since text
17 ends on the same leaf (f. 26^v) as 18 begins, and 18 ends on the
same leaf (f. 25^r) as 16 begins, it is clear that the scribe copied them
in the order set out below. Except for the first sixteen lines on f. 24^v
in Hand A, the texts throughout are in Hand D (perhaps the same
scribe writing anglicana), with Hand C adding titles later in the
middle of f. 25^r ('de fratribus peregre perficientibus') and at the foot
of f. 25^v ('de indulgenciis'). Item 16 breaks off in the middle of f. 23^v,
leaving the rest blank; f. 24^r is also blank.

17

Letter of Theobald, Bishop of Assisi (1296–1329), giving an account
of the circumstances of the Portiuncula Indulgence (ff. 24^v, 26^{r-v}).

   Rubric: 'Incipit indulgentia portiuncule sicut eam habuit beatus
Franciscus a domino.'

Frater Theobaldus dei gratia episcopus assisinas . . . In quorum omnium
testimonium et fidem certiorem presentes nostri sigilli appensione fecimus
communiri.

Theobald supports the indulgence against detractors, reporting
testimonies that Francis was granted the indulgence by the pope,
assuring the pope that he needed no written evidence. He criticizes

the many in the Curia who refuse to accept the authenticity of the indulgence.

Ed. Paul Sabatier, in *Fratris Francisci Bartholi de Assisio: Tractatus de Indulgentia S. Mariae de Portiuncula*, ii, pp. lxxvii–lxxix; also in *Acta Sanctorum*, ed. J. Bollandus and others (Antwerp, 1643–1940): October 11, 879–81. The original letter is dated the Feast of St Laurence (10 August) 1310.

18

Friar Michael Bernardi, Testimony to the Portiuncula Indulgence (ff. 26^v–27^v, 25^r).

In nomine indiuidue Trinitatis et beate Marie, ego Michael Bernardi olim de Spellonnis nunc habitator Assisi . . . fuerunt multi testes tam Perusio quam de aliis ciuitatibus et castris et contra.

On the testimony of the saint's companions, Bernardi reports that Christ granted the indulgence to Francis after he had resisted the temptations of Satan and mortified himself by jumping into a thorn bush. Francis then travelled to Rome to have the indulgence instituted by the pope and (with much resistance) promulgated by the bishops. The text is somewhat abbreviated and lacks the final paragraph of Sabatier's text in *Fratris Francisci Bartholi*, pp. lxxxii–lxxxvi.

16

Francesco della Rossa Bartholi (d. 1372?), *Tractatus de Indulgentia Sanctae Marie de Portiuncula*, cap. 37 (ff. 25^{r-v}, 23^{r-v}, breaks off incomplete, with the lower half of f. 23^v and the whole of 24^r blank).

Rubric: 'de fratribus peregre perficientibus'.

Anno domini m^o ccc^o viii xx die februarii, Frater Jacobus sacerdos & capellanus. . . . Crucifixus voluit propter amorem quem habet ad christianos quod esset citra mare. Et.

This extract describes how on 20 February 1328 a rich lady inhabited by a truth-telling demon affirmed the truth of the indulgence which is denied by many Dominicans. She agrees with a Franciscan that the Minorites are better and wiser than the Preachers. The extract ends at the point where she states that the power of the indulgence is such that a contrite man would be redeemed even if he had murdered everyone in the world. The *Tractatus* was completed in 1335, according to Sabatier, *Fratris Francisci Bartholi*, p. c.

Ed. *Fratris Francisci Bartholi*, 70–81, breaking off at p. 77, l. 1, having wrongly anticipated and crossed through p. 77, l. 5. Translation and discussion of all this material by Noel Muscat, ed., *In Defence of the Portiuncula Indulgence* (Malta, 2012), at http://i-tau.com/franstudies/texts/portiuncula_indul.pdf.

19. CHRIST ON THE CROSS   f. 28^{r–v}
DIMEV 3183 and 3341

The English text is embedded in well-known Latin pieces which commonly accompany their English translations and adaptations. See Ralph Hanna, 'Editing "Middle English Lyrics": The Case of *Candet Nudatum Pectus*', *Medium Ævum*, 80 (2011),189–200; Rita Copeland, 'The Middle English *Candet Nudatum Pectus* and Norms of Early Vernacular Translation Practice', *Leeds Studies in English*, NS 15 (1984), 57–81. Lines 1–16 of the English are introduced by a cue for 'Respice in faciem Christi tui', which is given in full in John of Grimestone's preaching book, Advocates 18.7.21, f. 117^r, as: 'Respice in faciem christi tui & inuenies eum in dorso flagellatum. Latere sauciatum. Capite spinis coronatum. Manibus perforatum. Pedibus confossum. Volue & reuolue dominicum corpus a latere vsque ad latus. A summa vsque deorsum & circumquaque inuenies dolorem & cruorem' (*Religious Lyrics of the XIVth Century*, ed. Carleton Brown (2nd edn., Oxford, 1957), 242). This is followed by a variant text of 'Candet nudatum pectus', by John of Fécamp, widely ascribed to Augustine; for the standard version, also in Grimestone's book with a translation (DIMEV 6540.5), see Woolf, *English Religious Lyric*, 29 n. 2. Following the English ll. 1–16 are a verse from Rev. 1: 5, two English lines (ll. 17–18), and a passage from Anselm's *Cur Deus Homo*, 2.20, stating Anselm's central theme of the necessity for Christ's sacrifice, which is then paraphrased in English (ll. 19–26). A very well-known Latin verse by Philip the Chancellor, 'O homo vide' (Walther, *Initia* 8401; printed in Woolf, *English Religious Lyric*, 37) is then quoted and translated (ll. 27–42). It is also quoted and translated in Grimestone's book (DIMEV 4849), ed. Brown, in *Religious Lyrics*, 88.

DIMEV records ll. 1–26 as no. 3183, 'a paraphrase of *Respice in faciem Christi tui*'. There is an earlier copy, 'Loke to þi louerd, man, þar hanget he a rode' in Cambridge, St John's College, MS A.15.

Another translation of *Respice*, 'Alle þat gos and rydys' (*DIMEV* 368) with some verbal correspondences is preserved in Lambeth Palace Library MS 557, a thirteenth-century sermon collection of Irish provenance, and is printed in Woolf, *English Religious Lyric*, 43. *DIMEV* records ll. 27–42 as no. 3341, describing it as 'a paraphrase of *O homo vide quid pro te pacior*, etc.' The best-known translation of 'Candet nudatum pectus' is 'Wit was his nakede brest' (*DIMEV* 6540, 6540.5), extant in many copies and versions. Other paraphrases of 'Respice' are *DIMEV* 3177 and 3336; of 'O homo vide' are *DIMEV* 805 (in *Fasciculus morum*, with Latin), 4849, 4850, 6110, and 6111. Woolf, *English Religious Lyric*, 19–44, has a full discussion.

Below the English text at the foot of f. 28ᵛ is an extract from *De doctrina cordis* (Gerardus Leodiensis, *Speculum concionatorum ad illustrandum pectora auditorium* (Naples, 1607), 6–8). This ends on f. 29ʳ, perhaps incomplete, leaving the remainder of the leaf blank.

f. 28ʳ Respice in faciem Christi tui etc. Augustinus.

Pendet nudatum pectus, rubet sanguineum latus, regia pallent ora, decora languent lumina, crura pendent marmorea. Rigat terebratos [*MS* terre beatos] pedes sanguinis unda. De istis auctoritatibus anglicum:

> Behold to þi Lord, man, whare he hangiþ on rode,
> And weep, if þou miȝt, teris al of blode;
> And loke to is heued, wiþ þornis al bewonde,
> And to is felle so bispette and to þe speris wnde.
> Bihold to is brest nakid, and is blodi side, 5
> Stiuiiþ is armis þat sprad beþ so wide;
> His fair lere falowiþ, and dimmiþ is siȝte,
> þerto is hendi bodi on rode so is ytiȝte.
> His lendin so hangiþ as cold as marbre stone,
> For luste of lechuri nas þer neuer none. 10
> Behold to is nailes in hond and ek in fote,
> And how þe stremis erniþ of is swet blode.
> Beginne at is heued and loke to is to:
> þou ne findest in is bodi bot anguis and wo.
> Turne him uppe, turne him doune, þi swete lemman; 15
> Ouer al þou findist him blodi oþer wan.

Dilexit nos et lauit nos a peccatis nostris in sanguine suo etc.

Leue, for þe mi brest nakid schiniþ, glisniing.
Mi side dep istunge, mi hondes sore bleding.

Quid misericordius ualet intelligi ipsi peccatori eternis tormentis f. 28ᵛ
dampnato et, vnde se redimat, non habenti quam ut dicat deus ipse
peccatori. Dicit enim deus pater: 'Accipe vnigenitum meum et da
pro te.' Et ille filius: 'Tolle me et redime te.' Anglicum expone:

> Man, þou hast þe forlor
> And ful nei[ʒ] to helle ibor.   20
> Wend aʒe and com to me
> And ich wol underfang þe.
> For first ich makid þe of noʒt,
> And siþ dere þe iboʒt,
> Whan ich mi lif ʒef for þe   25
> And ihang was on tre. Etc.

O homo, vide, quid pro te pacior! Sicut est dolor, sicut dolor, quo
crucior. Ad te clamo, qui pro te morior; uides penas, quibus afficior;
uide clauos, quibus confodior! Si est tantus dolor exterior, interius
est planctus grauior.

> Man, bihold what ich for þe
> þolid up þe rode-tre.
> Ne mai no kinnes wo be mare
> þan min was, þo ich heng þare.   30
> Hire me, man, to þe gredind,
> For loue of þe biter deiend.
> Loke mi pinis biter and strang,
> Wan ich was nailed þroʒ fot and hond.
> For þe ich ad hard stundis   35
> Dintes grete and sore wondes,
> For þe biter drink ich dronk,
> And þou cunnest me no þonk.
> Wiþvte ich was ipinid sore,
> Wiþin ich was mochil more.   40
> For þou nelt þonk me
> þe loue þat ich schowid þe. Etc.

Preparandum est cor hominis tamquam domus ad magnum hospitem
suscipiendum, Christum sanctum dominum. 'Ipse est enim tamquam
uir uagus super terram et declinans ad manendum.' Je. ix. 'Cuius

delicie sunt esse cum filiis hominum', ut dicitur Proverb. Qui in tuo negocio tantum laborauit, in hospicio cordis tui lassatus et wlneratus requiescere querit, dicens per Ysaiam: 'Hec requies mea, reficite lassum'. Lassum ergo Christum tuum refice, ut in te locum refeccionis et quietis inueniat, qui in te et a te | tanti causas laboris accepit. 'Laborem mihi prebuistis in iniquitatibus', Benedictus dicit ipse per Ysaiam. Quis pugilem suum de uictoria redeuntem gloriosum, asperum, sanguine liuidum, fessum, wlneratum, in domo sua gratanter non reciperet et cum honore non occurreret? Huius gracia ciues angelici non immemores, quos etiam non apprehendit, sicut dicit Apostolus, id est quorum naturam non assumpsit. Cum gloria ascendenti occurrerunt dicentes in Ysaya: 'Quis est iste, qui uenit de Edom etc., iste formosus in stola sua?' Ve ergo tibi, si ipse possit tibi improperare illud ewangelii: 'Hospes fui et non collegistis me'. Attende ergo, quod in tribus consistit preparacio hospicii cordis tui: primo, ut mundetur, secundo ut ornetur, tertio ut per te custodiantur. Munda ergo hospicium cordis tui, si uis Christum hospitem habere, quod fit per timorem, qui expellit et eicit peccata tamquam immundicias cordis, quia, sicut dicitur in Ecclesiastico: 'Timor domini expellit peccatum', per scopam confessionis etc., et non tantum domus cordis a squaloribus uiciorum mundanda est, sed etiam floribus uirtutum adornanda, vt humilitate fulgeat, castitate candeat, paciencia rutilet, caritate resplendeat.

[*Remainder of f. 29ʳ blank*].

20 nei3] neiþ   29 mare] o *altered to* a

f. 29ᵛ–31ʳ

20. FALL AND PASSION

DIMEV 5307

Written in alternately rhyming quatrains, as 'Sarmun', 'Fifteen Signs', and 'Ten Commandments', and in much the same style as these other metrical sermons. The poet surveys the history of salvation from the Fall of the Angels to the Resurrection, describing the Fall of Adam and Eve, the disobedience of mankind through Old Testament history, the life and death of Christ, and the Harrowing of Hell. For a poem covering the same ground cf. 'Louerd ass þu ard on God' (DIMEV 3187) in Cambridge, Trinity College MS B.14.39 (323), ed. in *Religiöse Dichtung*, 391–404.

þe grace of God ful of miȝt,   f. 29ᵛ
þat is king and euer was,
Mote amang vs aliȝt
And ȝiue vs alle is swet grace

Me to spek and ȝou to lere   5
þat hit be worsip, Lord, to þe,
Me to tech and ȝou to bere
þat helplich to ure sowles be;

þat ich mote wiþ moch worþing
þroȝ is miȝt so hit fulfille   10
To ȝov schow is vprising,
If hit be his swet wille.

Al þat God suffrid of pine,
Hit nas noȝt for is owen gilt,
Ok hit was, man, for sin þine   15
þat wer for sin in helle ipilt.

þo Lucifer steiȝ in pride
þat was angel in heuen so briȝte,
Vte of heuen he gan glide,
And into helle sone he liȝte.   20

And wiþ him mani and mo,
þat no tunge ne miȝt telle,
Wiþ him fille adune also
Into þe derk pit of helle.

Seue daies and seue niȝt,   25
As ȝe seeþ þat falliþ snowe,
Vte of heuen hi aliȝt
And into helle wer iþrow.

For þe prude of Lucifer
þe teþe angle fille into helle,   30
And al þat to him boxum were
Euer in pine hi mot dwelle.

Har stides forto fulfille
þat wer ifalle for prude and hore,
God makid Adam to is wille   35
To fille har stides þat wer ilor.

Skil, resun, and ek miȝt
He ȝef Adam in his mode
To be stidfast wiþ al riȝt
And leue þe harme and do gode.   40

God ȝaf him a gret maistri
Of al þat was in watir and londe,
Of Paradis al þe baly,
Whan him likid to is honde;

Foules, bestis and þe frute;   45
Saf o tre he him forbede,
Of Paradis þe grete dute,
And ȝit he sinied þroȝ iuil red.

To him þe deuil had envie
þat he in is stid schold be broȝte;   50
A serpent he com þroȝ felonie
And makid Eue chonge hir þoȝt.

Whi com he raþer to Eue
þan he com to Adam?
Ichul ȝou telle, sires, beleue,   55
For womman is lef euer to man;

f. 30ʳ Womman mai turne manis wille,
Whare ȝho wol pilt hir to;
þat is þe resun and skille
þat þe deuil com hir first to.   60

 'Ette', he seid, 'of þis appil,
If þat þou wolt witti be;
þe worþ as witti of miȝt and wille
As God himsilf in Trinite.'

Hi nad bot þat appil iȝette   65
þat þe sin nas ido;
Glad was þe deuil, wol ȝe iwit,
For þe sorow þat h[i] sold to.

Of Paradis hi wer utepilt
Wiþ trauail har liuelode to winne   70
And vteflemid for har gilt,
And neuer efte Paradis to com inne.

In þe vale of Ebron
His liuelod he most swink sore;
Wiþ sorow and care and dreri won   75
He liued nine hundred ȝer and more.

Aftir is lif he had here,
Nedis he most wend to helle
For þe trepas þat he did here;
þer he most bide and dwelle.   80

God makid mankin more,
Ok to helle þe deuil ham broȝt
And euer ham traiid þroȝ is lore;
Non fram him scapid noȝt.

God is prophetis to ham send   85
And seid hov hi sold be sauid,
As bi Moyses þat [to] am wend;
Aȝe þe propheci ȝit i sinid.

God wist wel bi þilk say
þat bi no man þat was ycor,   90
Whan bi prophetis no bi lai,
þat communelich hi ne wer forlor.

Holi bokis fort fulfil
God is angle anon forþ send,
As bi angle Gabriel   95
þat to þe maid was iwend.

Flees he tok of maid Mari,
God and manis kund togadir,
And þat was a gret maistri
þat þe doȝtir ber þe fader.   100

Maid bere heuen king
þat is al ure creatoure,
Maid ber þe swet þing,
þerfor sso ne les noȝt hir flure.

God him ȝed an erþ here   105
þritti winter and somdel mo,
As holi writ vs gan lere;
He suffrid boþe pine and wo.

Man aȝens God so gilt
To heuen non sowle ne miȝte   110
Fort Godis sone in rode was pilt
And wan vs heuen liȝt.

Iudas ne cuþe is lord noȝt hold,
His owen disciple ȝit he was;
For þritti peniis he him sold,   115
Ynom and ibund he was.

He was ibobid and ismitte
And hi spette in is face,
Hi bede him rede if he cuþe witte
Woch of ham al hit was.   120

He was ibund to a tre
And ibet wiþ scurges kene
þat al þe blode vt gan fle,
Ouer al is bodi hit was sene.

Siþ hi nom him as a þef   125
And lad him bifor Pilate
For he nas noȝt to ham lef;
Hi had to him grete hate.

Pilat bed ham do har best,
Aȝe þe law be he nold;   130
For no gilt bi him he nist
Warfor deþ suffri he ssold.

[Siþ hi seid at one mouþe
þat he wold destru temple and chirch,
And þat he was wel couþe   135
þat al falsnis schold wirche.

An vp Pilat hi cried apan,
Euchon at one vois,
þat he schold hold Baraban
And do Iesus on þe crois.]   140

Hi nailed him in hond and fete,
As ȝe mow al ise;
For þe appil þat Adam ete
Deþ he þolid opon þe tre.

þe wikkid men nol leue noȝt　　　　　　　　145
þat he wer fullich ded so,
Fort þat wiþ a sper hi ad him soȝt,
And clef is swet hert atwo.

þer was in þe lond a kniȝt
þat het Iosep of Arimathie,　　　　　　　150
þat louid Iesus wel ariȝt
And þoȝt is wel to honuri.

He wend to Pilat swiþe snel
And besoȝt him mercy,
If hit wer is wil　　　　　　　　　155
þe bodi grant biri.

þo Pilat had igrant is [bone],
Glade ynoȝ he was;
He nem þat swet bodi adoun
And biriid hit in a fair plas.　　　　　160

His moder stode him beside
And seint Ion ek also,
Bitter teris vte gan glide,
Hir þoȝt hir hert wol atwo.

Hit nas no wonder þoȝ ȝo wep　　　　　165
For hir swet child alowe;
Wiþ nailes he was ismit dep,
Wiþ sper hi delet him in two.

Al hir ioi was ago,
þo ȝo him sei dei in rode,　　　　　　170
Forto wep ȝo nad no mo
Bot fure bitter teris of blode.

Who spekiþ of deil aȝe þat del,　　　　f. 31ʳ
Neuer such nas þer none
As whan þat hi him beheld,　　　　　　175
As ȝho makid and seint Ion.

In þis maner he was ipinsed,
As his swet wil hit was,
And deþ for mankyn suffred;
þe þ[r]id dai vp he ros.　　　　　　　180

After þat he liȝt into helle,
þer al þe sowles wer iwisse,
Al his frendis he broȝt vt al
In to ioi and heuen blis.

Whan in helle was seint Ion,   185
Patriarkes and oþer mo,
Hit [is] isene þer scapid non,
Profetis þat God louid also.

Al in helle were ifast,
Fort Iesus Crist þroȝ is miȝte   190
Of þe pit vte he ham cast
And broȝt ham to heuen lyȝt.

þroȝ is deþ he ouercam,
As he is manhed siwed,
As profetis prechid in his name,   195
So þat he deþ suffrid.

þo he rose fram deþ to liue,
As telliþ Daui þe king,
Is godhed he gan to kiþe;
Holi Boke telliþ is uprising.   200

Iesus was sikir inoȝ
þat seid erlich 'ich wol riȝt me',
And a[ns]ward wiþvt woȝ,
'After þat deþ ouercom be'.

þe þrid dai he ros to liue,   205
Is lore riuedlich he send,
His deciplis he makid bliþe,
þerafter in þe world ham send

Of his lore forto preche,
Hou hi, Lord, ssold siu þe,   210
And þe sinful folk to tech,
Hou meri hit is to wiþ þe be.

þerafter he steiȝ to heuen aboue,
þer ioi is þat euer lest,
And þer he sal al vs loue   215
In his swet blisful fest. Amen.

68 hi] he   76 nine hundred] ix^c   87 to] *om.*   95 Gabriel] r *inserted*
another hand 106 þritti] xxx^{ti}   115 þritti] xxx   133–40 *These two stanzas*
follow l. 176   150 Arimathie] Arimathier   157 bone] luue (*?unclear*)
172 fure] iiii   180 þrid] þid   187 is] *om.*   203 answard] asnward
205 þrid] iij

21. TEN COMMANDMENTS   ff. 31ᵛ–32ʳ

DIMEV 3774

A number of early rhyming lists of the Ten Commandments are
printed in *English Lyrics*, ed. Brown, 33, 129, 181–2, and others in
Religiöse Dichtung, ed. Reichl, 334–7. The Auchinleck 'Iesu þat for vs
wolde die' (DIMEV 2914), ed. Eugen Kölbing, 'Kleine Publicatio-
nen aus der Auchinleck-HS', *Englische Studien* 9 (1886), 42–6, details
the Seven Sins (ll. 1–74), the Commandments (ll. 55–74), followed
by Pater Noster, Creed, Ave Maria, and Hours of the Cross.
Mannyng's *Handlyng Synne* offers the liveliest account. The struc-
ture of the poem here is unusual, with a prologue denouncing
swearing, i.e. the second Commandment, and introducing 'love thy
neighbour as thyself' as the fourth. The first three Commandments
are covered in some detail (ll. 33–64), but the treatment of the
seventh concerning one's neighbour consists of little more than a
rhymed list (ll. 65–80). Hand F has supplied brief annotations as
noted.

Nou, Iesus, for þi derworþ blode   f. 31ᵛ
þat þou schaddist for mankyn,
Ʒif vs grace to wirch workis gode,
To heuen þat we mot entri inn.

Man and womman, ich red be ware   5
Ʒure gret oþis þat ʒe beleue,
And bot ʒe nul, God nel ʒou spare,
Boþe lif and catel he wol ʒou reue.

Hit nis no wonder for soþ iwisse
þat gret wreche ne falliþ þerfor,   10
For we ne leuiþ of al is limmes
þat we ne habbiþ ham forswore.

Man is wors þan eni hunde,
Oþer he is to wild and wode,

þat we ssold edwite is worþi wound   15
þat he þolid for vre gode.

Be aware, whose-euer wol:
Al quelme and sorow þat euir is,
At þen end so find we sulle
þat for manis sin it is.   20

Ich rede þat euch be ware iwis,
In as moch as [h]e is man,
Whan ȝe sweriþ gret oþis
In rode þou piltist him apan.

God commandid [M]oysay   25
þat he ssold wend and prech,
þat was in þe hil of Syna[i],
Hou he ssold þe folk tech,

And to ssow ham Godis defens,
Boþe to ȝung and to olde,   30
Of þe Ten Commandemens;
Whos wold be sauid, ham ssold hold.

þe first Comondement is þis:
O God we ssul honuri,
þe heiȝ king of heuen blis,   35
His name wiþ wirssip to worþi.

Loue þou him, as he doþ þe,
Wiþ al þi miȝt and þi þoȝt;
We auȝt ful wel, for hit was he
þat vs wrecchis so dere boȝt.   40

More harm is we doþ noȝt so,
We louid þe ful dritte of grunde.
Alas! wrecchis, whi do we so?
Hit mai noȝt hold vre lif a stunde.

Ve! beþ hi þe deuil betauȝt   45
þat liuiþ op goddis mo þan one
And makiþ goddis þroȝ wichcraft;
þai ssul al to þe deuil gone.

þe secunde so is þis:
Sundai wel þat ȝe holde,   50
To serue God þilk dai wis,
Boþe ȝung and ek olde.

And now þe Sundai opunlich
Men holt al har cheping;
Wonder þat Gode ne sent wreech   55
Al an erþe vp mankyn.

þe þrid is fader, moder to honuri,
Fo[r] euch man aȝt ful wel.
Moch ten suffrid hi,
Her hi miȝt bring þe wrecch to wel.   60

Hit falliþ bi children þat beþ quede,   f. 32ʳ
As fariþ bi been in hiue:
Whan fader ȝiue[þ] ham londe and leede,
þe ȝung wol þe old ut driue.

þe verþ: loue þi neiȝbore as þine owe bodi,   65
Non oþer þou him wil;
þe fift: wit þe fram licheri;
þe sixt is: no gode of man þou ne stel.

þe sefþe: manslaȝt þou ne be,
Ne coueit noȝt neuer a del,   70
þoȝ þou be stuter þan is he,
No is wif no is catel.

Fals witnes þou ne ber
Forto des[tre]i pouer no riche;
Sore and bitter þe soule sal der,   75
For hit benimeþ heuenrich.

Besech we him mild of mode
þat sok þe milk of maidis brest,
þat boȝt vs wiþ is der blod,
Ȝiue vs euer in heuen rest! Amen.   80

22 he] þe   25 Moysay] to ysay   27 Synai] Syna   31 Ten] x
58 For] foȝ   63 ȝiueþ] ȝiuef   69 sefþe] vij   74 destrei] deserti

22. LULLABY

DIMEV 3302

Of several lyrics beginning 'Lullay, Lullay, little child', two in friar
John of Grimestone's sermon book are closely related to this one,
both addresses by the sinner to the Christ-child, lamenting the
sorrows he must suffer for our sins. 'Lullay, lullay litel child, child
reste þe a þrowe' (DIMEV 3300; *Religious Lyrics*, 83–4) has the same
stanza of seven-stress lines, with 'Lullay lullay' as the first words of
ll. 1 and 5 of each stanza. Either one author copied from the other, or
the poet wrote them as a pair. 'Lullay, lullay, litel child, / þu þat
were so sterne & wild' (DIMEV 3301; *Religious Lyrics*, 80–1) has this
poem's first line 'Lullay, lullay, litel child, qui wepest þu so sore?'as a
burden (see note to ll. 3 and 35). See Woolf, *English Religious Lyric*,
154–6 for discussion and comparison of these 'Lullay' poems.

The poem is of English provenance, the scribe altering some
features to his dialect. See Introduction, 'Language', p. xxix, and
note to l. 27. Lines from this poem are quoted in a fifteenth-century
Latin sermon in Worcester Cathedral Library MS F.10. The writer
first cites *Meditationes piissimae* (for details see headnote to 'Sarmun',
text 13): 'Consider, o man, what you were before your birth, and what
you are from birth to death, and what you will be after this life'
('Attende, o homo, quid fuisti ante ortum, et quid es ab ortu usque ad
occasum, atque quid eris post hanc vitam'), continuing: 'There used
to be a popular song as follows:

> þer nys no best olyue made of bon and blod
> þat hwen he cometȝ into world ne kan dun himself sum god
> But a barn unbliþe a brol of Adam blod.'

After commenting on the misery of life, the homilist says: 'Therefore
the quoted song begins as follows:

> Lullay, lullay litil schild, hwu wepust þou so sore
> Nede mot y wepe hyt was me ȝarkud ȝore
> For to liuen in sorwe and kare now and ewermore
> As myen eldres han don þat warn me beforne.

Behold, there is great wretchedness in man's coming into this world.'
(Quoted from Wenzel, *Preachers, Poets, and the Early English Lyric*,
165–6.)

The six-line stanzas rhyme aaaabb, with lines of six and seven stresses. The scribe marked each stanza with a paraph, the refrain with 'R', and the caesura with a punctus, generally preceding the last three stresses. The scribe's note at the head of the poem, 'Require ista in latino xii folio' refers to the Latin translation of the first two stanzas now at the end of the manuscript at the foot of f. 63ᵛ. Much of the last line of this has been lost by trimming the page.

Lollai, l[ollai], litil child, whi wepistou so sore?   f. 32ʳ
Nedis mostou wepe, hit was iȝarkid þe ȝore
Euer to lib in sorow and sich, and mourne euer[more],
As þin eldren did er þis, whil hi aliues w[o]re.
    Lollai, [lollai], litil child, child, lolai, lullow,   5
    Into vncuþ world icommen so ertow.

Bestis and þos foules, þe fisses in þe flode,
And euch schef aliues imakid of bone and blode,
Whan hi commiþ to þe world, hi doþ hamsilf sum gode,
Al bot þe wrech brol þat is of Adamis blode.   10
    Lollai, l[ollai], litil child, to kar ertou bemette,
    þou nost noȝt þis worldis wild bifor þe is isette.

Child, if betidith þat þou ssalt þriue and þe,
þench þou wer ifostred vp þi moder kne,
Euer hab mund in þi hert of þos þinges þre: 15
Whan þou commist, wha[t] þou art, and what ssal com of þe.
    Lollai, l[ollai], litil child, child, lollai, lollai,
    Wiþ sorow þou com into þis world, wiþ sorow ssalt wend awai.

Ne tristou to þis world, hit is þi ful vo,   f. 32ᵛ
þe rich he makiþ pouer, þe pore rich also;   20
Hit turneþ wo to wel and ek wel to wo;
Ne trist no man to þis world, whil hit turniþ so.
    Lollai, l[ollai], litil child, þe fote is in þe whele;
    þou nost whoder turne, to wo oþer wele.

Child, þou ert a pilgrim in wikidnis ibor[n],   25
þou wandrest in þis fals world, þou lok þe bifor[n]!
Deþ ssal com wiþ a blast vte of a wel dim hor[n],
Adamis kin dun to cast, himsilf haþ ido befor[n].
    Lollai, l[ollai], litil child, so wo þe wor[þ] Adam
    In þe lond of paradis, þroȝ wikidnes of Satan.   30

> Child, þou nert a pilgrim, bot an vncuþe g[e]st,
> þi dawes beþ itold, þi iurneis beþ i[ke]st;
> Whoder þou salt wend, norþ oþer est,
> Deþ þe sal betide, wiþ bitter bale in brest.
>> Lolla, l[ollai], litil chil, þis wo Adam þe wroȝt,   35
>> Whan he of þe appil ete and Eue hit him betacht.

f. 63ᵛ

> Lolla, lolla, paruule, cur fles tam amare?
> Oportet te plangere necnon suspirare,
> Te dolere grauiter, decet uegetare,
> Vt parentes exules nexerant ignare.   40
>> Lolla, lolla, paruule, natus mundo tristi.
>> Ignotum cum maximo dolore uenisti.

> Alites et bestie, pisces fluctuantes,
> Creature genite cuncte uegetantes
> Sibi prosunt aliquid uiuamen prestantes,   45
> Nisi tu miserrime uiuens inter fantes.
>> Lolla, l[olla], paruule, repletus dolore
>> . . . nesciens si fama . . . .

1, 11, 17, 23, 29 Lollai lollai] Lollai l   3 euermore] euer   4 wore] were
5 Lollai lollai] Lollai   16 what (1)] whan   25 iborn] ibor   26 biforn]
bifor   27 horn] horre   28 beforn] befor   29 worþ] worþ   31 gest]
gist   32 ikest] icast   35 Lolla lollai] Lolla l   45–6 *lines reversed and*
marked a, b   47 Lolla lolla] Lolla l   28 *line cropped*

ff. 32ᵛ–33ᵛ   23. LETTER FROM THE PRINCE OF HELL

Princeps regionis Gehennalis Ecclesiarum prelatis et clericis vniversis
salutem quam sibi. . . . Explicit inuectio subsanatoria diaboli contra totam
ecclesiam sanctam dei.

Addressed to all prelates and clerics. The devil praises their worship
of Venus and Mammon. The Dominicans, who excel all orders in
knowledge, are cruelly persecuted by our members. Franciscans have
refreshed our innards often, offering us a sacrifice of marrow with the
fat of lambs and the sacrifice of goats. Cistercians have attended to
acquiring goods, and their hunger is buried under the heap of wealth.
Hermits have recently been conflated from many orders, and
rejecting the desert have come into the towns: they should rather
be called 'urbanites'. Rough and ignorant, they have usurped the

office of preachers and given us excellent material. Only the Dominicans are disobedient.

Ed. from Reims, Bibliothèque Municipale MS 1275, by W. Wattenbach, 'Über erfundene Briefe in Handschriften des Mittelalters, besonders Teufelsbriefe', *Sitzungsberichte der Königlich Preussischen Akademie der Wissenschaften zu Berlin* (Berlin, 1892), 104–5. Also in Bodley MS Digby 166, part 5, ff. 46ra–48rb (with next); see A. G. Rigg, 'Medieval Latin Poetic Anthologies (III)', *Mediaeval Studies*, 41 (1979), 468–505 at 480. There is an extract in Bodley MS 851; see Rigg, 'Medieval Latin Poetic Anthologies (II)', *Mediaeval Studies*, 40 (1978), 387–407. On the 'Devils Letters' see Gianni Zippel, 'La lettera del Diavolo al clero dal sec. XII alla Riforma', *Bullettino dell'Istituto storico italiano per il medio evo*, 70 (1958), 125–79.

24. REPLY BY POPE DOSITHEUS   ff. 33^{v}–39^{r}

Rubric: 'Incipit Responsio Dosithei summi pontificis ecclesiam sanctam magnifice defendentis et responsionem in lectionibus exprimentis.'

Magnus mundi Monarcha christicolarum Calipha, Beelsebub demoniorum principi, confusione sua sicut deploide indui. . . . uix tenuiter potuerunt. Quippe quibus in solitudine uicinus non aderat.

Written as a papal bull to Beelzebub detailing the behaviour of the clergy. Pope Dositheus first describes the lechery and greed of the secular clerics, ironically praising their libidinous activities and their purloining of funds destined to the poor. Next his account of the Franciscans calls them 'principes cocorum', dwelling on their gluttony, as they indulge in competitive drinking in the English manner and eat everything under the sun. In this version, however, these gluttons are not identified, because the words 'minores fratres' (f. 36^{r}) have been entirely erased by an offended reader. The Cistercians are likewise characterized, and the extract breaks off during the description of the vices of the eremitical orders. For comment see Cartlidge, 'Festivity, Order, and Community', 46–7.

Ed. Wattenbach,'Über erfundene Briefe', 105–16, breaking off at par. 8, l. 17, on p. 113, leaving the rest of the page blank. In 'Beschreibung einer Handschrift der Stadtbibliothek zu Reims', 495, Wattenbach dates the composition to the 1280s.

25. HYMN ON THE WOUNDS OF CHRIST

Aue capud Christi gradum duris spinis coronatum . . . non conserua ne peccata uita priuent nos be[ata].

The hymn 'Ave fructus o Mariae', beginning with the third verse and ending with the ninth in *Analecta Hymnica Medii Aevi*, ed. Clemens Blume and Guido M. Dreves, xxxi (Leipzig, 1898), 90–1. Written by Hand E in the blank space following the 'Reply by Pope Dositheus'.

26. 'TROIA'

Pugnatum est annis x mensibus vij dies xij. . . . Andromachen et Helenum I CC, Hucusque historia Daretis scripta est.

Ten lines, giving figures for Greek and Trojan casualties and the numbers of those who followed Aeneas, Antenor, Andromache, and Helen at the conclusion of the Trojan war. This is the last chapter (44) of Dares, *Daretis Phrygii De Excidio Troiae Historia*, ed. Ferdinand Meister (Leipzig, 1873), 52.

27. LISTS OF TROJANS AND GREEKS

Troiani fuerunt: Laodemon cum filius Priamus . . . Ex parte grecorum plures ceciderunt per xxxij quam troianorum.

Lists of those killed on both sides in the Trojan War, appended to some copies of Dares; see Meister's edition, pp. viii–x.

28. FRANCISCAN CUSTODIES AND HOUSES

Hybernia habet 5 custodias. Loca 32. Anglia habet 7 custodias. Loca 58. Et duo loca Sancte Clare. . . . Prouincia Hybernie excedit 9 prouincias ordinis in conuentuum numero et in numero fratrum multo plures.

A total of thirty-four provinces listed with the numbers of their custodies and houses, from Ireland in the west to China in the east. Printed by P. Girolamo Golubovich, *Bibliteca bio-bibliografica della Terra Santa e dell'Oriente Francescano*, ii (Florence, 1913), 250–1. Compare the list of the English and Irish houses and custodies appended to the *Annals* of John Clyn, a Franciscan from Kilkenny, in *Friar John Clyn, The Annals of Ireland*, ed. Butler, 38–9. Clyn's list supplies the names of all the houses within each custody. His total of custodies and houses exactly matches the enumeration here, including the two English houses of poor Clares at London and Waterbeach, and presumably draws on the same source, which Clyn identifies as the list drawn up by the General Chapter (in Perpignan) in 1331. Fletcher, 'The Date of London, British Library, Harley MS 913', argues that the number of English houses (58) must include Ware, founded in 1338, and so dates the list after 1338 and before 1342, when the third English house of Poor Clares was founded at Denney. But in fact the same total in Clyn does not include Ware, as noted by A. G. Little, 'The Administrative Divisions of the Mendicant Orders in England', *English Historical Review*, 34 (1919), 205–9. For further comment see Little's *Studies in English Franciscan History* (Manchester, 1917), 235–8.

29. GLOSS ON 2 CORINTHIANS 11:24   f. 43ʳ

Quinquies quadragenas una minus accepi . . . accipiebat qui iuncti aliis faciunt xxxix.'

Ten lines. Based on Peter Lombard, *Collectanea in epistolas Pauli*, 2, ch. 2; in *PL* 192, col. 76C.

30. CALCULATION OF THE YEARS BETWEEN ADAM   f. 43ʳ
AND CHRIST

Ab adam usque ad diluuium anni duo milia ccxlvij . . .

Four lines, from Adam to the Flood, the Flood to Abraham, Abraham to Moses, Moses to Christ. The standard kind of chronology, as for instance in Jerome's *Chronicon*. See Chris Given-Wilson, *Chronicles: The Writing of History in Medieval England* (London, 2004), 114–21.

f. 43^v   31. EXTRACT FROM ST BONAVENTURE, *LEGENDA MAIOR SANCTI FRANCISCI*

Cum autem beatus Franciscus turbatus esset de statu et uita fratrum anxio spiritu . . . salua semper meo munere permanebit.

Eleven lines, from *Acta Sanctorum*, October, II, 763, col. 763D–E. Francis, concerned at the bad example set by some of his followers, is reassured by God that he will support his rule for ever. A more recent edition is *Legenda Maior Sancti Francisci*, ed. Michael Bihl, OFM, in *Legendae S. Francisci Assisiensis saeculis XIII et XIV conscriptae*, Analecta Franciscana, 10 (Quaracchi, 1926–41), 555–652.

ff. 43^v–44^r   32. DESCRIPTION OF BABYLON

Rubric: 'Historia tripartita'.

Ambitus Babilonie circumueniebant stadiis .cccc.lxxxvi. . . . unde humana uirtute destrui posse incredibile uidebatur.

In fact from Matthew Paris, *Chronica Majora*, ed. Henry Richards Luard (1872, repr. Cambridge, 2012), i. 53.
    The remainder of f. 44^r is blank.

ff. 44^v–47^v,   33. SONG ON THE TIMES
 52^{r–v}
                                          DIMEV 6633

Thomas Wright, who edited this poem in *Political Songs of England* in 1839, included a number of others in English, Latin, and French that make similar complaints, several of which he titled 'Song on the Times'. From the same period are 'Ich herde men vpo mold' in MS Harley 2253 (DIMEV 2198) and 'The Simonie' in the Auchinleck manuscript (DIMEV 6677).
    The scribe sets paraph markers fairly regularly every four lines, starting at l. 9, since the same rhymes run through the first eight lines. A later scribe has added a couple of headings: 'Brybit' (f. 44^v), 'The lyonys proclamacion' (f. 45^v). The four intervening leaves 48–51, containing the end of item 15, 'Seven Sins', and items 34–6 belong elsewhere. See Introduction, p. xvi.

Whose þenchiþ vp þis carful lif   f. 44ᵛ
Niȝte and dai þat we beþ inne,
So moch we seeþ of sorow and strif,
And lite þer is of worldis winne.

Hate and wreþ þer is wel riue,   5
And trew loue is ful þinne.
Men þat beþ in heiiȝist liue
Mest icharged beþ wiþ sinne.

Fals and liþer is þis lond,
As al dai we mai ise,   10
þerin is boþe hate and onde,
Ich wene þat euer so wol be.

Coueitise haþ þe law an honde
þat þe trewþe he ne mai ise,
Nov is maister prude and onde;   15
Alas, Louerde; whi suffriþ he?

Wold Holi Cherch pilt is miȝte
And law of lond pilt him to,
þan schold coueitise and vnriȝte
Vte of lond ben ydo.   20

Holi Cherch schold hold is riȝt
For no eie no for no loue,
þat hi ne schold schow har miȝt
For lordingen boste þat beþ aboue,

To entredite and amonsi   25 f. 45ʳ
Al þai, whate hi euir be,
þat lafful men doþ robbi,
Whate in lond, what in see.

And þos hoblurs namelich
þat husbond benimeþ eri of grund,   30
Men ne schold ham biri in non chirch,
Bot cast ham vte as a hund.

þos kingis ministris beþ ischend,
To riȝt and law þat ssold tak hede,
And al þe lond fort amend;   35
Of þos þeuis hi takeþ mede.

Be þe lafful man to deþ ibroȝt
And is catel awei ynom,
Of his deþ ne telliþ hi noȝt,
Bot of har prei hi hab som.   40

Hab hi þe siluer and þe mede
And þe catel vnderfo,
Of feloni hi ne takeþ hede;
Al þilk trepas is ago.

Of þos a uorbisen ich herd telle: 45
þe lion is king of alle beeste
And—herkniþ al to mi spelle—
In his lond he did an heste.

þe lyon lete cri as hit was do,
For he hird lome to telle,   50
And eke him was itold also,
þat þe wolf didde noȝt welle.

And þe fox, þat liþer grome,
Wiþ þe wolf iwreiid was.
Tofor har lord hi schold come   55
To amend har trepas.

And so men didde þat seli asse,
þat trepasid noȝt no did no gilte,
Wiþ ham boþe iwreiid was,
And in þe ditement was ipilt.   60

þe uoxe hird amang al menne,
And told þe wolf wiþ þe brode crune;
þat on him send gees and henne,
þat oþer geet and motune.

þe seli aasse wend [he] was saf,   65
For he ne eete noȝt bote grasse.
None ȝiftes he ne ȝaf,
No wend þat no harm nasse.

þo hi to har lord com to tune,
He told to ham law and skille.   70
þos wikid bestis lutid adune,
'Lord', hi seiid, 'What is þi wille?'

þo spek þe lion hem to,   f. 46ʳ
To þe fox anone his wille:
'Tel me, boi, what hast ido?   75
Men beþ aboute þe to spille.'

þo spek þe fox first anone:
'Lord king, nov þi wille,
þos men me wreiiþ of þe tune
And wold me gladlich forto spille.   80

  'Gees no hen nad ich noȝt,
Sire, for soþ ich þe sigge,
Bot as ich ham dere boȝt,
And bere ham vp myn owen rigge.'

'Godis grame most hi haue   85
þat in þe curte þe so pilt;
Whan hit is so, ich vouchesaue,
Ich forȝiue þe þis gilte.'

þe fals wolf stode behind.
He was doggid and ek felle.   90
'Ich am icom of grete kind,
Pes þou grant me, þat miȝt ful welle.'

  'What hast ido, belamy,
þat þou me so oxist pes?'
'Sire,' he seid, 'I nel noȝt lie,   95
If þou me woldist hire a res.

  'For ich huntid vp þe doune   f. 46ᵛ
To loke, sire, mi biȝete,
þer ich slow a motune,
Ȝe, Sire, and fewe gete.'   100

  'Ich am iwreiid, sire, to þe,
For þat ilk gilt.
Sire, ichul sker me:
Y ne ȝef ham dint no pilt.'

  'For soþ, I sigge þe, belami,   105
Hi nadde no gode munde,
þai þat wreiid þe to mei.
þou ne diddist noȝt bot þi kund.'

'Sei þou me, asse, wat hast ido?
Me þenchiþ þou cannist no gode.   110
Whi nadistou as oþer mo?
þou come of liþer stode.'

'Sertis, sire, not ich noȝt.
Ich ete sage a[nd] uil gras,
More harm ne did ich noȝt;   115
þerfor iwreiid ich was.'

'Belami, þat was misdo,
þat was aȝe þi kund
Forto et such gras so.
Hastilich ȝe him bind.   120

f. 47ʳ   'Al his bonis ȝe todraw.
Lok þat ȝe noȝt lete,
And þat ich ȝiue al for law,
þat his fleis be al ifrette.'

Al so hit fariþ nov in lond,   125
Whose wol tak þerto hede
Of þai þat habbiþ an hond:
Of þeuis hi takiþ mede.

þe lafful man ssal be ibund,
And ido in strang pine,   130
And ihold in fast prisund,
Fort þat he mak fine;

And þe þef to skap so
þat doþ euer aȝe þe riȝt!
God, tak hede þerto,   135
þat is al ful of miȝt.

þus fariþ al þe world nuþe,
As we mai al ise,
Boþe est and west, norþ and suþe,
God vs help and þe Trinite!   140

Trewþ is ifaillid wiþ fremid and sibbe
Also wide as al þis lond.
Ne mai no man þerin libbe,
What þroȝ couetise and þroȝ onde.

þo3 lafful man wold hold is lif   145 f. 47ᵛ
In loue, in charite and in pes,
Sone me ssul compas is lif,
And þat in a litil res.

Prude is maister and coueitise,
þe þrid broþer men clippeþ ond;   150
Ni3t and dai he fondiþ iwisse,
Lafful men to hab har lond.

Whan erþ haþ erþe igette
And of erþe so haþ inov3,
Whan he is þerin istekke   155
Wo is him þat was in wou3!

What is þe gode þat man ssal hab
Vte of þis world whan he ssal go?
A sori wede, whi ssal ich gab?
For he bro3t wiþ him no mo.   160

Ri3t as he com, he ssal wend,
In wo, in pine, in pouerte.
Takiþ gode hede, men, to 3ure end,
For as I sigge, so hit wol be.

Y not wharof beþ men so prute   165
Of erþe and axen, felle and bone.
Be þe soule enis vte,
A uilir caraing nis þer non.

þe caraing is so lolich to see   f. 52ʳ
þat vnder erþ men mot hit hide,   170
Boþe wif and child wol fram him fle,
þer nis no frend þat wol him bide.

What wol men for þe sowle del?
Corne no mel, wel þou wost,
Bot wel seld at þe mele   175
A row3 bare trenchur oþer a crust.

þe begger þat þe crust ssal hab,
Wel hokirlich he lokiþ þeran.
Soþ to sigge and no3t to gabbe,
Ri3t no3t he is ipaiid apan.   180

þan seiiþ þe begger in is mode:
'þe crust is boþe hard and tou[ʒ].
þe wrech was hard þat ow þe gode;
Hard for hard is gode ynowʒ.

'Moch misanter þat for him bidde   185
Pater Noster oþer Crede,
Bot let him hab as he didde,
For of þe ʒift naþ he no mede.'

Ich red vp no man þou hab triste,
No vppon non oþer,   190
Ok del hit wiþ ʒure owen fist;
Trist to soster no broþer.

f. 52ᵛ   Anuriþ God and Holi Chirch,
And ʒiueþ þe pouir þat habbiþ nede;
So Godis wille ʒe ssul wirche   195
And ioi of heuen hab to mede.

To whoch ioi vs bring
Iesus Crist, heuen king. Amen

65 he] *om.*   114 and uil] aluil, *perhaps for* a' uil   182 touʒ] touþ

f. 49ʳ⁻ᵛ   34. SINS AND VIRTUES

Lucifer . anthiocus . nemproth . nabugo . phariseus . [*In right margin*
Superbia] . . . Baltazar . Herodes . epulantur & olofernes'. [*In right margin*
Conuiuium]

Biblical figures representing the seven sins and the seven virtues,
concluding with nine banqueters. Above each of the names is the
biblical source.

f. 49ᵛ   35. RIDDLES

A. 'Nota de muliere que peperit puerum qui fuit filius eius frater eius et
auunculus filius auunculi & filius aui & nepos id est filius fratris . . .'

Similar riddles are found in *The Booke of Meery Riddles* (London,
1629), Riddle 71 and Proper Question 4. The type survived as a
country music song, 'I'm my own grandpa'.

B. 'Nota de illo qui fuit in pomario & portauit poma que oportebat dare tribus ianitoribus . . .'

This is riddle 38 in *The Booke of Meery Riddles*, where it is given in full.

C. 'Sex milia sex .dc. lxvi faciunt legionem'.

D. 'Prima trianglia . longa subanglia . curta sequatur . Greca sit ultima . talis in intima . cordis amatur . . .'

Cf. Walther, *Initia* 22376. A popular riddle discussed by Galloway, 'The Rhetoric of Riddling', 76. The solution, written above each element, is 'a-l-i-z a-m-o t-e'. For other significations of letters see text 1.

E. 'Porta salutis aue per quam fit exitus a ve uenit ab eua ue et ue quia tollis aue . . .'

Walther, *Initia* 14276.

36. PERS OF BERMINGHAM   ff. 50^r–51^v

DIMEV 4885

The poem celebrates the events of Trinity Sunday 1305, when Pers of Bermingham of Tethmoy invited his Gaelic neighbours from Offaly, the O'Conor clan, to dinner at his castle at Carrick and murdered them in retribution for plotting to kill Anglo-Irish leaders. He then sent their heads to Dublin and was well rewarded by the justiciar of Ireland. At his death in 1308 he was described as 'nobilis debellator Hibernicorum'. Not surprisingly, a less favourable account of the massacre is offered by the Irish princes in their *Remonstrance* to Pope John XXII. For an account see Introduction, 'Historical Context', pp. xxxii–iv. For elucidation of the poem in its context see Benskin, 'The Style and Authorship of the Kildare Poems' (with transcription); and Scattergood, 'Elegy for a Dangerous Man.'

Sith Gabriel gan grete   f. 50^r
Vre Leuedi Mari swete
    þat Godde wold in hir liȝte,
A þousand ȝer hit isse
þre hundred ful iwisse   5
    And ouer ȝeris eiȝte.

þan of þe eiȝt ȝere
Tak twies ten ifere,
   þat wol be tuenti fulle;
Apan þe tuentiþ dai   10
Of Aueril bifor Mai,
   So deþ vs gan to pulle.

He pullid us of on,
Al Irlond makiþ mon,
   Engelon ek as welle,   15
Ful wel ye witte his nam:
Sire Pers þe Brimgham,
   Non nede hit is to telle.

His nam hit was and isse,
Y sigge ȝou ful iwisse,   20
   þat vppe ssal arise;
In felle, flesse and bone
A better kniȝt nas none,
   No none of more prise.

Noble werrure he was   25
And gode castel in place,
   On stede þer he wold ride,
Wiþ his sper and scheld,
In hard wodde and feld
   No þef him durst abide.   30

f. 50ᵛ   Do þenchiþ al in him,
Wiþ weepin who wol win,
   Hou gode he was to nede.
In batail stif to stond
Iwis is pere nas nond;   35
   Alas, he sold be dede!

Al Englismen þat beþ
Sore mow wep is deþ
   þat such a kniȝt ssold falle;
þos kniȝtis euchone   40
Of him mai mak mone,
   As peruink of ham alle.

Peruink he miȝt be,
And þat for þinges þre
   He vssid oft and lome   45
þat was one of þe best:
He ne leet no þef hab rest,
   In no stid þer he come.

Anoþer þing also:
To Yrismen he was fo,   50
   þat wel widewhare.
Euer he rode aboute
Wiþ streinþ to hunt ham vte,
   As hunter doþ þe hare.

For whan hi wend best   55
In wildernis hab rest,
   þat no man ssold ham see,
þan he wold driue a quest
Anon to har nest,
   In stid þer hi wold be.   60

Of slep he wold ham wak;
For ferdnis hi wold quak
   And fond to sculk awai.
For þe hire of har bedde   f. 51ʳ
He tok har heuid to wedde,   65
   And so he taȝt ham plai.

þos Yrismen of þe lond,
Hi swor and tok an hond
   þe Englismen to trai,
And seid hi wold quelle   70
As fale, as ich ȝou telle,
   Al apon o dai.

þe erl of Vluester,
Sire Emond þe Botiler,
   Sire Ion le fiz Tomas,   75
Algate al bi name,
Sire Pers þe Brimghame,
   þis was har compas.

þis compasment com vte
Fram kniȝt to kniȝt abute,   80
   Hit nas noȝt lang ihidde;
þos kniȝtis preid al
þat meschans most ham fal
   Ȝif scape hi ssold þermidde;

And swor bi Godis name   85
To ȝild þe cuntrepane
   Whan hi miȝt com to,
And þat wiþvte lette
To certein dai isette
   þis þing ssold be do.   90

Lang er þis dai was com,
Hit was forȝit wiþ som
   þat neisse beþ to nede.
Alas, what ssold hi [be] ibor?
þroȝ ham þis lond is ilor   95
   To spille ale and bred.

f. 51ᵛ Sire Pers þe Brimgham,
On ernist and agam
   þis dai was in is þoȝt;
He þoȝt ordres to mak,   100
What time he miȝt ham tak;
   Of trauail nas him noȝt.

O'Konwir þat was king,
His keþerin he gan bring,
   þe maister heet Gilboie.   105
Riȝt at þe Trinite,
Whan hodes sold best be,
   To Pers in Totomoye.

And ȝite of oþer store
Com Eþe McMalmore   110
   And oþer fale bi name.
Sire Pers lokid vte,
He seei such a rute,
   Him þoȝt hit nas no game.

Sir Pers sei ham com,   115
He receiuid al and som,
   No3t on iwernd nas;
Siþ hoodis he let mak,
No3t on nas forsak,
   Bot al he did ham grace.   120

Saue o wrech þat þer was,
He cuþe no3t red in place
   No sing whar he com.
He was of Caymis kinne,
And he refusid him;   125
   He wend vnhodid hom.

He þat þis sang let mak
For sir Persis sake,
   Wel wid haþ igo,
Widwhar iso3t   130
And god pardon ibro3t,
   Two hundrid daies and mo.
      Explicit.

2 Leuedi] le'di   9 tuenti] XX^{ti} 10 tuentiþ] XX   16 ye] *altered from* þe
94 be] *om.*   109 store] *written above* stoore *or* sttore *in another ink*

37. RECIPES FOR PREPARING PIGMENTS   ff. 52^{v}–53^{v}

De temperatura azorii. Azorium bonum molitur cum aqua . . . extendans
corium & superponas vassillum illo erit ruber.

Other headings are: 'De temperaturo uermiculi', 'De uiridi ad usum
scribendi', 'De synoblo', 'De assiso ponendo sub auro in libro'.
   This follows the last six lines of 'Song on the Times'. MS Harley
2253, f. 52^{v}, has similar recipes in English.

38. PROPHETIC VERSES ON SCOTLAND   f. 53^{v}

Bruti posteritas albanis associata . . . Hostibus expulsis iudicis vsque diem.

Eight lines; Hand C. For similar verses, widely copied, see *Reliquiæ
Antiquæ*, ii. 245–6. See Lesley A. Coote, *Prophecy and Public Affairs in*

Later Medieval England (Woodbridge, 2000), 116, who lists other copies on pp. 255, 256, 263, and 278. F. 54ʳ is blank.

ff. 54ᵛ
and 62ʳ

39. ELDE

DIMEV 1183

First-person laments for old age are modelled on the Elegies of Maximian, which were, curiously, a standard school text throughout the Middle Ages. To Maximian's description of physical decay, impotence, loss of memory, and regret for the lost pleasures of youth were added the enumeration of the Signs of Death, ultimately derived from the medical work of Hippocrates, but popular in Middle English in many versions, represented by 'Wanne mine eyhnen misten' (DIMEV 6383, ed. *English Lyrics*, 130). See Woolf, *English Religious Lyric*, 78–82, 103–4, and Rossell Hope Robbins, 'Signs of Death in Middle English', *Mediaeval Studies*, 32 (1970), 282–98.

With 'Elde' may be compared two other dramatic monologues on old age: 'Le Regret de Maximian' (DIMEV 1769) in MS Digby 86, ed. *English Lyrics*, 92–100 (there is another version, 'Maximion', in MS Harley 2253, ed. *Altenglische Dichtungen*, 245–53), and 'Heʒe louerd, þou here my bone' (DIMEV 2025), also in Harley 2253, *Religious Lyrics*, 3–7; all are discussed by Woolf, *English Religious Lyric*, 104–7, and see notes to ll. 5, 19, 48, 59. Descriptions in *Cursor Mundi*, ll. 3555–94 and *Prick of Conscience*, ll. 766–801 are also to be compared; see notes to ll. 8, 13, 54.

While the other two monologues powerfully present the pleasures of youth to evoke a moving contrast with the miseries of age, 'Elde' is a static portrait of physical decay and humiliation. Its power lies in its metrical and lexical extravagance.

The title 'Age' is added by Hand F.

f. 54ᵛ

    Elde makiþ me geld and growen al grai,
    When eld me wol feld, nykkest þer no nai.
    Eld nul meld no murþes of Mai,
    When eld me wol aweld, mi wele is awai.
    Eld wol keld and cling so þe clai,   5
    Wiþ eld I mot held and hien to mi dai.
    When eld blowid he is b[ol]de; his ble is sone abatid.
    Al we wilniþ to ben old; wy is eld ihatid?

Moch me anueþ
þat mi dribil druiþ,   10
   And mi wrot wet;
Eld me awarpeþ,
þat mi schuldren scharpiþ,
   And ʒouþe me haþ let.

Ihc ne mai no more   15
Grope vnder gore,
   þoʒ mi wil wold ʒete;
Yʒoket ich am of ʒore
Wiþ last and luþer lore,
   And sunne me haþ biset.   20

Iset ich am wiþ sunne
þat I ne mai noʒt munne
   Non murþis wiþ muþe.
Eld me haþ amarrid,
Ich wene he be bicharred   25
   þat trusteþ to ʒuþe.

Al þus eld me fordede,
þus he toggiþ vte mi ted
   And drawiþ ham on rewe.
Y ne mai no more of loue done,   30
Mi pilkoc pisseþ on mi schone,
   Vch schenlon me bischrew.

Mine hed is hore and al forfare,
Ihewid as a grei mare,
   Mi bodi wexit lewe;   35
When I bihold on mi schennen,
Min [ein] dimmiþ, al fordwynnen,
   Mi frendis waxiþ fewe.

Now I pirtle, I pofte, I poute,
I snurpe, I snobbe, I sneipe on snovte,   40
   þroʒ kund I comble and kelde.
I lench, I len, on lyme I lasse,   f. 62ʳ
I poke, I pomple, I palle, I passe
   As galliþ gome igeld.

I riuele, I roxle, I rake, I rouwe,   45
I clyng, I cluche, I croke, I couwe,
 þus he wol me aweld.
I grunt, I grone, I grenne, I gruche,
I nese, I nappe, I nifle, I nuche,
 And al þis wilneþ eld.   50

I stunt, I stomere, I stomble as sledde,
I blind, I bleri, I b[l]ert in bedde,
 Such sond is me sent!
I spitte, I spatle in spech, I sporne,
I werne, I lutle, þerfor I murne,   55
 þus is mi wel iwent.

Ispend and marrit is mi main,
And wold wil ȝuþe aȝayn,
 As falc I falow and felde.
I was heordmon, nov am holle,   60
Al folk of me beþ wel folle.
 Such willing is after elde!

Eld me haþ so hard ihent,
Seo, wouw spak[l]y he me spent,
Vch toþ fram oþer is trent,   65
 Arerid is of rote.
þe tunge wlaseþ, wend þerwiþ,
Lostles lowtiþ in uch a liþ,
I mot be þer eld beþ,
 He fint me vnder fote. Amen.   70

7 bolde] blode 17 ȝete] *altered from* ȝite 37 ein] *om.* 52 blert] bert
64 spakly] spakky (-kk- *overwritten*)

ff. 64, 61,   # 40. THE WALLING OF NEW ROSS
55, 56   ## Dean no. 58

The poem describes how the citizens of New Ross in County
Wexford built defences for their town in 1265. The poet says the
need for the defences was occasioned by the civil strife between two
Norman lords, Maurice Fitzgerald and Walter de Burgh (l. 13),
although he later remarks that, when completed, the walls will
protect the town from the Irish (l. 200). He describes the building

of the fosse in progress, and looks forward to the completion of
the work (l. 162). The burgesses hire (Irish?) workmen who prove
unsatisfactory, so it is agreed that the townspeople must carry out the
work themselves, involving all the gilds, the vintners, sailors, and so
on; twenty trades are named, as well as priests and women. The work
of each group is described, together with the arms, equipment, and
soldiers that the citizens assemble. Later records of the walls include
references in the Irish Memoranda Rolls for 1279 and murage taxes
for their repair. See Keith V. Sinclair, '*The Walling of New Ross*: An
Anglo-Norman Satirical *Dit*', *Zeitschrift für französische Sprache und
Literatur*, 105 (1995), 240–80 at 263. The poem is edited and
translated by Hugh Shields, 'The Walling of New Ross: A Thir-
teenth-Century Poem in French', *Long Room* (Dublin), 12–13 (1975–
6), 24–33. For further historical and textual studies see Sinclair, 'On
the Text of the Anglo-Norman Poem *The Walling of New Ross*'
Romanische Forschungen 106 (1994), 225–35.

Compare the description of the town and the enumeration of trades
in 'Satire'(item 4). A Middle English poem from 1458 about a similar
collaborative civic building project is edited and discussed by Ralph
Hanna, '*The Bridges at Abingdon*: An Unnoticed Alliterative Poem', in
Michael Calabrese and Stephen H. A. Shepherd (ed.), *Yee? Baw for
Bokes* (Los Angeles, 2013), 31–44.

The account is written in rough octosyllabic couplets with rhymes
that are sometimes only approximate. The leaves of the manuscript
are disordered, with the poem following the order ff. 64, 61, 55, 56.
The poet's record of numbers of workers have often been noted in the
margin in another hand, including (next to l. 124) 'numerus non est'.
Doubtful readings have been checked against Ware's transcription in
BL MS Lansdowne 418, as noted.

Rithmus facture ville de Rosse.   f. 64ʳ

    Talent me prent de rimaunceir
    S'il vous plet de escoteir,
    Kar parole qe n'est oie
    Ne uaut pas vn aillie.
    Pur ce vous prie d'escoter,   5
    Si me oiés ben aucer
    De vne vile en Ireland,
    La plus bele de sa grand
    Qe ie sache en nule tere.

Mes poure auoint de vn gerre   10
Qe fu par entre deus barouns,
Vei ci escrit amdeus lur nuns:
Sire Morice e Sire Wauter.
Le noun de la vile voil nomer:
Ros le deuez apeler,   15
C'est le nouel pont de Ros;
Ce fu lur poure ke ne furent clos.
A lur conseil vn ioure alerent
E tot la commune ense[mbl]erent;
Lur conseil pristerent en tele maner: 20
Qe vn mure de morter e de pere
Voilent enture la vile feire,
Qe poure auoint de cel geere.
A la Chandeler commencerent,
De mercher la fosse y alerent,   25
Coment le mure dut aler.
Aleint liz prodoms mercher;
E [quant] auoint le mure merché
Pur ouerors vnt tost mandé,
f. 64ᵛ   Cent ov plus chescun iour   30
I vont ouerer od grand honur.
Les burgeis entur la fosse alerent,
E gent lowis poi espleiterent;
E a lure conseil realerent
E vn purueans purparlerent,   35
Ke vnkes tele purueance
Ne fu en Engleter ne en France.
E l'endemain en firent crier,
E tot la commune ensembler;
La purueance fu la mustré,   40
E tot la commune ben paié.
Vne prodome susleua,
La purueans i mustra.
   Ke le lundi tot primers,
Irrunt a la fosse le vineters,   45
Mercers, marchans e drapers,
Ensemblement od lez vineters.
De l'oure de prime deke nune sonee
Dussent ouerer au fossee.

Et si si funt eus mult bonement,   50
I uont ouerir od bele gent,
Mil e plus, pur voir vous die,
I uont ouerir chescun lundi,
O beles baners e grantz honurs,
E od floites e taburs.   55
E ausi tost cum noune soune
I uont al ostel li prodome;
Lure baners y vont deuant.   f. 61ʳ
La ieuene gent haut chantant
Par tot la vile karoler,   60
Oue grant ioi vount laborer.
E les prestres, quan ont chanté,
Si vont ouerir au fossé,
E trauellent mut durement
Plus qe ne funt autre gent,   65
Kar i sunt ieuenz e envuysés,
E grans e forts, ben soiornés.
Le mariners kant al ostel sunt,
En bele maner au fossé vount,
Lure baner en vete deuont,   70
La nef dedens est depoint.
E apres la baner vont suent
Bien sis cenz de bel gent,
E si fusent tuz al outeus,
Tuz le nefs e bateus,   75
Plus i auereit de vnze cens,
Sachez pur ueir, de bone gens.
Le mardi prochein suent apres
I vont taillurs e parm[en]ters,
Tenturers, fulrurs, e celers,   80
Bele gent sunt de lur mesters;
I vont ouerir cum dit deuant;
Mes ne sunt tant de gent,
Mes bien sunt quatre cens,
Sachez pur veir, de bele gens.   85
    Le mekirdi prochein suant   f. 61ᵛ
I vont autre maner de gent,
Cordiwaners, tannors, macecrers,
Mult i a de beus bachelers;

Lur baners en sunt depeint   90
Si com a lur mester apeint.
Treis cens sunt, si cum ie quit,
Qe oue grant e oue petit,
E hautement vont karoler,
Ausi com funt li primer.   95
   Le Iudi vont li pesturs,
E lez regraturs trestuz,
Qe ble uendunt e peissuns;
Diuers sunt lur gonfanuns.
Bien y vont en icel iure,   100
Quatre cens od grant honur,
E karolent e chantent haut
Com le primers par deuant.
Lez waynpayns i vunt ausi
Meimes en icel iudi,   105
Apres les autres vont derer,
E par deuant vnt bele baner
Le esquele e le peissun par dedens
En lur baner en est depeins.
Issi vont eus au fossee,   110
Trent e deus sunt pur verité.
   Le p[or]turs vont le uendredi,
Bien sunt treis cens e demy.

f. 55^r

[L]ur baners en sunt deuant
[A]l orle de fosse en estant.   115
[Le]z carpenters vont le samadi,
[E] feuers e masuns autresi.
Mult bele gent sunt ie vous pleui;
Ben sunt treis cens e demy,
E tuz vont ouerir od bon corage,   120
Sach[e]z de ce en funt qe sage.
   Le demainge les dames i vont,
Sachez de ueires bon ouere i funt.
Le nombre ne sai de cert nomer,
Nule hom viuant ne les puit conter.   125
Totz la pere i vont ieter,
E hors de fosse aporter.
Kiqe la fut pur esgarder,
Meint bele dame y put il veer,

Meint mantel de escarlet,   130
E de verd e de burnet,
E meint bone roket bien ridee,
Meint blank fem ben colouree;
Ke vnkes en tere ou ie ai esté,
Tantz bele dames ne vi en fossee,   135
Mult fu cil en bon vre nee
Ke purreit choiser a sa uolunté.

Meint bele baner lur sunt deuant,
Tant cum sunt la pere p[or]tant;
E quant ont la pere aportee,   140 f. 55ᵛ
Tant cum plest a uolunté,
Entur la fosse vont chanter,
Auant qe en vile volen entrer.

E quant en la uile sunt entrés,
Les richez dames sunt ensemblés   145
E iuent e beiuent e karolent
E de bons enueisurus en parolent;
E chescun a autre en confort,
E dient qe ferunt vn port,
La Port de Dames auera a noune,   150
E la en ferunt lur prisune.

E qi en lur prisun est entré
De tut n'en auera sa uolunté.
Ie ne di pas pur nule blame,
Bon serreit estre en prisun de dame,   155
Kar bone dame est deboner,
Qe ia ne li leireit vilein fere.

   De dames ore me voil lesser,
E du fossé plus enparler.
Le fossé est vint pees parfunt,   160
E vne lue de vei teint ben de lung.
Al oure qe serra tot parfeit,
Ia n'auera mester de auer gayte,
Mes dormir puunt surement;
Ia n'auerunt gard de male gent.   165
Me ke uenissent quarant mile
Ia n'en entrunt dedens la vile.
Kar eus vnt acez de garnesuns,   f. 56ʳ
Meint blanc auberk e aubersuns,

Meint parpunt e meint aketun;   170
E meint sauage garsun
E mult de bon arblasters,
E de arc de main mult bons archers,
Qe vnkes en vile ou ie ai estee
Ne vi tant de bone glenné,   175
Ne tant arblestes au pareis pendre,
Ne tant de quarels pur despendre,
E chescun oustel plein de maces,
E bonez escuz e tolfaces.
Bein sunt garnis, ie vous pleuis,   180
Pur bien defendre de lur enemis.
Qe arblaster, vus di pur vers,
Treis cens sunt seissant e treis
Ke a lur mostresun furent contez,
E en loure rol sunt arollez,   185
E de autres archers duze cens,
Sachez pur ueir, de bon gens.
E de autre part furent treis mile
O lances e od haches de me[im]es la uile.
E gens a chiual cent e quater,   190
Bien furent armés pur combater.
Me ie vous die tot, sanz faille,
Eus ne desirent nule bataile,
Mes lur vile voleint garder
De maueis gent a lur pouer.   195
f. 56ᵛ   Nule home de ce ne lez dut blamer
Qe lur vile voleint fermer,
Qe quant la uile serra fermé
E [d]e mure tot viroré,
N'ad Ires en Irland si hardi,   200
Qi l'oserent asailler, ie vus pleui,
Qe kant vnt vn corne deus feez cornee;
Tantost la commune est ensemblee,
E as armes vont tost corant.
Chescun a envie pur aler deuant,   205
Tant sunt coraius e hardi
Pur eus uenger de lur enemi.
Deu lur doint si en venger
E la vile a honur garder,

Qe Deus en seit de tot paié,   210
E tuz diez amen pur charité.
Kar ce est la plus franch uile
Qe seit en certein ne en yle;
E tot hom estrange est ben venu,
E de grant ioi est rescev,   215
E chater e vendre en pute ben,
Qe nul hom ne li demandra reen.
A Deu la uile ie command,
E tous qe dedens sunt habitand. Amen, amen, amen.

Ce fu fet l'an de l'incarnacion Nostre Seignur
1265.

19 ensemblerent] en senterent   21 vn] i; de (2)] de de   28 quant] *om.*
73 sis] vj   76 vnze] xi   78 apres] *unclear; sic Lansdowne*
79 parmenters] parmters   84 quatre] iiij   92 Treis cens] CCC. 100
iure] *unclear; sic Lansdowne*   101 Quatre cens] CCCC   106 autres]
illegible; sic Lansdowne 109 en] *illegible; sic Lansdowne* 111 Trent e deus]
xxxij   112 porturs] *parturs*   113 treis cens] ccc   114-17 *initial letters
lost*   119 treis cens] CCC   121 Sachez] Sachz   139 portant] *partant*
160 vint] xx   166 quarant] xl   183 Treis cens] CCC; sunt] *followed by
erasure*; seissant e treis] lxiij   186 duze] xii   188 treis] iij   189 meimes]
membles   190 cent] C   199 de] le   202 vn] j   deus] ij
Explicit 1265] M.CC.LXV

41. METRA DE MONACHIS CARNALIBUS   f. 57^r

Walther, *Initia* 16086

Quis nescit quam sit monacorum nobilis ordo? In omnem terram exiuit
sonus eorum. [Ps. 18.5] . . . Dum uiuunt monachi nec amant nec amantur ab
ullo: Fiant tanquam fenum tectorum quia priusquam euellatur etc. [Ps.
128.6]

Eleven couplets, each consisting of a hexameter and a verse from the
Psalms, in mock praise of the gluttony of monks.

    Ed. A. George Rigg, '"Metra de Monachis Carnalibus": The
Three Versions', *Mittellateinisches Jahrbuch*, 15 (1980), 134-42, also
reprinting a later Continental version ed. by Lehmann, *Die Parodie im
Mittelalter*, 194-5. Rigg notes that the Harley text is closest to that in
Oxford, St John's College, MS 178 (s. xiii in.), f. 411^v. Another copy,
not noted by Rigg, is in Dublin, Trinity College MS 347, f. 9^r, an

Irish Franciscan miscellany of the late thirteenth century, perhaps from Multyfarnham. See Colker, *Trinity College Library Dublin* i. 710–41.

f. 57ᵛ

42. JOHN PECHAM'S 'DE CORPORE CHRISTI'

Walther, *Initia* 2023

Rubric: 'Hanc meditacionem de corpore Christi composuit Frater Johannes Pecham de ordine fratrum Minorum, archiepiscopus Cantuarensis. In eleuacione corporis Christi dicitur hec antiphona.' After verse 2 is the rubric 'Oratio post eleuacionem'.

Aue uiuens hostia . ueritas & uita . . . per te tandem cernere . da remunerator. Amen

Verses 1–2 and 13–15 in *Analecta Hymnica Medii Aevi*, xxxi. 111–13. Many manuscripts; widely attributed to John Pecham (*c*.1225–92), archbishop of Canterbury 1279–92.

f. 58ʳ

43. REPENTANCE OF LOVE

DIMEV 3269

This is a poetic exercise with run-over rhymes, internal rhyme, end-rhyme, and alliteration. Early Irish verse has examples of *aicill*, 'rhyme of the end-word of one line with a word in the beginning or interior of the next line', commonly with alliteration; see Murphy, *Early Irish Metrics*, 83. The same device is found in Latin in the verse of Reginald of Canterbury (*c*.1100) and Michael of Cornwall (fl. 1250s); for examples see Rigg, *History of Anglo-Latin Literature*, 29 and 197. Compare also the complex verbal and metrical patterns of the French 'Proverbia comitis Desmonie' (text 11).

　　Written on the upper half of the leaf, leaving the lower half blank.

f. 58ʳ

[L]oue hauiþ me broȝt in liþir þoȝt,
þoȝt ich ab to blinne;
Blinne to þench hit is for noȝt,
Noȝt is loue of sinne.

[S]inne me hauiþ in care ibroȝt,　　　　5
Broȝt in mochil vnwinne;
Winne to weld ich had iþoȝt;

þoȝt is þat ich am inne.

[I]n me is care how I ssal fare,
Fare ich wol and funde;   10
F[unde] ich wiþouten are,
Ar I be broȝt to grunde.

1, 5, 9 *the rubricator has missed the opening letter of each stanza*   11 Funde] fare

44. NEGO   f. 58ᵛ

DIMEV 2750

A Latin poem, 'Meum est propositum gentis imperitæ', similarly
mocking scholars who spend time in dialectics to no purpose, is
edited in *Political Songs*, 206–10. Cf. note to l. 6 here. The
Franciscan 'doctor subtilis' Duns Scotus (d. 1308) would have cast
a dark shadow over any Franciscan student of the time; see note to
l. 20.

Hit nis bot trewþ iwend an afte   f. 58ᵛ
Forte sette 'nego' in eni crafte.
Trewþ so drawiþ to heuen blisse,
'Nego' doþ noȝt so iwisse.
'Forsak' and 'saue' is þef in lore,   5
'Nego' is pouer clerk in store.
Whan menne horliþ ham here and þare,
'Nego' sauiþ ham fram care.
Awei wiþ 'nego'! Vte of place,
Whose wol haue Goddis grace!   10
Whoso wol aȝens þe deuil fiȝte,
þer mai 'nego' sit ariȝte,
Ak loke þat we neuer more
'Nego' sette in trew lore,
For whoso can lite, haþ sone ido,   15
Anone he draweþ to 'nego'.
Now o clerk seiiþ 'nego',
And þat oþer 'dubito',
Seiiþ anoþer 'concedo',
And anoþer 'obligo',   20
'Verum falsum' sette þerto,

þan is al þe lore ido.
þus þe fals clerkes of har heuid
Makiþ men trewþ of ham be reuid.

45 · BEATI QUI ESURIUNT

Walther, *Initia* 2098

Beati qui esuriunt & scitiunt & faciunt iusticiam . . . In hoc malum faciunt & patriam decipiunt nemini parcentes.

144 lines of verse, written as prose. The lawcourts are wedded to money; not just the judges themselves but the range of court officials who demand bribes for access to the court. The sheriffs ('vice-comites') travel the country demanding fine dinners and rich robes for their wives. Officials amass lands, grow proud, and become 'wise'.

Ed. by Wright as 'Song on the Venality of the Judges', in *Political Songs* , 224–30. Also ed. James M. Dean, in *Medieval English Political Writings* (Kalamazoo, 1996). There are two other copies in early fourteenth-century manuscripts of English provenance: Lambeth Palace MS 179, f. 136^v, a text of Statutes, added in another hand on a blank page; and BL MS Royal 12 C.xii, f. 1^v, copied by the scribe of MS Harley 2253.

46 · 'PASSIO UNIUS MONACHI LACIUII'

In antiquis temporibus sub aprilis idibus, monachus quidam postquam incaluerat mero hillario solito factus timens ne per continenciam morbus perriperet ad uitalia. . . . Per aliam uiam reuersus est monachus ad claustrum suum. Amen.

A monk develops a passion for a woman he meets. After giving her 10 marks he is allowed to sleep with her, but in the middle of the night the master bursts in the bedroom and cuts off those parts of the monk that have offended God and men. The story is told by way of biblical quotations, so the lustful exchange between the monk and the woman is: '"Delectasti me, domine, in factura tua." At illa subridens ait: "Quam dulcia faucibus meis eloquia tua, super mel ori meo!"' (quoting Ps. 91: 5 (AV 92: 4) and 118 (AV 119): 103), and the castration of the monk adapts Ps. 77 (AV 78): 66: 'Et percussit eum in posteriori parte, et opprobrium sempiternum dedit illi.'

The story exists in several quite different versions. A much longer version is edited by Lehmann, *Die Parodie im Mittelalter*, 224–31. A different short version from the fifteenth century is printed by Julius Feifalik, 'Studien zur Geschichte der altböhmischen Literatur V', *Sitzungsberichte der Kaiserlichen Akademie der Wissenschaften: Philosophisch-Historische Classe*, 36 (1861), 174–5, under the title 'Passio cuiusdam nigri monachi secundam luxuriam'. See Lehmann, *Die Parodie im Mittelalter*, 121–2; Cartlidge, 'Festivity, Order, and Community', 40.

47. 'HOSPITALITAS MONACHORUM'   f. 60ᵛ

Walther, *Initia* 1894

Rubric: 'Hospitalitas Monachorum & salutes in claustro'.

Aue capitale . signum manuale . patens hospitale. horridus barbale . jereptum iumsale . sordidum mappale. panis coctus male . vinum tale . quale olus sine sale. Ouum canonicale. cubile brutale . vade sine uale . mancipium rusticale.

Four lines satirizing the monks' poor provisions. Walther lists no other copy. Below this at the foot of the page the scribe has written (boxed): 'Serua [*read* Sola?] grece monos . xl . eres . Misperei [*sic*] perdere seruicium . deus miserere.'

48. EARTH   ff. 62ʳ–63ᵛ

DIMEV 6292

This is one of a number of poems based on the words from the liturgy for Ash Wednesday: 'Memento homo quod cinis es et in cinerem reverteris': 'Remember man that you are dust and to dust you shall return', ultimately from Gen. 3: 19. Hence *erþ* can mean 'man', 'body', 'the world', 'the surface of the earth', 'the grave', 'riches', as well as 'earth'. The poem expands the most pointed of these lyrics, in Harley 2253 (DIMEV 6292), ed. G. L. Brook, in *The Harley Lyrics* (4th edn., Manchester, 1968), 29:

> Erþe toc of erþe erþe wyþ woh,
> Erþe oþer erþe to þe erþe droh,
> Erþe leyde erþe in erþene þroh,
> þo heuede erþe of erþe erþe ynoh.

The most popular of these expansions begins 'Erthe oute of erthe ys wonderly wrought' (DIMEV 1170, listing eighteen copies), with several variant versions, e.g. 'Erthe vpon erth is waxin and wrought' in CUL MS Ii.4.9 (DIMEV 1171), which shows knowledge of the version in Harley 913 (see notes to ll. 13–18, 49–54, 63, 65–6). There are also versions of the poem on later tombstones. Yet another version, beginning 'Whanne eorthe hath eorthe wiþ wrong igete' (DIMEV 6293), is accompanied by translations into Anglo-Norman and (as here) into Latin. All ed. Hilda M. R. Murray, in *The Middle English Poem Erthe upon Erthe*, EETS os 141 (1911).

f. 62ʳ

Whan erþ haþ erþ iwonne wiþ wow,
þan erþ mai of erþ nim hir inow;
Erþ vp erþ falliþ fol frow,
Erþ toward erþ delful him drow.
Of erþ þou were makid, and mon þou art ilich;   5
In on erþ awaked þe pore and þe riche.

Terram per iniuriam cum terra lucratur,
Tunc de terra cepiam terra sorciatur.

f. 62ᵛ

Terra super aream subito frustratur;
Se traxit ad aridam terraque tristatur.   10
De terra plasmaris, es similis virroni,
Vna terra pauperes ac dites sunt proni.

Erþ geþ on erþ wrikkend in weden,
Erþ toward erþ wormes to feden;
Erþ berriþ to erþ al is lif-deden;   15
When erþ is in erþe, h[o] muntid þi meden?
When erþ is in erþe, þe rof is on þe chynne;
þan schullen an hundred wormes wroten on þe skin.

Vesta pergit uestibus super uestem vare,
Artatur et uermibus vesta pastum dare;   20
Ac cum gestis omnibus ad uestam migrare;
Cum uesta sit scrobibus, quis wlt suspirare?
Cum sit uesta ponita, doma tangit mentum;
Tunc in cute candida verrunt uermes centum.

Erþ askiþ erþ, and erþ hir answerid,   25
Whi erþ hatid erþ, and erþ erþ verrid.
Erþ haþ erþ, and erþ erþ teriþ,

Erþ geeþ on erþ, and erþ erþ berriþ.
Of erþ þow were bigun, on erþ þou schalt end;
Al þat þou in erþ wonne, to erþ schal hit wend.   30

Humus humum repetit, et responsum datur,
Humum quare negligit, et humo fruatur.
Humus humum porrigit, sic et operatur,
Super humum peragit, humo quod portatur.
Humo sic inciperis, ac humo meabis;   35
Quod humo quesieris, humo totum dabis.

Erþ get hit on erþ maistri and miȝte,   f. 63ʳ
Al we beþ erþ, to erþ we beþ idiȝte;
Erþ askeþ carayne of king and of kniȝt,
Whan erþ is in erþ, so lowȝ he be liȝt.   40
Whan þi riȝt and þi wowȝ wendiþ þe bifor,
Be þou þre niȝt in a þrouȝ, þi frendschip is ilor.

Terra uimque brauivm terra collucratur;
Totus cetus hominvm de terra p[a]tratur;
Ops cadauer militvm que regis scrutatur;   45
Cum detur in tumulvm, mox terra voratur.
Cum ius et iusticivm coram te migrabunt,
Pauci per trinoccivm mortem deplorabunt.

Erþ is a palfrei to king and to quene,
Erþ is ar lang wei, þouw we lutil wene,   50
þat weriþ grouer and groy and schrud so schene,
Whan erþ makiþ is liuerei, he grauiþ vs in grene.
Whan erþ haþ erþ wiþ streinþ þus geten,
Alast he haþ is leinþ miseislich imeten.

Dic uestam dextrarium regique regine,   55
Iter longum marium, quod est sine fine,
Indumentum uarium dans cedit sentine,
Quando dat corrodium, nos tradit ruine.
Cum per fortitudinem tenet hanc lucratam,
Capit longitudinem misere metatam.   60

Erþ gette on erþ gersom and gold,
Erþ is þi moder, in erþ is þi mold.
Erþ uppon erþ, be þi soule hold;
Er erþe go to erþe, bild þi long bold.

Erþ bilt castles, and erþe bilt toures;   65
Whan erþ is on erþe, blak beþ þe boures.

Humus querit plurima super humum bona,
Humus est mater tua, in qua sumas dona.
Anime sis famula super humum prona;
Domum dei perpetra mundo cum corona.   70
Ops turres edificat ac castra de petra;
Quando fatum capiat, penora sunt tetra.

þenk man in lond on þi last ende,
Wharof þou com and whoder schaltou wend;
Make þe wel at on wiþ him þat is so hend,   75
And dred þe of þe dome lest sin þe schend;
For he is king of blis, and mon of moch mede,
þat deliþ þe dai fram niȝt, and leniþ lif and dede.

De fine nouissimo mauors mediteris,
Huc quo ueneris uico, dic quo gradieris.   80
Miti prudentissimo concordare deris,
Hesides iudic[i]o, ne noxa dampneris.
Quia rex est glorie, dans mensura restat;
Mutat noctem de die, vitam mortem prestat.
     Amen.

---

16 ho] heo   17 chynne] *corrected from* schynne   44 patratur] pᵃrtratur *or*
pᵒrtratur (*first* r *possibly subpuncted*)   82 iudicio] iudico

APPENDIX

BL MS LANSDOWNE 418

In 1608 Sir James Ware, auditor-general in Ireland, transcribed texts from Harley 913, five of which are now missing from the manuscript. BL MS Lansdowne 418 is an assembly of his papers. Ware was evidently especially interested in the texts relating to Irish politics. With one exception, all his copies are from texts that are now towards the end of Harley, on fols. 50–60, items 36–46.

f. 88ʳ

Heading: 'Out of a smale olde booke in parchment called the booke of Rosse or of Waterford. Febr. 1608.'

Pers of Bermingham (Harley item 36)

'Sith Gabriell gan grete . . . Two hundred daies and mo. Explicit.'

f. 88ᵛ

Prophetic Verses on Scotland (Harley item 38)

'Bruti posteritas albanis associata . . . Hostibus expulsis judicis vsque diem.'

ff. 88ᵛ–89ʳ

'Litera Domini Ade de Briton militis' (not in Harley)

'Excelso leoni crities prolixos rubeos . . . vsquam adventum scolaris in hyberniam. Carmen hic ita deest.'

Sixty-eight lines of prose. A letter to the lion of St Brigid's town (Kildare) and his lioness and cubs. He is identified at the end as R. filii Mauritii (Fitz Maurice). The author, Adam de Briton, who has long studied the Prophecies of Merlin, interprets the events of the Bruce invasion as a fulfilment of them. A great battle at Mullaghmast (Co. Kildare) is mentioned, as is Adam's informant, Robert Waleys (Walensi).

Robert fitz Maurice, fl. 1328–46, was seneschal of Kildare c.1330 and sheriff later in that decade. In 1331, after the death of the short-lived third earl of Kildare, he and John Barby were described as assigning guards to the castle of Rathangan.[1] In 1335 and again in 1345 he is listed among those who stood surety for Maurice fitz Thomas, the young fourth earl. An Adam Bretoun was seneschal of Carlow in 1316, and was rewarded in 1318 following the Bruce invasion.[2] Perhaps it was the same Adam Bretton or Bruton who was seneschal of the liberty of Kildare in 1327.[3]

This is followed on f. 89^r by: 'Carmen non vituperes : licet egi male : vel quamvis sit aliquid verbum criminale; Sit sermo vel carmen, folis sum fole: leo tibi dico: vale, vale, vale.'

f. 89^r

Letter from the Prince of Hell (Harley item 23)

'Princeps regionis gehennalis . . . Explicit inveccio subsanatoria diaboli contra ecclesiam sanctam dei.'

ff. 89^v–90^r

Metra de monachis carnalibus (Harley item 41)

'Quis nescit quam sit monacorum nobilis ordo . . . Fiant tanquam fenam tectorum quod priusquam evellatur etc.'

f. 90^{r-v}

Passio vnius Monachi (Harley item 46)

'In antiquis temporibus . . . Per aliam viam reversus est monachus ad claustrum suum. Amen.'

f. 90^v

An acrostic hymn to the Virgin (not in Harley)

> Celi reginam laudemus crebro Mariam
> Reginam mitem regnantis querite matrem
> Laudemus regnantis nomen celica dantis

---

[1] *The Red Book of the Earls of Kildare*, ed. G. Mac Niocaill (Dublin, 1964), 102. All ex info Robin Frame.

[2] G. H. Orpen, *Ireland under the Normans*, 4 vols. (Oxford, 1911–20), iv. 175n, 208.

[3] *Red Book*, no. 160.

Crebro querite celica consolamina sacra
Mariam matrem dantis sacra magnificemus

List of Twelve Tribes and their symbols (not in Harley)

'Ruben Mandragora . . . Azer Ante edes habebat pelvim et desuper obumbrantem oleum.'

On the list see Charles D. Wright, 'The Lion Standard in *Exodus*: Jewish Legend, Germanic Tradition, and Christian Typology', in R. M. Liuzza (ed.), *The Poems of MS Junius 11* (London, 2002), 188–202. Wright has a set of depictions of the twelve from an eleventh-century manuscript, and quotes a later Irish poem. There is another copy of the list in Dublin, Trinity College MS 53 (s. xii, Winchester).

ff. 91ʳ–93ʳ

Walling of New Ross (Harley item 40)

'Rithmus faite ville de Rosse'. 'Talent me prent de rimaunceir . . . E deus qe dedens sunt habitan. Amen amen amen. Ce fait fet lan du l'incarnacion du nostre seignur m.cc.lxv.' Copied in two different hands.

f. 93ʳ

Young men of Waterford (not in Harley)

'There is in this booke a longe discourse in meter putting the youth of Waterford in mind of harme taken by the Povers, and wishing them to beware for yᵉ time to come. I have written out yᵉ first staffe only.

    Yung men of Waterford lernith now to plei
    For ȝure mere is plowis ilad beth awey
    Scure ȝe ȝur hanfelis þat lang habith ilei
    And fend ȝou of the pouers that waltith bi the wey
      Ich rede   5
      For if hi takith ȝou on and on
      Frame ham scapith ther never one
      I swer bi Christ and St Jon
        That of goth ȝur hede

    Now hi walkith etc.'   10

On the le Poers, their influence in Waterford, and their conflict with
Maurice fitz Thomas Fitzgerald, earl of Desmond, see Introduction,
'Historical Context', pp. xxxiv–v. Line 3 *Scure ʒe ʒur hanfelis*: 'Polish
up your anvils'. In l. 4 *waltith* is an error for *walkith*, as in l. 10.

f. 93^v

Chant for Archbishop Thomas (not in Harley)

'Gloriose presul Thome / Solvus istud auxioma . . . Quo fex caule
conditur.'

Eighteen lines on two rhymes; chant for Thomas, presumably of
Canterbury, but possibly of Hereford. Not in Walther, but cf. *Initia*
7258, 'Gloriose celi presul' (on Thomas of Canterbury).

COMMENTARY ON EDITED POEMS

2. THE LAND OF COKAYGNE

1 *bi west Spayngne*: 'to the west of Spain' (OE *be-westan*). Cf. Laȝamon's *Brut* 1068: 'bi westen (Otho *weste*) Sæuarne'. The Dutch texts say that half of Cokaygne is better than the whole of Spain: 'Dye eyn helft is beter dan all Hyspaniën' (Pleij, *Dreaming of Cockaigne*, text B, l. 12), and for discussion Pleij, pp. 267–8. Trevisa explains that Spain is so called after Hesperia, 'þe weeste eve sterre', and describes its many attractions (*On the Properties of Things*, gen. ed. M. C. Seymour (Oxford, 1975), 766/21). Everyone knew, of course, that the real Earthly Paradise lay in the east (e.g. *Isidori Hispalensis Episcopi Etymologiarum sive Originum libri XX*, ed. W. M. Lindsay (Oxford, 1911), 14. 3. 2).

2 *Cokaygne*: For theories of the origin of the name see Pleij, *Dreaming of Cockaigne*, 391–402. Its first literary occurrence (*c*.1200) is in the *Carmina Burana*, 'Ego sum abbas Cucaniensis', in which the abbot frequents the tavern to play dice. See Dronke, '*Land of Cokaygne*', 69–70. Dronke also cites a mock letter of the thirteenth century to the abbess and other nuns of Cokaygne ('Cucanacensi') inviting them 'to pay tribute unceasingly to bountiful Venus whose representatives you are' (pp. 70–1).

10 So Gen. 1: 29: 'I give you all the seed-bearing plants . . . and all the trees with seed-bearing fruit; this shall be your food.'

12 Gen. 2: 10: 'A river flowed from Eden to water the garden.' The first wine-bibber was Noah (Gen. 9: 20–1).

14 In the Earthy Paradise Elias (Elijah) and Enoch await the coming of Antichrist; see Mary Lascelles, 'Alexander and the Earthly Paradise in Mediaeval English Writings', *Medium Ævum*, 5 (1936), 31–47; Thomas D. Hill, 'Parody and Theme in the Middle English "Land of Cokaygne"', *Notes & Queries*, 220 (1975), 55–9.

15 *elinglich*: 'with tedium, drearily' (OE *ælenge*), because there is no company.

18 *how*: 'trouble' (OE *hogu*).

19 *trie*: cf. 'Satire', 4.23.

20 *russin*: 'snack' (Ir *ruisín*), evidently between the midday meal (*none*) and supper. Not elsewhere in English.

26 Cf. Owein's visit to the Earthly Paradise in *St Patrick's Purgatory*, where 'Nox illam nunquam obscurat' (*Tractatus de Purgatorio Sancti Patricii*,

l. 796). This is translated in *The South English Legendary*, ed. Charlotte d'Evelyn and Anna J. Mill, EETS OS 235 (1956), as 'Hit was þar euere iliche liȝt . and euere it was day' (*St Patrick*, l. 541). The source is Rev. 21: 25. Hill, 'Parody and Theme', 57, quotes from *Collectanea pseudo-Bedae*, which reports that in Heaven is 'vita sine morte, juventus sine senectute, lux sine tenebris, gaudium sine tristitia, pax sine discordia, voluntas sine injuria, regnum sine commutatione'. For this text see headnote to 'Fifteen Signs' (item 14).

34 *horwȝ*: 'dirt'; cf. 'Fall and Passion', 20.34. Presumably there is no need to clean up after the farm animals.

35 Both *harace* (OF) and *stod* (OE) mean 'stud-farm, collection of horses kept for breeding'.

40 Of course there was 'non vile worme' in Ireland since 'Sein Patrik bad oure Louerd Crist . þat þe lond delyuered were / Of þulke voule wormes . þat non ne come þere' (*St Patrick*, ll. 5–6) in *The South English Legendary*.

45–6 In the *Apocalypse of Paul* (*Visio Sancti Pauli*) Paul is granted a vision of the Heavenly City in which 'there was a river of honey, and a river of milk, and a river of wine, and a river of oil' (James, in *Apocryphal New Testament*, 538). The angel guide identifies the rivers as Phison, Euphrates, Geon, and Tigris, the four rivers that flow from the earthly paradise (Gen. 2: 11–14).

52 Not two orders, as has been suggested. Cistercians, whose habit was undyed wool, were referred to as both grey and white monks, as explained by Walter Map in the course of his denunciation of their practices: 'nos uel albos nominamus monachos uel grisos. . . . ut qualem ouis gesserit lanam textam habeant, alieni coloris nesciam' (Map, *De Nugis Curialium*, ed. M. R. James, rev. C. N. L. Brooke and R. A. B. Mynors (Oxford, 1983), 84). Cf. *MED grei* adj. & n. 1(c); *whit* adj. 2(b). Critics have speculated on what light this throws on the relationship between Cistercians and Franciscans in Ireland, and on the identity of the 'fair abbei'. See esp. P. L. Henry, 'The Land of Cokaygne: Cultures in Contact in Medieval Ireland', *Studia Hibernica*, 12 (1972), 120–41. It is true that the 'Letter from the Prince of Hell' and the 'Reply of Pope Dositheus' (items 23 and 24) both include trenchant attacks on the Cistercians. However, it is more likely that the identification of Cistercians should be seen as a satiric allusion to a Cistercian production immensely popular in Ireland as elsewhere, *St Patrick's Purgatory*, in which Owein reports that the monks he met in Paradise were Cistercians, as the order pre-eminent in glory. See *Tractatus de Purgatorio Sancti Patricii*, ll. 1081–5, and Easting's note on the Cistercians' conviction that they were all saved. The passage is translated in the *South English Legendary*: 'As him þoȝte greie monekes . in mest ioie he sei þere / None men in so gret ioye . ne so gret honur he ne say / Ne no wonder sikerliche . for þe ordre is noble & hei' (*St Patrick*, ll. 706–8).

57 *fluren*: 'made of flour' (not elsewhere recorded); *schingles*: roof-tiles. A standard feature in the Cokaygne texts; cf. the Dutch text B, l. 34, where the houses are tiled with tarts (*vladen*).

59 *pinnes*: 'pegs'; *podinges*: 'sausages'. In the Dutch text B the fences are made of sausages (l. 20) and the joists of butter (l. 26). In the French 'Cocagne' the houses have sturgeon rafters, bacon roofs, and sausage battens (ll. 33–5).

68–70 In the Auchinleck version of *St Patrick's Purgatory*, Owein arrives at the gate of the Earthly Paradise made of 'Jaspers, topes and cristal, / Margarites and coral' (*Owayne Miles*, 131.1–2, ed. Easting, in *St Patrick's Purgatory*). See also the list of gems below, ll. 89–94. The model for such lists is Rev. 21: 19–20.

69 *bas*: The emendation is supported by *MED bas(e* 1(b); *capitale*: much the earliest instance in English for 'head of a pillar' though *AND capital* cites a parallel from Thomas of Kent, *Roman de toute chevalerie* (*c*.1175).

73 *galingale*: an aromatic root, often paired with ginger in recipes. In *Kyng Alisaunder*, ed. G. V. Smithers, EETS os 227, 237 (1952, 1957), 6782–7 Alexander visits the trees of the sun and moon which smell of *note-muge*, *setewale*, *galyngale*, *caneil*, *lycorys*, *gylofre*, *quybibbe*, *mace*, *gyngyuer*, and *comyn*, most of which appear here. Cf. also the list of spices to which the lady is compared in the Harley Lyric 'Annot and John', ed. G. L. Brook, in *The Harley Lyrics*, ll. 37–40. The ultimate source is Song of Songs 4: 13–14.

74 *siouns*: 'scions, shoots' (AN *ciun*); the earliest English citation in *MED*. *sedwale*: the spice 'setwall' (AN *sedewale*).

78 *cucubes*: 'cubebs' (AN), a spice berry.

85 *piement*: 'spiced wine', often used medicinally.

86 *rent*: 'produce, output'. *MED rent(e* 1(f) translates the phrase as 'to flow without diminishing'.

87 *þai stremes*: The commentary in *Early Middle English Verse and Prose*, 340, takes *stremes* to be a verb, 'overflow with moisture (intrans.), be drenched', but the glossary interprets it as a noun, which must be right since the pr. 3 sg. ending is always -þ. 'All the bed of those streams is precious stones and gold.'

89 *vniune*: a pearl (Lat.): 'Of þe whiche margaritis, some ben ycleped *vniones* and hauen a couenable name for oonliche oon is yfounde and neuer two or mo togidre' (Trevisa, *Properties*, 856/18–20). The author must have consulted a lapidary for these lines.

90 *astriune*: '*Astrion* is a precious stoon of Ynde nigh liche to cristalle. In þe myddel þerof schyneþ a sterre wiþ clerenesse of þe fulle moone and haþ þat name of *astris*, "sterris", for if it is ysette in þe sterres light it takeþ light of hem, as Isider seiþ' (Trevisa, *Properties*, 836/1–5).

91 *lugre*: 'ligure' (*OED*). '*Ligurius* is a stone like to *electrum* in colour and haþ þat name, as Isider seiþ, of a beste þat hatte *linx*. þis stoon *ligurius* is ygendred among grauelle of þe vryne of a beste' (Trevisa, *Properties*, 855/30–2). *prassiune*: 'prasine'. '*Prassius* is a stoon grene as leeke, and conforteþ feble sight, and is somtyme yfounde wiþ rede dropes and is somtyme distyngued wiþ white dropes' (*Properties*, 864/31–3).

94 *epetite*: '*Epistites* is a litel stoon bright and rody, and makeþ a man siker þat bereþ it in þe hert syde' (Trevisa, *Properties*, 848/5–6).

96 *þrostil* and *þruisse* both referred to songbirds of the thrush family, the former often glossed *merula*, 'blackbird'. The two are distinct in *The Owl and Nightingale*, ed. Neil Cartlidge (Exeter, 2001), l. 1659: 'þrusche & þrostle & wudewale'. See P. R. Kitson, 'Old English Bird-Names (I)', *English Studies*, 78 (1997), 481–505 at 484–5.

97 *chalandre*: 'lark'. See Kitson 'Bird-Names', 489. *MED* glosses 'calander lark', a bird restricted to the Mediterranean, but the poet is unlikely to be so precise, and this is not evidence for a French source, as suggested by T. J. Garbáty, 'Studies in the Franciscan "The Land of Cokaygne"', *Franziskanische Studien*, 45 (1963), 139–63. Bibbesworth's *Tretiz* lists the *chalaundre* among the woodland birds, where it is glossed *wodelarke* (*AND*). *wodwale*: used of various songbirds; Kitson, 'Bird-Names', 497.

102 Ready-cooked birds flying into one's mouth are regular inhabitants of Cokaygne. See Dutch text B, ll. 72–5, in Pleij, *Dreaming of Cockaigne*, 38 (translation) and 436, and discussion pp. 137–46.

103 *Fleeþ*: the scribe writes ʒ for þ. For the reverse see *neiþ* for *neiʒ* 19.20, *touþ* for *touʒ* 33.182, and *þe* for *ʒe* in 5.21. Interchange between þ and ʒ is not uncommon in scribes more accustomed to writing Latin.

105 *garlek*: In the French 'Cocagne' meat turns itself on the spit and covers itself with garlic sauce, 'blanche aillie', l. 42.

109 *stu*: 'cook-pot' (OF *estuve*).

111 *spech*: *MED spech(e* 5(a) glosses 'mention of something in a text', but more appropriate would be 4(b), 'argument'. 'There's no question of doing without drink.'

113 *geeþ*: pr. pl. There is no need to emend to *goþ*. The vowel is by analogy with 3 sg.; cf. *geeþ* 48.28. So too *geþ* in ll. 141 and 145.

132 *in o randun*: *MED randoun* glosses 'with (great) speed or violence', but 'one after another' would be appropriate; see *AND randun*.

135–6 There has been a clumsy attempt to make the maiden plural, by erasing *a* before *maidin* (there is no room to add *-s*) and altering *hir* to *har*.

142 *þakkeþ*: 'stroke, pat' (OE *þaccian*). Used in a sexual sense also of Nicholas's actions in the Miller's Tale (*CT* A.3304).

149 Cf. l. 45n. Alluding ironically to the *Apocalypse of Paul*, in which the river of milk is for the Holy Innocents and 'all they that keep chastity in cleanness' (p. 539). See Hill, 'Parody and Theme', 58.

158 *sleilich*: either 'surreptitiously' or 'dexterously' would suit the context.

159 *þat hi seeþ*: 'they see that'.

164 There were at least two abbeys called 'the Grey Abbey'; one at Mainster Liath on the Ards Penisula near Newtownlands (Cistercian), another at Kildare (Franciscan), and attempts have been made to identify this with one or other. But this is just a title for any Cistercian Abbey, and refers to the same abbey mentioned in l. 51. Cf. the Life of Becket in the *South English Legendary*: 'a grei abbeye / þat me clupeþ Cler Mareis [Clairmarais, Pas-de-Calais] of greie monkes iwis' (1234–5).

165 *oreisun*: the poet is presumably thinking of prostrate prayer; see *MED orisoun* 1(d), 'lien in orisoun'.

166 *iambleue*: 'legs lifted'. *AND jambe* cites the sexual sense from *La Chanson de Guillaume* 2618: 'Quant es colché, ben es acuvetee, si te fais futre a la jambe levee.'

168 Presumably some proverbial expression lies behind this line. Cf. (possibly) the modern 'set your cap at someone'.

169 *wiþoute danger*: 'without opposition', or 'with no difficulty'.

171 Alluding to the distinction between salvation by right or by grace, as expressed, e.g., by Langland on the salvation of the poor: 'þei han Eritage in heuene, and by trewe riȝte, / Ther riche men no riȝt may cleyme, but of ruþe and grace' (*Piers Plowman* B.10.341–2).

173 For a celebration of monastic sleep see 'Hore Sompnolentium' (text 7).

179–80 The earthly paradise is cut off by a barrier of some sort. In *St Patrick's Purgatory* it is a wall. Elsewhere it is a mountain or the sea; see Howard R. Patch, *The Other World* (Cambridge, Mass., 1950), 134–74, and cf. the river in *Pearl*. In the sixteenth-century Dutch text on Luilekkerland the visitor has to eat his way through a three-mile mountain of buckwheat porridge 'ende langhen bergh van boecweytenbry, wel drie mijlen breet oft dicke'; Pleij, *Dreaming of Cockaigne*, 40, 438.

185 *stond to ȝure cheance*: 'risk your luck'; *MED stonden* 8(a).

4. SATIRE

1 The Archangel appropriately heads the series of five saints. He is often depicted weighing souls, but sometimes, as here, slaying the dragon with a spear, with reference to Rev. 12: 7–9. In an alabaster in the V&A (A.209–1946) he is both slaying and weighing. For a contemporary example, see the Stowe Breviary (BL MS Stowe 12), f. 305, with a red cape as here.

7 Christopher's long staff sprouted leaves and fruit at Christ's command. He is pictured with it in very frequent illustrations of his legend, as in an alabaster at the V&A (A.2–1912). The east window at All Saints, North Street, York, as well as wall paintings at Newnham, Hertfordshire, Woodeaton, Oxfordshire, and Slapton, Northamptonshire, depict the fish at the saint's feet.

10 West Cheap, later Cheapside, was the site of London's food market.

13 For an early English version of the life of Mary Magdalen in Bodleian Library, Laud Misc. 108 (*c.*1300) see *The Early South-English Legendary*, ed. Carl Horstmann, EETS os 87 (1887), 462–80; also *Middle English Legends of Women Saints*, ed. Sherry L. Reames (Kalamazoo, 2003), with a full account of the legend. In that text (DIMEV 4928) Mary is guilty of lechery and pride in her appearance: 'þaron was al hire þouȝht, and faire hire to schruyde' (l. 50). Following Luke 7:37, she anoints Christ: 'Out of hire boxe heo nam oynement ful guod, / And smeorede ore louerdes heued with ful blisful mod' (ll. 97–8). Hence her emblem is a box of ointment. See Katherine Ludwig Jansen, *The Making of the Magdalen: Preaching and Popular Devotion in the Later Middle Ages* (Princeton, 2000). The attributes here are all Mary's, not her bastard son's, who is probably the poet's satiric invention. This is the only stanza not beginning 'Hail!' until the last two, and emendation is attractive.

19–20 The Thornham Parva retable (1330s) from the Dominican priory at Thetford depicts Dominic with a book and a staff with cross, not, as here, a crosier. See Ann Massing (ed.), *The Thornham Parva Retable* (Turnhout, 2003).

22 The Dominicans were much criticized for their pride, as in *Pierce the Ploughmans Crede*, ed. Walter W. Skeat, EETS os 30 (1867): 'For wiþ þe princes of pride þe prechours dwellen' (354).

25–7 For Francis preaching to the birds see Bonaventure's *Legenda Maior*, XII. 3. Item 31 is an extract from the *Legenda*. The scene is often illustrated.

28 *Mani bold begger*: For the controversy about able-bodied begging, see Introduction, 'The Franciscans in Ireland'.

31–2 The Carmelites or White Friars wore a white mantel over a brown habit. St Mary the Virgin, their house in Drogheda, was founded in the late thirteenth century. See A. Gwynn and R. N. Hadcock, *Medieval Religious Houses: Ireland* (London, 1970), 288. Drogheda was a major trading port and centre of shipbuilding; see J. Bradley, 'The Topography and Layout of Medieval Drogheda', *Co. Louth Archaeological and Historical Journal*, 19 (1978), 98–127.

33 The Carmelites 'raken aboute / At feires & at ful ales & fyllen þe cuppe' (*Pierce the Ploughmans Crede*, ll. 72–3).

34 *watir-daissers*: *MED*, s.v. *dasher*, glosses '? A brush for sprinkling holy water' (from *dashen* v.) If so, he would indeed be an excellent master 'þat þis sentence vnderstode'.

36 *sentence*: In context the primary meaning is probably 'statement', *MED sentence* 5(a), but other senses such as 'wise saying', 'authoritative teaching', are also relevant.

37 *Gilmins* (OF *Guillemin*): The Williamites were an eremitical order founded in the mid-twelfth century by St William of Maleval (d. 1157). In 1256 Pope Alexander IV ordered that they should amalgamate with the Augustinian hermits as the Austin Friars and accept their rule and their black habit. However, they protested and were permitted to revert to their former status, which many of them did. See Francis Roth, *The English Austin Friars 1249–1538* (New York, 1966), i. 16–17. The poet here describes the Austin Friars, who arrived in Dublin *c.*1280, and established four more houses in Ireland by the end of the century (Roth, i. 26), including one in Drogheda (Gwynn and Hadcock, *Medieval Religious Houses: Ireland*, 298).

38 Originally eremitical, the Williamites and Austin friars first lived in remote areas, but then moved into towns; see *Pierce the Ploughmans Crede*, ll. 308–16. It is a point made by Satan in the 'Letter from the Prince of Hell' (item 23).

39 Perhaps this means they live as Franciscans (*menur*) in the wilderness but behave grandly as Dominicans (*prechur*) in towns.

40 The reader expects a physical description of the friars' habit, but *abite* refers instead to their customary activity of *gadering*, accumulating wealth (*MED gaderinge* 2c).

42 *adun ileiid*: 'written down', in contrast to *iseid* (*MED leien* v.^{1}, 11b); or 'set aside' (*MED adoun* adv. 5).

43 'The Abbot of Gloucester's Feast' (item 6) is a satire on the drunkeness of the Benedictines. Among countless other examples, the *Ordre de bel eyse* (Harley 2253) remarks that the Black Monks love drinking and 'E fount cheschun jour yvre' (*Anglo-Norman Political Songs*, no. 12, l. 97). The word *corrin*, 'drinking vessel', is used three times in 'The Abbot of Gloucester's

Feast' (*currinum*, 68.1, 70.3, 71.2), but nowhere else. It is of Celtic origin (cf. Irish *cuirin*).

46 St Benedict is sometimes depicted with a scourge symbolizing discipline, as in Fra Angelico's fresco in San Marco, Florence. The line presumably has sexual implications: tempted to run off with a fair woman, the saint 'Himsulf he strupte naked anon . among þornes he wende / And breres, & turnde her & þer . and al is fleiss torende' (*The South English Legendary* (1956), 122, ll. 23–4).

49 The Augustinian abbey of St Mary de Hogges in Dublin was founded *c*.1146 as the first house of Irish nuns; see Gwynn and Hadcock, *Medieval Religious Houses: Ireland*, 316. There were, of course, other nunneries in Ireland dedicated to Mary.

51 'You go often astray'; the clear sexual reference picks up the hints of *bourmaidnes* and *spouse*. For the locution, see *Hoccleve's Minor Poems*, ed. I. Gollancz EETS ES 73 (1897), *Jonathas*, l. 66: 'swich oon as hath trode hir shoo amis'. *OED* cites later examples s.v. *mistread* and *shoe* n. 2 1.

52 'A curse on the cobbler who tans your hide!' Mannyng uses *lepir* contemptuously of women's flesh in *Handlyng Synne*, ed. Frederick J. Furnivall, EETS OS 119, 123 (1901, 1903), l. 3448.

56 *crokes*: 'curly locks' (*MED crok* 5(a)). The tonsure was prescribed for all those in holy orders. 'The Simonie' (DIMEV 6677, in *Medieval English Political Writings*, ed. Dean, criticizes acolites who, having given up their curly locks for the tonsure, conceal it when they go out on the town: 'Summe bereþ croune of acolite for þe crumponde crok, . . . At euen he set vpon a koife and kembeþ þe croket' (115–17). *Crok* also has the sense 'dirty trick', as in 'sich wylys and crokys' (*The Towneley Plays*, ed. Martin Stevens and A. C. Cawley, EETS SS 13–14 (Oxford, 1994), 16.337).

57 *Ȝow*: an early example as a nominative form. *deleþ bot ahouue*: 'give only in moderation', i.e. stingily (*MED ahove, hof*, cf. ON *hóf*). The merchants are similarly criticized in the next stanza. *lewid men* generally has the sense 'laity', but here its primary sense 'ignorant people' must be involved (*MED leued man*).

58 *holibrede*: bread that has been blessed but not consecrated, distributed to those who have not received the Eucharist at Mass.

61 The eight stanzas on tradespeople begin with the rich merchants and end with two stanzas devoted to tradeswomen. Cf. 'Walling of New Ross' (text 40), which enumerates many of the same trades. *auoir-depeise*: 'goods by weight'; see quotations in *AND aver*[1].

67 The duplicity of tailors was proverbial: see Whiting T13. Compare the next stanzas with Dunbar's poem 'To The Merchants of Edinburgh': 'Tailȝouris, soutteris and craftis vyll / The fairest of ȝour streittis dois fyll', ll. 36–7 (*The Poems of William Dunbar*, ed. James Kinsley (Oxford, 1979).

69 *Aȝens*: 'in preparation for', though hot needles would hardly be suitable for sewing.

71 *baston*: 'verse'; cf. l. 77. Mannyng uses the term in the prologue of his *Chronicle* to denote a particular kind of verse distinct from *ryme couwee*, 'tail-rhyme', and other sophisticated forms that *lewed men* would find difficult (Robert Mannyng of Brunne, *The Chronicle*, ed. Idelle Sullens (Binghamton, 1996), 1. 79–92).

75 These are all evidently cobblers' implements. For *trobles* see *AND truble*, *trobile*, glossed 'shovel' (MedL *tribula*). For *treisuses* see *MED traisus*, citing a gloss for MedL *tramellum*, 'hopper'; *AND tramel* glosses 'funnel' and also 'spool'. *bochevampe* is from *bocchen*, 'mend' (cf. ModE *botch*), plus *vaumpe*, 'front part of shoe' (*AND vampe*); *alles* are awls for piercing leather (*MED al*).

76 *route*: *MED rout(e* n.(1), 4(b), glosses 'collection or group of objects', but the reference is to the cobblers not their implements, so sense 3(a) 'gang of rascals' is appropriate; cf. l. 28.

79 *drenche-kiue*: 'soaking vat'. *OED drench* n. 5 gives a nineteenth-century example meaning 'preparation in which skins are steeped'.

80 *wo is him aliue*: *MED alive* 3 cites the expression from Laȝamon and elsewhere.

81 This plays upon portentous weather prognostications, which begin 'When it thundreth in Ariete . . .' etc., as in Curt F. Bühler, 'Astrological Prognostications in MS. 775 of the Pierpont Morgan Library', *Modern Language Notes*, 56 (1941), 351–5.

85 *bochers*: the error *potters* is difficult to account for, but the stanza clearly describes butchers with their meat axes and wearing aprons, standing at their stalls surrounded by flies.

86 *barmhatres*: 'lap-garments', i.e. aprons.

87 *schamil*: 'shambles' (as in York). *MED shamel* (b) gives examples of the meaning 'butcher's stall'.

93 *pincheþ on*: 'are mean with', 'give short measure on', as implied by the *louis smale*; cf. ModE *penny-pinching*. White bread is made from more refined and therefore more expensive flour.

94 *OED baker* quotes Heywood's proverb of 1562: 'I feare we parte not yeet, Quoth the baker to the pylorie.'

97 *brewesters*: female brewers, as Langland's Beton (*Piers Plowman* B.5.299), for whom the cucking-stool was considered appropriate punishment. See

Judith M. Bennett, *Ale, Beer and Brewsters in England: Women's Work in a Changing World 1300–1600* (Oxford, 1996), 104–5.

98 *Potels* hold half a gallon, and *quartes* a quarter. In 1310 potters were forbidden to 'make any other measures than gallons, potells, and quarts' (Henry Thomas Riley, *Memorials of London and London Life* (London, 1868), 78.

99 They make profit by cheating; like Chaucer's Miller, they have thumbs of gold (*CT* 1.563).

103 *hokesters*: 'peddlers', here female, as often in early use.

106 *tromcheri*: 'liver', from Irish. See Andrew Breeze, 'Middle English *tromcheri* and Irish *tromchroí* "Liver"', *Notes and Queries*, 238 (1993), 16. *inne*: 'stall'; *MED in* n. 3(a) misleadingly cites this in the sense 'permanent dwelling'.

109 *Fi a debles*: For the imprecation, see *AND fi*[3]. It occurs several times in English texts. See also *MED debles*.

110 *tronn* (see *AND trone*): the public weighing machine, used also for shaming false tradesmen (*OED tron* 1 b). Scottish records refer to the punishment of nailing an ear to the *tron*; see citations s.v. *DOST tron(e* 2.

111 *goshorne*: a horn for calling geese, so 'an obnoxious noise?' (*MED gos* 4(c)). But is *goshorne* rather the loud noise made by geese? Cf. the Owl's voice in *The Owl and the Nightingale* 'ilich one grete horne', l. 318.

112 *hechil*: a (metal) wool-comb. Possibly the poet is alluding to a gruesome passage in 'Als I lay in a winteris nyt' (DIMEV 605) in which the soul is dragged off to hell sitting on a very uncomfortable saddle 'Fol of scharpe pikes schote / Alse a hechele onne to ride', ll. 542–3, ed. John W. Conlee, in *Middle English Debate Poetry* (East Lansing, Mich., 1991).

5. SONG OF MICHAEL KILDARE

9 Cf. l. 139; and 'Sarmun' 13.225 for the heavenly vision of the Trinity.

15 *iclung so clai*: Context suggests 'destined to die'; cf. the Vernon lyric 'Nou Bernes, Buirdus bolde and blyþe' (DIMEV 3717), in *Religious Lyrics of the XIV*[th] *Century*, Brown, 134–6: 'to amende þat we mis-do / In Clei or þat we clynge and cleue' (ll. 53–4). Elsewhere the phrase appears to mean 'be dismayed'; cf. the description of the Crucifixion in 'I syke when y singe' (DIMEV 2279), in *Harley Lyrics*, ed. Brook, 59–60: 'his frendes aren afered / and clyngeþ so þe clay' (ll. 16–17); also *The N-Town Play*, ed. Stephen Spector, EETS ss 11–12 (1991), 5.164, when Abraham is ordered to kill Isaac: 'My hert doth clynge and cleue as clay.' Other senses of the collocation are 'congeal' and 'shrivel up', as in 'Elde' 39.5, but these seem less appropriate.

17 *rai*: 'king' (OF); much earlier than examples cited by *MED roi(e*. The rhyme scheme requires emendation of *king*.

21 *ʒe*: For the writing of *þ* for *ʒ*, see note to 2.103.

22 *denne*: 'house', though it can also mean 'hiding-place'.

29 The image of trees to be cut down and burnt runs through the next stanzas. See note to l. 53.

30 *kiue*: literally a vat, as in 'Satire' 4.79.

37 *þe bow is bend*: 'The process has begun'. Cf. *Lear* III. i. 137; and *N-Town Plays* 5.140: 'Alas, þat evyr þis bowe was bent.'

47 *hori ding*: 'filthy muck' (OE *dung, dingc*). For the form *ding* (also in rhyme) see also 'Fall and Passion' 20.31.

53 *tre*: the image is suggested by Innocent III, *De miseria conditionis humane* 1.8 (ed. Robert E. Lewis (Athens, Ga., 1978)), quoted and translated in *Prick of Conscience*, ed. Hanna and Wood, ll. 666–87.

56 This is the last line of the *Proverbs of Hending* (DIMEV 3383 and 2800), copies of which are in MSS Harley 2253, Digby 86, and CUL Gg.1.1 (probably from Ireland). The stanza as in *Hending* is quoted by Grimestone, ed. Wilson, *Descriptive Index*, 25, as: 'Seket soule bote / For wan ʒe wenen alþerbest / To hauen helþe pes an rest / þe ex is at þe rote' (DIMEV 4475); and in a Latin treatise on the vices, likening a sinner to a tree that bears no fruit; see Wenzel, *Preachers, Poets, and the Early English Lyric*, 119.

57 'The wicked fiend regards it as a pleasure.'

59 *So mote ich þe*: 'as I hope to prosper', i.e. 'you can believe me'. Cf. l. 107.

60 For *sowleis bote* see note to l. 56.

63 *þou doist no streinþ of*: 'You place no importance on.' This sense of *strength* is common in *Ancrene Wisse*, ed. Bella Millett and Richard Dance, EETS OS 325–6 (2005–6): e.g. 'Lutel strengðe Ich do of ham', 7.370–1.

69 *qwest*: 'search for escape'.

70 *blench*: 'avoid'. Cf. the Body and Soul debate 'Als I lay in a winteris nyt' (DIMEV 605), ed. in *Middle English Debate Poetry*: 'Hellehoundes cometh nou sone / Forþi ne mouwe we noyþer blenche' (ll. 447–8).

78 The pronoun *me* is construed with plural *sul*, as in 33.147.

84 *deuist*: 'deafen' (*MED deven* v.(1)). But the reading could be *denist*, 'resound in' (*MED dinen* v.(1)).

85 *Hungir-bitte*: cf. *Cleanness*, ed. J. J. Anderson (Manchester, 1977), l. 1243: 'so biten with þe bale hunger'.

92 *wiþir witte*: 'perverse mind'; referring to the parable of Dives and Lazarus where Dives was 'clothed in purple and fine linen' (Luke 16: 19–31).

97 *flitte*: 'strife, struggle, tumult' (OE *geflit*). Note the *rime riche* with l. 95.

99 *is knot to knitte*: 'to fasten his fetters', or more figuratively, 'to put an end to him'; cf. the Auchinleck 'þe siker soþe' (DIMEV 5460), ed. *Religious Lyrics*, 32–5: Death has 'ouer him y-knett his knott / Vnder his clay kist' (ll. 75–6).

102 The poet extends the image of the body as a tree, here the withered tree of the pauper.

107 'Without a doubt, if Christ should see it.'

109 *icrauid*: 'demanded'; i.e. you will be held to account for his death.

112 *lake*: 'pit', used of hell in *St Erkenwald*, l. 302: 'We are dampnyd dulfully into þe depe lake' (in *Alliterative Poetry of the Later Middle Ages*, ed. Turville-Petre). The usage is from the Vulgate *lacus*, e.g. 'Domine eduxisti ab inferno animam meam, salvasti me a descendentibus in lacum' (Ps. 29: 4). See also *Seinte Marherete*, ed. Frances M. Mack, EETS os 193 (1934), 32/24–5: 'þe ladliche lake of þet suti sunne', though *MED lak(e* n.(1), 2(c), glosses both instances '?a marsh, slough'.

117 *dri þe stak*: *MED stake* 1(a) suggests '?to take an irrevocable action', though cites no support and it is not appropriate. Perhaps 'endure the punishment'; *MED drien* v.(2); *stake* sense 2(a), post for punishment or restraint.

122 *sadde*: 'slow'; *MED* does not record this sense, which is derived from *sad* 1(a) 'sated' and 3(c) 'heavy'. See also *MED sadli* 2(d).

124 *techith*: the ending is assimilated for the rhyme.

135 *ʒem*: 'protect'. Cf. 'Fifteen Signs' 14.4.

141 *menur*: A word of about five letters has been erased after *frere*. Heuser reasonably suggested that the correct reading should be *menur*, though under ultra-violet the erased word seems likely to be *p(re)chu(re)*, i.e. Dominican. Perhaps the scribe realized his error and forgot to supply the correction. There was no Dominican friary at Kildare, but there was one at nearby Athy. In the 'Reply by Pope Dositheus' (item 24) 'minores fratres' has been erased with more reason.

143 *toure*: Cf. Rolle, 'Mercy es maste' (DIMEV 3483), ed. in *Religious Lyrics*, 98–9: 'And bring me til þe rial toure / Whare I mai se mi God sa brygh[t]' (ll. 31–2), Chaucer's *ABC* 154: 'the hye tour of Paradys', and of course Langland's 'tour on a toft' (*Piers Plowman* B.Prol. 14), on which see the long note in Andrew Galloway, *The Penn Commentary on Piers Plowman*, i (Philadephia, 2006), 43–5, citing Jerome's commentary on Isa. 21: 8, 'I am upon the watchtower of the Lord.'

145 The bower is a nice contrast to the tower, though its connotations are more commonly favourable.

149–50 Cf. the Body and Soul debate in MS Harley 2253, 'In a þestri stude y stod' (DIMEV 2462), in *Altenglische Dichtungen*, ed. K. Böddeker (Berlin, 1878): 'shild me from helle shoures' (l. 80). *schoure* is commonly used in ME of an attack or bout of pain. Rhyming with it is *sure*, 'bitter' (*MED sour*, 3(a)), not 'sure'.

11. TWO ALLITERATING FRENCH VERSES

(1) 3–4 'Falsehoods make folly strong, cause a proud man to be flattered by sweet talking'.

13. SARMUN

Heading in Hand B: 'Thema: Si quis centiret, quo tendit & vnde weniret . Numquam gauderet, sed in omni tempore fleret' (Walther, *Proverbia* 29074).

1 Cf. the opening lines of 'Fall and Passion' ('þe grace of God ful of miȝt'), and 'Fifteen Signs' ('þe grace of Iesu full of miȝte').

5 Hand F writes 'Of deth' in the margin.

7–8 Cf. *Meditationes* on looking into the graves of ancestors: 'Cum eorum sepulcra respicio, non invenio in eis nisi cinerem et vermem, fetorem et horrorem' (section 4).

9–12 Cf. *Meditationes*: 'Attende, homo, quid fuisti ante ortum, et quid es ab ortu usque ad occasum, atque quid eris post hanc vitam. . . . Sic in non hominem vertitur omnis homo. . . . Quid superbis, pulvis et cinis, cujus conceptus culpa, nasci miseria, vivere poena, mori angustia?' (8).

15 *to be hend*: In his edition, *Altenglische Sprachproben*, i: *Poesie*, 115, Mätzner plausibly emends *to þe hend*, i.e. 'end'.

16 *file*: 'vile'. Cf. *Meditationes*: 'Si diligenter consideres, quid per os et nares caeterosque corporis meatus egrediatur, vilius sterquilinium nunquam vidisti' (7), quoted and translated in *Prick of Conscience* 620–8. 'The Sayings of St Bernard' in Bodley MS Laud Misc. 108 (ed. *Minor Poems of the Vernon Manuscript*, ll. 55–60) translates this as:

> A, man, ne beo nouȝht þi-sulf vnkouth,
> Loke ȝwat comez out of þi mouth,
> And elles-ȝware with-oute.
> ȝif þou wolt nime wel guod kepe,
> þou ne findest bote a foul doung hepe,
> þei þou loke þe al a-boute.

21–4 This little cameo of the body as a hunting park is suggested by Innocent III, *De miseria conditionis humane* 1.8, ed. Lewis, 105–7; *PL* 217, col. 705: 'O vilis conditionis humanae indignitas, o indigna vilitatis humanae conditio! Herbas et arbores investiga. Illae de se producunt flores et frondes, et fructus: et heu tu de te lendes et pediculos et lumbricos', quoted and translated in *Prick of Conscience* as:

> þis gret clerk telles þus in a buke:
> 'Behald', he says, 'Graythely and loke
> Herbes and trese þat þou sees spryng
> And take gude kepe what þai forth bryng.
> Herbes forth bringes floures and sede,
> And tres fair fruyt and braunches to sprede,
> And þou forth brynges of þiself here
> Nites, lyse, and other vermyn sere.' (644–51)

23 *I ne hold no pride*: 'I don't think much of'; *MED holden* v.(1), 10(b).

25–8 Cf. *Meditationes*: 'Cur ergo superbis, homo, attendens quod fuisti vile semen et sanguis coagulatus in utero, deinde miseriis hujus vitae expositus et peccato, postea vermis et cibus vermium futurus in tumulo?' (8).

27 *wormeis meisse*: 'food for worms'. Cf. 'Seven Sins' 15.13; and *Towneley Plays*: 'It shall be wormes mese' (31.118).

29 At the top of the page Hand F has written the heading: 'Agaynste pride'.

29–32 *Meditationes*: 'Nihil aliud est homo quam sperma fetidum, saccus stercorum, cibus vermium. Post hominem vermis, post vermem foetor et horror' (8). The image of the sack of dung became a commonplace: *MED sak* 2a(c). *Prick of Conscience* translates as:

> Saynt Bernard says, als þe buke telles,
> þat 'Man here es nathyng elles
> Bot a foul slyme, wlatsom til men,
> And a sekful of stynkand fen. (562–5)

31 *Ipudrid*: 'powdered, sprinkled', hence 'spattered' (*MED poudren* 2(c)).

42 *icrop*: 'that have crawled', i.e. 'crawling'.

45–50 Cf. *Meditationes*: 'Cur carnem tuam pretiosis rebus impinguas et adornas, quam post paucos dies vermes devoraturi sunt in sepulcro?' (8).

49 *wiked wede*: 'wretched cloth'; cf. l. 163.

50 *forsoȝt*: In *MED*'s three other instances the sense is 'seek out'. OE *forsecan* has the sense 'seek with hostile intent', hence 'afflict, attack' (*DOE*), which would be appropriate here.

55 *dwelle*: 'illusion' (OE), as at l. 111.

57 At the top of the page Hand F has written the heading: 'Agaynste couetise'.

65 *mister-men*: 'kinds of people' (AN *mester*, 'function, activity').

70 *a lone*: 'on loan'. *MED* takes MS *alone* as *a-lone*, adv. 4(b), 'only'. Rather it is *lone* n.(1), 2; cf. the phrase *lent lone* used of God's temporary gift, as in the Auchinleck MS 'þe siker soþe' (DIMEV 5460, ed. *Religious Lyrics*, 32–5: 'Y tel it bot a lent lan / When al the welþ of our wan / þus oway wites' (ll. 30–2)). Cf. l. 102.

74 *ȝime in store*: i.e. 'hoard'. *Meditationes* has nothing of this description of the miser. Cf. Mannyng's extensive treatment of *negons* in *Handlyng Synne*, ll. 6055–228.

81 *wrechis*: specifically 'misers'; see *OED wretch* n. and adj. 4, quoting Mannyng and Chaucer. *wringit*: *MED wringen* 3(b) glosses 'hold on to (sth.) avariciously', but this is entirely contextual. Rather, cf. the modern expression 'to squeeze blood from a stone' for the image. *mok*: *OED muck* n.[1] 4, and cf. the earlier *moker*; also *mukerer* and *mokerard*, 'miser'.

85 At the top of the page Hand F has written the heading: 'The rychman'.

85 *wringer*: Again *MED* tries too hard to find an appropriate sense, s.v. *wringer(e*: '?One who extorts or financially oppresses; ?a stingy person, penny pincher'. See note to l. 81.

89–92 Matt. 19: 24.

91 *bring*: Perhaps emend to *spring*, which would avoid the repetition and would better translate 'intrare'.

107 'But no-one will take heed of any other consideration' (*MED other* pron. 4(b)).

108 *Fort*: 'until' (MS *For*). Cf. 'Fall and Passion' 20.190.

111 'a tale' is written in the right margin in the main hand.

112 *Wlonchargan*: Otherwise unrecorded. *MED* interprets this as a name formed on *wlonk* (*wlonk* 3).

121–36 For the signs before Judgement see Heist, *The Fifteen Signs before Doomsday*, and the methodical treatment in the next text, 'Fifteen Signs'.

121 'The water shall then cover the Earth' (*MED spreden* 8(a)).

122 *Route*: 'surge' (OE *hrūtan*); cf. *Cursor Mundi*, ed. R. Morris, EETS os 57, 59, 62, 66, 99, 101 (1874–93), l. 21869: 'þe see sal rise and rute'. *for wode* 'in a fury' (*MED wod(e* n.(3), 2(c)).

129–30 *Les Quinze signes du jugement dernier*, ed. von Kræmer, the main source of 'Fifteen Signs', has 'Li ciés, la terre tout ardra' (335).

131 *rede*: 'fate' (*MED red* n.(1), 3(c)). *Les Quinze signes* has 'O vous,

pecheor, / Fuiez trestuit, vez ci lou jor / Tout plain de grant mesavanture'
(343–5).

135 Quaking angels are the tenth sign before Judgement in 'Fifteen Signs'
14.151–2 (see note there), citing the authority of Jerome and Gregory. See
Heist, *Fifteen Signs*, 69, 92. Cf. also *Ancrene Wisse*, 2.1038–9: 'ȝef þet ha
þencheð wel o þe dom of Domesdei, þer þe engles schule cwakien'.

138 *com to hepe*: 'come to pass' (*MED hep*, 4(b)). With this rather curious
expression, cf. *Piers Plowman* C.X.190 and 192, *brynge to hepe*, 'bring about'.

140 For bloody tears see 'Fall and Passion' 20.172 and note; and 'Christ on
the Cross' 19.2.

141 At the top of the page Hand F has written the heading: 'Loke þi last
end man'.

146 *þeran*: 'therein'; cf. *an* 'in' 214.

153 Cf. e.g. Ps. 143: 4.

155–6 'Look how he manages to be cheerful as if all the world might be
his.' See *MED though* conj. 2a (d).

157–60 Cf. *Meditationes*: 'Profecto fuit quando non eras: postea de vili
materia factus, et vilissimo panno involutus' (8).

161–72 For these same lines see 'Song on the Times' 33.157–68.

163 *wikid wede*: cf. l. 49.

171 'For once the soul has departed.'

179 *broþin*: 'degenerate' (*MED brethen* v.(2), 'be discomforted, perish'); the
p.p. has the same sense in OE (OE *ābrēoðan* 'to go to ruin, fail').

180 'What was yours will all belong to others.'

184 *be we fre*: 'let us be generous'.

185–8 This stanza is repeated at the end of 'Song on the Times' 33.193–6.

186 *helpiþ þai*: For the form of the demons. pronoun see Glossary, s.v. *þai*.
'Song on the Times' has instead 'ȝiueþ þe pouir' (33.194).

196 *dar*: 'need' (*MED durren*, 2(b)).

197 At the top of the page Hand F has written the heading: 'The lyfe
euerlasting'.

199 Isa. 30: 26. In *Hali Meiðhad*, ed. Bella Millett and Jocelyn Wogan-
Browne, in *Medieval English Prose for Women* (Oxford, 1990), Christ
embraces the ugliest of all 'ant makeð ham seouesiðe schenre þen þe
sunne' (36.6–7). *Meditationes*, quoting Matt. 13: 43, has 'ubi similes erunt
homines angelis Dei et fulgebunt justi sicut sol in regno Patris eorum.
Qualis, putas, tunc erit splendor animarum quando solis splendorem habebit
lux corporum?' (36).

205 'There is no want of food and drink' (*MED ned(e* 1(b)), rather than 'there is no need to eat and drink', since the ultimate source is Rev. 7: 16: 'Non esurient, necque sitient amplius.' In *Meditationes* this becomes 'Nulla est ibi aegritudo, nulla omnino necessitas; non est ibi fames, non sitis', continuing that those in heaven 'securi in propria patria manebunt, semper laeti, semper satiati de visione Dei' (37).

209 John 14: 2.

211 A proverb quoted also in Bodleian Library MS Douce 52 (Whiting W598). Walther, *Proverbia* 9536 has 'Finis coronat opus'. Cf. also Chaucer, *Troilus and Criseyde* 2.260: 'th'ende is every tales strengthe'. *bint*: 'binds'. *MED binden*, 15, glosses 'consummate', but perhaps 'encapsulates' is closer.

213–28 This account of the joys of Heaven may be compared to that in the seventh part of *Prick of Conscience*, ll. 7530 ff. There is not enough detail to identify a particular source.

218–19 Cf. *Prick of Conscience*: 'þare sall ilk man als wele knaw other / Als a man here knawes hys syster or brother' (8274–5).

221 *Prick of Conscience* has: 'þai sall allswa se þare apertly / His blysfull moder saint Mary' (8678–9).

225–6 Cf. *Prick of Conscience*: 'Bot þair mast ioy in heven sal be / þe blisful sight of þe Trinite' (9372–3).

230 *fest*: The emendation is supported by sense and rhyme.

233–5 For the same lines see 'Ten Commandments' 21.77–9.

239 *were*: 'apprehension' (*MED wer(e* n.(5)) .

14. FIFTEEN SIGNS

1–3 Cf. 'Fall and Passion' 20.1–3.

10 Isaiah is listed as just one of many authorities in *QSJD* 56. There are few specific parallels, though see notes to ll. 37–40, 53–4, 61–4, 86–8.

13–16 *holi boke*: e.g. Dan. 12: 1, Matt. 24: 21, Mark 13: 19, Rev. 6: 12–7, 16: 1–21.

17–20 Translating *QSJD* 49–52: 'N'a sou ciel homme tant felon, / Se vers Dieu a s'antancion, / S'un petit m'escoute parler / Qu'il ne lou coveigne plorer?'

23–32 Perhaps some lines have been lost, since in *QSJD* and *Cursor Mundi* the first sign is a bloody rain at which unborn children cry. These lines translate *QSJD* 77–86:

> Li enfant qui né ne seront
> Dedanz les vantres crïeront

A clere vouiz mont hautemant:
'Merci, vrai Diex omnipotant!
Sire, nos ne querons ja naitre.
Miez volons touz jorz noianz estre
Que nasquissens a icest jour
Que toute riens soffre dolor!'
Li enfent crïeront einsi,
Et se diront 'Jhesu, merci!'

In 'Les xv singnes de domesdai' in MS Digby 86, on the first day it rains blood, so that 'Children vnborene þat nout ne beþ / Of þare tokne adred hy beþ / And greteþ help of oure driȝte / Riȝt also hy speken miȝte' (*Codicem manu scriptum Digby 86*, 53–7, ll. 9–12).

26 When the infinitive is separated from its auxiliary, particularly 'shall', it is preceded by *to*. Other instances are in ll. 47–8, 138. On the other hand, when 'shall' immediately precedes, as in l. 139, 'sold tofal', it is more probable that *to* is the intensifying prefix, *MED to* pref.(2). So also 'tofalle' 92, 'toberst' 95, 'todriue' 122. See Tauno F. Mustanoja, *A Middle English Syntax* (Helsinki, 1955), 522.

27 *red vs rede*: 'guide us'; for the collocation, see *MED reden* v.(1), 8a(c).

29–30 'Lord, we wish that we had not been born into the world.'

33–5 *QSJD* 87–8: 'Li premiers jorz sera itaus, / Mais li secons sera plus max.' Cf. *Cursor Mundi* 22475–6: 'þe toþer dai to bide iwisse / It sal be well war þan þis.' The lines *follow* the first 'token' and introduce the second, 'þat oþer', so that the marginal note here, 'The first tokyn', is misplaced.

37–40 Cf. Isa. 13: 10: 'quoniam stellae caeli et splendor earum non expandent lumen suum'; Matt. 24: 29: 'luna non dabit lumen suum et stellae cadent de caelo': similarly Mark 13: 25, Rev. 6: 13. In pseudo-Bede and its derivatives, including Comestor, the sign on the twelfth day is 'cadent stellae et signa de coelo'. It is the second sign in *QSJD* and *Cursor Mundi* 22475–92.

42 *QSJD* 101: 'Noires seront comme charbons'. *Cursor Mundi* 22489: 'Worth al black sum ani cole'.

45–50 *stidfast man*: Apparently the author has misunderstood the French, in which it is the stars that were once fixed that now run around the earth like lightning and descend to the abyss: 'Nule n'i ert si bien fichiee / Qui a ce jor dou ciel ne chiee / Et courront si tost desor terre / Comme foudre' (*QSJD* 91–4).

52 'They will avoid neither sea nor land' in their desire to escape (*MED sparen* 7(a)). Cf. *Sir Orfeo*, ed. A. J. Bliss (Oxford, 1954): 'He no spard noiþer stub no ston' (346).

53–4 In Pseudo-Bede it is on the thirteenth day that 'congregabuntur ossa defunctorum, et exsurgent usque ad sepulcrum'. Cf. Isa. 26: 19, etc. *Prick of Conscience* has: 'þe thredend day sal dede men banes / Be sett togyder, and ryse al attanes, / And aboven on þair graves stand' (4804–6). This is not in the French.

61–4 *QSJD* 107–9: 'Quar li solois que vos veez, / Qui tant est bien enluminez / Qu'il enlumine tote rien'. Cf. Isa. 13: 10: 'Obtenebratus est sol in ortu suo.' This takes place on the fourth day in *Cursor Mundi*.

65 *QSJD* 113: 'en droit midi'.

66 The poet substitutes the conventional image (repeating l. 42) for the French 'plus noirs que nul haire' (111), i.e. sackcloth, as in Rev. 6: 12, 'niger tanquam saccus cilicinus'.

69 *son*: In *QSJD* 125 and Digby 86 it is the moon that turns red on the fourth day. In *Cursor Mundi* on the third day the moon 'Sal becum rede als any blod / Thoru dred of him was don on rode' (22497–8).

71–2 *QSJD* 131–2: 'Pour eschiver le jour de l'ire / Que nos mousterra nostre Sire'.

74–80 *QSJD* 137–40: 'Quar trestoutes les mues bestes / Vers le ciel leveront les testes: / A Dieu vourront merci crïer, / Mais eles ne pourront paller.' On the fifth day in the seven-sign scheme in the Harley 2253 version of 'In a þestri stude y stod' (DIMEV 2462) 'Eueruch best þat lyues ys / toward heuene ys hed halt, /Ant þuncheþ wonder whet þis by halt, / ant wolde clepe to oure dryhte / ah hy to speke ne habbeþ myhte' (ed. *Altenglische Dichtungen*, 138–42). This is not in the version in MS Digby 86. The fourth sign in 'In a þestri stude y stod' corresponds to ll. 85–92 here; again Digby differs.

81 *tak*: 'get'. The French is not parallel.

85 Exactly translating *QSJD* 149: 'Lou siste jour ne larai pas.'

86–8 Cf. Isa. 40: 4.

89–96 *QSJD* 156–9: 'Et tant fort crolera la terre / Qu'il n'a so ciel si ferme tour / Qui ne chiee jus a cel jour, / Et lors charront trestuit cil abre.'

98 *crop*: 'top' (*MED crop* 2(c) and (d)). Cf. *QSJD* 165–6. *Cursor Mundi* translates similarly 'Dun þe croppe, vpward þe rote' (22549).

101–4 Bleeding trees are not in the French but are from pseudo-Bede: 'Sexta die omnes herbae et arbores sanguineum rorem dabunt.'

104 *Vnkundlich*: 'unnatural'.

105–12 Loosely translating *QSJD* 171–6: 'Que devanront lors vos maisons, / Vos beles habitations? / Toutes les covandra failir. / Pres sera li monz de fenir / Et lors covanra toute jant / Morir a mervoileus tormant.'

113–15 *QSJD* 177–8: 'Li octieves ert mont doteus / Et plus que tuit cist angoisseus.'

118 The simile is from the first sign in pseudo-Bede, where the sea rises 'quasi murus'.

121–4 *QSJD* 187–90: 'Li poisson qui anz sont enclos, / Don nos faisons sovant grant los, / Dendanz terre feront lor voie / Et cuideront que Diex nes voie.'

125–8 *QSJD* 191–4: 'Donc revanra la mers arriere: / Comme chose qui tant iert fiere / Enterra s'an en son rivaige / Et les aigues an lor estaige.'

127 *uerisse water*: *MED fresh* 5(d) glosses the phrase 'a body or stream of fresh water'.

129–31 *QSJD* 195–6: 'Li novoimes ert mont despers / E de ces signes mont divers.' Hence *deuers* means 'diversify, be different' (*MED diversen*). For 'E de ces signes' other manuscripts have 'Sur tous les autres', evidently the reading of the poet's source.

133 *QSJD* 199: 'J'an trai a garant Augustin.'

134 *skeis*: *QSJD* 197 has instead: 'tuit li flueve [*var.* aigues] parleront'. *Cursor Mundi* 22581 has 'al thing'.

135 *QSJD* 200: 'Qui de cest siegle [*var.* monde] dist la fin'.

138 *QSJD* 198: 'voiz d'omme'.

143–4 'Let us never be destroyed on account of the (covetous?) gaze of sinful man.' The French text is particularly unstable at this point and offers no help.

145 This is the tenth sign, a verse announcing this having presumably been lost; cf. *QSJD* 207–10.

146 *ferred*: 'company' (OE *geferrǣden*).

148 *QSJD* 210: 'Qui de ce signe n'oit paour'.

149–52 Jerome, Gregory, and trembling seraphim and cherubim are all in *QSJD* 211–14. Heist, *The Fifteen Signs*, 59–61, discounts the influence of Gregory.

157–68 In the French poem St Peter looks on silently in wonder as the damned emerge from Hell as St Paul had said, and are so terrified that they beg to be returned to their home.

162 *men har mone*: 'lament' (*MED menen* v.(2)).

163 *lede*: 'behave'(*MED leden* v.(1), 4(e)).

167 *QSJD* 237: 'Ren nos nostre herbergerie'.

171 'All the devils will be terrified of that.'

179 *fiz Mari*: 'le fil Marie' (*QSJD* 272).

15. SEVEN SINS

5 'In honouring the king of heaven'.

8 'So as to greatly disgrace and dishonour the Devil', taking *schame* and *schonde* as verbs.

10 'And grant that you may keep to it'. As in l. 7, the *þat*-clauses continue the hortatory subjunctive of the first stanza.

13 *meiis*: *MED* records this line under both *mes* n.(2), 'food', and *mei*, 'male kinsman' (OE *mǣg*); the latter is correct. *meiis and mowe* is 'men and women', as in 'þene latemeste dai' (DIMEV 5640), ed. *English Lyrics*, 46–9: 'Nou nis offered of þe, þi mei ne þi mouwe' (37); and see *MED moue* n.(1) (OE *māge*).

14 *isowe*: 'begotten'; *MED souen* v.(1), 4(a).

18 *gond*: pr. p. 'going', i.e. 'vanishing'; *MED gon* 12(b). Or it may be a reverse spelling for p.p. *gon*; cf. the rhyme *stond : nond* 36.35, and Introduction, 'Language', p. xxv.

47 *lusting*: 'happiness', the only citation in *MED*.

55 *heuid-sinnes*: For frequent examples of 'the seven head-sins' see *MED hed* n.(1), 5b(b).

59 *bipeche*: 'deceive' (OE). Cf. l. 103.

61–2 Cf. 'Seven Sins' (DIMV 2932) in MS Laud Misc. 463, ed. *Die Kildare Gedichte*, 186–97: 'At pride first I wile begynne, / For it is hed of al oure sinne.'

65 Lucifer is commonly held up as the original example of pride in poems on the sins. See also 'Fall and Passion' 20.29, and *Speculum Vitae*, ed. Ralph Hanna, EETS os 331–2 (2008), ll. 645–6.

71–6 i.e. Lucifer's only sin, for which he was driven from heaven, was 'a litil prude'.

80 *Whannin*: 'from where?' (OE *hwanon*), *MED whenne*. The question is answered in 90–4.

81 *Mid whate*: 'with which'; *MED what* pron., 3(b).

89–90 *Man and womman* is followed by the sg. imperatives *vnderstond* and *Betak*. Mustanoja, *Syntax*, 63–5 and 474, has nothing quite parallel.

90–4 'If each beast takes back what belongs to it, which you are so nicely dressed in . . . of which you are so proud, it won't leave you a single piece of clothing.' (After the Fall Adam and Eve were supplied with 'tunicas pelliceas'.) The poet's point works well enough for woollens, gloves, and shoes, though not for linen, but the source of this passage is Odo of Cheriton's fable of the upstart crow, ed. Léopold Hervieux, in *Les Fabulistes*

latins depuis le siècle d'Auguste jusqu'à la fin du moyen âge (2nd edn., Paris,
1893–9), iv. 180–1: 'Sic miser homo de ornatu suo superbit. Set accipiat ouis
lanam suam, terra li[m]um, boues et capri corium suum, cirogrilli et agni
suas pelles, et remanebit miser homo nudus et turpis.' In fact *limum* 'muck'
here is the editor's emendation of *linum*, 'linen'.

104 *iteiȝte*: *MED* takes this s.v. *itechen* 2(b) 'give instruction', but elsewhere
in the MS the p.p. is *taȝt*. Rather it is *MED teien*, 'bound, fettered'. Cf. the
version of *Cursor Mundi* in Cambridge, Trinity College MS R. 3. 8 (588), ll.
23307–8: 'tyed . . . wiþ synnes sere'.

111 *He*: i.e. the miser.

128 i.e. 'rather than nourish his soul as he should do'.

129 *abrode*: *MED abrod(e* adv.(1), 4(a) glosses 'out of doors', which has no
point. More appropriate would be sense 5, 'Across the breadth of some-
thing, from one side to the other'. But the phrase 'sit abrode' suggests
instead a figurative use of *abrode* adv.(2), 'on his brood, brooding'; cf. *Owl
and Nightingale*: 'þu sittest a brode'(518).

138 *hold*: 'safe and sound'; *MED hol(e* adj.(2). For the *-d* see Introduction,
'Language', p. xxv.

143 'The devil destroys him on account of his possessions.' *MED deren*
misinterprets, evidently taking *is gode* as 'his God' in apposition to *þe fend*.

161 *is was*: 'was his'.

181 *Areri cuntake*: 'provoke strife'. The poem breaks off with these words.

<h2 style="text-align:center">19. CHRIST ON THE CROSS</h2>

1–14 The earlier version of these lines in Cambridge, St John's College,
MS A.15, f. 72ʳ, is ed. in *Religious Lyrics*, 2, and Woolf, *English Religious
Lyric*, 31–2 with discussion. Variants are as follows:

1 Behold] Loke; whare he hangiþ] þar hanget he. **3** And] Vor; to] hu; wiþ]
biis mid; al] *om.* **4** felle] neb. **5–6** *follow* 7–8. **5** Bihold to] Blickied; is blodi]
bledet hiis. **6** sprad] istreid. **7** H f l f] F h f l; dimmiþ] desewet. **8** þerto . . .
ytiȝte] Drowepet his hendi bodi þat on rode biis itiht. **9–10**] *om.* **11** Behold
to is] Loke to þe; in (1)] on; ek in] on. **12** And] *om.*; is] þat. **13** heued] molde.
14 þou . . . bodi] Ne saltu no wit vinde. **15–16** *om.*

2 For tears of blood see 'Fall and Passion' 20.172 and note, and 'Sarmun'
13.140.

9–10 These lines are not in the Cambridge version, though the marble-
stone is in the source quoted in the headnote. The version in MS Digby 55
(*c*.1270) translates as 'þine þedes hongen colde also þe marbre ston' (quoted

by Woolf, *English Religious Lyric*, 29). The poet has added the reference to lechery.

15–16 These rather odd lines, though not in the Cambridge version, are a translation of 'volue & revolue'.

19 *þe forlor*: 'brought yourself to perdition'.

20 *neiȝ*: The scribe has written *þ* for *ȝ*. For the reverse, see *Fleeȝ* 2.103.

38 'And you felt no gratitude towards me'; *MED connen* 6 (g).

20. FALL AND PASSION

At the top of the leaf is the heading 'Adams is laps' in Hand F.

3 For the same line see 'Fifteen Signs' 14.3.

7 *bere*: *MED beren* (v.(1)), 9(a) glosses 'endure', which hardly seems appropriate! More probably it is sense 12(a), 'conduct oneself': 'behave in such a way that may be helpful to our souls'. Heuser proposed emendation to *here*, but the form in this dialect is always *hire*.

9 *worþing*: 'reverence', as often in *Ancrene Wisse*.

16 *wer*: i.e. *þou wer*.

17–20 Biblical passages used as the basis of the story of the Fall of the Angels are Isa. 14: 12–15, Ezek. 28: 1–19, Luke 10: 18, and Rev. 12: 7–9.

25 In *Piers Plowman* B.1.121, as in *Paradise Lost* 6.871, the angels fall for nine days.

26 The same image is used of the falling angels in *Cleanness* l. 222, 'as þe snaw þikke'.

30 *þe teþe angle*: Lucifer represents the tenth order of angels, as in *Piers Plowman* B.1.105. Cf. also *Towneley Plays* 1.254–6: 'X orders in heuen were, . . . The x parte fell downe with me.' There were nine named good orders, on which see *OED order* n. 1.

33 'To take the places of those . . .'. Cf. *South English Legendary*: 'þanne is man iwroȝt / To folfelle þe teþe ordre þat of heuene was ibroȝt' (*St Michael*, ll. 213–14).

47 *dute*: 'joy' (OF *deduit*), as in 'Cokaygne' 2.9.

57 At the top of the leaf is the heading 'The incarnacyon' in Hand F.

58 *pilt her to*: *MED pilten* 4 suggests 'apply oneself to'. Perhaps sense 1(c) 'thrust herself forward, assert herself' is closer; cf. the expression 'pilt him forth' cited there.

63 *þe worþ*: An impersonal construction: 'you will become', as in OE; see Bruce Mitchell, *Old English Syntax* (Oxford, 1985), i. 436 (paras. 1047–9).

68 *hi sold to*: 'they should (come) to', emending the reading *he*.

73 *Ebron*: Previously misread as *Eboir*. See Frontispiece. *Cursor Mundi* ll. 405–6 and 1415–15 follows the tradition that Adam was created and buried in the vale of Hebron.

87 *am:* = *ham*, 'them'. 'As (he did) through the agency of Moses who came to them.'

88 *i*: = *hi*, 'they'. 'Even so they sinned in the face of the prophecy of Moses.'

89–92 'God perceived by this test that even through the agency of a man who was chosen, even when (they were instructed) through prophets or commandments, would the whole human race not be lost' (i.e. would it be saved). *Whan* might be emended to *What*, 'whether'; cf. 'Song on the Times', 33.28.

99–100 The paradox is expressed in Latin hymns, and thence in Friar William Herebert's poem 'þou wommon boute uere', which continues 'þyn oune uader bere; / Gret wonder þys was / þat on wommon was moder / To uader and hyre broþer' (ed. *Religious Lyrics*, 18–20). See the Latin parallel in *Religious Lyrics*, 248, and discussion by Woolf, *English Religious Lyric*, 131–4.

104 'In consequence of which she did not lose her virginity'.

109–11 'Man so sinned against God that no soul could go to heaven until God's son was placed upon the cross.'

113 *hold*: 'be faithful to'; cf. *MED holden* v.(1), 19(a), and *hold* adj., 'loyal'.

119 'They told him to say if he could discover.' *MED reden* v.(1), 5b(a).

131 'Since he knew no guilt concerning him'.

133–40 These two stanzas, which follow l. 176 in the manuscript, obviously belong here.

145 *nol leue noȝt*: 'will not believe'. Or *nol* is for *nold*, 'would not'.

147 *soȝt*: 'pierced'; *MED sechen*, 11(c). 'Until they had pierced him there with a spear'.

152 *wel*: 'corpse' (OE *wæl*); the last recorded use except in the compound *walkyries* in *Cleanness* l. 1577.

157 *bone*: The reading appears to be *luue*, which is obviously corrupt. Some of the readings to the foot of f. 30ᵛ are unclear.

166 *alowe*: 'below' (in the tomb); *MED aloue*. Editors emend unnecessarily to *also*.

172 *teris of blode*: cf. 'Christ on the Cross', 19.2. On the tradition see Andrew Breeze, 'The Virgin's Tears of Blood', *Celtica*, 20 (1988), 110–22.

The detail of four tears is not found elsewhere, but perhaps they represent the three nails and the spear.

173 'To speak of sorrow in comparison to that sorrow'. From Lam. 1: 12,'Videte si est dolor sicut dolor meus', words frequently spoken by Christ on the cross, as most powerfully in the York *Crucifixion Play* (*The York Plays*, ed. Richard Beadle, EETS ss 23–4 (2009–13), 35. 253–8); see Woolf, *English Religious Lyric*, 36–44.

177 *ipinsed* 'tortured' (OF *pincier*), the only citation in *MED*.

185 *seint Ion*: the Baptist, not, as in l. 176, the Evangelist.

190–216 Some of the readings to the foot of f. 31ʳ are unclear.

194 *siwed*: *MED seuen* v.(1), 5(b), 'to act in accordance with'.

198 Specifically in Ps. 16: 8–11, quoted in the context of Christ's Resurrection in Acts 2: 25–8.

202 *riȝt me*: 'stand up, rise', *MED righten* 1(b). Alluding to Christ's foretelling of his Resurrection; e.g. Mark 10: 34, Luke 18: 33.

203 *wiþvt woȝ*: Implying 'without transgressing the law of God' (as opposed to natural law). *MED wough* n.(2).

206 'He sent his teaching far and wide'.

214 For the same line see 'Sarmun' 13.236.

21. TEN COMMANDMENTS

Heading 'Agaynst swerynge' in Hand F.

6 *beleue*: 'desist from' (*MED bileven* v.(1) 1(b)). On the topic of denunciation of swearers, common in sermons, see Woolf, *English Religious Lyric*, 395–400. By swearing on Christ's body we tear him limb from limb; see ll. 11–12. Mannyng treats the subject extensively in *Handlyng Synne* under the Second Commandment, especially ll. 665–88.

12 *forswore*: 'sworn profanely', *MED forsweren*, 4, citing the Vernon lyric 'Bi west vnder a wylde wode-syde' (DIMEV 950; *Religious Lyrics*, 125–31): 'We stunte neiþer for schame ne drede / To teren vr god from top to to, / Forswere his soule, his herte also, / And alle þe Menbres þat we cun Mynge' (ll. 151–4). So the lines mean: 'For we spare none of his limbs without profaning them.'

15 *edwite*: 'censure', so here 'speak disrespectfully of'.

25 *Moysay*: The form is not given in *MED*; it derives from the French or inflected Latin *Moise*. For the rhyme with *Synay*, cf. the version of *Seynt Katerine* in Cambridge, Gonville and Caius MS 175/96 (DIMEV 1881), ed. in *Altenglische Legenden: Neue Folge*, ed. Carl Horstmann (Heilbronn, 1881),

259: 'In þe mount off Synay / þere gaff þe lawe god off heuene / Vnto þe prophete Moysy' (ll. 760–2). The reading *to ysay* must be wrong since it is impossible to believe that the poet could have confused Isaiah with Moses.

29 *defens*: 'prohibition', i.e. the prohibitions listed in the commandments.

33 'X precepta' in left margin in Hand F. Each commandment is numbered in the margin.

45 *Ve*: 'alas'. Editors emend to *ȝe*, but *ve* is MedL (Lat. *vae*) Also cf. *MED we* and *wei* interj. *betauȝt*: 'consigned to': 'Alas, if they are given over to the devil.' Cf. Mannyng, *Handlyng Synne* (also on witchcraft): 'Swych beyn þe deuyl betaght' (l. 481).

47 Mannyng gives an account of different forms of witchcraft in his analysis of the First Commandment, *Handlyng Synne*, ll. 339–62, 480–500.

60 Presumably *hi* refers to children and *wrecch* to their parents, whose sufferings on behalf of their children should be alleviated by their ungrateful offspring.

64 Behaviour not characteristic of bees, either in nature or in lore. Bartholomaeus Anglicus describes how wicked king bees who consume too much honey are killed (Trevisa, *Properties*, 1147).

65 Not from the Decalogue but from Matt. 22: 39. The poet includes Christ's 'revision' of the Ten Commandments, since 'on these two commandments dependeth the whole law'. John Audelay does the same in his Ten Commandments carol, beginning 'loue þi God ouer al þyng, / þi neȝbore as þiselfe I say' (DIMEV 525), repeated in DIMEV 2512, ll. 144–5; both ed. in *Poems of John Audelay*, 6 and 181.

71 *stuter*: 'stronger' or 'more violent' (*MED stout(e)*).

77–9 For the same lines see 'Sarmun' 13.233–5.

22. LULLABY

2 In the version in Worcester Cathedral MS F.10, quoted in the headnote, it is the child who speaks.

3 *euermore*: The reading in the copy in the Worcester sermon. The scribe repeats *euer* from the beginning of the line, losing the rhyme and so altering *wore* in l. 4 for the new rhyme. Having made this error, he breaks the line with a punctus after *sorow*, taking *sich* as a verb parallel to *mourne*, and all editors have followed. The line is metrical with *sich* as a noun, 'sighing', parallel to *sorow* in the a-verse. Cf. *MED sik(e* for regular collocation with *sorow*. This is supported by the sermon's 'sorwe and kare'.

6 *vncuþ*: 'alien', because the child is a stranger (l. 31). In Grimestone's

'Lullay, lullay litel child, child reste þe a þrowe' (*Religious Lyrics*, 83–4) the Christ child is 'vnkut & vnknowe' (l. 3).

8–10 Cf. the lines quoted in the Worcester sermon.

8 *schef*: 'created thing' (OE *sceaft*).

11 *bemette*: 'destined' (not elsewhere); cf. *MED meten* v.(1), 'mete out'.

16 Cf. *Meditationes piissimae*, cited in the Worcester sermon.

19–23 Cf. the quatrain incorporated into *Fasciculus Morum*: 'The lade dame Fortune is bothe frende & foo, / Of pore hoe maketh riche and ryche of pore also, / Hee turneth woo to wele and wele also to woo; / Ne trust noght to his word þe whele turneth so' (in Bodleian Library, MS Rawlinson C.670). There are at least sixteen copies, conveniently reproduced as DIMEV 5367. Variant readings in the last line include 'No tryst now to thys wordl þe wyle he turneth soo' in Durham University Library, MS Cosin V.iv.2. So the child has already set his foot on Fortune's wheel.

24 'You don't know which way (it will) turn.'

25 The traditional metaphor of the pilgrim is abruptly overturned in the next stanza. St Paul is the source for the image of man as both a pilgrim and a guest in this world: 'peregrini et hospites sunt super terram' (Hebr. 11: 13), though Paul is referring to those faithful who recognized that their true home is elsewhere. Here the metaphor reminds us that after our miserable passage through life we are hell-bound. For the same combination of metaphors, cf. 'Man ys dethys vnderlyng, / Man ys a gest in hys dwellyng, / Man ys a pylgrym in his pasyng' (transcribed DIMEV 3365).

27 *horn*: MS *horre* is OE *heorr*, 'hinge' (e.g. of a door), so possibly, in this instance only, 'door'. But the scribe has been prompted to this reading by loss, as is usual in his language, of the p.p. ending -*n* in l. 25 (*ibore*), and loss of -*n* in *bifor* in ll. 26 and 28 (see Introduction, 'Language', p. xxvii). The emendations are made by Douglas Gray in his edition, *A Selection of Religious Lyrics* (Oxford, 1975), 83–4. For the blast of death's horn, cf. 'Fare well this world I take my leue foreuere' (DIMEV 1271; ed. Gray, 93–4) with the lines 'Wold to God I had remembyrd me beforne / I sey no more but be ware of ane horne' (20–1), and *Everyman*, ed. A. C. Cawley (Manchester, 1961), l. 843: 'When Death bloweth his blast'. Both examples are cited by Woolf, *English Religious Lyric*, 354 n. 3, who wonders if this instance is too early (p. 155 n. 6), though the biblical trumpets in Revelation and elsewhere would seem sufficient precedent for the image. For *dim* applied to horn-blast see *Sir Orfeo*, l. 285, 'dim cri & bloweing'.

28 'To destroy the children of Adam as he had previously destroyed Adam himself.'

29 *worp* (ms. *worþ*): 'cast', i.e. 'destined', rather than 'contrived' as glossed by *MED werpen* 10(b). In *Religious Lyrics*, 255, Brown pertinently compares the Harley Lyric 'Middelerd for mon wes mad' (DIMEV 3490), *Harley Lyrics*, 29–31, l. 65: 'wo him wes ywarpe ȝore'. Cf. l. 35.

31 *gest*: See note to l. 25. The comforting metaphor of the pilgrim is exchanged for that of the stranger.

32 *iurneis*: 'days', synonymous with *dawes*: 'Your days have been counted, the length of your life predetermined.'

35 'Adam caused you this sorrow.' In Grimestone's 'Lullay, lullay litel child, / þu þat were so sterne & wild', ll. 9–16, the speaker acknowledges his sin in taking the apple.

33. SONG ON THE TIMES

13 'Greed controls the law so that it is blind to true justice.'

15 Cf. ll. 149–50, and the complaint 'Bi west vnder a wylde wode-syde' (DIMEV 950) ll. 149–50, 'Who is a mayster now but meede / And pruide þat wakened al vr wo?' (*Religious Lyrics*, 125–31).

16 *whi suffriþ he*: 'why does he allow it'.

17 *pilt*: 'push' (*MED pilten*, 1(a)), so 'assert'. For the verb in a different sense, see ll. 60 and 86; for the noun l. 104.

21 *hold is riȝt*: 'maintain its justice', therefore support what is just.

22 *For no eie no for no loue*: For the phrase see *MED loue* n.(1) 1b, glossing 'on no account', but here it has its literal sense, 'without fear or favour'.

25 *entredite and amonsi*: both verbs mean 'excommunicate', the former OF, the latter OE.

29 *hoblurs*: riders on hobbies, small horses (AN *hobeler*). Here they are local officials, similarly described as horse-riders, *prikyares*, in 'Ich herde men vpo mold', l. 24 (ed. in *Alliterative Poetry*, 17–20). For complaints from Ireland about the destruction caused by hoblers, see Introduction, 'Historical Context', p. xxxvi.

30 The riders prevent the husbandmen from ploughing their land. Cf. 'Ich herde men vpo mold': 'Ar londes ant ar leodes liggeþ fol lene / þorh biddyng of baylyfs such harm hem haþ hiht' (ll. 27–8), and 'To seche seluer to þe kyng y mi sede solde, / Forþi mi lond leye liþ ant leorneþ to slepe' (ll. 63–4). *MED ere-grund* doubtfully suggests emending to *eri-grund*, so 'who deprive the farmers of ploughland', but there is no other citation for the compound. Bliss and Long, 'Literature', 720, suggest derivation from Irish *ériac*, but this is not appropriate.

45 The earliest version of this fable is perhaps Odo of Cheriton's 'De lupo, vulpe et asino' (after 1225) in which the wolf calls the animals to confession. The fox, admitting stealing hens, is pardoned because he acted according to his nature. The ass confesses to picking up a sheaf of hay fallen from a cart, and is condemned to be hanged (ed. Hervieux, *Les Fabulistes*, iv. 255). Two versions of *c*.1320 are closer, and both originate with the friars. In the *Promptuarium exemplorum*, ed. Karl Warnke, in *Die Fabeln der Marie de France* (Halle, 1898), p. lxiv, the appended moral is that 'fratres bonos pauperes qui portant honus religionis' are punished by prelates. The same conclusion is reached in the version by Nicolas Bozon, a Nottingham Franciscan, in *Les Contes moralisés de Nicole Bozon*, ed. Lucy Toulmin Smith and Paul Meyer, Société des anciens textes français (Paris, 1889), no. 4, pp. 10–11: prelates and bailiffs 'esparnunt les pussantz et les doggetz, et defoulent les simples gentz sovent sanz reisoun'. Only in the present poem is the fable given a political interpretation. See Jill Mann, *From Aesop to Reynard: Beast Literature in Medieval Britain* (Oxford, 2009), 38 and nn. 46–7.

48 The *Promptuarium exemplorum* begins: 'Leo mandauit omnibus bestiis ut uenirent ad penitentiam.'

53 *liþer*: 'wicked, deceitful'. Cf. ll. 9, 112.

54 *iwreiid*: 'accused' (*MED wreien*). Cf. l. 101, etc. On legal terminology in the poem see Wendy Scase, *Literature and Complaint in England, 1272–1553* (Oxford, 2007), 49–52.

60 *ditement*: 'indictment'; an aphetic form not recorded elsewhere by *MED*. *ipilt*, 'placed', so 'named' (on the charge), *MED pilten*, 2(a). Cf. also l. 86, and (in a different sense) l. 17.

63–4 'One (the fox) sent him (the lion) geese and hens; the other (the wolf) goats and sheep'; i.e. they both bribe the judge. The ass gives nothing (l. 67). The complaint on the judicial system, 'Beati qui esuriunt' (text 45), describes the same situation, in which the poor man is told 'Si nichil attuleris / Stabis omnino foras' (45.86–7).

77–8 In the right margin is written and boxed (by hand A?) 'at on rime'. Presumably this points to the repeated rhyme on *wille* through these three stanzas.

81 In the *Promptuarium exemplorum* the fox admits to taking capons, geese, and hens.

90 *doggid*: 'dog-like', i.e. 'fierce'. Bozon comments that it is the powerful and 'les doggetz' who are spared. *AND dogget* suggests this is the English word.

92 'Grant me pardon, as you have full power to do.'

96 'If you will listen to me for a moment'. For this sense of *res* see *MED res* 5, and cf. l. 148.

97 *vp þe doune*: *MED up-the-doun* glosses 'from top to bottom'. Rather, it is 'upon the hill' where the wolf hunts.

99–100 In the *Promptuarium exemplorum* the wolf takes cows, oxen, and horses. Bozon's wolf takes sheep ('berbis').

108 Similarly, Bozon's lion tells the wolf: 'ceo est ta nature de beiser le moton'. In the *Promptuarium exemplorum* the lion acknowledges that the wolf is incorrigible because 'tu vere animosus es'.

112 *stod*: 'breed' (ModE *stud*).

114 In both the closest analogues the crime of the ass is to eat sage leaves: 'inuenit saluiam et comedit tria folia' (*Promptuarium exemplorum*); 'un bouchee de sauge pris' (Bozon).

121–4 Bozon's lion has the ass 'bien batu e pus eschorchee'.

131 *prisund*: 'prison'; for the form, rhyming with *ibund*, see Introduction, 'Language', p. xxv.

132 'Until he pays up'. To *mak fine* was to pay to escape punishment or to make a settlement (*MED fin* n.(2), 8(a),10(a)).

141 'Loyalty has been lost between strangers and between kin.'

149–50 Cf. ll. 13–15.

153–4 As in 'Earth' (text 48), *erþ* signifies the human made of dust, landed wealth, and the grave. The version in Harley 2253 (DIMEV 6292) ends: 'þo heuede erþe of erþe erþe ynoh' (*Harley Lyrics*, 29). See notes to 'Earth'.

157–68 For these same lines see *Sarmun*, 13.161–72.

183 *ow þe gode*: 'possesses the goods'.

184 'Hard-heartedness is a good enough exchange for hard bread', playing on the senses of *hard* and *gode* in ll. 182–3.

185 *Moch misanter þat*: 'Bad luck to anyone who'.

187 i.e. he will get no spiritual reward for the gift of a crust. The poet plays on the senses of *mede*, from 'bribe', ll. 36, 41, 128, to 'reward in heaven', ll. 188, 196. Recourse to the former results in loss of the latter.

193–6 For the same lines see *Sarmun*, 185–8.

36. PERS OF BERMINGHAM

1–6 Pers of Bermingham died in 1308. There were various dates for reckoning the start of the year; here it is Lady Day, the feast of the Annunciation (25 March), as elaborately established by the first three lines.

See C. R. Cheney, *Handbook of Dates* (repr. Cambridge, 1996), 3–6. Pers was buried at Kildare in the Franciscan Grey Abbey.

7–8 'Take twice ten (days) in the eighth year (i.e. 1308).' Twenty days after Lady Day; i.e. 13 April. Thus l. 11 is in parenthesis: 'This was in April that precedes May.' Some sources give the date of Pers's death as 'idibus Aprilis' and 'in vigilia Pasche', i.e. 13 April, since Easter fell on 14 April. See Benskin 'Style and Authorship', 72–3.

12 *pulle*: 'deprive, rob'; *MED pullen* 4(c).

21 The subject is *his nam*, 'his reputation', which will increase.

26 *castel*: 'protector'; *MED castel* 2(b).

31–3 'Everyone who wishes to succeed with weapon (i.e. every warrior), consider in his case how good he was at time of need.'

35 *nond*: 'none', a reverse spelling, depending on the loss of /d/ after /n/. Cf. the rhyme in ll. 22–3, and see Introduction, 'Language', p. xxv.

42 *peruink*: the periwinkle is usually used as an image of womanly excellence; cf. 'Blow northerne wynd' (DIMEV 2325; ed. *Harley Lyrics*, 48–50): 'Heo is lilie of largesse; heo is paruenke of prouesse' (ll. 51–2).

58 *driue a quest*: 'drive (the hounds) out on the chase'; *quest* is a hunting term; *MED quest(e* 6(a).

63 *skulk*: (ON); much the earliest record of the verb in English.

65 *to wedde*: 'as a security' (for their bed-hire). See Benskin, 'Style and Authorship', 63.

66 *plai*: probably noun, but possibly verb. Both include the sense of warlike play; *MED plei(e* 4, *pleien* v.(1), 4; e.g. Laȝamon: *Brut*, ed. G. L. Brook and R. F. Leslie, EETS os 250, 277 (1963, 1978), 4188–90: 'þa gunnen heo to pleien / summe mid foten ueire igerede / summe an heorse hehliche iscrudde'. On the violent implications of 'teach one to play' see further Scattergood, 'Elegy', 100–1.

69 *trai*: *MED* takes this as *treien* (OE *tregian*), 'annoy', but rather it is *traien* (AN *traier*), 'attack perfidiously'.

73–5 For Richard de Burgh, earl of Ulster see Seán Duffy, 'Burgh, Richard de, second earl of Ulster (b. in or after 1259, d. 1326)',*ODNB*. Sir Edmund Butler acted as deputy justiciar of Ireland in 1304–5, and was knighted in 1309. In 1302 he married Joan, daughter of John fitz Thomas Fitzgerald. See Robin Frame, 'Butler, Edmund, earl of Carrick (d. 1321)', *ODNB*. John fitz Thomas Fitzgerald, lord of Offaly, was created earl of Kildare in 1316 and died the same year, and was buried in the Franciscan friary at Kildare. His son Thomas married Joan, daughter of Richard de Burgh, in 1312. See Ó Cléirigh, 'Fitzgerald, John fitz Thomas', *ODNB*.

84 'If they were to get away with it'.

86 'To get their own back'. Cf. *AND contrepan*, citing *Manuel des pechez* 8943 'le cuntrepan li rendez', referring to paying the devil back by confessing sins. This is translated by Mannyng as 'ȝelde hym þe countre paye' (*Handlyng Synne* 12155). As Benskin points out, 'Style and Authorship', 73, *cuntrepane* is a legal term: a matching pledge; see *OED counterpane*[1], 'the counterpart of an indenture'.

87 *com to*: 'succeed, manage'. Cf. Mannyng, *Handlyng Synne* l. 2672: 'he myȝt neuer come to to do'.

93 *neisse*: 'feeble', referring to the lords who reneged on their compact.

94 'Why should they have been born?'

96 Evidently colloquial for 'to sit about idly'. The old man in the version of 'Maximion' in MS Harley 2253 (DIMEV 1769; ed. in *Altenglische Dichtungen*) resents his wife calling him 'Spille bred' (l. 148).

98 The phrase meaning 'in all circumstances' (*MED agame*), picks up the sense of *plai* in l. 66.

100 *ordres to mak*: not 'to issue orders', though there is a pun on that sense, but 'to strike off opponents' heads', to 'crown' someone; a jocular allusion to cutting the tonsure (or 'crown') at the ordination ceremony. *MED ordre* 7(e) offers several examples of the phrase, including *Gamelyn* l. 533 where 'Gamelyn made ordres of monkes and frere' with good strokes of an oak staff. See Scattergood, 'Elegy', 103, who quotes the Auchinleck *Otuel* ll. 184–6; and see note to l. 126.

102 'It was not too great a task for him.'

103 Murtagh O'Conor, king of Offaly (Muirchertach Ó Conchobuir Fhailgi).

104 *keþerin*: 'band of foot soldiers' (Irish *ceithern*). *MED* has separate entries for *ketherin* and *kerne*.

105 *Gilboie*: An anglicization of the name Gilla Buidhe.

106 Trinity Sunday fell on 13 June in 1305.

107 Presumably to celebrate Trinity Sunday people wore their best hoods. Benskin, 'Style and Authorship', 64, aptly compares Easter bonnets.

108 Piers was lord of Tethmoy in Offaly. His ruined castle where the massacre occurred stands at Carrick, Co. Kildare. See Scattergood, 'Elegy', 91, for illustrations.

110 *Eþe McMalmore*: *The Annals of the Kingdom of Ireland by the Four Masters*, ed. John O'Donovan (Dublin, 1856), iii. 480–1, lists Aedh Maol Mordha (Maelmora), O'Conor's kinsman, among the slain.

118 For the hoods see l. 107. Benskin, 'Style and Authorship', 65, suggests they also denote the leather bags in which Pers sent his guests' heads to Dublin for a reward.

121–6 Like Grendel, this descendant of Cain is excluded from the feast. Unworthy of celebrating Pers's 'Mass', he is the only one to go home untonsured. The records do not note that anyone escaped with their heads unbagged. For the senses of *red* and *sing*, 'celebrate Mass', see *MED reden* v.(1), 2b(b); and see *place* 6(c) for the sense 'church'.

126 *vnhodid*: 'not ordained' (OE *ungehādod*), with a pun on 'unhooded'. See Benskin, 'Style and Authorship', 65. The first sense relates to l. 100: Pers did not 'crown' him; the second sense to ll. 107 and 118: Pers did not provide him with a hood. See *The Owl and the Nightingale*, where the Owl objects to the Nightingale's invocation of the Almighty on the grounds that he is no priest; 'Hartu ihoded, / Oþer þu kursest al unihoded?' (ll. 1177–8).

127 Referring to the poet's patron or superior.

131 For another pardon, see the last line of 'Sarmun', 13.240.

39. ELDE

1 *geld*: 'impotent'. Cf. l. 44.

2 *feld*: 'bend' or 'make stoop' (OE *fealdan*). Cf. l. 59.

3 *meld*: *MED melden* glosses '?to expatiate (on sth.)'. More probably it is a form of *MED medlen* 2a(a), 'have to do with'.

5 *keld*: 'make cold' (OE *cealdian*), as again in l. 41. Cf. 'mi nose koldet' in 'Wanne mine eyhnen misten' l. 3; 'min herte keldeþ' in 'Le Regret de Maximian' (Digby version), l. 64. *cling*: 'cause to shrivel, moulder away' as at l. 46. For the conventional collocation with *clai*, cf. 'Song of Michael Kildare' 5.15.

6 *held*: *MED helden* 2 b(a) glosses 'bow, stoop'. Rather it is sense 4, 'go', as frequently in Laȝamon. *dai*: 'appointed day', 'death day'; cf. *Lambeth Homilies* 35: 'forð he scal þenne is dei cumeð' (cited *MED dai* 10 (b)).

7 *blowid*: perhaps 'is full of pride'; *MED blouen* v.(1) 7 'brag' (OE *blāwan*), often collated with *bost*, or, in view of the reference to the impairment of his complexion, *ble*, a figurative use of v.(2), 'bloom, flourish' (OE *blōwan*). The verb is pr. 3 sg.; the spelling ⟨-d⟩ for ⟨-þ⟩ is also in ll. 27–8, and for the reverse see probably l. 44. See also the rhymes in 'Earth' 25–8. Jordan, *Handbook*, 187, has an inconclusive discussion.

8 'We all want to reach old age.' Cf. *Cursor Mundi*: 'Eild es þou a selcut thing / þat al it gerns þat er ying; / Quen þai it haue þai are vnfayn / And wald ha youthed þan again' (ll. 3589–92).

9–10 'It annoys me greatly that my saliva dries up.'

11 *wrot*: 'snout'(OE), elsewhere used only of animals.

12 *awarpeþ*: elsewhere the sense is 'overcomes', but it has perhaps developed the sense 'twist out of shape', like *werpen* itself (ModE *warp*).

13 Traditionally it is the old man's nose that becomes pointed as one of the signs of approaching death (*MED sharpen* (c)), but that would lose the alliteration with *schuldren*. Cf. *Prick of Conscience* l. 820 'His nese at þe poynt es sharp and smalle'.

14 *let*: 'deserted, departed from'; *MED leten* 6a.

16 *gore*: Cf. *The Owl and the Nightingale*: 'Habbe he istunge under gore, / Ne last his luue no lenger more' (l. 515).

19 *lore*: 'behaviour', cf. 'Le Regret de Maximian' 22–3: 'þo gon him rewen sore / Al his wilde lore.'

22 *munne*: 'recall' (*MED monen* v.(1)). In collocation with *wiþ muþe*, the usual verb is *minnen*.

24 *amarrid*: 'destroyed'. For the rhyme cf. Laȝamon's *Brut*: 'we sculle[ð] heom bi-charren & seo[ð]ðen heom amarren' (l. 2671).

27–8 *fordede / ted*: ⟨d⟩ for ⟨þ⟩; see n. to l. 7. So the verb is present tense.

29 *on rewe*: 'one after another' (*MED reue* n.(2)).

31 *pilkoc*: *MED* records use only as a personal name apart from this instance. It became common later as *pillicock* and *pillock*.

32 *schenlon*: 'fellow'. Evidently rare, since it is glossed 'puer' by the main scribe. There does not seem any merit in *MED*'s suggestion that it may be an error for *shende* + *-lou*, a variant of the rare derivational suffix *-leue*. *bischrew*: apparently pr. 3 sg., despite the form to rhyme with *rewe*.

35 *lewe*: 'frail' (*MED leu(e* adj.(3); OE *-læw*), glossed 'debile' by the main scribe.

37 *ein*: lost after *Min*. Cf. 'Wanne mine eyhnen misten' (l. 1). *fordwynnen*: 'become feeble'; used several times in *South English Legendary* in relation to approaching death.

39 *pirtle*: 'babble'? Not found elsewhere; cf. *OED prattle* (from *prate* + suffix) and *prittle-prattle*. *pofte*: 'pant'? *MED* compares *puffen*. *poute*: uncommon in ME and its etymology is uncertain. Here perhaps 'puff'.

40 *snurpe*: not elsewhere. *MED* compares MLG *snorpe*, 'sneezing' or Norw. *snerpa*, 'shrivel'. *OED* offers the latter, comparing ModE dialect *snurp*, but the former sense is more appropriate here. *sneipe*: 'sniff'? (ON?); not elsewhere.

41 *þroȝ kund*: i.e. as a result of my physical condition. *comble*: 'become numb' (OF); *MED comelen* and *acombled*.

42 'I stoop, I lean, my limbs shrink.' *lench* is only here in ME, though *OED* cites Halliwell's *Dictionary* (1847) '*Lench*, to stoop in walking. *Linc.*'. Cf. OE *ge-hlenced* 'twisted' (twice in Bald's *Leechbook*).

43 *poke*: 'stoop' (Du?). *pomple*: origin and meaning unknown. *pall*: 'grow weak' (OF); the first instance. *passe*: *MED passen* glosses 'move, advance, travel' (sense 1), but it is sense 5b, 'advance in years'.

44 *galliþ*: probably ⟨þ⟩ for ⟨d⟩, so p.p. 'afflicted with sores'. The verb appears to be a back-formation from the adj. (see *OED gall* v.¹ and *galled* adj.²), and all *MED*'s citations s.v. *gallen* are otherwise of the adj. and refer to horses.

45 *roxle*: 'grow feeble'? Only elsewhere, as a variant to *roileþ*, in *Piers Plowman* A.11.209. Cf. in later dialect *OED rox* 'decay'. *rake*: in this instance *MED* suggests 'wander, roam; ?also, wander in the mind'. *rouwe*: *MED roughen*, 'cough' (OE). *OED rough* v.¹ cites Skelton's *Colyn Cloute* 1223 'Let hym cough, rough, or sneuyll'.

48 Cf. 'Le Regret de Maximian' 37: 'Ofte ich grunte and grone.' *grenne*: 'grimace', or more probably 'gape'; cf. 'Wanne mine eynen misten': 'mine lippes blaken, / and mi muþ grennet' (6–7). The sense 'smile' is post-medieval.

49 *nese*: 'sneeze' (ON). *nifle*, 'snivel', as several times in *Ancrene Wisse*. *nuche*: only here, and not recorded in *OED*. Halliwell's *Dictionary* lists 'NUCH. To tremble. *Northumb.*'

50 *wilneþ*: 'demands'.

51 *stunt*: 'stand still' (*MED stinten*). With this passage compare the lament of Pathnucius over the death of his daughter in the Life of St Euphrosine in the Vernon *Golden Legend* (DIMEV 2467), in *Sammlung altenglischer Legenden*, ed. Carl Horstmann (Helibronn, 1878), 178, ll. 387–90: 'Allas, for deol I droupe and dare, / I clynge as cley3, Icau3t in care, / I wayle, I wandre, I wake, I walke, / I stunte, I stonde, vnstabli I stalke.'

52 *b[l]ert*: 'snore'; the alliteration supports *MED*'s suggested emendation s.v. *berten*, though the word is not elsewhere recorded in ME. *OED* s.v. *blurt* v. quotes Cotgrave's definition from 1611 'to puffe, or blurt out puffes, in sleeping'.

54 *spatle*: 'spit' (OE *spatlian*); cf. the description of the dragons in Robert Mannyng's *Chronicle*, Pt. 1 (MS P): 'Spatled, spouted, belewed, & byten' (l. 8082). *sporne*: cf. *Cursor Mundi* 3575: 'þan es eth þe fote to spurn'.

55 *werne*: 'fade, waste away'; *MED wernen* v.(2) (OE *weornian*).

57 *Ispend*: p.p. 'used up, exhausted', or pr., as *I spend*, 'I use up my energy'.

58 *wil*: 'agreeable' (*MED wille* adj. and *iwil* adj.). 'And I long for my lovely youth back.' Cf. the lines from *Cursor Mundi* quoted in note to l. 8.

59 *falc*: not elsewhere. *MED* suggests derivation from OE *fealg* and glosses '?fallow land'. *felde*: 'fold', i.e. 'grow weak' (*MED folden* v.(2), 2(b)). Cf. 'Maximion' (Harley version): 'Care & kunde of elde / makeþ mi body felde / þat y ne mai stonde vpriht' (ll. 34–6).

60 *heordmon*: originally 'household retainer', as in *Battle of Maldon* l. 261, and later Laȝamon and *Sir Gawain and the Green Knight*. Here, more generally, 'gentleman'. *holle*: (OE *hol*), with a range of senses; see *MED hol(e* adj.(1). Used particularly of eyes, 'sunken': e.g. *Awntyrs off Arthure*, ed. Ralph Hanna (Manchester, 1974), l. 116: 'With eighen holked ful holle'.

61 *folle*, 'fed up' (*MED ful* adj., 2(b)).

62 'So much is the attraction for old age.'

64 *wouw*: 'how'; for the form see Introduction, 'Language', p. xxix. *spent*: 'used up' (cf. l. 57); the subject is Elde.

65 *trent*: 'torn apart'; probably a form of *torenden*, but cf. German *trennen*, 'separate'.

67 *wlaseþ*: 'mumbles'; *MED* emends to *wlafeþ* (OE *wlaffian*). *wend*: pr. 3 sg.? 'Moves about as it does so'?

68 *Lostles*: 'the listless person'.

70 i.e. 'He has me in his control'.

40. THE WALLING OF NEW ROSS

1 Compare the opening line of *Trailbaston* (Dean, no. 93) in MS Harley 2253 (ed. in *Anglo-Norman Political Songs*, 66–78): 'Talent me prent de rymer e de geste fere.'

4 *Ne uaut pas vn aillie*: 'is worth nothing'. *AND ail* quotes from Bibbesworth's *Tretiz* 1082, which has the gloss 'pile of garlec'.

6 *aucer*: *AND* glosses 'to speak of (?)', perhaps for *ahucier*. But it may be for *anuncer*, 'announce, relate', as Shields, 'Walling of New Ross', suggests.

13 Maurice Fitzgerald and Walter de Burgh. Henry III created de Burgh earl of Ulster by 1264, in which year de Burgh seized the Connacht castles of the Fitzgeralds, his rivals in the south. In retaliation Fitzgerald imprisoned the royal justiciar, Richard de la Rochelle. See Introduction, 'Historical Context', p. xxxi. The burgesses of New Ross may have felt particularly vulnerable in this conflict since they had detained ships bound for the royal town of Waterford, claiming the authorization of Fitzgerald, which he denied (Sinclair 'Satirical *Dit*', 246–9).

16 The town was also known as 'villa novi pontis' (Orpen, *Ireland under the Normans*, ii. 244–5), referring to the bridge over the Barrow built by

William Marshall (d. 1219), who had married the Clare heiress who inherited the lordship of Leinster, including County Wexford.

19 *ensemblerent*: Shields's emendation. Sinclair, 'On the Text', 227, suggests the manuscript reading *en senterent* might represent *asenterent*, 'agreed'.

27 *prodoms*: 'freeholders of standing in the guild merchant, and chosen annually by the whole community' (Sinclair, 'On the Text', 227, referring also to *OED prudhomme*).

32 *la fosse alerent*: Since the fosse is not complete, Sinclair, 'On the Text', 228, suggests 'inspected (rather than 'went round') the fosse'.

38–9 Since *firent* is causative, Sinclair, 'On the Text', 228, translates: 'They had a crier announce it and summon the community to a moot.'

74 *al outeus*: 'at home' (*AND ostel*). Sinclair, 'On the Text', 229–30, would emend the reading *alouteus* to *a lor leus*, 'in their places', 'at their moorings'.

86–113 The leaf is badly stained, and some letters are difficult to read. They have been checked against Ware's transcription.

89 *bachelers*: For the sense 'junior member of gild', see *AND bacheler*, and *MED bacheler* 6.

97 *regraturs*: See John A. Alford, *Piers Plowman: A Glossary of Legal Diction* (Cambridge, 1988), 129, s.v. *regrater*: 'A retailer who buys goods in order to sell them again at higher prices. . . . The term usually applies to retailers of victuals; . . . it was subject to numerous regulations.'

104 *waynpayns*: See *MED wain-pain*, literally 'one who earns his bread'; here a labourer.

113–15 The initial letters are torn away and were probably lost to Ware, who guesses [S]*ur*, [*e*]*l*, [*Le*]*z*.

130–1 *escarlet*: *MED scarlet*, 2 'a kind of rich cloth', cites many examples of collocation with *grene*. *MED* defines *burnet* as 'a brown woollen cloth of fine quality', *AND brunet* as 'fine, dark cloth'. See Sinclair, 'On the Text', 231.

141 'As long as it pleases and is to their liking' (Sinclair, 'On the Text', 232).

150 *La Port de Dames*: Sinclair, '*The Walling of New Ross*', 263, notes an early record of 'Maiden's Gate' near the church of St Mary. P. H. Hore, *History of the Town and County of Wexford*, 6 vols. (London, 1900–2), i. 51 n. 1, notes that one of the town's four gates was 'the Bishop's Gate, known also as the Maiden, or Fair Gate'; see Hore's town plan, loc. cit. The ruins of a later structure still stand.

153 Not 'will lose his liberty entirely' (Shields, 'Walling', 33), but 'will not thereby have his own way entirely' (Sinclair, '*Walling*', 264).

155 An allusion to the metaphor of the prisoner of love. In Chrétien's

Yvain, when the damsel warns Yvain that her lady wishes to keep him imprisoned, he replies: ' "I'm very willing to be in her prison!" . . . for there is no lover who is not imprisoned' (*Arthurian Romances*, trans. D. D. R. Owen (2nd edn., London, 1993), 307).

157 *vilein fere*: Shields, 'Walling', 33, takes *vilein* as an unattested form of *vilenie*, translating 'evil action'. Sinclair, 'On the Text', 232, suggests the phrase *fere vilein* means 'to acquire a villain or villein', which seems inappropriate. Rather, the phrase means 'act as a villein', i.e. discourteously.

167 'They will never thereby (because of their large numbers) enter the town' (Sinclair, 'On the Text', 233).

179 *tolfaces*: cf. *MED talevace*, 'shield', citing *Havelok*, ed. G. V. Smithers (Oxford, 1987), 2323, and *Ywain and Gawain*, ed. Albert B. Friedman and Norman T. Harrington, EETS os 254 (London, 1964): 'A mikel rownd talvace / And a klub ful grete and lang' (ll. 3158–9). From Lat. *tavola*, 'table'.

211 *amen pur charité*: The phrase is quite commonly used to end a Middle English text; see *MED charite* 4. 'Cokaygne' ends 'Amen par seint charite' (2.190).

212 *la plus franch uile*: 'The epithet alludes to the liberties or freedom from taxes granted to the burgesses in their foundation charter' (Sinclair, 'On the Text', 234).

214 *hom estrange*: Sinclair, '*Walling*', 259, explains this as 'a trader outside the community', a *mercator extraneus*, subject to a number of regulations.

43. REPENTANCE OF LOVE

1 *poȝt*: 'distress' (*MED thought* 5(a)). Cf. 'The Way of Woman's Love' (DIMEV 3136), ed. in *Harley Lyrics*, 71–2: 'for my leof icham in grete þohte / Y þenche on hire þat y ne seo nout ofte' (ll. 7–8).

2 *poȝt*: n. 'intention', or p.p. 'intended'.

3 'It's impossible to stop brooding.'

7 'I'd anticipated enjoying happiness.'

8 'I am in distress.'

9–12 'I'm anxious about how I shall proceed; I want to move on and advance; I'll strive without (my dear one's) favour until I am dead and buried.' There is play on different senses of *funde* (see *MED founden* v.(1), 1 and 5), and on the homonyms *MED or(e* n.(2) and *er* conj.(1).

44. NEGO

1 *iwend an afte*: 'turned backwards', i.e. distorted (OE *æftan*). *OED* compares *abaft* in the same sense.

2 *nego*: 'I deny'. *crafte*: 'method of teaching' or 'branch of learning' (*MED craft* n.(1), 5). *Nego* and the other Latin terms in the poem are from scholastic debates. See Ignacio Angelelli, 'The Techniques of Disputation in the History of Logic', *Journal of Philosophy*, 67 (1970), 800–15 at 803: 'The game is started by the *opponens* and goes on by alternating moves. The *opponens* has two possible moves: "I propose that you assert A₁," (*pono tibi* A₁, *positio*) and "I propose that you deny A₁" (*depono tibi* A₁, *depositio*). The *respondens* has three possible answers: "I accept" (*consedo, admitto*), "I deny" (*nego*), and "I doubt" (*dubito*).'

5 *Forsak*: 'deny', as in *Sir Gawain and the Green Knight*, ed. J. R. R. Tolkien and E. V. Gordon, rev. Norman Davis (2nd edn., Oxford, 1967), 475: 'I haf sen a selly, I may not forsake'; so translating 'nego'. *saue*: 'but, on the contrary', i.e. qualifying the truth; *MED sauf* prep. 4 (as conj.). *þef in lore*: 'dishonesty in learning'; cf. *MED thef* 2(d), 'a liar' .

6 ' "Nego" is a scholar poor in possessions.' The Latin satire explains: 'Why do you consume your time upon dialectics, thou who receivest no income from other sources?' (*Political Songs*, 209).

7–8 'When men hurl themselves about (in disputation), they escape from trouble with a "nego".'

9 *vt of place*: 'Be gone!'; *MED place* 8(c).

11–12 i.e. 'I say no' is appropriate in dealing with the Devil, but it is improper to deny the truth as a stratagem in disputation.

15: 'For someone who knows little is quickly done', i.e. a fool's bolt is soon shot, and he falls back on a scholastic device.

20 *obligo*: 'Obligation is the *respondens*' commitment to avoid falling into a contradiction once he has accepted or denied an initial sentence proposed by the *opponens*' (Angelelli, 'Techniques', 803). It is an aspect of the *ars obligatoria*; on Duns Scotus's approval of the art of obligations, see Antonie Vos, *The Philosophy of John Duns Scotus* (Edinburgh, 2006), 196–222, who explains: 'It is the task of the opponent to trap the respondent into a pair of contradictory propositions. When the opponent has achieved this aim, he concludes "Cedat tempus" and the debate is over' (p. 199).

21 *verum falsum*: 'true / false'. Boethius stated: 'Propositio est oratio verum falsumve significans', that a proposition is a statement signifying true or false, the basis of dialectics. See Taki Suto, *Boethius on Mind, Grammar and Logic* (Leiden, 2012), 17–42. The *ars obligatoria* develops this: 'what is incompatible with the *positum* (*repugnans posito*) is in fact a truth (*verum*), although such a truth has to be denied within the game of the dispute, because its denial is assumed in the game. The rule of negation is governed partly by the internal rules of the game of obligation and partly by the external requirements of truth and falsehood in reality' (Vos, *Philosophy*, 211).

23 *of har heuid*: 'from their own speculation'; *MED hed* n.(1), 3(b).

24 'Cause men to be deprived of truth'.

48. EARTH

1 *wow* (OE *wōh*): The Latin translation takes this in the sense 'injustice'. For ll. 1–2 and 4 cf. the poem in MS Harley 2253 quoted in the headnote.

2 *hir*: In OE *eorðe* is feminine. Cf. l. 25 and contrast *him* in l. 4.

3 *frow*: Etymology uncertain; the usual sense is 'weak', often collocated with *fals*. Here evidently used as adv.: *MED frough* 2(a) suggests 'in crumbling fashion, as dust', but the scribe glosses the word as *festine*, 'quickly', and it is translated by *subito* in the Latin version l. 9.

5 *ilich*: *MED iliche* interprets as adv., 'also', but the next line together with the Latin 'similis virroni' (11) suggests adj., 'resembling' (other men).

6 *awaked*: *MED awaken* 3(a) suggests 'created, originate in', but the parallels are not convincing. Nor does 'awoke' seem possible. The Latin has 'Rich and poor are laid low in the same earth' (12), which suggests derivation from OE *awācian*, 'grow weak', hence 'declined'. Cf. *MED woken*.

13–18 With this stanza, cf. the version in CUL Ii.4.9 (*Middle English Poem Erthe upon Erthe*, 32–4):

> Ffor erth gos in erth walkand in vede,
> And erthe rydys on erth on a fayr stede,
> When he was gotyn in erth erth to his mede,
> Than is erth layde in erthe wormys to fede.
> Whylke are the wormys the flesch brede?
> God wote the wormys for to ryght rede (41–6).

13 *wrikkend*: 'moving about' (cf. Du *wrikken*). Recorded only here and once in the *South English Legendary* in *MED*.

16 *ho*: The Latin translation, though not literal, indicates that *heo*, 'she', is an error for *ho*, 'who'. For the form see *LALME* iv. 283. There is no instance of *heo* for 'she' in the manuscript. *muntid* (for *muntiþ*): 'gives out, pays'; glossed in margin 'metitur'. *MED minten* 1(b) interprets 'determine (someone's) just deserts', but this has no support and makes poor sense. Cf.

'Ich herde men vpo mold'(DIMEV 2198), l. 53: 'Mede y mot munten a marke oþer more', and 'Ne mai no lewed lued' (DIMEV 3683), l. 29: 'y mot for menske munte sum mede', both in MS Harley 2253, ed. in *Alliterative Poetry*, 17–20, 28–31.

17 Cf. 'þene latemeste dai' (DIMEV 5640), ed. in *English Lyrics*, 46–9: 'Boþe þe wirst & þe rouf sal liggen uppon þin chinne' (l. 30), and the version of *Erthe* in CUL Ii.4.9, ll. 25–6: 'When erthe is in erth for wormys wyn, / The rof of his hows xal ly on his chyn.'

18 *wroten*: 'wriggle' (OE *wrōtan*). Cf. the pains of Hell in *Cursor Mundi* (Trinity text) 23281:'þo wormes euer shul on hem wrote'.

24 *verrunt*: 'scour'. Glossed 'trahunt' in the margin.

25 *answerid*: The rhyme scheme shows this is a spelling for *answeriþ*.

26 *verrid* (for *verriþ*): Perhaps in the sense 'wears', taking *erþ* here in the more specific sense of 'clothes, jewels, etc.'. But the Latin *fruatur* suggests the sense 'makes use of' (possessions); *MED weren* v.(1) (OE *werian*, 'guard') 4(b), or *weren* v.(2), (OE *werian*, 'clothe') 4. Thus: why does man hate the grave since he makes use of possessions?

27 *teriþ*: 'covers with earth' (*AND terrer*[4]; ultimately < Lat. *terra*).

30 *wonne*: Glossed 'lucrataris' in margin.

37 *get hit*: 'gets for itself', glossed 'lucratur' above.

41 *wendiþ þe bifor*: 'depart from you'; cf. 'migrabunt' in the translation l. 47.

42 The abandonment of the body by friends is a standard feature in 'Body and Soul' poems. Cf. 'In a þestri stude y stod' in MS Harley 2253 (DIMEV 2462), ed. in *Altenglische Dichtungen*, 235–43, ll. 201–2: 'Ne haueþ he frend on erþe / þat þenkeþ opon hym'; and *The Grave* (DIMEV 5543), ed. in *Middle English Debate Poetry*, l. 18.

49–54 With this stanza, cf. the version in CUL Ii.4.9: 'Erth vpon erthe gos in the weye, / Prykys and prankys on a palfreye; / When erth has gotyn erth alle that he maye, / He schal haue but seven fote at his last daye' (19–22).

49 *palfrei*: an elegant riding horse, and so both a rich possession and a means of getting somewhere. The Latin *dextrarium* is a *destrier*, the horse Sir Thopas rides. See Thorlac Turville-Petre, 'Alliterative Horses', *Journal of English and Germanic Philology*, 112 (2013), 154–68.

50 *ar lang wei*: 'their long journey', i.e. through life, as in *Ancrene Wisse*, 6.31: 'ha beon i worltlich wei'. The Latin has 'a long sea-journey' (56) instead. For the form *ar*, 'their', see *LALME* iv. 14 (west Worcs.).

51 *grouer*: a kind of fur (OF *gros vair*) in contrast to miniver (OF *menu vair*). *groy*: 'grey fur' (*MED grei* n.(2)).

52 In contrast to the rich grey furs, Earth's livery is green. The Latin translates *liuerei* as 'corrodium' (58), i.e. grant of provisions to a vassal. There is play on two senses of *grauiþ vs in grene*: 'decorates us in green robes' and 'buries us in the ground'. For the latter sense see *Pride of Life*, ed. Davis, l. 443: 'Qwhen þou art grauen on grene'; further involving a pun on *greithen in grene*, 'attired in green', as in *Awntyrs off Arthure* 508: 'Gawyn was gaily graþed in grene.'

53 *streinþ*: 'force'. Cf. the Latin, l. 59, and *The Peterborough Chronicle,* ed. Cecily Clark (2nd edn., Oxford, 1970) for 1119: 'Sume þa castelas he mid strengðe genam.'

54 'In the end he (the man) has measured/stretched his full length uncomfortably.' The concept of measuring the dead body is central to *The Grave*, e.g. l. 6: 'Nu me scæl þe meten & þa molde seoðða'. Here the poet plays with another sense of *meten length*, 'lie prostrate', not recognized by *MED*, but cf. *Midsummer Night's Dream* III. ii. 428–9 'Faintness constraineth me / To measure out my length on this cold bed.'

62 Cf. Gower, *Confessio Amantis*, in *The Complete Works of John Gower*, ed. G. C. Macaulay, 4 vols. (Oxford, 1899–1902), 7.4743–4: 'therthe of every mannes kinde / Is Moder', here with reference to one's native soil.

63 'While you are on Earth, be loyal to your soul'. Cf. the Latin text, and the version in CUL Ii.4.9: 'Be ware, erth, for erthe, for sake of thi sowle' (38).

64 'Build your long house before you die.' The Latin interprets this as a church, which makes good sense in context, but there is also a play on the sense 'grave', as in the opening line of *The Grave*: 'ðe wes bold ȝebyld er þu iboren were'; and cf. the Harley 'In a þestri stude y stod' ll. 233–4: 'Fare we shule to a bour / þat is oure long hom', involving both spacial and temporal senses of 'long'. See *MED hom* n. 2(c); *OED home* 3 also citing OE instances.

65–6 Cf. the version in CUL Ii.4.9: 'Erthe bygyth hallys & erth bygith towres, / When erth is layd in erth, blayke is his bours' (63–4).

65 *bilt* present; glossed 'bildiþ' in margin.

75 'Reconcile yourself to him . . .'.

GLOSSARIES

The Glossaries include every word, but not every instance of every word, in the English and Anglo-Norman texts. Listings are generally restricted to three instances of a word or meaning. Abbreviations for grammatical categories are those prescribed by EETS and set out in the Guidelines for editors, p. 18, at http://users.ox.ac.uk/~eets/guidelines.html. Also abbreviated are *def(inite)*, *indef(inite)*, and in the Anglo-Norman glossary *cond(itional)*, *fut(ure)*, *imperf(ect)*, *pret(erite)*. Emendations are starred.

MIDDLE ENGLISH

A

a *indef. art.* a 2.2, 148, 4.3, **an** (before vowel and *h*) 2.165, 15.157, 22.31, one 48.18

a *interj.* ah! 5.87, 13.9

a *prep.* on 5.68, **an** (before vowel or *h*) 4.24, 110, 21.56 [see **on** *prep.*]

ab, abbiþ *see* **hab**

abatid *p.p.* diminished 39.7

abbei *n.* abbey 2.51, 83, 147, **abbai** 2.103

abbot *n.* abbot 2.127, 133, 176

abide *v.* stand and fight 36.30

abigge *v.* pay for 15.77

abite *n.* habit 4.40n

aboue *adv.* on high 14.38, 20.213, in authority 33.24, **abow** on high 14.145

aboue *prep.* above, over 13.228

aboute, abute *adv.* around 36.52, everywhere 36.80, covering (the body) 13.49, *ben* ~ are ready 33.76

aboute, abute *prep.* around 2.141, 4.9, 33, around, covering 13.47, around (time) 14.65; *al* ~ everywhere around 13.18

abrode *adv.* brooding 15.129n

ac *conj.* but 2.28, 13.107, 14.40, **ak** 2.129, 13.113, **ok** 2.43, 20.15, **oc** 15.136

acuntis *n. pl.* final statements 13.97

ad *see* **hab**

adoun, adun(e) *adv.* down 20.23, 159, 15.140, facing down 14.98

adrad(de) *adj.* terrified 5.125, 14.155

aferd *adj.* frightened 14.149

afte *adv.* in *an* ~ backwards 44.1n

after, aftir *conj.* 20.77, after 15.180, 20.181 ~ *þat* 20.204; *prep.* after 2.122, 143, 13.64, for 39.62

agam *adv.* in jest [*see* **ernist**]

agast *p.p.* dismayed 13.7

ago *p.p.* gone 20.169, passed away 15.148, forgotten 33.44

agris(e) *v.* become terrified 14.46, 55, 171

aȝayn *adv.* back 39.58

aȝe *adv.* back 2.188, 14.168,19.21, backwards 14.97, 125

aȝe *prep.* towards 14.50, contrary to 33.118, 134, in the face of 20.88n, in contravention of 20.130, in comparison to 20.173

aȝens *prep.* against 20.109, 44.11, in preparation for 4.69, in contravention of 4.93

aȝtist *pa. 2 sg.* (with pr. sense) ought 14.5, 163; **aȝt** *3 sg.* should, ought to 13.139, 21.58, must 2.82; **aȝt** *pl.* 13.43, 105, 14.83, **auȝt** 21.39

ahouue *adv.* in moderation, stingily 4.57n

ai *adv.* always, the whole time 5.19, 82

ak *see* **ac**

al *pron.* everything 2.26, 43, 13.122, everyone 13.237, ~ *we* all of us 5.15, 15.13, ~ *ure* of us all 20.102, ~ *and som* every one of them 36.116; **alle** *pl.* all of them 15.57, *vs* ~ all of us 13.228, 20.4, *hem* ~ all of them 36.42; **alir** *pl. gen.* of all 13.232

al *adv.* all 2.141, quite, just 2.129, entirely 2.171, 4.15, thoroughly 13.50, everywhere 4.33, ~ *so* just in this way 15.154, 33.125

al *adj. see* **al(le)**

alas *interj.* alas! 5.21, 13.51, 14.81

alast *adv.* finally 48.54

ale *n.* ale 4.44, 36.96

algate *adv.* all together 36.76

aliȝt(e) *v.* descend 14.3, 20.3; **aliȝt** *pa. pl.* 20.27

aliue *adj.* living 14.17, 45, 15.113, (to be) alive 4.80
aliues *adv.* living 22.4, 8
al(le) *adj.* all 2.57, 4.45, 14.94, the whole of 36.14
alles *n. pl.* cobblers' awls 4.75n
allirkin *adj. gen.* in ~ *maner* of every kind 14.75
almiȝt(e) *adj.* almighty, in *God* ~ 14.120, 15.42
alowe *adv.* below 20.166n
also *adv.* also, as well 2.14, 22.20, 33.51, in addition 13.201, 36.49, too 14.150, 20.23, **also . . . as** as . . . as 33.142
am *see* **be, hi**
amang *prep.* among 14.3, 20.3, from amongst 33.6, **amangis** amongst 15.44
amarrid *p.p.* destroyed 39.24
amen *interj.* amen 2.189
amend *v.* improve 33.35, make amends for 33.56, **amendie** amend 15.35; **amend** *pr. pl. subj.* reform 5.39
ametist *n.* amethyst (purple gem) 2.93
amonsi *v.* excommunicate 33.25
amorow *adv.* in *þan* ~ on the next morning 14.57
amoue *v.* be stirred (by fear) 14.147
an *see* **a** *prep.*
and *conj.* and 5.4, 33.57, **an** 20.137 (otherwise always a' or tironian nota), if 5.108, since 48.26
angil *n.* angel 14.153, **angel** 20.18, **angle** 4.4, 20.30; **angles** *pl.* 13.135, 214, 14.152
anguis *n.* anguish 19.14, **angus** agony 14.115
ani *see* **eni**
anon(e) *adv.* then 2.161, 33.74, 44.16, at once 36.59, ~ *(vp) to* even (up) to 2.181, 4.3
anoþer *adj.* another 2.147, 36.49
anoþir *pron.* another one 4.24, someone else 15.178, 180
an(o)uriþ *see* **honuri**
answerid *pr. 3 sg.* answers 48.25n; **answard** *pa. 3 sg.* 20.203*
anueþ *pr. 3 sg.* in *me* ~ it annoys me 39.9
apan *adv.* in *þench* ~ reflect on it 13.148, 14.19
apan *prep.* upon 15.129, on 36.10, upon (it) 21.24, **apon** on 36.72, **opon** upon

4.110, 112, 20.144, **uppon** 48.63, **vppon** 33.190
appil *n.* apple 20.61, 65, 22.36
ar *conj.* before 43.12 [*see* **er**]
ar *see* **hi**
are *n.* favour 43.11
areri *v.* provoke 15.181; **arerid** *p.p.* lifted 39.66
ariȝt(e) *adv.* properly 2.168, suitably 4.78, in the right way 13.101, *wel* ~ very much 20.151
arise *v.* rise up 14.53, *vppe* ~ increase 36.21
armis *pl.* arms 19.6
art, artow *see* **be**
as, als *conj.* as 4.20, 5.102, 33.10, as if 14.139, just as 20.87, in the way that 20.95; as *adv.* 13.40, ~ . . . ~ 14.41
askiþ *see* **oxist**
asse *n.* donkey 33.57, 109, **aase** 33.65
astriune *n.* astrion 2.90*n
at *prep.* at 4.10, 19.13, 33.175, with 15.61, 20.138
atwo *adv.* in two 20.148, 164
Aue Marie *n.* Hail Mary (prayer) 15.41
Aueril *n.* April 36.11
auoir-depeise *n.* goods sold by weight 4.62n
awai *adv.* away 4.99, 5.11, 22.18, past 39.4, **awei** 33.38, ~ *wiþ* off with! 44.9
awaked *pa. pl.* declined? 48.6n
aware *adj.* aware 21.17 [*cf.* **ware**]
awarpeþ *pr. 3 sg.* distorts 39.12n
aweld *v.* defeat 39.4, govern, overcome 39.47
ax *n.* axe 5.56
axen *n. pl.* ashes 13.11, 33.166, **axin** 13.170, 15.23

B

bak *n.* back 4.21
bakers *n. pl.* bakers 4.91
bale *n.* misery 22.34
baly *n.* jurisdiction 20.43
bare *adj.* destitute 13.174, empty 33.176
baret *n.* struggle 2.27
barmhatres *n. pl.* aprons 4.86
barun *n.* baron 5.71, 14.108
bas *n.* base 2.69*
bastard *n.* illegitimate child 4.13
baston *n.* verse 4.71n, **bastun** 4.76, 90
batail *n.* battle 36.34

baum *n.* balm 2.85
be *v.* 2.44, 167, 19.29, **ben** 14.144, 33.20, **bene** 14.30; **am** *pr. 1 sg.* 5.106; 33. 91, 39.18; **ert** *2 sg.* 4.4, 13.25, 14.180; **art** 5.5, 14.164; **artow** (with pron.) 15.78, **ertow** 22.6; **is** *3 sg.* 2.2, 147, 4.5, **iss(e)** 36.4, 19, **beþ** 39.69; **beþ** *pl.* are 2.13, 3.7, 4.33, will be 5.35, exist 36.37; **be** *1 sg. subj.* 43.12; *2 sg.* 4.22; *3 sg.* 2.5, 4.56; 5.52, may be 13.4, (in condit. clause) if (he) is 33.37; **beþ** *pl.* if (they) are 21.45; **be** *imp. sg.* 4.22, 5.3; **beþ** *pl.* 4.100; **was** *pa. 1 sg.* 19.34, 39.60; **wer(e)** *pa. 2 sg.* 4.16, 20.16, 48.5; **was** *3. sg.* 4.14, 30, 5.2; **wasse** 2.120; **wer** *pl.* 13.67, 14.31, 20.31, **wore** 22.4*; **wer(e)** *3 sg. subj.* would/should be, 4.42, 83 (2×), might be 15.114, *as hit ~ as* if it were 14.70, 136; **ibe** *p.p.* been 13.97
becom *v.* go 14.128; **becommiþ** *pr. 3 sg.* becomes 13.73; **becom** *p.p.* 13.75, turned 14.42
bed(e) *see* biddiþ
bed(de) *n.* bed 2.38, 39.52; **bedde** *pl. (or distributive sg.)* 36.64
been *n. pl.* bees 21.62
beeste *n. coll.* beasts 33.46; **bestis** *pl.* 33.71
befal(le) *v.* happen 13.226, take place 14.74
befor *see* bifor
beforn *adv.* earlier 22.28
begger *n.* beggar 4.28, 33.177
begin *v.* begin 15.61; **beginne** *imp. sg.* start 19.13; **bigun** *p.p.* created 48.29
beginninge *n.* start 15.4
behind *adv.* behind 33.89
behold *v.* look 14.77; **bihold** *pr. 1 sg.* 39.36; *imp. sg.* 19.5, 27, **behold** 15.20, *~ to* look at, observe 19.1; **beheld** *pa. pl.* gazed on 20.175
belamy *n.* dear friend 33.93, 105, 117
beleue *adv.* at once 20.55
beleue *pr. pl. subj.* give up 21.6n
bemette *p.p.* destined 22.11
bench *n.* seat 2.11, 5.68
bend *p.p.* bent (of bow) 5.37
benimeþ, -iþ *pr. 3 sg.* takes away (from) 15.141, 21.76; *pl.* prevent 33.30n; **benome** *p.p.* 15.74, 122
bere *n.* bier 5.73, 88
ber(e) *v.* carry 5.23, take 5.44; hold on to

13.175, behave 20.7; **berrist** *pr. 2 sg.* carry 4.15, 20; **berriþ** *3 sg.* 48.15, 28; *pl.* 2.163, 4.99; **ber** *imp. sg.* bear (witness) 21.73; **bere** *pa. 1 sg.* carried 33.84; **ber(e)** *3 sg.* 4.8, gave birth to 5.137, 20.100, 101, 104; **ibor(n)** *p.p.* born 22.25, 36.94, *þe ~* (have) carried yourself 19.20
beril *n.* beryl (transparent gem) 2.92
berne *v.* burn 13.127, 130
bernes *n. pl.* men 4.87
besech *pr. 1 sg.* beseech 5.133, **biseche** beg 15.31; **besech** *pl. subj.* in *~ we* let us implore 13.233, 21.77; **besoȝt** *pa. 3 sg.* begged for 20.154
beside *prep.* beside 20.161
best *n.* best (thing) 13.232, 20.129, 36.46
beste *n.* animal 14.74, 15.90; **bestis** *pl.* 4.74, 14.49, 22.7
betacht *pa. 3 sg.* handed over to 22.36; **betauȝt** *p.p.* handed over 21.45
betak *3. sg. subj. sg.* take back 15.90
beþench *imp. sg.* consider 5.80, bear in mind 15.22, *~ þe* reflect 5.51, consider 15.88
betide *v.* happen to 22.34; **betidith** *pr. 3 sg.* (it) happens 22.13
betiþ *pr. 3 sg.* beats 2.137; **ibet** *p.p.* 20.122
bet(t)ir, better *adj. comp.* better 13.160, 210, 36.23; **best** *superl.* best 4.4, 13.212 (2), 36.107
bettir *adv. comp.* 2.124; **best** *superl.* best 2.106,173,13.212 (1), most 36.55, most pleasantly 5.65
bewonde *p.p.* bound round 19.3
bi *prep.* by 3.6, 4.103, through the agency of 20.87n, 90, concerning 20.131, in relation to, as applied to 21.61, 62, about 13.87, through 2.124
bible *n.* Bible 4.21
bicharred *p.p.* led astray, deluded 39.25
biddiþ *pr. 3 sg.* orders 2.130; **bit** prays 5.81; **bidde** *3 sg. subj.* prays 33.185; **bed** *pa. 3 sg.* ordered 20.129; **bad** commanded, urged 5.129; **bede** *pl.* 20.119
bide *v.* remain 20.80, stay with 33.172
bifor, befor *prep.* in front of (place) 5.101, in the presence of 14.72, 20.126, before (time) 14.7, 36.11, ahead of 22.12, **biforn** 22.26*
bigon *p.p.* in *~ mid* covered with 15.91

bigun *see* begin

bi3ete *n.* winnings, prey 33.98

bihold *see* behold

bild *imp. sg.* build 48.64; bilt *pa. 3 sg.*
48.65

bint *pr. 3 sg.* binds 13.211n; bind *imp. pl.*
33.120; ibund *p.p.* bound, fettered
5.104, 20.116, 33.129, confined 15.70

bipeche *v.* seduce 15.59; bipei3te *p.p.*
deceived 15.103

biri *v.* bury 33.31, *grant* ~ allow to be
buried 20.156; biriid *pa. 3 sg.* buried
20.160; ibiriid *p.p.* 5.92

biriles *n.* grave 13.39; biriles *pl.* tombs
14.54

bischrew *pr. 3 sg.* (?) curses 39.32n

bise *n.* dark fur 13.46

biseche *see* besech

biset *p.p.* encompassed 39.20

bispette *p.p.* spat upon 19.4

bissop *n.* bishop 3.1

bit *see* biddiþ

bit(t)er *adj.* cruel 5.30, 19.33, bitter
(taste) 19.37, severe 13.134, sorrowful
20.163, 172, 22.34

bit(t)er *adv.* bitterly 13.152, cruelly
19.32, 21.75

blak(e) *adj.* black 4.37, 14.42, 5.115, dark
48.66, blakke 13.32

blast *n.* trumpet-blast 22.27

ble *n.* complexion, hue colour 2.79, 5.7,
39.7

blede *v.* bleed 14.101; bleding *pr. p.*
bleeding 19.18

blench *v.* escape 5.70n

bleri *pr. 1 sg.* grow bleary 39.52

blert *pr. 1 sg.* snore 39.52*n

blind *pr. 1 sg.* go blind 39.52; iblend *p.p.*
blinded 13.66

blinde *adj.* blind 2.42

blinne *v.* stop, desist 43.2, 3

blis(se) *n.* heavenly bliss 13.92, 15.53,
20.184, joy 15.154, happiness 2.24,
13.88

blisful *adj.* blessed 5.128, blissful 20.216

bliþe *adj.* happy 20.207

blod(e) *n.* blood 13.117, 19.2, 21.79,
kindred 22.10

blodi *adj.* bloody 13.140, 19.5, 16

blote *adj.* supple 4.74

blow *v.* blow 13.127

blowid *pr. 3 sg.* swells with pride, blooms
39.7n

bochers *n. pl.* butchers 4.85*

bochevampe *n.* shoemakers' tool 4.75n

bodi *n.* body 5.66, 13.201, 15.11

bo3t *pa. 1 sg.* bought 33.83; *3 sg.*
redeemed 13.235, 21.40, 79; bo3te *p.p.*
bought 15.110, ibo3t 19.24

boi *n.* fellow 33.75

bok(e) *n.* book 4.21, 13.6, 135n, *holi* ~
the Bible 13.194, 14.13, 15.64; bokes
pl. 4.55, (liturgical) books 2.118, bokis
20.93

bold *n.* house 48.64

bold(e) *adj.* confident 5.68, brave 39.7*,
able-bodied 4.28n; *as n.* self-confident
people 2.64

bole-ax *n.* large axe 4.85

bone *n.*[1] bone 13.47, 15.84, 33.166; bonis
pl. bones 33.121

bone *n.*[2] request 20.157

boste *n.* arrogance 33.24

bote *n.*[1] boat 2.152

bote *n.*[2] salvation 5.60, benefit 15.11

bot(e) *adv.* only 4.57, merely 15.16, 86,
nothing but, only 5.53, 90, *nis* ~ is
merely 13.30, *no3t* ~ only 33.66, 108,
botte just 4.58; *conj.* (with subj.) unless
5.39, 13.101, if (in neg.) 21.7; *prep.*
except 2.8, 20.172, except as 13.70, but
except 15.126, boute without 2.21,
15.82

boþe *adj.* both 33.59; *adv.* in ~ . . . *and*
2.154, 13.213, 20.108

boure *n.* room 2.58, bure 2.11, *helle* ~
the enclosure of hell 5.145n; *pl.* bowris
2.53, boures chambers 48.66

bourmaidnes *n. pl.* female servants 4.50

bouse *v.* booze, drink 4.45

boute *see* bot(e)

bow *n.* bow (for shooting) 5.37n

bowris *see* boure

box *n.* box 4.15

boxum *adj.* obedient 20.31

bred *n.* bread 4.92, 36.99

brek *v.* break 15.38

brenne *v.* burn 5.29

brest *n.* breast 13.234, 19.5, 21.78, heart
22.34

breþ *n.* breath, life 15.141

breþerin *see* broþer

brewesters *n. pl.* brewers (female) 4.97

briddes *n. pl.* birds 2.95, 98

bri3t *adv.* brightly 14.61

bri3t(e) *adj.* bright 2.5, 14.37, 20.18,

beautiful 13.221, radiant 5.7, 15.65;
 briȝtir *comp.* brighter 13.199
brimme *n.* water 2.157
bring *v.* bring 13.89, 21.60, 36.104;
 bringeþ *pr. pl.* 2.105; **bring** *3 sg. subj.*
 33.197; *imp. sg.* 5.143; **broȝt** *pa. 3 sg.*
 13.158, 20.82, 183; **broȝt(e)** *p.p.* 20.50,
 43.1, **ybroȝt, ibroȝt** 4.6, 36.131, 43.5,
 brought about 14.87, ~ *to grund*
 brought low 5.106, buried 43.12, *in* ~
 taken in (to hell) 13.108, ~ *to deþ*
 killed 33.37
brod(e) *adj.* broad 2.66, 4.8, 33.62, large
 4.55, 87
brol *n.* brat 22.10
broþer *n.* brother 33.192, (fig.) 33.150,
 i.e. brother in God 15.102, 177;
 breþerin *pl.* 15.167
broþin *p.p.* degenerate 13.179n
brotil *adj.* brittle 5.53
bure *see* **boure**; **but** *see* **bot(e)**

C

cakes *n. pl.* cakes 2.57
calcedun *n.* chalcedony (gem) 2.94
camel *n.* camel 13.90
can *v.* in *sul* ~ *no gode* shall have no
 sense 14.51; **can** *pr. 1 sg.* am able
 13.193; **cannist** *2 sg.* are capable of
 33.110, **cunnest** ~ *þonk* offer thanks
 19.38; **can** *3 sg.* is able 14.47, knows
 44.15, **kan** 2.168, *if gode he* ~ if he has
 any sense 13.35; **can** *pl.* can, are able
 to 13.194, **cun** 4.45, 15.171, ~ *no witte*
 have lost their senses 14.56; **cuþe** *pa. 3
 sg.* was able to 20.113, 119, 36.122; **cuþ**
 p.p. offered 2.107, **couþe** in *wel* ~
 widely known 20.135
candles *n. pl.* candles 4.104
canel *n.* cinnamon 2.76, 110
capil *n.* farm horse 2.32
capitale *n.* capital (of pillar) 2.69n
caraing *n.* body, corpse 13.172, 33.168,
 169, **carayne** 48.39
carbuncle *n.* carbuncle (red gem) 2.90
care *n.* sorrow 43.5, 44.8, suffering 5.148,
 worry 2.18, anxiety 20.75, 43.9,
 concern, interest 4.45, **kar** sorrow
 22.11
carful *adj.* sorrowful 33.1
cast *v.* throw 22.28, 33.32; **cast** *imp. sg.*
 in ~ *awai* banish 5.148; **cast** *pa. 3 sg.*

cast 20.191; *p.p.* thrown 14.40, 15.76,
 ikest predestined 22.32*
castel *n.* castle 14.89, 109, stronghold
 36.26n; **castles** *pl.* 48.65
catel *n.* possessions 5.26, 13.57, 21.8,
 goods, wealth 15.111
certein *adj.* a particular 36.89
chalandre *n.* lark 2.97n
charite *n.* love 33.146, *par* ~ in the
 name of charity 15.40, in your
 compassion 5.105, *par seint* ~ by holy
 charity 2.190n
chasur *n.* hunting horse 14.110
cheance *n.* fate, luck 2.185
cheping *n.* trading 21.54
cherubin *n.* cherubim 14.151
chest *n.* casket, coffin 5.67
child *n.* child 15.30, 20.166, 22.1, **chil**
 22.35; **children** *pl.* 14.23, 21.61
chirch *n.* church 20.134, 33.31, **cherch**
 2.58; **churchis** *pl.* 4.34 [*and see*
 Holi ~]
chonge *v.* change 20.52
chynne *n.* chin 2.181, 48.17
clai *n.* earth, mud 5.15, 87, 39.5
clansi *imp. sg.* in ~ *þe* of purify yourself
 from 15.25
clere *adj.* clear 2.19
clerk *n.* cleric, scholar, learned man 4.22,
 59, 44.6, 17; **clerkes** *pl.* 44.23, **clerkis**
 clerics 14.14
cleue *v.* split 13.139; **clef** *pa. pl.* 20.148
cling *pr. 1 sg.* wither, shrivel 39.5n, 46;
 iclung *p.p.* shrivelled 5.15n
clippeþ *pr. pl.* call, name 33.150
cloister *n.* cloister (covered walk) 2.58,
 65, 67
cloþ *n.* clothing 2.29, 38
clotte *n.* lump 5.87
cloute *n.* shred of cloth 15.94; **clute** rag
 15.157
cluche *pr. 1 sg.* bend 39.46
coking-stole *n.* ducking stool 4.100
cold *adj.* 15.156, 19.9
cole *n.* coal 14.42, 66
collacione *n.* (gathering for) supper
 2.145
com(e) *v.* come 2.177, 13.197, 14.7, **cum**
 15.121, ~ *to hepe* come about 13.138n;
 ~ *of* become of, happen to 22.16; ~ *to*
 succeed 36.87n; **commist** *pr. 2 sg.*
 22.16; **commiþ** *3. sg.* 13.10, 20, 15.80,
 106; *pl.* 2.161, 22.9; ~*bifor* will precede

14.22; **com** *imp. sg.* 19.21; **com(e)** *pa.
2 sg.* came 22.17, 33.112, 48.74; *3 sg.*
4.12, 20.53, 36.48, became 20.51, ~ *vte*
became known 36.79; **com** *p.p.* arrived
36.91, **icom** come 14.30, **icommen**
22.6, **icom(m)in** assembled 13.237, ~
of descended from 33.91
comble *pr. 1 sg.* become numb 39.41n
commandid *pr. 3 sg.* 21.25
commune *adj.* in ~ *to* owned in
common by 2.63
communelich *adv.* as a body, without
exception 20.92
Comondement *n.* Commandment 21.33;
Commandemens *pl.* 21.31
compas *n.* plot, stratagem 36.78
compas *v.* make plots against 33.1467
compasment *n.* scheme 36.79
concedo (Lat.) I accept 44.19
consonans *n. pl.* consonants 4.18
copis *n. pl.* cloaks 4.31
corale *n.* coral 2.70
corne *n.* corn 33.174
corrin *n.* cup 4.43n
couþe *see* **can**
couwe *pr. 1 sg.* cough 39.46
coueit *imp. sg.* covet 21.70
coue(i)tise *n.* greed, avarice 13.66,
15.101, 33.144
coueituse *adj.* avaricious 15.105
crafte *n.* learning 44.2n
craftfullich *adv.* skilfully 4.90
craftilich *adj.* skilful 4.60
creatoure *n.* creator 20.102
Crede *n.* the Creed 33.186
cri(e) *v.* cry out 13.120, 14.26, call for
14.79, announce 33.49; **crie** *pr. 1 sg.*
call for 15.40; **crieþ** *imp. pl.* cry out
5.19; **cried** *pa. pl.* in ~ *apan* called on
20.137
crisolite *n.* crysolite (green gem) 2.94
cristal(e) *n.* crystal 2.68, 11
Cristin *adj.* Christian 13.216
crois *n.* cross 20.140
croke *pr. 1 sg.* become crooked 39.46
crokes *n. pl.* pastoral staffs 4.56n
crokid *adj.* bent 4.20
crop *n.* top 14.98n
crowis *n. pl.* crows 4.26
crune *n.* top of head 4.56, head 33.62
crust *n.* crust of bread 33.176, 177, 182
cucubes *n. pl.* cubeb berries 2.78n
cum *see* **com(e)**; **cun(nest)** *see* **can**

cuntake *n.* strife 15.181
cuntrepane *n.* matching pledge 36.86n
curte *n.* royal court 33.86
curteisie *n.* elegant behaviour (ironic)
4.82
cuþe *see* **can**

D

dai *n.* day 2.26, 5.12, 14.55, death-day
39.6, *to* ~ on a day 36.89; **daies** *pl.*
20.25, 36.132, **dawes** 22.32
dalis *n. pl.* valleys 14.88
danger *n.* in *wiþoute* ~ with no problem
2.169
dar *pr. 3 sg.* need 13.196n
daþeit *interj.* curses on! 4.52, 82
debles *n.* (AN) devil, in *fi a* ~ to hell
with you! 4.109n
deciplis *see* **disciple**
ded(e) *n.*[1] deed 14.104, 15.96
dede *n.*[2] dead people 13.8, 14.53, death
48.77
ded(e) *adj.* dead 13.95, 14.112, 20.146
dedlich *adj.* in ~ *sinne* mortal sin 5.135
dedute *n.* pleasure 2.50
defens *n.* prohibition 21.29n
dei *v.* die 5.105, 13.83, 14.105; *pr. sg.
subj.* 5.108; **deiend** *pr. p.* dying 19.32
deil *n.* sorrow 20.173, **del** 20.173
del *n.* in *neuer a* ~ not at all 21.70
del *v.* distribute (as alms) 33.173; **deliþ**
pr. 3 sg. separates 48.77; **deleþ** *pl.*
distribute 4.57, **deliþ** 4.58; **del** *imp. sg.*
handle 33.191; **delet** *pa. pl.* split 20.168
delful *adj.* miserable 48.4
denne *n.* dwelling 5.22n
dep(e) *adj.* deep 4.100, 14.88, profound
4.114; *adv.* deeply 4.45, 19.18, 20.167
der *v.* injure 21.75; **deriiþ** *pr. 3 sg.* does
harm 15.143
der *adj.* precious 13.235, 21.79; **dere** *as
n.* beloved one 19.24; *adv.* at a high
price 15.110, at great cost 33.83, 21.40
dere *n.* animals 13.24
derk *adj.* dark 20.24, **durke** 14.43
derworþ *adj.* precious 21.1
destru *v.* destroy 20.134, **destrei** 21.74*
deþ *n.* death 2.28, 5.64, 13.67
deþ *see* **do**
deuers *v.* be distinguished 14.131n
deuil *n.* the Devil 13.84, 20.49, 21.45,

wend a ~ *wai!* go to hell! 5.83; **deuilis** *gen.* 13.75, 15.38

deuist *pr. 2 sg.* deafen 5.84

dew *n.* dew 5.12

diche *n.* pit (of hell) 5.96

didde *see* **do**

dim *adj.* muffled, faint 22.27n

dimmiþ *pr. 3 sg.* grows dim 19.7; *pl.* 39.37

din *n.* loud noise 14.158

ding *n.* dung 13.31, (fig.) 5.47n

dint *n.* blow 33.104; **dintes** *pl.* 19.36

disciple *n.* disciple 20.114; **deciplis** *pl.* 20.207

disciplineþ *pr. pl.* inflict discipline, flog 4.46

ditee *n.* poem 4.54

ditement *n.* indictment 33.60n

ditid *pa. 3 sg.* composed 4.84

do *v.* do 2.178, 20.40, put 20.140, bring 2.172, behave 13.212, **don(e)** act, perform 39.30, ~ *to wit* inform 15.63, *ded sal* ~ will perform 14.104; **do** *pr. 1 sg.* ~ *to witte* tell 2.101; **doist** *2 sg.* 5.63; **doþ** *3 sg.* sets 2.174, does 15.152, 21.37, acts 33.134, **deþ** 15.142; **doþ** *pl.* act 21.41, (auxil. with infin.) 33.27, do (followed by pron.) 21.43, *refl.* in ~ *ham* go 2.153, 158, 160; **do** *imp. sg.* bring about 5.60, ~ *vs* cause us to 5.9, bring us 5.139; **do** *pl.* (emphatic) come! 36.31; **diddist** *pa. 2 sg.* did 33.108; **didde** *3 sg.* behaved 33.52, acted 33.187; *pl.* (representing previous v.) 33.57; **do** *p.p.* carried out 33.49, accomplished 36.90, **ido** done, 22.28, 33.75, committed (sin) 20.66, finished 44.15n, 22, **ydo** put, driven 33.20, ~ *in* subjected to 33.130

doȝtir *n.* daughter 20.100

doggid *adj.* fierce 33.90n

dome *n.* judgement 48.76, Day of Judgement 13.96, 14.7, 15.54, Last Judgement 13.134

dotus *adj.* terrifying 14.113

doune *n.* hill 33.97

doune *see* **dun(e)**

doute *n.* doubt 15.82, *hit nis no* ~ it is certain 13.95

draperie *n.* cloth 4.62

draw *v.* in ~ *ifere* come into one mass 14.117, ~ *aȝe* pull back (of the sea) 14.125; **drawiþ** *pr. 3 sg.* draws, leads

44.3, pulls out 39.29, **draweþ** in ~ *to* resorts to 44.16; **drow** *pa. 3 sg.* in *him* ~ approached 48.4

drede *n.* terror 15.118, *hab* ~ be terrified 15.88, have reverence 15.98

drede *v.* dread, fear 14.16, be terrified 13.7, 115, 196; *pr. 2 sg. subj.* fear 5.76; **dred** *imp. sg.* in ~ *þe* be afraid 48.76

drench-kiue *n.* vat for soaking skins 4.79n

dreri *adj.* sad 20.75

dri *imp. sg.* endure 5.117

dribil *n.* spittle 39.10

drink *n.* drink 2.17, 13.205, 19.37, alcoholic drink 2.111

drink *v.* drink 2.144; **drinkeþ** *imp. pl.* 4.116, **drinkiþ** 4.118; **dronk** *pa. 1 sg.* drank 19.37

dritte *n.* shit 2.179, excrement 13.31, ordure 21.42

driue *v.* drive forward 13.122, drive (hounds) 36.58n, ~ *ut* force out 21.64

drow *see* **draw**

druiþ *pr. 3 sg.* dries up 39.10; **idriid** *p.p.* dried up, withered 5.102

dubito (Lat.) I doubt 44.18

duble *adj.* double 14.176

dun(e) *adv.* down 2.140, 4.103, 22.28, **doune** 19.15

dunnir *n.* thunder 2.39

durke *see* **derk**

durst *pa. 3 sg.* dared to 36.30

duste *n.* dust 13.12

dute *n.* pleasure 2.9, joy 20.47 [cf. **dedute**]

dute *v.* be afraid 14.24

dwel *n.* portion 5.32n [see **del** *n.*]

dwelle *n.* vanity 13.55, a fairy tale 13.111

dwel(le) *v.* dwell, stay 14.176, remain 20.32, 80

E

edwite *v.* disrespect 21.15

efte *adv.* again 20.72

ei *n.* eye 13.90; **ein** *pl.* 13.17, 39.37*, **eiine** 13.140

eie *n.* fear 33.22

eiȝt *adj.* eighth 14.113, 36.7

eiȝte *num.* eight 36.6

ein-siȝt *n.* gaze 14.143n

eir *n.* heir 13.174, 175, 179

ek(e) *adv.* also 2.85, 4.63, 33.51

eld(e) *n.* old age 39.1, 2, 3
eldren *n. pl.* ancestors 22.4
elemens *n. pl.* elements 14.177
elinglich *adv.* drearily 2.15n
end(e) *n.* end 21.19, an end 13.10, end
    (of life) 13.167, 15.130, 33.163, *ouir* ~
    top 4.20, *last* ~ death 48.73
end *v.* end 48.29.
ending *n.* death 15.46, ~ *worldis* end of
    the world 14.6
endlefte *adj.* elleventh 14.169*
Englismen *n. pl.* Englishmen 36.37, 69
eni *adj.* any 13.34, 21.13, 44.2, ani
    15.124
enis *adv.* once 13.171, 33.167
entredite *v.* excommunicate 33.25
entri *v.* enter 21.4
envie *n.* hatred 20.49
epetite *n.* hepatite (gem) 2.94
er *adv.* before 14.96, 36.91; *prep.* in ~ *þis*
    previously 22.4 [*see* ar]
ere *n.* ear 5.84; eris *pl.* 13.18
eri *v.* in ~ *of grund* plough the field
    33.30n
erl *n.* earl 14.108, 36.73
erlich *adv.* from early on 20.202
erne *v.* run 14.50; erniþ *pr. pl.* 19.12;
    ernend *pr. p.* 2.86
ernist *n.* in *on* ~ *and agam* in all
    circumstances 36.98n
ert, ertow *see* be
erþ(e) *n.* the Earth, 4.24, 5.31, 14.40,
    earth, soil 2.22, 13.11, 14.93, 48.1(1),
    dust 15.23, 33.166, 48.29 (1), the body
    48.1 (2), 2 (2), the ground 5.78, 33.170,
    48.3 (2), man 48.4 (1), 13 (1), 14 (1),
    humans 33.153 (1), the grave 48.4 (2),
    6, 14 (2), wealth 33.153 (2), possessions
    48.26 (4), the world 48.49, life 48.50, *in*
    ~ in life 48.30, *uppon* ~ while alive
    48.63, *on* ~ in the world 48.13 (2), 28,
    37
est *n.* east 5.69, 33.139; *adv.* 22.33
et *v.* eat 2.56, 61, 33.119; ette *imp. sg.*
    20.61; ete *pa. 1 sg.* ate 33.114; *3 sg.*
    20.143, 22.36, eete 33.66; iȝette *p.p.*
    eaten 20.65
eþe *adj.* easy 13.89
euch *pron.* everyone 21.21
euch *adj.* every 2.121, 4.78, 13.215, uche
    5.81, vch 39.32, ~ *a* every 39.68
euchon(e) *pron.* everyone 20.138, every
    one 36.40

euer, euir *adv.* always 2.28, 5.3, 13.80,
    15.115, ever 4.4, 21.18
euer-glowind *adj.* ever-burning 5.40
euerich *adj.* every 2.49*
euermore, euirmore *adv.* for all time
    5.18, 13.106, 15.3
euesang *n.* evensong 2.130
executur *n.* executor 15.145

F

face *n.* face 20.118
fader *n.* father 13.219, 14.31, 20.100,
    uadir father (ecclesiastical) 2.176
fail *v.* be unsuccessful 13.175; ifaillid
    p.p. lacking 33.141
fair *adj.* handsome, excellent 2.51, 4.2,
    beautiful 13.202, 14.41, lovely 15.68,
    19.7, (ironic) 4.94; fairir *comp.* more
    lovely 2.6; fairist *superl.* loveliest 15.66
fair *adv.* decently 14.163, beautifully
    15.91, pleasantly 15.175
fal(le) *v.* fall 14.170, 15.140, fall from
    grace 15.60, befall 36.83; falliþ *pr. 3
    sg.* falls 20.26, 48.3, befalls 21.10, is
    distributed 15.169, ~ *bi* happens with
    21.61, fallit ~ *to* come by right
    13.195; falleþ *imp. pl.* fall 5.27; fille
    pa. 3 sg. fell 20.30; *pl.* 20.23; ifalle *p.p.*
    fallen 20.34
falc *n.* fallow land? 39.59n
fale *adj.* many
    2.95, 4.92, 36.71, fele 15.107
falow *pr. 1 sg.* fade away 39.59; faloweþ
    pr. 3 sg. fades 2.81, falowiþ becomes
    pale 19.7
fals *adj.* false 21.73, deceptive 33.9,
    deceitful 22.26, 33.89, fraudulent 44.23
falsnis *n.* wickedness 20.136
fare *v.* go 5.146, proceed 43.9, 10; fariþ
    pr. 3 sg. goes 15.154, happens 33.125, it
    happens in 33.136, ~ *bi* happens with
    21.62
fast *adj.* fastened, hooked up 4.108,
    firmly rooted 14.93, secure 33.131
fast *adv.* firmly 13.79, 14.38, securely
    15.112, 120 vigorously 13.81; faster
    comp. more quickly 15.116
fat *adj.* fat 2.59
fax *n. pl.* hairs 4.86
fe *n.* wealth 5.55
fede *v.* feed 13.207, 15.126, feden 48.14

fel(le) *n.* skin 13.30, 159, 170, **velle** 13.26

felaw *n.* your companion 13.59

feld *n.* open field 36.29

feld *v.* bend 39.2; **felde** *pr. 1 sg.* grow weak 39.59

fele *see* fale

felle *n.* skin 15.86, 19.4, 33.166

felle *adj.* cruel 5.120, 33.90

feloni(e) *n.* wickedness, treachery 20.51, crime 33.43

fend *n.* the Devil 15.2, 8, **fent** fiend, devil 5.57, 99; **fendis** *pl.* 14.157, 5.120, **fentis** 14.162, 5.115

fenestres *n. pl.* windows 2.114

fenne *n.* dirt, trash 5.25

ferd *n.* fear 14.71

ferdnis *n.* fear 36.62

feriiþ *pr. 3 sg.* carries 15.144

ferlich *adj.* intimidating 4.87

ferred *n.* fellowship 14.146n

ferþ *adj.* fourth 14.69, **verþ** 21.65

ferþing *n.* farthing 5.49, **verþing** 13.99

fest *n.* feast (fig.) 13.230*, heavenly feast 20.216; **festis** *pl.* feasts 13.94

fet(e) *see* fote

few *n.* few people 5.13

fewe *adj.* a few 33.100, few 39.38

fiȝte *v.* fight 15.39, 44.11

fift(e) *adj.* fifth 14.73, 21.67

fiftene *num.* fifteen 14.9*

file *see* vile; **fille** *see* fal(le)

fille *n.* in ȝur ~ as much as you want 4.116

fille *v.* fill 14.88, occupy 20.36, ~ *of* fill up with 5.22; **filleþ** *pr. pl.* occupy 4.38; **ifillid** *p.p.* in ~ *of* filled with 4.44

find *v.* discover 13.36, 21.19; **findest** *pr. 2 sg.* 19.14, **findist** 19.16; **fint** *3 sg.* finds 39.70; **fint** *pl.* 14.60; **ifund** *p.p.* discovered to be 15.69

fine *n.* end 14.135, *mak* ~ pays a fine 33.132

fine *adj.* excellent 2.45

fire *n.* fire 5.37, 13.125, 14.70

first *adj.* first 14.33, 21.33; *adv.* firstly 15.61, 19.23, 20.60

fisse *n.* fish 2.55; **fissis** *pl.* 14.121, 22.7

fist *n.* fist 33.191

fiue *num.* five 3.7, 5.28

fiz *n.* son of 14.179

fle(e) *n.* flea 2.37, 13.22

fle(e) *v.* flee 5.59, 13.118, 14.48, fly 2.127,

run (of blood) 20.123; **fleeþ** *pr. pl.* fly 2.103*, 2.132, 134; **fleing** *pr. p.* flying 2.124

flei *n.* fly 2.37; **fleiis** *pl.* 4.88

fleis(se) *n.* meat 2.55, flesh 13.25, 14.102, 15.84, **flees** 20.97

flitte *n.* strife 5.97n

flitte *v.* escape 5.95

flode *n.* water, river 22.7

flure *n.* blossom 2.8, 75, flower 5.147, virginity 20.104

fluren *adj.* made of flour 2.57

fo *n.* an enemy 36.50, **vo** 22.19

fole *n.* fool 13.54

folk *n.* people 20.211, 21.28, 39.61

fol(le) *see* ful(le)

folowith *pr. pl.* follow 4.88

fond *v.* attempt 36.63; **fondiþ** *pr. 3 sg.* tries 33.151

for *conj.* because 5.29, 13.36, 20.56; *prep.* as 14.12, in consequence of 14.39, 20.29, because of 20.143

forbede *pr. 1 sg.* forbid 15.95, 150; **forbede** *pa. 3 sg.* forbad 20.46

fordede *pr. 3 sg.* destroys 39.27n

fordwynnen *p.p.* enfeebled 39.37

forfare *p.p.* ruined, disfigured 39.33

forȝite *imp. sg.* forget 13.148; **forȝit** *p.p.* forgotten 36.92

forȝiue *pr. 1 sg.* forgive 33.88

forlor *p.p.* lost 20.92, *þe* ~ destroyed yourself 19.19

forroti *v.* rot away 15.23

forsak *v.* deny 44.5; *p.p.* omitted 36.119

forsoȝt *p.p.* afflicted 13.50n

forswore *p.p.* profaned 21.12n

fort *conj.* (with subj.) until 2.185, 13.108, 20.111, ~ *þat* until 33.132, 20.147

forþ *adv.* forth 20.94, out, away 2.153, 160, 163

forþi *adv.* therefore 14.51

forto *prep.* (introd. infin.) to, in order to 2.75, 13.89, 13.133, **fortto** 13.71, **fort(e)** 13.150, 44.2

fote *n.* foot 4.3, 19.11, 22.23, (after num.) feet (in length) 5.54, *vnder* ~ in subjection 39.70; **fet(e)** *pl.* feet 4.9, 13.117, 20.141

foule *adj.* filthy 15.14

foulis *see* fule

fow *n.* particoloured fur 5.89

fox *n.* fox 2.31, 33.53, **uoxe** 33.61

fram *prep.* from 2.134, 5.4, 13.19, ~ *зer to зere* over the years 13.100

fre *adj.* noble 5.1, 131, 137, generous 13.184

fremid *n.* stranger 33.141

frend *n.* friend 13.218, 15.28, 33.172; **frendis** *pl.* 4.115, 15.31, 39.38, followers 20.183

frendschip *n.* friends 48.42

frere *n.* friar 5.141, 144; **freris** *pl.* 4.31, 13.109

fro *prep.* away from 13.203

frow *adv.* quickly? 48.3n

frute *n.* fruit 2.10, 49, 20.45

fule *n.* bird 2.123; **foulis** *n. pl.* 4.25, **foules** 20.45, 22.7

ful(e) *adj.* foul 21.42, 15.126, ugly 15.69

fulfil(le) *v.* accomplish 20.10, occupy 20.33, fulfil 20.93; **fulfille** *pr. pl. subj.* carry out 2.186

ful(le) *adj.* full 2.36, 20.1, 13.222, complete 22.19, **folle** fed up 39.61n, ~ *wiþ* full of 13.31

ful(le) *adv.* fully 36.5, 9, completely 13.231, very 2.178, 4.29, 14.11, **fol** 48.3

fullich *adv.* completely 20.146

funde *v.* go 43.10, strive 43.11

fure *num.* four 2.83*, 4.27, 14.169

fur(re) *adv.* far 13.203, far away 2.1, 155; a long way 4.30; in *of wel* ~ from very far away 4.6; **furre** *comp.* further 2.132

G

gab(be) *v.* lie 13.164, 191, 33.159, 179

gadering *vbl. n.* acquisition 4.40

gaderiþ *pr. 3 sg.* hoards 15.116; **gadred** *pa. 3 sg.* 15.161

gaffe *n.* iron hook 4.20

galingale *n.* galingale (spice) 2.73n

galliþ *p.p.*? afflicted with sores 39.44n

galuns *n. pl.* vessels holding a gallon 4.97

game *n.* fun 2.43, *no* ~ serious business 36.114

gan *pa. 3 sg.* (forming pa. with infin.) 36.1, 20.19, 107, 166

garlek *n.* garlic 2.105

gees *n. pl.* geese 2.102, 104, 33.63, **ges** 4.27

geet *see* **gote**; **ge(e)þ** *see* **go**

geld *adj.* impotent 39.1

gentilman *n.* gentleman 13.33

gersom *n.* treasure 48.61

gest *n.* stranger 22.31*

get(te) *pr. 3 sg.* earns 48.37, acquires 48.61; **geten** *p.p.* taken 48.53, **igette** acquired 33.153

gile *n.* deception 13.56, 57, **gyle** trickery 4.99

gilofre *n.* gillyflower, clove 2.77, 2.110

gilt *pa. 3 sg.* sinned 20.109

gilt(e) *n.* sin 20.14, 71, wrong 33.58, crime, transgression 15.71, 33.88, 102

gingeuir *n.* ginger 2.73

girdil *n.* belt 13.19

glad(de) *adj.* glad 4.115, happy 5.129, 13.155, pleased 20.67, 158

gladieþ *imp. pl.* rejoice 4.116

gladlich *adv.* with pleasure 33.80

glasse *n.* glass 2.114, 119

glede *n.* coals 5.40

gle(e) *n.* merriment 2.43, fun 2.128

glide *v.* pass 20.20, flow 20.166

glisniing *pr. p.* glistening (with sweat) 19.17

glouis *n. pl.* gloves 15.92

gnede *adj.* miserly 5.38

go *v.* go 2.15, 13.163, gone 21.48, ~ *to* set to, get started 13.126; **goþ** *pr. 3 sg.* 13.55, 85, **geþ** walks 48.13, **geeþ** goes 48.28; **goþ** *pl.* 2.122, **geeþ** 2.113n, **geþ** 2.141, 144, 160; **go** *3 sg. subj.* 48.64; **gond** *pr. p.* vanishing 15.18n; **gon** *p.p.* 5.11, **igo** travelled 36.129

God(de) *n.* God 2.34, 4.4, 5.31; **Go(d)dis** *gen.* 5.14, 63, 33.195, **Goddes** 4.50; **goddis** *pl.* 21.46

god(e) *n.* good 13.63, 22.9, what is good 20.40, goods, wealth 13.68, 86, 102, 21.68, 33.157, possessions 15.124, 143, good things 2.36, charity, gifts 5.82, benefit 21.16, good action 33.110

gode *adj.* good 2.77, 167, 4.113, 33.184

godhed *n.* divinity 20.199

godmen *n. pl.* (as address) dear people 14.21

godnis *n.* excellence 2.4

gold(e) *n.* gold 2.88, 4.63, 5.55, gold colour 4.15

golokes *n. pl.* tubs (*MED collok*) 4.104

gome *n.*[1] heed 14.5, 21, 15.51

gome *n.*[2] man 39.44

gond, gon(e) *see* **go**

gore *n.* skirt 39.16; **gores** *pl.* (triangular) pieces of cloth 4.68

goshorne *n.* goosehorn 4.111n

gospel *n.* gospel, teachings 15.49

Gost *n.* in *Holi* ∼ Holy Spirit 14.11

gote *n.* goat 2.33; geet *pl.* 33.64, gete 33.100

goþ *see* go

grace *n.* grace 2.171n, 13.1, 15.45

grace *v.* honour 36.120

grai *n.* grey fur 5.89

grai *adj.* grey, grey-haired 39.1, grei 2.52n, 164, 39.34

grame *n.* anger 33.85

grant *v.* permit 20.156; *imp. sg.* grant 33.92; igrant *p.p.* 20.158

gras(se) *n.* grass, greenery 2.8, 5.12, 33.66

grauiþ *n.* buries, decorates 48.52n

grede *v.* lament 13.129, call out 14.25, 137; grediþ *pr. 3 sg.* cries out 5.103; *pl.* 2.104; gredind *pr. p.* weeping 19.31

grei *see* grai

gremful *adj.* wrathful 14.156

grene *n.* green 48.52

grene *adj.* green 2.8, 70, 14.63

grenne *pr. 1 sg.* have mouth open 39.48

gret(e) *adj.* great 2.9, 14.158, large 2.45, 4.9, noble 33.91, severe 19.36

grete *v.* greet with the news 36.1

greue *v.* injure, cause pain 13.204

grimme *adj.* grim 5.120

grisful *adj.* horrible 13.133, terrifying 14.16, 58

grome *n.* servant, subject 33.53

grone *pr. 1 sg.* groan 39.48

grope *v.* grope (sexually) 39.16

grouer *n.* rich fur 48.51

grow *v.* grow 14.97, growen become 39.1

groy *n.* grey fur 48.51

gruche *pr. 1 sg.* grumble 39.48

grund(e) *n.* ground 5.106, earth 21.42

grunt *pr. 1 sg.* grunt 39.48

gunes *n. pl.* gowns 4.37

3

3af *see* 3iue

3e *pron. 2 pl. nom.* you 2.180, 4.31, 5.23, ye (altered from *þe*) 36.16, 3ow 4.57; 3ou, 3ow *acc. & dat.* you 2.101, 4.88, 5.31, 3ov 5.32; 3eu *refl.* yourself 5.39; 3our(e) *gen.* your 4.73, 74, 15.35, 3ur(e) 2.185, 4.37, 5.19, 13.167 [see þou etc.]

3e *interj.* yes, indeed 13.98, 33.100

3ed *pa. 3 sg. him* ∼ came, walked 20.105

3ef *see* 3iue

3eld *v.* yield, give 13.96, 3ild *v.* pay back 36.86

3em(e) *v.* protect 13.48, 14.4, 3ime ∼ *in store* hoard 13.74n; 3em *imp. sg.* protect 5.135

3er(e) *n.* year 2.170, 36.7; 3er(e) *pl.* (after num.) 2.179, 13.240, 20.76, 3eris 36.5

3ho *see* 3o

3ift *n.* gift 33.188; 3iftes *n. pl.* presents, bribes 33.67

3ime *see* 3eme

3it *conj.* even though 20.114

3it(e) *adv.* even so 13.83, 20.48, one day 13.113, furthermore 36.109, ∼ *mo* furthermore 2.101, 3ete still 39.17

3iue *v.* give 2.116, 5.49, 13.97; *pr. 1 sg.* allow 33.123; *pl.* give 4.64; *pr. 2 sg. subj.* 5.110; *3 sg.* 15.47; 3if *imp. sg.* 13.3, 21.3, 14.167, 3iue 21.80, 13.326; *pl.* (followed by pron.) 4.58, 3iueþ give to 33.194; 3ef *pa. 1 sg.* gave 19.25, 33.104; *3 sg.* 20.38, 3af 20.4, 33.67

3o *pron. 3 sg. fem. nom.* she 20.165, 170, 172, 3ho 20.58, 176, sso 20.104; hir *acc. and dat.* her 20.160, 36.3, 48.2; hir *gen.* 2.142, 13.223, 20.52 [*see* hi, þai etc.]

3olow *adj.* yellow 4.86

3ore *adv.* long ago 22.2, *of* ∼ of old, from long ago 39.18

3ou, 3ow, 3our(e) *see* 3e

3(o)uþe *n.* youth 39.14, 26, 58

3ung *adj.* young 2.121, 152, 3.3; *as n.* young 2.63, young people 14.8, 15.32

3ur(e) *see* 3e

H

hab *v.* have 2.169, 13.44, 14.135, haue 33.85, 44.10; ab *pr. 1 sg.* 43.2; hast *2 sg.* 4.3, 13.61, have you 33.75; hauiþ *3 sg.* has 5.31, 32, 15.74, haþ 33.13; habbiþ *pl.* 4.32, 4.117, 13.50, habiþ 13.186, habbeþ 4.117, 5.140, abbiþ 14.82, haþ 15.178, hab (followed by pron.) 4.118; hab *sg. subj.* 13.101, 14.28, 15.88; haue *pl. subj.* 13.183, hab 33.40, 41; hab *imp. sg.* 4.99, 13.9; had *pa. 1 sg.* 43.7, ad 19.35; had *3 sg.* 20.49, 77; had *pl.* 20.128, ad 20.147

hail *interj.* greetings! 4.1, 7, 19; *adj.* in ∼
    be all the best! 4.31, 37
halle *n.* hall 2.11, 58; *pl.* halles 2.53
halt *see* hold(e)
halwei *n.* healing lotion 2.84
ham *see* hi
hamsilf *pron. pl.* they themselves 13.108;
    hamsilf *acc and dat.* themselves 13.82,
    15.175, 22.9
hangiþ *pr. 3 sg.* hangs 19.1; *pl.* hang
    down 19.9; heng *pa. 1 sg.* hung 19.30;
    ihang *p.p.* 19.26
har *see* hi
harace *n.* stud 2.35
hard *adj.* hard 33.182, callous 33.183,
    painful 19.35, perilous ? 36.29; *as n.* in
    ∼ *for* ∼ hard-heartedness in exchange
    for hard-heartedness 33.184
hard *adv.* firmly, roughly 39.63, violently
    14.121
hare *n.* hare 36.54
harm(e) *n.* harm 33.68, 115, damage
    21.41, loss, matter for regret 4.42, what
    is wrong 20.40
hast *see* hab
hastilich *adv.* quickly 33.120
hate *n.* hatred 20.128, 33.5, 11
hatid *pa. 3 sg.* hated 48.26; ihatid *p.p.*
    hated 39.8
hauk *n.* hawk 2.123
haue, hauiþ *see* hab
hawle *n.* hail 2.39
he *pron. 3 sg. masc. nom.* he 2.128, 4.35,
    5.33, of inanimate objects 14.71 (sun),
    14.127 (water), 22.20 (world); him *acc.*
    & dat. him 2.134, 175; *refl.* himself
    33.18, for himself 2.133, for itself 4.78;
    is *gen.* his 2.134, 5.99, 13.52, his 4.50,
    13.13, belonging to him 13.69 [*see* hit
    etc.]
hechil *n.* comb 4.112n
hed *see* heued
hed(e) *n.* heed 4.47, 94
hede *v.* take account of 15.125
heet *see* het
hei, heiȝ *adj.* high 2.125, 13.213, 14.72,
    loud 14.178, arrogant 4.22; *as n.* in *an*
    ∼ heaped up high 4.110, on high, in
    heaven 13.92, 14.100, at the top 14.98;
    heiiȝist *superl.* most noble 33.7
held *v.* go 39.6n
heliþ *pr. 3 sg.* covers 15.84; ihelid *p.p.*
    15.159

helle *n.* hell 5.5, 36, 14.157; *gen.* of hell
    5.30, 5.93, 97, hel 13.196
help *v.* help 13.72, 14.109; *pr. 3. sg. subj.*
    33.140; *imp. sg.* 5.103; helpiþ *pl.*
    13.186
helplich *adj.* beneficial 13.4, 62, useful
    20.8
hen *n.* hen 33.81; henne *pl.* 33.63
hend *adj.* gracious 2.183, 5.1, 48.75,
    generous 4.16, well behaved, obedient
    13.14
hendi *adj.* lovely 19.8
heng *see* hangiþ
henne *adv.* away from here 5.23, hen
    5.146
heordmon *n.* retainer 39.60n
hepe *n.* in *com to* ∼ 13.138 [*see* com]
her *see* hi
herapan *adv.* upon this 13.148
herbergi *n.* place of refuge 14.167
here *n.* hair, thread 5.90
her(e) *adv.* here 13.147, 15.153, 21.60,
    here (in this life) 13.48, ∼ *and þare*
    everywhere 5.150, all over the place
    44.7, hither and thither 14.50
hering *n.* herring 4.10
herinne *adv.* here on earth 5.6
herkne *imp. sg.* listen 15.102; herkniþ *pl.*
    15.33, 167, 33.47
hert *n.* heart 13.44, 15.96, 20.148
hest(e) *n.* command 5.63, *did an* ∼ issued
    a decree 33.48
het *pa. 3 sg.* was called 20.150, heet
    36.105; ihote *p.p.* 2.2
heued *n.* head 19.3, 13, heuid 36.65,
    chief 15.62, hed 39.33, *of har* ∼ from
    their speculation 44.23n; heuedes *pl.*
    4.105
heuen(e) *n.* heaven 2.23, 5.131, 14.38;
    heuen *gen.* 15.53, 20.112, 44.3
heuen(e)riche *n.* the kingdom of heaven
    2.3, 5.10, 21.76
heuen-kyng *n.* king of heaven 3.6
heuid-sinnes *n. pl.* deadly sins 15.55n
hewid *p.p.* coloured 39.34
hi *pron. 3 pl. nom.* they 2.15, 4.70, 13.66,
    i 20.88n; ham *acc.& dat* 2.130, 13.68,
    14.41, am 20.87; har *gen.* 2.69, 126,
    13.77, 80, ar 48.50n, her 2.143, 13.149,
    14.123 [*see* þai, and he etc.]
hide *v.* hide 13.114, 14.47, 33.170; hidde
    p.p. concealed 5.35, ihidde 36.81;
    ihuddid 13.48

hides *n. pl.* animal skins 4.74
hien *v.* hurry 39.6
hil *n.* hill 21.27; hille *pl.* 14.86
him *see* he
himsilf *pron. nom.* (emphasizing) he
  himself 13.35, 15.49, 20.64; *acc.* himself
  2.172, 22.28
hir *see* 30
hire *n.* hire 36.64
hir(e) *v.* hear 13.134, 14.159, 33.96;
  hirist *pr. 2 sg.* 13.136; hire *imp. sg.*
  5.7, 19.31; herd *pa. 1 sg.* in ~ *telle* was
  told 33.45; hird *3 sg.* heard 33.50, 61;
  ihird *p.p.* 4.117
his *see* he
hit *pron. 3 sg. neut. nom.* it 2.4, 4.6, 5.23,
  it 2.34; hit *acc. and dat.* 2.175, 4.23,
  13.50; is *gen.* its 2.22 (land), 33.17, 21
  (Holy Church), what belongs to it
  15.90n [*see* he etc.]
hiue *n.* beehive 21.62
hiwe *n.* colour 14.43
ho *see* who
hoblurs *n. pl.* riders 33.29n
hode *n.* hood 2.126, 2.168n; ho(o)des *pl.*
  hoods 4.68, 36.107, 36.118n
hokesters *n. pl.* hucksters, peddlers
  (female) 4.103
hokirlich *adv.* scornfully 33.178
hold *adj.¹* loyal to 48.63, ~ *to* attached to
  5.48
hold *adj.²* secure 15.138n
hold(e) *v.* keep 15.10, retain 13.79,
  20.139, observe 21.32, 50, preserve
  21.44, maintain 33.21, conduct (life)
  33.145, be faithful to 20.113n; hold *pr.*
  1 sg. in ~ *no pride of* hold in no regard
  13.23, ~ *þat* suppose that 13.54;
  holdiþ *3 sg.* arranges (feast) 13.94,
  halt in ~ *to gle* thinks it fun 5.57n,
  holt in ~ *for* regards as 2.128; holt *pl.*
  engage in 21.54; ihold *p.p.* restrained,
  locked up 33.131
holi *adj.* holy 4.43, 14.133, 15.45
Holi Boke *n.* the Bible 20.200
Holi Cherch *n.* Holy Church 33.17, 21,
  ~ Chirch(e) 13.1, 33.193, ~ Church
  5.124
holibrede *n.* blessed bread 4.58n
holle *adj.* sunken 39.60n
hom *adv.* home 2.144, 36.126
hond(e) *n.* hand 4.15, 19.11, 34, control
  20.44, *an* ~ in control 33.13, *habbiþ an*

~ have power 33.127; *(sg. or pl.)* 2.137;
  hond *pl.* hands 20.141, hondes 13.117,
  19.18
honi *n.* honey 2.46
honur *n.* honour 5.147, 14.111
honuri *v.* honour 20.152, 21.34, 57;
  anouriþ *imp. pl.* worship, revere
  13.185, anuriþ 33.193
hoppe *n.* hope 2.175, source of hope 5.8
hore *n.* corruption 20.34
hore *adj.* grey 39.33
hori *adj.* filthy 4.76, 100, 5.47, 15.86
horliþ *pr. pl.* in ~ *ham* throw themselves
  44.7
horn *n.* trumpet 22.27*
hors *n.* riding horse 2.32
horwȝ *n.* dirt 2.34n
hosse *n.* leggings 13.19
hot(e) *adj.* hot 2.104, 151, 4.69
hou, how *adv.* how 4.10, 5.33, 15.148,
  (with adj.) to what extent 36.33, in
  what condition? 13.38, in what way
  13.155, hov 20.86, wouw 39.64
house *see* hus(e)
how *n.* trouble 2.18
hund(e) *n.* dog 21.13, 33.32
hundred *num.* hundred 36.5, 48.18,
  hundrid 36.132
hungre *n.* hunger 5.104, hungir 13.206;
  hungir-bitte *adj.* starving 5.85
hunt *v.* hunt 36.53, hunti 13.22; huntid
  pa. 1 sg. 33.97
hunter *n.* huntsman 36.54
husbond *n.* farmer 33.30
hus(e) *n.* house, friary 4.32, house house
  2.38, nunnery 4.49, *Godis* ~ the
  Church 15.43, heaven 15.106

I

I *see* ich
ibe *see* be; ibet *see* betiþ; ibiriid *see*
  biri; iblend *see* blind
iblessid *p.p.* blessed 4.120, 5.132
ibobid *p.p.* struck 20.117
iboȝt *see* boȝt; ibor(n) *see* ber; ibroȝt *see*
  bring; ibund *see* bint
ich *pron. 1 sg. nom.* I 4.21, 94, 14.132,
  ihc 13.54, 39.15, I 2.21, 3.6, Y 33.104,
  39.30; me *acc. & dat.* me 4.47, 58,
  mei *dat.* (in rhyme) 33.107; mi *gen.*
  my 4.115, 13.61, 15.31, min(e) (before

vowel) 5.84, 33.84, 39.33, belonging to
me 19.30 [*see* **we** etc.]
icharged *p.p.* loaded up 33.8
ichul *see* **wol**
icloþed *p.p.* dressed 4.14
iclung *see* **cling**; **icom, icommen,
icommin** *see* **com(e)**
ycor *p.p.* chosen 20.90
icrauid *p.p.* demanded, required 5.109
icrop *p.p.* crawling 13.42n
idiʒt *p.p.* prepared 2.106, 109, destined
48.38
ido *see* **do**; **idriid** *see* **druiþ**
if *conj.* if 5.35, 13.15, 19.2, ∼ *þat* if 20.62
ifaillid *see* **fail**
ifast *p.p.* imprisoned 20.189
ifere *adv.* together 14.117, added together
36.8
ifesid *p.p.* driven 14.172
ifillid *see* **fille**
ifostred *p.p.* nurtured, brought up 22.14
ifrette *p.p.* devoured 33.124
ifund *see* **find**
igeld *p.p.* gelded 39.44
igette *see* **get(te)**; **igo** *see* **go**
iʒarkid *p.p.* arranged, destined 22.2
iʒette *see* **ette**
yʒoket *p.p.* yoked, harnessed 39.18
ihang *see* **hangiþ**; **ihatid** *see* **hated**; **ihc**
see **ich**; **ihelid** *see* **heliþ**
ihent *p.p.* seized 39.63
ihidde *see* **hide**; **ihird** *see* **hir(e)**; **ihold**
see **hold(e)**; **ihote** *see* **het**; **ihuddid** *see*
hide; **ikest** *see* **cast**
ilappid *p.p.* covered 13.159
ileiid *p.p.* in *up* ∼ put away 2.118, *adun*
∼ dropped, set aside 4.42n
ilend, ilent *see* **leniþ**
ilich *adv.* equally 15.170
ilich(e) *adj.* like 2.4, 15.20, equal 14.107,
resembling 48.5n
ilk *adj.* particular 33.102, *þat* ∼ that same
13.113, that 14.76 [*see* **þilk**]
iloke *p.p.* locked (fig.) 13.145
ilor *see* **lesist**; **imakid** *see* **mak(e)**
imeten *p.p.* measured 48.54n
in *adv.* within 13.217, **inne** 33.2
in, inn(e) *prep.* in 2.1, 20.72, 21.4, into
5.40, on 5.73, during 5.12, ∼ *rode* on
the cross 20.111, 170
incom *p.p.* in *him was* ∼ had entered
him 15.73
incomming *vbl. n.* arrival, birth 5.41

inne *n.* peddler's booth 4.106n
inoʒ *n.* plenty 2.61, enough 2.112, **inovʒ**
33.154, **ynowʒ** 33.184, **inow** 48.2;
ynow *adj.* many 4.88; **inoʒ** *adv.* very
20.201, **ynoʒ** 20.158
inom *see* **nim**
into *prep.* into 2.115, 5.79, 13.158
ipaiid *p.p.* in ∼ *apan* gratified by it
33.180
ipeintid *p.p.* painted, decorated 4.15
ipiʒt(e) *p.p.* organized 4.77, fixed, planted
14.94
ipilt(e) *see* **pilt**
ipinid *p.p.* tortured 19.39
ipinsed *p.p.* tortured 20.177n
ipudrid *see* **pudrid**
Yrismen *n. pl.* Irishmen 36.50, 67
irostid *p.p.* roasted 2.102
is *see* **be, he, hit**
ischaue *p.p.* shaved 4.56
ischend *see* **schend**
ischrid *p.p.* clothed, adorned 5.55, ∼
aboute dressed in 15.81
ise(e) *v.* see 2.187, 14.8, 13.58; **iseeþ** *pr.
3 sg.* realizes (*him* for himself) 2.133; *pl.*
see 2.139; **ise** *3 sg. subj.* may see
15.160; **isene** *p.p.* 20.187 [*see* **se(e)**]
iseid *see* **sigge**; **isent** *see* **sent**; **iset(te)**
see **set(te)**
ismit(te) *p.p.* wounded 20.167, hit 20.117
isoʒt *see* **soʒt**; **isold** *see* **sold**
isowe *p.p.* begotten 15.14
ispend *see* **spen(e)**; **ispoke** *see* **speke**;
iss(e) *see* **be**
istekke *p.p.* stuck 33.155
istrawʒt *p.p.* stretched out 5.2
istunge *p.p.* pierced 19.18
it *see* **hit**; **itake** *see* **tak(e)**
iteiʒte *p.p.* bound 15.104n, **itiʒte**
stretched out 5.73, 19.8
itend *p.p.* lit (of fire) 5.37
iþoʒt *see* **þench**
iþrow *p.p.* thrown 20.28
itold *see* **tel(le)**; **iturned** *see* **turn(e)**
ivette *p.p.* fetched 4.30
iuil *n.* suffering, misfortune 13.203
iuil *adj.* wicked 20.48
iwar(e) *adj.* aware 13.107, 143, *beþ* ∼ *of*
watch out for 4.100 [*cf.* **ware**]
iwend *see* **wend**
iwernd *pp.* refused 36.117
iwis(se) *adv.* indeed 2.23, 4.96, 13.71,

truly 13.224, *ful* ~ quite certainly
36.20

iwitte *v.* know, understand 2.180, *wol ʒe*
~ you may believe 20.67; **iwit** *pr. 2 sg.*
realize 15.85

iwonne *see* **win(ne)**

iworþe *v.* become 15.22; **iworþ** *pr. pl.*
(they) will be 14.154

iwritte *p.p.* written 13.6, 14.13, 15.64,
inscribed 13.44

iwroʒt *see* **wirch(e)**

J

iambleue *n.* legs aloft 2.166n

iaspe *n.* jasper (quartz) 2.70

ioi *n.* joy 2.9, 13.110, 20.169; **iois** *pl.*
13.231

iurneis *n. pl.* days 22.32n

K

kaitefs *n. pl.* wretches 4.109*

kan *see* **can**

kar *n. see* **care**

kar *v.* be concerned 13.206

keld *v.* chill 39.5n; **kelde** *pr. 1 sg.* grow
cold 39.41

kemiþ *pr. pl.* comb 4.109

kene *adj.* sharp 20.122

kepe *n.* attention, in *tak* ~ take account
14.18

keþerin *n.* footsoldiers 36.104n

kin *n.* kindred, family 13.219, 22.28,
kinne race 36.124; **kinnes** *gen.* in *no* ~
of no kind 19.29

kind *see* **kund(e)**

kine *n. pl.* in ~ *fete* feet of cattle 4.105

king *n.* king 5.131, 13.228, 14.108; **kingis**
gen. 33.33; **kinges** *pl.* 60

kirtil *n.* coat 4.3

kites *n. pl.* kites (bird) 4.26

kiþe *v.* reveal 20.199.

kiue *n.* vat, (fig.) pit 5.30n

kne *n.* knee 22.14; **knen** *pl.* 5.27

kniʒt(e) *n.* knight 5.71, 14.108, 20.149;
pl. **kniʒtis** 36.40, 82

knitte *v.* tie, fasten 5.99

knot *n.* tie, fetters 5.99n

know *v.* recognize 13.218

kowe *n.* cow 2.32

kund(e) *n.* nature 20.98, 39.41n, natural
form, body 13.11, *þi* ~ what was

natural to you 33.108, 117, **kind**
kindred, ancestry 33.91

kunger *n.* conger eel 4.9

L

la *interj.* indeed 2.34, look! 4.23

lac *n.* shortage 2.29; **lakke** 2.78

lad(de) *see* **lede**

lafful *adj.* law-abiding 33.27, 37, 129

lai *n.* law 20.91

lak(e) *n.* lake, water 4.8, 100, 103, pit
5.112n

lang *adv.* for a long time 36.81, 91, **long**
long (of time) 4.115

lang(e) *adj.* long 2.66, 4.1, 48.50, **long**
48.64

lasse *pr. 1 sg.* become smaller 39.42

last *n.*[1] sin 39.19

last *n.*[2] in *at þe* ~ in the end 13.63, 83

last *see* **lest** *v.*

late *adj.* late 13.141; **last** *superl.* final
13.211, last 48.73

late *adv.* late 4.44; **last** *superl.* in *nou* ~
just now 13.5n

Latin *n.* Latin 13.6

law *n.* law 20.130, 33.13, divine law 4.93,
~ *of lond* the law of the land 33.18, *for*
~ in accord with the law 33.123

lech *n.* healer 5.126

lechuri *n.* lechery 19.10

lede *n.* property 13.93, **leede** 21.63, *on* ~
on Earth 5.136

lede *v.* take 5.78, conduct (life) 15.26, ~
þe behave yourself 14.163n; **lediþ** *pr. 3
sg.* leads, conducts 13.88; *pl.* 13.80;
lede *imp. sg.* conduct (life) 15.97, 117;
lad *pa. pl.* led 20.126; **ladde** *p.p.*
conducted 5.120

lef *see* **leue** *v.*[2], **leue** *adj.*

leinþ *n.* length 48.54

lemman *n.* darling 19.15

len *pr. 1 sg.* lean 39.42

lench *pr. 1 sg.* stoop 39.42n

lendin *n. pl.* limbs 19.9

leniþ *pr. 3 sg.* grants 48.77; **ilent** *p.p.*
5.32, **ilend** bestowed upon, granted
13.70, 102

lepiþ *pr. pl.* leap 2.157

lere *n.* face, complexion 19.7

lere *v.* learn 20.5, teach 20.107

lerne *imp. sg.* learn 15.26

les *n.* falsehood 13.37

lesist *pr. 2 sg.* (as fut.) will lose 13.103;
 lesiþ *pl.* lose 15.56; **les** *pa. 3 sg.* lost
 20.104; **ilor** *p.p.* 20.36, 48.42, destroyed
 36.95
lest *v.* last 14.76, endure 13.236, **last**
 15.75; **lest** *pr. 3 sg.* 20.214; **lestiþ** *pl.*
 last 4.70
lest *conj.* for fear that 15.122, lest 48.76
lest *see* litil *adj.*
lestes *n. pl.* shoemakers' lasts (for
 shaping shoes) 4.73
let *v.* in ~ *mak* caused to be made
 36.118, 127; **let** *pr. 3 sg. subj.* 15.37;
 lete *pl. subj.* show mercy 33.122; **let**
 imp. sg. allow (to) 5.5, 13.126, 14.144;
 leet *pa. 3 sg.* allowed 36.47, lete in ~
 cri had it proclaimed 33.49; **let** *p.p.*
 deserted 39.14
leþir *n.* leather, hide 4.52n
lette *n.* delay 36.88
leue *n.* dear one 19.17
leue *adj.* dear 15.31, 50, 102, **lef** 20.56,
 127; **leuer** *comp.* in *wer* ~ had rather
 13.67, ~ *him wer* he would rather
 15.123
leue *v.*[1] believe 13.137, 202, 20.145; **liuiþ**
 pr. pl. 21.46
leue *v.*[2] leave 13.60, 174, desist from
 20.40; *þe* ~ remain to you 15.93; **lef**
 pr. 1 sg. omit 14.85; **leuith** *pl.* go away
 from 4.38, ~ *of* leave out, spare 21.11;
 leueþ *imp. pl.* give up 5.19
Leuedi *n.* lady (Virgin Mary) 5.147, 14.2,
 ~ *Oure* the Virgin Mary 13.221
leuerokes *n. pl.* larks 2.107
lewe *adj.* frail 39.35n
lewid *adj.* ignorant 4.57
lib(be) *v.* live 13.71, 15.171, 22.3, **liuie**
 15.139; **libbe** *pr. 1 sg.*; **libbeþ** *pl.*
 13.76; **liue** *imp. sg.* in ~ *is lore* live in
 accordance with his teaching 13.144;
 liued *pa. 3 sg.* 20.76
liche *n.* dead body 15.156
licheri *n.* lechery 21.67
lie *v.* tell a lie 15.52, 33.95; **list(e)** *pr. 2
 sg.* lie 5.73, 88
lif *n.* life 2.28, 4.107, 5.94, **liue** 5.26, 121
lif-deden *n.* actions 48.15
lifte *n.* sky 2.124
liȝt *adj.* bright 2.65
liȝt(e) *n.* light 2.116, 14.39, 20.112,
 daylight 5.79
liȝt(e) *v.* alight, land, come down 2.130,

138, descend (into the Virgin) 36.3;
 liȝtiþ *pr. pl.* land 2.131, fall 2.108;
 liȝt(e) *pa. 3 sg.* descended 20.20, 181;
 liȝt *p.p.* 48.40
likam *n.* body 2.174
likful *adj.* attractive 2.72, 80; **likfullist**
 superl. most delightful 2.56
likid *pa. 3 sg.* in *him* ~ it pleased him
 20.44
lilie *n.* lilly 2.80
lime *n.* lime 14.91
lyme *n.* in *in* ~ in stature 39.42;
 limmes *pl.* limbs 21.11
linnin *n.* linen 15.92
lion *n.* lion 33.46, 73, **lyon** 33.49
list(e) *see* lie
lite *n.* little 33.4, 44.15
liþ *n.* limb, joint 39.68
liþ *pr. 3 sg.* lies 15.70, 156
liþer *adj.* wicked, harmful 3.7, evil 33.9,
 53, 112, painful 43.1, **luþer** 39.19
litil *n.* little 4.58, 64
litil *adj.* little 4.70, 22.1, a small amount
 of 13.86, 15.73, short 5.32; **lest** *superl.*
 smallest 13.217
litil *adv.* in *wel* ~ scarcely 13.160, **lutil**
 little 48.50
liue *see* lib(be), **lif**; **liuiþ** *see* leue *v.*[1];
 liued, liuie *see* lib(be)
liuelod(e) *n.* livelihood 20.70, 74
liuerei *n.* livery 48.52
lo *interj.* indeed 13.57
loke *v.* look 13.14, look at 13.8, 133, look
 for 33.98, see 14.15; **lokiþ** *pr. 3 sg.*
 looks 33.178; **loke** *2 sg. subj.* consider
 13.38; *imp. sg.* look 13.39, 19.3, look at,
 consider 13.17, look out 22.26; **lok(e)**
 pl. make sure 33.122, ~ *þat* ensure that
 13.239; **lokid** *pa. 3 sg.* looked 36.112
lol(l)ai *interj.* hush! 22.1, 5, 11, **lullow**
 22.5
lolich *adj.* foul 13.8, horrible 33.169,
 loþlich ugly 4.76; **lolich** *adv.* foully
 13.32
lome *adj.* crooked 4.68
lome *adv.* often 4.46, 33.50, *oft(e) and* ~
 very frequently 13.13, 94, all the time
 36.45
lond(e) *n.* land 2.2, 23, 20.42, the
 country 4.117, ground 2.138, *in* ~
 everywhere 33.125; **londis** *pl.* 4.33
lone *n.* in *a* ~ on loan 13.70n
long *see* lang(e)

lord *n.* lord 20.113, 33.55, 69, Christ 19.1, 20.6, **louerd(e)** lord 4.8, 5.103, 14.81, Lord (Christ) 14.27, 29, Lord God 33.16, ~ *King* God 5.47

lordinges *n. pl.* (in address) sirs 2.183; **lordingen** *gen.* of lords 33.24

lore *n.* learning 4.66, 14, 22, 44.5, teaching 5.14, 13.144, 15.6, behaviour 39.19n

lorles *adj.* without learning 3.1

lostles *adj. as n.* the listless one 39.68n

loþlich *see* **lolich**

loue *n.* love 5.11, 15.179, 33.6, sex 39.30, favour 33.22n

loue *v.* love 20.215, **loui** 15.98; **louiþ** *pr. 3 sg.* 5.130; *pl.* 5.14, 15.108; **loue** *imp. sg.* 21.37, 65; *pa. 3 sg.* 20.151; **louid** *pl.* 21.42

louerd(e) *see* **lord**

louis *n. pl.* loaves 4.91

lowȝ *adv.* low 48.40

lowse *n.* louse 2.37, **luse** 13.22

lowtiþ *pr. 3 sg.* bows down 39.68; **lutid** *pa. pl.* bowed 33.71

lude *adv.* loudly 13.125, 14.137

lugre *n.* ligure (gemstone) 2.91n

lullow *see* **lol(l)ai**

luste *n.* desire 19.10

lusting *n.* happiness 15.47n

luþer *see* **liþer**; **lutid** *see* **lowtiþ**; **lutil** *see* **litil**

lutle *pr. 1 sg.* shrink 39.55

M

maces *n. pl.* nutmegs 2.75

madde *adj.* foolish 5.121

mageste *n.* majesty, glory 13.227

Mai *n.* May 36.11, 39.3

mai *pr. 1 sg.* am able to 13.87, 14.132; **miȝt(e)** *2 sg.* 5.70, 19.2; *pr. or pa. 2 sg.* can, could 5.129, 13.22, 24, (as fut.) will be able 13.118; **mai** *3 sg.* may 2.44, can 4.96, 5.100, 14.15, **mei** 13.35, is able to 13.155; **mai** *pl.* may 2.15, 106, **mou** 13.202, 14.36, **mov** 13.58, 14.62, **mow** 4.48, 13.58, 14.14; **miȝt** *3. sg. subj.* might 13.156, 20.22; **miȝt(e)** *pa. 3. sg.* (often with pr. sense) 13.155, 20.22, has the power to 33.92, would be able to 36.87, might go 20.110; **miȝt** *pl.* would be able to 21.60

maid *n.* girl 2.140, virgin (Mary) 5.137,

20.96, 101, **maidin** 2.135; **maidis** *gen.* Virgin's 13.234, 21.78

main *n.* strength 5.75, 39.57

maister *n.* learned man 4.35, master 33.15, 149, captain 36.105

maistri *n.* authority 20.41, miracle 20.99, power 48.37

mak(e) *v.* make 4.68, 36.100, cause (to) 2.138, 15.60; **makiþ** *pr. 3 sg.* makes 22.20, 39.1, causes to 5.48; *pl.* make 4.32, construct 21.47, cause 44.24, *refl.* in ~ *ham nakid* strip off 2.156; **mak** *pr. 3 sg. subj.* makes 33.132; **mak(e)** *imp. sg.* in ~ *þi wei* go along 5.117, ~ *þe* make yourself 48.75; **makiþ** *imp. pl.* in ~ *glad* be cheerful 4.115, 118; **makid** *pa. 3 sg.* made 4.4, 54, 20.35, composed 4.90, forced (someone) to 4.112; *pl.* made 4.111; **imakid** *p.p.* 4.17, 22.8, 15.24, constructed 14.91, **makid** 19.23, 48.5

man *n.* man 2.30, a person 13.69, 14.5, (in address) sir 13.9, 25, mankind 5.48, 13.195, **mon** 48.5; **manis** *gen.* 2.12, 13.153, 14.39; **men** *pl.* 2.13, 4.32, 33.150, **menne** 33.61; **men** *gen.* 4.117

man *pron. indef.* (any)one 2.56, 61, 106, me one, people 5.78, (*with pl. v.*) 33.147

maner *n.* sort of 2.49, 15.166, 20.177

manhed *n.* manhood 20.194

mani *pron.* many 20.21; *adj.* many 2.25, 4.9, 5.86, (*with sg. n.*) 15.103

mankin *n.* people 20.81, mankind 21.2, **mankynne** 5.8

manslaȝt *n.* murderer 21.69

marbre *n.* in ~ *stone* marble 19.9

marchans *n. pl.* merchants 4.61

mare *n.* mare 39.34

mare *see* **more**

markes *n. pl.* marks (two-thirds of a pound sterling) 4.63

marrit *p.p.* depleted 39.57

Masse *n.* Mass 2.113; **Masses** *pl.* 2.117

maugrei *prep.* despite, in ~ *ham* against their wishes 14.175

me *see* **ich, man**

mede *n.* reward 5.36, 13.212, (heavenly) reward 33.188, bribe 33.128, 36, money 33.41, generosity 48.77, *to* ~ as a reward 13.189, 33.196; **meden** *pl.* rewards, wages 48.16

mei *see* **ich, mai**

meiis *n. pl.* men 15.13n
meisse *n.* food 13.27n
mek *adj.* humble 13.233, *as n.* humble
people 2.64
meklich *adv.* meekly, obediently 2.144
mel *n.* flour 33.174
meld *v.* engage in 39.3n
mele *n.* meal-time 33.175
melk *see* **milk(e)**; **men** *see* **man**
men *v.* bewail 14.162n
meniuer *n.* squirrel fur 13.46
menur *n.* friar minor, Franciscan 4.39,
frere ~ 5.141*
merci(e) *n.* mercy 14.28, 79, have mercy!
14.140, be merciful 14.141, favour
20.154
meri *see* **miri**
meschans *n.* misfortune 36.83
mest *see* **more**
met *n.* food, meal 2.10, 17, 13.205
mi *see* **ich**
miche *n.* loaf of bread 5.98
mid *prep.* with 5.3, 14.94, 15.1
middai *n.* midday 14.65
midwinter *n.* mid-winter 4.69
miȝt(e) *n.* might 48.37, power 20.1, 14.1,
33.17, strength 21.38, *bi har* ~ with all
their strength 2.99
miȝt(e) *see* **mai**
mild *adj.* gentle 21.77
milk(e) *n.* milk 2.149, 13.234, 21.78,
melk 2.46
min(e) *see* **ich**
ministris *n. pl.* ministers 33.33
miri *adj.* delightful 2.5, 13.208, **meri**
joyous 20.212
miri *adv.* joyfully 2.100
misanter *n.* misfortune 33.185n
misdede *n.* sin 15.25
misdo *p.p.* done wrong 13.128, wickedly
done 33.117
miseislich *adv.* uncomfortably 48.54
miste *n.* mist 15.152
mister-men *n. pl.* kinds of men 13.65n
mistrediþ *pr. pl.* tread wrongly 4.51n
mo *adj.* more (in number) 2.16, *as pron.*
in *no* ~ nothing more 13.165, 33.160;
adv. more 2.101, more, besides 20.106
moch *n.* a great amount 4.99, *so* ~ so
much 33.3
moch *adj.* great 2.128, 14.111, much
14.59, 21.59, 33.185

moch *adv.* greatly 15.147, 39.9, *in as* ~
as as surely as, considering that 21.22
mochil *adj.* much 2.24, 4.40 great 2.164,
15.11, **mochel** 15.118
mochil *adv.* greatly 15.8, 164, much
19.40
mode *n.* mind 20.38, thought 33.181,
heart 21.77, 13.233, spirit 2.125
moder *n.* mother 20.161, 21.57, 48.62;
moder *gen.* mother's 14.23, 25, 22.14
mok *see* **muk(ke)**
mold(e) *n.* earth, ground 2.87, grave
48.62, *to* ~ into the ground 5.44
mon *see* **man**
mon(e) *n.* lamentation 14.159, 162, *mak*,
makiþ ~ lament(s) 36.14, 41
monke *n.* monk 2.162, 173; **monkes** *pl.*
2.113, 121, 4.43
montis *n. pl.* mountains 14.86
more *adj. comp.* more 2.116, 20.76, 36.24,
greater 15.71, 21.41, more severely
19.40, **mare** 19.29; **more** *as n.* a
greater amount 15.115; **mest** *adj.*
superl. greatest 5.63, 13.226, most 33.8
mot(e) *pr. 1 sg.* may 5.59, 107, 20.8,
must 39.6, 69; **mostou** *pr. 2 sg.* +
pron. you must 22.2; **mot(e)** *3 sg.* must
2.178, 179, may (wish) 2.188; *pl.* may
2.187, 21.4, could 4.81,120, must
14.175, 20.32, 33.170; *subj. sg.* may
(expressing wish) 5.132, 14.3; *pl.* 2.184,
most 33.85, 36.83; **mote** *imp. sg.* may
20.3; **most** *pa. 3 sg.* had to 20.74, 80
motune *n.* mutton, sheep 33.64, 99
mou, mov, mow *see* **mai**
mourne *v.* 22.3; **murne** *pr. 1 sg.* am
sorrowful 39.55
mouþ(e) *see* **muþ**
mowe *n. pl.* women 15.13n
muk(ke) *n.* filth, (fig.) wealth 5.22, lucre
15.120, 122, **mok** 13.81n
mund(e) *n.* minds 14.78, intention
33.106, *hab* ~ bear in mind 13.9,
remember 22.15
munne *v.* in ~ *wiþ muþe* speak about
39.22n
muntid *pr. 3 sg.* pays 48.16n
murne *see* **mourne**
murþes *n. pl.* joys 39.3, 23
muþ *n.* mouth 2.108, **mouþ(e)** 13.18, *at*
one ~ with one voice 20.133

N

nab *see* nastou

nai *n.* refusal 39.2; *adv.* no 5.24

nailed *pa. pl.* nailed 20.141; *p.p.* 19.34

nailes *n. pl.* nails (in the cross) 13.119, 20.167, fingernails 19.11

nakid *adj.* naked 2.156, 15.21, 19.5

nam(e) *n.* name 15.34, 20.195, 36.16, fame 36.19, *bi* ~ as they were called 36.76; namis *pl.* 15.58

namelich *adv.* especially 33.29

nappe *pr. 1 sg.* doze 39.49

nas(se) *see* nert

nastou *pr. 2 sg. + pron* you have not 5.75, 90; naþ *3 sg.* 13.72, 14.102, will not have 33.188; nab *pl. subj.* have not 13.239; *imp. sg.* 15.28, 151; nad *pa. 1 sg.* 33.81; nadistou *2 sg. + pron.* had you not done 33.111; nad *3 sg.* 15.71, 20.171; nad(de) *pl.* 33.106, *hi* ~ *bot* no sooner had they 20.65

naþeles *adv.* nevertheless 2.129

na(u)зte *n.* worth nothing 13.24, ~ *bot* nothing but, merely 13.27

ne *adv.* not (before v.) 4.118, 5.43, 13.23

neb *n.* face 13.223

nede *n.* need 4.118, 5.140, necessity 36.18, affliction, poverty 13.186, 33.194, *to* ~ at time of need 36.33, 93, ~ *to* lack of 13.205n

nedful *adj. (as n.)* needy person 13.72

nedi *adj.* in want 15.176

nedis *adv.* in ~ *most* of necessity 20.78, 22.2

neзbor *n.* neighbour, fellow human being 13.38, neiзbore 21.65

nego (Lat.) I deny 44.2n, 4, 6

neiз *adv.* nearly 19.20*

neisse *adj.* weak 36.93

neldis *n. gen.* needle's 13.90; neldes *pl.* 4.69

nelle *pr. 1 sg.* will not 15.52; nelt *2 sg.* 19.41, *but þou* ~ unless you will 13.63; neltov *2 sg. + pron.* will you not 5.64, 13.137; nel(le) *3 sg.* will not (fut.) 21.7, 13.59, 15.111, nul 39.3; *pl.* 13.74, 21.7, nol 20.145 (or *pa.*); nold *pa. 3 sg.* did not wish 20.130; *sg. subj.* would not (expressing condit. fut.) 14.20, 15.113; *pl.* 13.114 [*see* wol]

nemeni *v.* name 15.57

nert *pr. 2 sg.* are not 22.31; nis *3 sg.* is

not 2.3, 4.77, 5.121, ~ *bot* is merely 13.57, 70; nere *pr. 3 sg. subj.* might not be 15.113; nas *pa. 3 sg.* was not 15.67, 19.10, 20.14; nasse in *no harm* ~ there was no harm in it 33.68; ner *pa. pl. subj.* were not 14.29n [*see* be]

nese *pr. 1 sg.* sneeze 39.49

nest *n.* nest, resting place 5.67, den, lair 36.59

neuer *adv.* never 2.81, 5.95, 14.144, *ne be þou/he* ~ *so riche* however rich you are/he is 15.19, 155; ~ *a* not a single 15.93

neuermore *adv.* never again 2.187

niзte *n.* night 2.26, 5.79, 13.76; niзt(e) *(adv.)* ~ *and dai* day and night 33.2, 151; niзt *pl.* (after num.) 20.25, 48.42

niзtingale *n.* nightingale 2.96

nifle *pr. 1 sg.* snivel 39.49

nykkest *pr. 3 sg.* in ~ *þer no nai* it cannot be refused 39.2

nim *v.* ~ *hir* take to itself 48.2; nimiþ *imp. pl.* in ~ *gome* pay attention 15.51; nem *pa. 3 sg.* 20.159; nom *pl.* took 20.125; ynom *p.p.* taken, captured 20.116, 33.38

nine *num.* 20.76*

ninþe *adj.* ninth 14.129*

nis *see* nert; nist *see* not(e)

no *adj.* no 2.13, 111, 4.96; non (before vowel or h) 2.34, 21.66

no *conj.* nor 2.1, 5.89, 14.52, ~ . . . *no* neither , . . nor 21.72

noble *adj.* noble 36.25, excellent 4.12, 113

noзt *adv.* not 2.62, 5.5, 13.191, *riзt* ~ not at all 14.80

noзt(e) *n.* evil 43.4, nothing 13.52, 181 19.23, nowзte 4.72, *riзt* ~ absolutely nothing 13.79, 160, *for* ~ without success 43.3

nol(d) *see* nelle; nom *see* nim; non *see* no

none *n.* midday meal 2.20

non(e) *pron.* none, not any 13.45, 72, no-one 13.107, 15.69, 20.84; nond 36.35n

nonnes *see* nunnes

norþ *n.* north 33.139; *adv.* 22.33

nosse *n.* nose 13.17

not(e) *pr. 1 sg.* do not know 4.24, 13.169, 33.113; nost *2 sg.* 22.12, 24; nist *pa. 3 sg.* 20.131

noþer *adv. and conj.* nor 2.27, 35, ~ . . .
no neither . . . nor 5.75

noþing *n.* nothing 2.47

noþing *adv.* in no way 5.70

nouþe, nowþe *see* nuþe

now, nou, nov *adv.* now 4.116, 5.61,
33.125

now3te *see* no3t(e)

nuche *pr. 1 sg.* tremble? 39.49n

nul *see* nelle

nunnerie *adj.* nunnery 2.148

nunnes *n. pl.* nuns 2.152, 161, 165,
nonnes 4.49

nuþe adv. now 14.3, 15.164, nouþe
13.65, 181, nowþe 5.3

O

o *interj.* oh! 13.131

o *see* on

obligo (Lat.) I bind, place under an
obligation 44.20n

oc *see* ac

odur *n.* scent 2.76

of *prep.* of 2.4, 4.65, 20.150, with 4.44,
13.117, 19.12, made of 2.114, 4.92,
13.11, consisting of 4.18, some of
15.123, 20.61, from 2.135, 4.11, 13.21,
concerning 2.175, with regard to 4.107,
in the way of 20.13, 33.4, by 4.119,
5.7, about 20.173

ofte *adv.* often 4.51, 13.13

oile *n.* oil 2.46

ok *see* ac

old *adj.* old 39.8, 15.157; *as n.* old people
2.63, 14.8, 15.32

on *num and adj.* one, a single 2.162,
4.112, 21.46, one person 36.13, the
same 48.6, o 15.52, 20.46, 36.72; on
pron. in þat ~ one of them 33.63, at ~
reconciled 48.75

on *adv.* on you 15.83

on *prep.* on 2.22, 5.12, 39.31, in 13.173, o
5.27

ond(e) *n.* envy 15.163, malice 33.11, 15,
144, 150

one *adj.* alone 15.29

onix *n.* onyx (gemstone) 2.92

op *see* vp; opon *see* apan

opunlich *adv.* openly 21.53

ordres *n. pl.* tonsures 36.100n

ore *n.* in þin ~ have mercy! 5.20, 13.141

oreisun *n.* prayer (fig.) 2.165

oris *n. pl.* oars 2.154

oþer *pron.* anything other 13.107n, the
other 39.65, other substance 13.34,
oþir one another 14.50, þat ~ the
second 14.35, 15.101 the others 14.131,
in ~ mo others as well 20.186; oþeris
gen. belonging to another 13.180

oþer *adj.* other 2.36, 4.57, 13.64

oþer *conj.* or 5.71, 19.16, 21.14, oþir
13.26

oþis *n. pl.* oaths 21.6, 23

oules *n. pl.* owls 4.26

oure, ous *see* we; oute *see* vte

outegoing *vbl. n.* departure, death 5.42

ouer *adv.* in addition 36.6

ouer *prep.* over 4.8, 19.16, 20.124, above,
beyond 14.131, throughout 4.98, 111

ouercam *pa. 3 sg.* achieved victory
20.193; ouercom *p.p.* defeated 20.204

ouir *adj.* upper 4.20

ow *pr. 3 sg.* owns 33.183n [*see* a3tist]

owen *adj.* own 4.50, 15.83, 20.14, owin
13.218, 14.128, owe in þine ~ bodi
yourself 21.65

ox *n.* ox 2.32

oxist *pr. 2 sg.* ask for 33.94; askiþ *pr. 3
sg.* asks 48.25; askeþ *pr. 3 sg.* claims
48.39

P

packes *n. pl.* bundles 4.61

palfrei *n.* riding horse 14.110, 48.49n

palle *pr. 1 sg.* grow weak 39.43n

paradis *n.* paradise 20.43, 47, 69, 22.30

pardo(u)n *n.* pardon 36.131, to ~ as
pardon 13.240

park *n.* hunting park 13.23

passe *pr. 1 sg.* grow older 39.43n

pasteiis *n. pl.* pies 2.54

Pater Noster *n.* Our Father (prayer)
15.41, 33.186

patriarkes *n. pl.* Old Testament
patriarchs 20.186

pe(e)s *n.* peace 15.43, 33.146, pardon
33.92, 94

penance *n.* penance 2.178, 186, 5.120

peni *n.* a penny 4.10, 5.44; peniis *pl.*
pence 20.115

pere *n.* equal 2.22, 36.35

peruink *n.* flower 36.42n, 43

piement *n.* spiced wine 2.85

pilers *n. pl.* pillars 2.67

pilgrim *n.* pilgrim 22.25, 31

pilkoc *n.* penis 39.31

pillori *n.* pillory 4.94

pilt *n.* attack, buffet 33.104

pilt *v.* assert 33.17n, 18, ~ *hir to* assert herself 20.58n; **piltist** *pr. 2 sg.* place 21.24; **pilt** *pa. pl.* accused 33.86; *p.p.* placed (on cross) 20.112, **ipilt(e)** placed (on a charge) 33.60n, thrust 20.16, ~ *of* driven out from 15.72

pincheþ *pr. pl.* scrimp 4.93n

pine *n.* misery 14.68, 166, suffering 20.13, 108, torment 13.104, 105, 110, agony (of hell) 20.32, torture 33.130, struggle 13.178, 33.162, **pinne** suffering 13.80; **pinis** *n. pl.* torments 5.149, sufferings 19.33

pining *n.* in *in* ~ to those suffering 5.49

pinnes *n. pl.* tile-pegs 2.59

pirtle *pr. 1 sg.* babble? 39.39n

pisseþ *pr. 3 sg.* pisses 39.31

pit(te) *n.* pit 5.93, pit (of hell) 20.24, 191

place *n.* place, church 15.48, 36.122n, *in* ~ there 36.26, *vte of* ~ be gone! 44.9, **plas** position 14.128, spot 20.160

plai *n.* play, pleasure 5.19, 36.66n

plai *v.* have fun 2.122, **plei** 2.156

plente *n.* plentiful amount, abundance 2.105, 150

podinges *n. pl.* sausages 2.60n

pofte *pr. 1 sg.* pant? 39.39n

poke *pr. 1 sg.* stoop 39.43n

pomple *pr. 1 sg.* (meaning unknown) 39.43n

potels *n. pl.* vessels holding half a gallon 4.98

pottes *n. pl.* pots 4.104

poucok *n.* peacock 4.27

poute *pr. 1 sg.* puff? 39.39n

pouer *n.* poor people 4.64, 14.105, 15.32, **pouir** 33.194, **pore** 22.20, 48.6

pouer *adj.* poor, without possessions 5.41, 22.20, 44.6, humble, simple 5.67, 74

pouerte *n.* poverty 13.166, 33.162

praer *n.* meadow 2.71

prassiune *n.* prasine (green gem) 2.91n

prech(e) *v.* preach 20.209, 21.26; *pr. pl. subj.* 13.109; **prechid** *pa. sg.* 14.12; *pl.* 20.195

prechur *n.* preacher, Dominican 4.39

preciuse *adj.* precious 2.88

predicacioune *n.* sermon 15.9

prei *n.* prey 2.163, stolen property 33.40

prest *n.* priest 5.118; **prestis** *pl.* 4.55

prey *pr. 2 pl. subj.* in ~ *we* let us pray 2.188; **preid** *pa. 3 pl.* 36.82

pride *see* **prude**

prier *n.* prayer 14.2

prince *n.* prince 5.17; **princez** *pl.* princes 2.60

prise *n.* honour 36.24

prisund *n.* prison 33.131

processione *n.* procession (of monks) 2.146

profecie *n.* prophecy 14.12, **propheci** 20.88

profetis *n. pl.* prophets 20.188, 195; **prophetis** 20.85, 91

prude *n.* pride 13.146, 15.61, 33.15, *whate* ~ what splendid thing 13.41, **pride** 13.52, 20.17, regard 13.23 [*see* **hold(e)**]

prute *adj.* proud 13.25, 28, 40, 33.165

pudrid *p.p.* garnished 2.110, **ipudrid** spattered 13.31

pulle *v.* rob 36.12; **pullid** *pa. 3 sg.* 36.13

pundes *n. pl.* pounds (money) 4.63

put *pr. 3 sg.* in ~ *in writte* set in writing 4.66

Q

quak(e) *v.* tremble 13.135, 14.75, 36.62

quartes *n. pl.* vessels holding a quarter of a gallon 4.98

quede *adj.* wicked 21.61

quelle *v.* kill 36.70

quelme *n.* affliction, misery 21.18

queme *v.* please 15.100; **quemiþ** *pr. pl.* 15.165

quench *v.* quench 2.12, **qwench** extinguish, destroy 5.66

quene *n.* queen 48.49

qwest *n.* search 5.69n, **quest** 36.58n

R

radde *see* **rede** *v.*

rai *n.*[1] striped cloth 5.89

rai *n.*[2] king 5.17*

rake *v.* in ~ *fram* leave, depart from 5.119; *pr. 1 sg.* wander 39.45n

randun *n.* in *in o* ~ one after another 2.132n

raþe *adv.* early 4.44; **raþer** *comp.* previously 2.120, sooner 20.53

receiuid *pa. 3 sg.* wecomed 36.116

reche *see* **rich(e)**

rechles *adj.* reckless 3.3

recning *n.* statement of accounts 13.96

red(e) *n.* advice 13.61, counsel 20.48, fate 13.131n, decree 15.97

rede *n.* red cloth 5.89

rede *adj.* red 2.70, 4.3, 14.70

red(e) *v.* read 13.194, 14.14, read Mass 36.122n, advise 20.119; *pr. 1 sg.* 5.34, 21.5, 33.189; *imp. sg.* in ~ vs rede offer us guidance 14.27n; **radde** *pa. 3 sg.* 5.127

redeles *adj.* without judgement 3.2

refusid *pa. 3 sg.* denied admission 36.125

rein *n.* rain 2.41

reinbow *n.* rainbow 14.170

ren *v.* in ~ *of* flow with 13.117; *imp. pl.* run 5.27

rent *n.* output 2.86n

res *n.* short time 33.96, *a litel* ~ a short time 33.148

rest *n.* rest, repose 5.62, 15.119, peace 21.80, *to* ~ at rest 2.174, *hab* ~ be at peace 36.47, 56

resun *n.* (capacity of) reason 20.37, reason, motive 20.59

reue *v.* take away from 21.8; **reuid** *p.p.* taken away 44.24

reuenes *n. pl.* ravens 4.26

rew *v.* grieve for 5.16, regret 13.152

rewe *n.* in *on* ~ one after another 39.29

rewful *adj.* sorrowful 5.45

rewþ *n.* a pitiful thing 15.162

rich(e) *n.* rich people 14.105, 21.74, 22.20 (1), **reche** 15.32

rich(e) *adj.* wealthy 5.21, 15.114, 22.20 (2), mighty 15.54, valuable 4.63, luxurious 2.55, 60

ride *v.* ride 36.27; **rode** *pa. 3 sg.* 36.52

rigge *n.* back 33.84

riʒt *n.* justice 33.21, 48.41, lawful entitlement 2.171, *þe* ~ what is right 33.134, *wiþ* ~ virtuously 2.62, *wiþ al* ~ in strict justice 20.39

riʒt *v.* in ~ *me* arise 20.202n

riʒt(e) *adj.* proper, correct 2.86, true, 4.93, just 5.77, rightful 15.87

riʒt(e) *adv.* exactly 36.106, ~ *as* just as, 13.165, 33.161, ~ *no(w)ʒt* not at all 4.72, 33.180

rime *n.* rhyme 4.23

rind *n.* bark 2.76

ris *n.* branch 2.8

rise *v.* rise up (of wind) 14.169; *imp. sg.* get up 5.111; **ros(e)** *pa. 3 sg.* rose 20.180, 197

riue *adv.* abundantly 33.5

riuedlich *adv.* far and wide 20.206

riuele *pr. 1 sg.* shrivel 39.45

riuer *n.* river 2.149, 153; **riuers** *pl.* 2.45

ro *n.* peace 5.62

robbi *v.* rob 33.27; **robbiþ** *pr. pl.* in ~ *of* steal (something) from 4.34

rode *n.* cross 5.127, 13.119, 19.1, **rode-tre** 5.2, 19.28

rode *see* **ride**

rof *n.* roof 48.17

roilend *pr. p.* roaming 4.33

ropis *n. pl.* ropes 4.32

ros(e) *see* **rise**

rosis *n. pl.* roses 2.79

rote *n.* root 2.73, 5.56, 14.98; **rotis** *pl.* 14.94

rote *v.* in *adun to* ~ to cut off at the root 5.58

route *n.* company 4.28, 76n, company of nuns 2.135, **rute** retinue 36.113

route *v.* surge 13.122n

rouwe *pr. 1 sg.* cough, splutter 39.45n

rowʒ *adj.* roughly made 33.176

roxle *pr. 1 sg.* grow feeble? 39.45n

russin *n.* snack 2.20n

rute *see* **route** *n.*

S

sadde *adj.* slow 5.120n

sadde *see* **schaddist**

saf *adj.* safe 33.65

saf *prep. see* **saue**

sage *n.* sage (herb) 33.114

sake *n.* sake 36.128

sakke *n.* bag 13.30

sal *pr. 1 sg.* shall 13.193, 43.9; **ssal** 33.159; **schalt** *pr. 2 sg.* 5.114, **salt** 5.72, 13.60, 14.62, **ssalt** 5.43, **saltou** (with pron.) 13.41, **schaltou** 48.74; **schal** *3 sg.* shall (auxil. forming future) 2.169, 182, 5.33, 69, **sal** will (fut.) 5.50, 66, 13.163, will be 13.177, **ssal** 5.42, 67, 79, 14.6, **salle** 14.90, **sel** 14.117, **schel** 15.140, shall (go) 15.134; **sul** *pl.* (future) 5.39, 78n, 13.83, **ssul** 21.34, **sulle** 5.25, 13.64, 97, **schul** 13.29, **schulliþ** 13.12, **schullen** 48.18, sal 14.131, 134; sold *pa. 1 sg.* should 13.164, 14.71; **schold** *3 sg.* ought to do 15.128, should 20.50, 36.107, **ssold** 20.132; **schold** *pl.* ought to 5.16, **sold** 14.139, 20.86, 36.107, **ssold** 20.210, 21.15

saluacioune *n.* salvation 15.12

sang *n.* song, poem 5.141, 36.127, **song** 4.119

saphir *n.* sapphire 2.89

sarmun *n.* sermon 13.238

saue *prep.* apart from 20.46, 36.121; *conj.* on the contrary 44.5n

saui *v.* save 14.4; **sauiþ** *pr. 3 sg.* relieves 44.8; **sauid** *p.p.* redeemed 20.86, 21.32

say *n.* test 20.89

scape *v.* get away 36.84n; **scapid** *pa. 3 sg.* escaped 20.84; *pl.* 20.187

schaddist *pa. 2 sg.* shed 21.2; **sadde** *3 sg.* 13.124

schade *n.* shadow 13.153

schal(t), schaltou *see* **sal**

schame *n.* disgrace 4.40; in ~ *hab* shame upon 4.99

schame *v.* shame 15.8

schamil *n.* butcher's stall 4.87

scharpe *adj.* sharp 4.67

scharpiþ *pr. pl.* become pointed 39.13n

schef *n.* creature 22.8n

schel *see* **sal**

scheld *n.* shield 36.28

schend *pr. 3 sg. subj.* destroy 48.76; **ischend** *p.p.* destroyed 14.144, disgraced 33.33, **ischent** ruined 5.35

schene *adj.* bright 48.51

schenlon *n.* person 39.32n

schennen *n. pl.* shins 39.36

schepe *n.* sheep 2.33; **schepen** *pl. gen.* 4.105

schild *imp. sg.* shield, protect 5.4, 145, **sild** 5.150

schindes *n. pl.* humiliations (*MED shende*) 4.110

schingles *n. pl.* roof-tiles 2.57n

schiniþ *pr. 3 sg.* shines 14.61, 19.17

schite *v.* shit 4.81

schold *see* **sal**

scholder *n.* shoulder 4.2; **schuldres** *pl.* 13.21, **schuldren** 39.13

schond *n.* shame 15.83

schonde *v.* dishonour 15.8

schone *n. pl.* shoes 4.51, 15.92, 39.31

schorte *adj.* short 5.54

schoure *n.* assault 5.149

schow *v.* describe 20.11, reveal 33.23, **ssow** show 21.29; **schowid** *pa. sg.* bestowed on 19.42

schrute *n.* clothing 15.80, **schrud** 48.51

schul, schullen, schulliþ *see* **sal**; **schuldres, schuldren** *see* **scholder**

sculk *v.* in ~ *awai* steal away 36.63n

sculle *n.* skull 4.110

scurge *n.* scourge, whip 4.46n; **scurges** *pl.* 20.122

sech *see* **such**

secunde *adj.* second 21.49

sedwale *n.* setwall (spice) 2.74

see *n.* sea 2.1, 14.52, 33.28

se(e) *v.* see 2.72, 4.48, 5.25, observe 36.57, look at 33.169; **seiist** *pr. 2 sg.* see 5.82, **sest** 14.37, **seest** 14.41; **seeþ** *3 sg.* 2.127; *pl.* 2.159, 20.26, 33.3; **seo** *imp. sg.* look! 39.64; **sei** *pa. 3 sg.* saw 20.170, 36.115, **seei** 36.113; **sene** *p.p.* visible 20.124

sefþe *adj.* seventh 14.97, 21.69*

sei, sei(i)þ, sei(i)d *see* **sigge**

seint *n.* saint 14.145

selcuþ *adj.* various 4.74

seld *adv.* seldom 33.175

seli *adj.* innocent 33.57, 65

sembli *adj.* beautiful 2.66

semes *n. pl.* seams 4.70

semiþ *pr. pl.* appear 4.70

sendale *n.* fine fabric 13.45

sent *pr. 3 sg.* sends 21.55; **send** *pa. 3 sg.* 13.68, 20.85, 33.63; **isend** *p.p.* 13.104, **isent** 5.31, **sent** 39.53

sentence *n.* statement 4.36

seo *see* **se(e)**

seraphin *n.* seraphim 14.151

serpent *n.* snake 2.31, 20.51

sertis *adv.* certainly, indeed 33.113

serue *v.* serve 21.51; **seruiþ** *pr. 3 sg.* serves, is good 2.47

set(te) *v.* put on 2.168; place 44.2, 13; *imp. sg.* place 44.21; **iset(te)** *p.p.* composed 4.29, fixed 22.12, 36.89, ~ *wiþ* immersed in 39.21

seue *num.* seven 2.179, 20.25, 5.54, **seuene** 15.55

shores *n. pl.* shears, scissors 4.67

sibbe *n.* kin, family 33.141

sibbe *adj.* in *frendis* ~ supportive relatives 15.172

sich *n.* grief 22.3n

side *n.* side of body 13.21, 116, 19.5,
   direction 13.215
siȝt(e) *n.* sight, view 13.43, 103, 207,
   eyesight 19.7, appearance 2.6, 66, 5.77,
   thing to see 2.25; in *to* ~ for looking at
   2.48
sigge *v.* say 14.67; *pr. 1 sg.* 2.21, 13.168,
   tell 33.105, 36.20; seiiþ *3 sg.* says 13.9,
   15.49, 33.181, seiþ 13.13, 135; sei *imp.
   sg.* 13.137, tell 33.109; seid *pa. 3 sg.*
   said 20.61, 202; *pl.* 20.133, 36.70, seiid
   33.72; iseiid *p.p.* 2.117, iseid spoken
   4.41, yseid in ~ *of* spoken by, uttered
   by 4.119
sikir *adj.* trustworthy 20.201
sikirlich *adv.* certainly 4.59, sikerlich
   4.101
sild *see* schild
silf, silue *adj.* in *þat/ þilk* ~ the same
   14.70, 96, *þis* ~ this 15.48
silk *n.* silk 2.150, 13.45
siluer *n.* silver 4.63, 15.127, 137, silver
   goods 33.41
sinful *adj.* sinful 13.120, 15.35, 20.211
sing *v.* sing 2.100, sing Mass 36.123
sinied *pa. 3 sg.* sinned 20.48; sinid *pl.*
   20.88
sin(ne) *n.* sin 5.4, 14.39, 43.4, sunne
   39.20; sinne *gen.* 5.112; sinnes *pl.*
   5.118
siouns *n. pl.* shoots 2.74n
sire *n.* (in address) sir 13.33, 33.82, lord
   14.72, (title) 36.17; sires *pl.* (in
   address) 20.55
sit(te) *v.* sit 4.112, 5.97, 14.54, ~ *ariȝte*
   be appropriate 44.12; sittist *pr. 2 sg.*
   5.68; sit *3 sg.* 14.100, 15.129; sitte *refl.*
   in *him* ~ is placed 4.78; sitteþ *pl.* sit
   4.115, sit are positioned 14.38
siþ *adv.* then, afterwards 2.143, 19.24,
   20.125; *conj.* since 13.85, 36.1, ~ *þat*
   since 13.181
siþis *n. pl.* times 13.199
siu *v.* follow 20.210; siwiþ *pr. 3 sg.* 4.28;
   siwed *pa. 3 sg.* 20.194n
sixt(e) *adj.* sixth 14.85, 21.68
skap *v.* escape (punishment) 33.133
skeis *n. pl.* skies 14.134
sker *v.* exonerate, in ~ *me* clear myself
   33.103
skil(le) *n.* understanding, judgement
   20.37, explanation 20.59
skin *n.* skin 48.18

skinners *n. pl.* skinners, furriers 4.79
skriche *v.* scream 5.100
sle *v.* kill 13.24; slow *pa. 1 sg.* 33.99
slech *adj.* skilful 4.48, sleiȝ 4.65
sledde *n.* sledge 39.51
sleilich *adv.* secretly 2.158n, skilfully,
   cunningly 4.41, 102
slep(e) *n.* sleep 15.121, 36.61
slepiþ *pr. 3 sg.* sleeps 2.173; slepe *pa. 3
   sg.* 4.72
slete *n.* sleet 2.39
sleuis *n. pl.* sleeves 2.126
slow *see* sle
smakke *n.* taste 2.77
smale *adj.* small 4.91
smaragde *n.* emerald (green gem) 2.90
smilliþ *pr. 3 sg.* sniffs 4.80
snawile *n.* snail 2.40
sneipe *pr. 1 sg.* sniff? 39.40n
snel *adv.* quickly 20.152
snellich *adv.* quickly 2.163
snobbe *pr. 1 sg.* sob 39.40
snovte *n.* snout, nose 39.40
snowe *n.* snow 20.26
snurpe *pr. 1 sg.* sneeze? 39.40n
so *adv.* just so 5.42, to such a degree
   4.54, 95, so (intensifying) 5.7, 13.8,
   15.109, in that way 2.24, 5. 119,
   20.146, in this way 21.41, 22.6, 33.195,
   thus 2.188, 13.13, (*quasi-prep.*) like
   5.12, 15, ~ *hit is* that's how it is 13.36,
   ~ *is þis* is like this 21.49
so *conj.* to the extent which 15.115, in the
   manner in which 15.152
soch *see* such
socure *n.* comfort 5.142
soȝt *p.p.* pierced 20.147n; isoȝt searched
   36.130
sok(e) *pa. 3 sg.* sucked 13.234, 21.78
solas *n.* joy 2.50, delight 13.198, solace
   2.172
sold *pa. 3 sg.* sold 20.115; isold *p.p.*
   13.177
sold *see* sal; som *see* sum
somdel *n.* a little bit 20.106
someris *n. gen.* summer's 2.151, 5.12
sond *n.* destiny 39.53
son(e) *see* sun
sone *n.* son 4.13, 15.99, 20.111
sone *adv.* immediately 20.20, quickly
   44.15, soon 2.176, 14.112, before long
   33.147
song *see* sang

sopper *n.* supper 2.20

sore *n.* sorrow, suffering 5.16, 15.118, misery 13.76

sore *adj.* cruel 19.36

sore *adv.* bitterly 5.100, 13.115, 14.20, cruelly 19.18, 39, painfully 13.152, 21.75, hard 15.173, 20.74

sorful *adj.* miserable 5.72, 96, 116, pitiful 5.86, **sorwȝful** 5.77

sori *adj.* poor 33.159, ∼ *of* miserable about 4.107

sorow *n.* sorrow 14.59, 20.68, 22.3

soster *n.* sister 33.192

soþ *n.* the truth 13.37, 191, 33.176, *for* ∼ truly 2.21, 148, 13.151, 14.36, *al for* ∼ without any doubt 14.87, ∼ *iwisse* truly, without a doubt 13.99

sotter *n.* shoemaker 4.52; **sutters** *pl.* 73

soule *n.* soul 13.171, 15.11, 21.75, **sowle** 20.110, 33.173; **sowleis** *gen.*; 5.60; **sowles** *pl.* 13.4, 20.8, 182

spakly *adv.* quickly 39.64*

spare *v.* shun 14.52n, refrain from punishing 21.7

spatle *pr. 1 sg.* spit 39.54

spech *n.* speech 39.54, voice, words 5.128, 15.33, mention 2.111n, *hab* ∼ talk 14.154

spek *v.* speak 14.80, 15.37, 20.5, **spec** 14.134, **spekin** 15.6; **spekiþ** *3 sg.* 20.173; *imp. pl.* 4.116; **speke** *pa. 1 sg.* 13.5; **spek** *3 sg.* spoke, said 33.73, 77; **ispoke** *p.p.* 13.147

spelle *n.* story 33.47

spen(e) *v.* spend 13.68, 74, 15.111, **spened** (in rhyme) spend money 13.82; **speniþ** *pr. 3 sg.* use (time); **spen** *2 sg. subj.* use (goods) 13.62; **spent** *pa. 3 sg.* used up 39.64; *p.p.* spent (time) 5.33, **ispend** 13.101, 14.142, exhausted 39.57n

sper *n.* spear 4.1, 13.119, 20.147; **speris** *gen.* 19.4

spicis *n. pl.* spices 4.16

spille *v.* kill 33.76, 80, waste 36.96n

spitte *n.* spit (for roasting) 2.102

spitte *pr. 1 sg.* spit 39.54; **spette** *pa. pl.* 20.118

sporne *pr. 1 sg.* stumble 39.54

spouse *n. pl.* brides 4.50

sprede *v.* cover 13.121; **spradde** *pa. 3 sg.* stretched out 5.127; **sprad** *p.p.* spread 19.6

spring *v.* flow (of light) 13.223; ∼ *of* crawl out of 13.29

ssal(t) *see* sal

ssamles *adj.* withoute shame 3.5

sso *see* ȝo; **ssold** *see* sal; **ssow** *see* schow; **ssul** *see* sal

staf(fe) *n.* staff 4.19, 15.38

stak(e) *n.* staff 4.7, (post for) punishment 5.117n

stalun *n.* stallion (fig.) 2.167

state *n.* in *in* ∼ in the condition 2.120

stede *n.* warhorse 14.110, horse 36.27

steiȝ *pa. 3 sg.* increased, grew 20.17, rose 20.213

stel *imp. sg.* steal 21.68

stench *n.* stench 13.42

stere *n.* rudder 2.154

sterne *adj. as n.* fierce ones 2.64

sterris *n. pl.* stars 14.37

steuen(e) *n.* voice, sound 14.136, 166, 178

stid *n.* place 20.50, 36.48, position 14.126; **stides** *pl.* places 20.33, 36

stidfast *adj.* resolute 14.45, firm 20.39

stif *adj.* firm 36.34

stille *adj.* still, not moving 4.115

stinkiþ *pr. 3 sg.* stinks 13.32; **stinkeþ** *pl.* make smell 4.82; **stinkind** *pr. p.* 13.159

stinteþ *see* stunt

stiuiiþ *pr. pl.* grow stiff 19.6

stode *n.* horse-breeding establishment 2.35, breed 33.112

stomble *pr. 1 sg.* stumble, stagger 39.51

stomere *pr. 1 sg.* stammer 39.51

ston *n.* stone 14.91; **stonis** *pl.* gems 2.88, stones 4.63

stond *v.* stand 14.118, withstand 36.34; **stondiþ** *pr. pl.* stand 4.87; **stond** *pl. subj.* in ∼ *to* submit to 2.185n; **stode** *pa. 3 sg.* stood 20.161, 33.89

store *n.* store-room 13.74, possessions 44.6, group of people 36.109, *to* ∼ in reserve 15.116

storme *n.* storm 2.41

stoute *adj. as n.* brave ones 2.64; **stuter** *comp.* stronger 21.71n

strang *adj.* strong 13.202, harsh 19.33, severe 33.130

streinþ *n.* armed force 36.53, *wiþ* ∼ by force 48.53, *doist no* ∼ *of* are indifferent to 5.63n

stremis *n. pl.* rivers 2.87n, (blood)streams 19.12

strete *n.* street 4.82
strif *n.* contention 2.27, strife 33.3.
stu *n.* stewpot 2.109
stunde *n.* moment 21.44, *þat* ~ then
5.108; **stundis** *pl.* in *hard* ~ times of
suffering 19.35
stunt *pr. 1 sg.* stand still 39.51; **stinteþ**
pl. stop 2.99
stuter *see* **stoute**
such *adj.* such 4.108, 13.23, 36.39, **sech**
4.111, **soch** 13.3, like that 4.24, 20.174
suche *pron. pl.* such people 15.107
suffri *v.* suffer 14.32, 20.132; **suffriþ** *pr.*
3 sg. permits 33.16; **suffrid** *pa. sg.*
endured 20.13, 178; *pl.* suffered 21.59
sul(le) *see* **sal**
sum *pron.* some 4.16, some people
15.171, 177, **som** a part 33.40, some
people 36.92
sum *adj.* a certain amount of 22.9
sun *n.* sun 13.199; **son(e)** *n.* 14.61, 69
Sundai *n.* Sunday 21.50, 53
sunne *see* **sin(ne)**
sure *adj.* bitter 5.149n
susteni *v.* support 15.175
suþe *n.* south 33.139
sutters *see* **sotter**
swer *pr. 1 sg.* swear 3.6; **sweriþ** *pl.*
21.23; **swor** *pa. pl.* pledged 36.68, 85
swet(e) *adj.* dear 5.1, 14.2, 20.12, sweet
(taste) 2.149, fragrant 2.76, lovely 2.82,
13.198, delightful 2.25, precious 19.12,
20.4, glorious 20.216
swetlich *adj.* sweetly, tenderly 5.138
swifte *adj.* swift 2.123
swimme *v.* swim 2.158; **swimmeþ** *pr. 3*
sg. 4.9
swine *n.* pig 2.33; **swineis** *gen.* 2.179
swink *v.* work for 20.74; **swinkiþ** *pr. pl.*
work 15.173
swink(e) *n.* work, labour 2.18, 143, effort
2.112
swiþe *adv.* very 2.72, 4.30, 15.110, *ful* ~
extremely 2.109
swolowiþ *pr. pl.* swallow 4.88
swor *see* **swer**

T

taburs *n. pl.* little drums (fig.) 2.137
taȝt *see* **tech**
tailurs *n. pl.* tailors 4.67
tak(e) *v.* take 2.112, seize 36.101, receive

14.81n, ~ *hede to* take account of
33.34; **takeþ** *pr. 3 sg.* takes 2.135, *him*
~ takes for himself 2.162; **takiþ** *pl.*
2.152, 14.21, 33.128, **takeþ** 33.36, ~
hede of care about 33.43, ~ *gode hede*
pay close attention 13.167, 33.163;
tak(e) *imp. sg.* take 36.8, ~ *gode hede*
5.52, ~ *wrech of* exact retribution from
13.120, **takeþ** *pl.* 4.47; **tak** *subj. pl.*
4.94; **tok** *pa. 3 sg.* took 36.65, assumed
20.97; *pl.* ~ *an hond* undertook 36.68;
itake *p.p.* captured 5.113
tale *n.*[1] number, in *wiþout* ~ innumerable
2.98
tale *n.*[2] story, argument 13.211
tawiþ *pr. 3 sg.* tans 4.52
te *v.* go 5.5; *pr. 3 sg. subj.* 15.2
tech(e) *v.* teach 20.7, 21.28, 15.36;
techiþ *pr. 3 sg.* 5.124,13.13, 14.10; *pl.*
2.165; **taȝt** *pa. 3 sg.* 14.11, 36.66
ted *see* **toþ**
tel(le) *v.* tell 4.96, 14.132, 15.50, describe
13.192, 14.9, ~ *bi* say about 13.87;
telliþ *pr. 3 sg.* tells 14.133, 149,
20.198, relates 5.91; *pl.* in ~ *of* speak
about 13.112, ~ *of* regard as 33.39;
tel(le) *imp. sg.* confess 5.118, tell 33.75;
told *pa. 3 sg.* 33.70; **itold** *p.p.* 33.51,
reckoned 22.32
temple *n.* temple 20.134
ten *num.* ten 36.8, 21.31*
tendre *adj.* tender 4.51
ten(e) *n.* distress 14.32, suffering 14.115,
hardship 21.59
tere *n.* tear 5.86; **teris** *pl.* 13.140, 19.2,
20.163
teriþ *pr. 3 sg.* covers with earth 48.27n
teþ *see* **toþ**
teþe *adj.* tenth 20.30
þai *pron. 3 pl. nom.* they 2.81, 5.17,
21.48; *pron. demons. nom.* in ~ *þat*
those who 33.107; *acc.* 5.6, 13.186, in
al ~ all those 33.26; *dat.* in *of* ~ *þat* of
those who 33.127; *as. adj.?* those 2.87n
[see **hi** etc.]
þakkeþ *pr. pl.* smack 2.142
þan *adv.* then 5.79, 13.118, 14.53
þan *conj.* than 2.125, 13.34, 19.30
þar(e) *see* **þer** *adv.*
þat *pron.* that 2.139, 4.40, who 2.44, 4.36,
13.67, (the one) who 4.54, 60, he who
48.51, you who 5.68, 33.92, that which
13.48, what 14.22, 43.8; *al* ~ the whole

thing 13.111; **þan** *dat.* (after prep.) 15.180

þat *adj.* that 2.103, 5.16, 15.43 (1); *conj.* that 2.134, 4.48, 39.10, so that (with cl. of result) 2.187, with consequence that 14.113, 15.99, in that, because 36.39

þe *def. art.* the 2.19, 4.1, 13.1; **þen** *dat.* in ~ end 21.19

þe *v.* prosper 22.13, *so mot I* ~ on my life! 5.59, 107

þe *see* **þou**; **þe(i)ȝ** *see* **þoȝ**

þef *n.* thief 20.125, criminal 33.133, 36.30, 47, dishonesty 44.5n; **þeuis** *pl.* criminals 33.36, 128

þench *v.* think, reflect 13.149, 14.19, 43.3, ~ *of* think about 5.64, ~ *in* reflect on 15.136; **þenchith** *pr. 3 sg.* 15.130, **þenchit** 13.173, **þenchiþ** in ~ *vp* thinks about 33.1; **þench** *imp. sg.* reflect 13.148, 22.14, **þenk** 48.73; **þenchiþ** *pl.* think 36.31 (after *do*); **þoȝt** *pa. 3 sg.* intended 20.152, 36.100; **iþoȝt** *p.p.* imagined 43.7

þenchiþ *pr. impers.* in *me* ~ it seems to me 33.110, **þenchit** in *him* ~ seems to him 13.111; **þoȝt** *pa. impers.* 20.164, 36.114

þer *adv.* there, in that place 2.3, 33.99, 13.201, (introductory) 13.10, 20.187, **þar(e)** (in rhyme only) 12.150, 13.208, 14.50, ~ *beþ / is* there are / is 5.13, 33.4

þer *conj.* where 15.77, 36.27, 39.69

þerafter *adv.* after that 20.208, 213

þeramang *adv.* at the same time 2.129

þeran *adv.* over it 13.159, within 13.146, at it 33.178

þerbi *adv.* nearby 2.147

þerfor *adv.* therefore 13.9, 15.74, for that reason 4.112, because of that 21.10, about that 14.24

þerin *adv.* in there 4.81, 5.113, 13.216

þermidde *adv.* with that 36.84

þerof *adv.* thereof 2.61, of it 4.64, of that 14.18, 46, by that 14.147, about that 5.125

þerto *adv.* to that 33.126, 135, at it 4.80, in addition 15.40, 19.8, 44.21

þerwiþ *adv.* at the same time 39.67

þes *see* **þis**; **þi**, **þin(e)** *see* **þou**

þilk *adj.* that (same) 2.173, 14.55, 21.51, this 20.89, such 33.44

þing *n.* thing 13.28, 14.101, 36.49;

business 36.90, literary work 4.84, *no* ~ nothing 13.47, *swet* ~ dear one 20.103; **þing** *pl.* things 3.7, 14.104, possessions 5.43, **þinges** 22.15, 36.44

þinne *adj.* scarce 33.6

þis *adj.* this 4.5, 5.11, 14.6; **þes** *pl.* these 13.5, 14.86

þo *adv.* then 33.73, 77; *conj.* when 19.30, 20.17, 197

þoȝ *conj.* although (with subj.) 2.5, 4.22, 13.69, as if 13.156n, ~ *þat* even though 14.80, **þeȝ** 5.50, 109, **þeiȝ** 13.93, 109, **þouw** 48.50

þoȝt *n.* thought 14.78, mind 14.84, 20.52, 36.99, misery 43.1n, 8, intention 43.2, concern 13.77, *in* ~ in mind 13.106, *on is* ~ in his mind 13.173

þoȝt *see* **þench**, **þenchith**

þole *v.* suffer 14.44, 68; **þolid** *pa. sg.* 19.28, 20.144, 21.16, **þoliid** 5.28

þonk *n.* gratitude 19.38

þonk *v.* thank for 19.41

þonneriþ *pr. 3 sg.* thunders 4.81

þornis *n. pl.* thorns 19.3

þos *pron. pl.* those 3.7, 33.45; *adj.* 13.147, 14.119, 22.7 [*see* **þis**]

þou *pron. 2 sg. nom.* thou 4.3, 5.5, 14.5; **þe** *acc.* thee 13.60; *refl.* 21.67; **þi** *gen.* thy 4.2, 5.60, 13.38, **þin(e)** (before vowel) 5.20, 13.17, 15.83; **þine** belonging to you 13.180, (following noun) 20.15 [*see* **ȝe** etc.]

þousand *num.* thousand 36.4

þouw *see* **þoȝ**

þowmes *n. pl.* thumbs 4.99

þralle *n.* slave (to money) 13.73, (to devil) 13.75

þre *num.* three 22.15, 36.5, 48.42

þrid *adj.* third 14.57, 15.163, 20.205

þritti *num.* thirty 20.106*

þriue *v.* thrive 22.13; *pr. 1 sg.* prosper, in *so mote I* ~ on my life! 5.24

þroȝ *prep.* through, because of 2.171, 13.66, 14.2, as a result of 33.144

þroȝute *adv.* through and through 13.139

þrostil *n.* thrush, blackbird 2.96n

þrouȝ *n.* grave 48.42

þrow *n.* instant 15.17

þruisse *n.* thrush 2.96

þurst *n.* thirst 2.12

þus *adv.* thus 5.127, 14.149, as follows 14.129, in this way 39.27, **þusse** 14.33

time *n.* 14.65, 142, occasion 36.101, time on earth 13.100

tiþing *n.* piece of information 5.45

to *n.* toe 19.13

to *adv.* too 4.22, 13.141, 15.107, as well 33.18

to *prep.* (introd. infin.) to 2.122, 5.18, to (place) 2.138, (following noun) 2.177, for 2.130, towards 5.27, for (value) 4.10, as far as 13.19

toberst *v.* crash 14.95

todai *n.* 15.3, 36, 38

todraw *imp. pl.* pull apart 33.121

tofor *prep.* before, in front of 33.55

todriue *v.* dash about 14.122

tofal(le) *v.* tumble 14.92, 139

togadir *adv.* together 20.98

toggiþ *pr. 3 sg.* tugs 39.28

tok *see* tak(e)

tokin *n.* sign 14.129, 148

tokning *n.* sign 14.33, 73; tokingis *pl.* 14.9, tokninges 14.21

told *see* tel(le)

topasiune *n.* topaz 2.92

toþ *n.* tooth 39.65; teþ *pl.* 4.76, ted 39.28

touȝ *adj.* tough, chewy 33.182*

toune(s) *see* tun(e)

toure *n.* tower (of heaven) 5.143n, ture castle tower 14.89, 109; toures *pl.* 48.65

toute *n.* bum 2.136, 142

toward *prep.* towards 48.4, 14, towar in the direction of 14.77

trai *v.* plot against 36.69n; traiid *pa. 3 sg.* deceived 20.83

trauail *n.* toil 20.70, hard work 36.102

tre *n.* tree 2.71, 5.53, 14.93, cross 19.26; trenne *pl.* trees 5.29, tren 14.101

treisuses *n. pl.* cobblers' tools 4.75n

trenchur *n.* plate 33.176

trent *p.p.* torn 39.65n

trepas *n.* transgression 20.79, criminal act 33.44, trespas 33.56

trepasid *pa. 3 sg.* committed crime 33.58

tresure *n.* treasure 15.146

trew *adj.* true 33.6, 44.14

trewlich *adv.* truly 13.58

trewþ(e) *n.* justice 33.14, honesty 33.141, truth 44.1, 24

triacle *n.* medicinal salve 2.84

trie *adj.* excellent 2.19, 75, 4.23

Trinite *n.* Trinity 5.9, 13.2, 20.64, feast of the Trinity 36.106n

tripis *n. pl.* tripe 4.105

trist *pr. 3 sg.* in ~ *to* trusts in 15.147, trusteþ 39.26; trist *imp. sg.* 33.192, ~ *to* 22.22; tristou *imp. 2 sg.* + *pron.* 22.19

triste *n.* trust 33.189, ~ *to* confidence in 15.28, 151

trobles *n. pl.* cobblers' implements 4.75n

tromcheri *n.* liver, offal 4.106n

tronn *n.* scales 4.110n

tuenti *num.* twenty 4.27, 36.9*

tuentiþ *adj.* twentieth 36.10*

tun(e) *n.* town 4.89, 33.69, 79, toune habitation 2.38; *pl.* tunis towns 4.38, tounes 4.98

tung(e) *n.* tongue 4.96, 13.192, 20.22

ture *see* tour(e)

turn(e) *v.* turn (of wheel) 22.24, change 5.79, bend 20.57, ~ *aȝe* return 2.187, ~ *to* become 13.52; turniþ *pr. 3 sg.* turns 2.136, 22.22, changes 2.119, turneþ 22.21; *pl.* change 2.115; turne *imp. sg.* turn 19.15; iturned *p.p.* shaped (by rotating) 2.68

twelfte *adj.* twelfth 14.177*

twelue *num.* twelve 2.170*

twies *adv.* twice 36.8

two *num.* two 2.13, 14.152, 20.168

U

uch(e) *see* euch(e)

vnbeȝet *p.p.* not begotten, unborn 14.31

vncuþ *adj.* alien 22.6n, 31

vnder *prep.* under 2.3, 5.138, 33.170

vnderfong *v.* receive 13.150, underfang 19.22; vnderfo *p.p.* seized 33.42

vnderstond(e) *v.* understand 15.7, 133; *imp. sg.* 15.89; vnderstode *pa. 3 sg.* 4.36, 114; *pl.* 4.53

vndo *imp. sg.* unlock (fig.) 13.144, 145

vnfre *adj.* evil 5.57

vnhodid *adj.* unordained 36.126n

vniune *n.* pearl 2.89n

vnkundlich *adv.* unnaturally 14.104

vnliche *adv.* unevenly 15.169

vnriȝte *n.* injustice 33.19

vnseli *adj.* miserable 13.157

vnwinne *n.* unhappiness 43.6

vp *adv.* upwards 2.136, up 2.166, uppe upright 19.15

vp *prep.* upon 2.149, 4.2, 19.28, on 33.97,
op upon 21.46
uppon *see* apan
upri3t *adv.* upright 14.118
vprising *n.* Resurrection 20.11, 200
ur(e), vs(e) *see* we
vssid *pa. 3 sg.* practiced, carried out
36.45
vte *adv.* out 20.19, 33.32, 36.53, away
33.167, out(e) 13.162, 171
vteflemid *p.p.* banished 20.71
utepilt *p.p.* thrust out 20.69

V

uadir *see* fader
vale *n.* vale 20.73
vanite *n.* illusion 13.182; wanite 13.56
ve *interj.* alas! 21.45n
velle *see* felle
uerisse *adj.* fresh 14.127
verrid *pr. 3 sg.* uses 48.26n
uers *n.* verse 4.5, 11, 17
verþ *see* ferþ, verþing *see* ferþing
uertu *n.* power 13.2
verum falsum (Lat.) true-false 44.21n
vile *adj.* vile 2.40, hideous 13.20, file
13.16, uil worthless 33.114; uilir *comp.*
fouler 13.172, 33.168
vo *see* fo
vode *n.* food (fig.) 13.229
uois *n.* voice 14.138, *at one* ~ in accord
20.138
uorbisen *n.* parable 33.45
vouchesaue *pr. 1 sg.* consent 33.87
uoxe *see* fox

W

wade *v.* wade 2.180
wai *see* wei
waiissing *n.* washing 2.48
wailowai *interj.* alas! 5.87, wailawai
14.67, weilawai 5.13
wak *v.* wake 36.61; wake *imp. sg.* 5.111;
woke *pa. 3 sg.* stayed awake 4.72
walle *n.* wall 14.118; walles *pl.* 2.54
wan *adj.* dim 14.43, 63, pale 19.16
wan *see* win(ne), whan
wandrest *pr. 2 sg.* roam about 22.26
wanite *see* vanite
ware *adj.* in *be* ~ be on guard 13.43,
105, make sure 21.5, be aware 21.21
war(for) *see* whar(for)

warne *pr. 1 sg.* warn 13.177
was, wasse *see* be
wast *n.* in *in* ~ wastefully 15.111
wast *v.* dissipate 13.176, 179
wat(e) *see* whate
watir *n.* water 2.12, 13.121, 20.42, mass
of water 14.127n; watris *pl.* 14.119
watir-daissers *n. pl.* holy-water
sprinklers? 4.33n
we *pron. 1 pl.* we 2.189, 5.16, 13.7; us
acc. & dat. us 4.16, 5.9, 13.16, vs 5.3,
13.13, vse 15.44, ous 13.3; ur(e) *gen.*
our 4.8, 13.4, 14.167, vre 13.44, oure
13.221, 224 [see ich etc.]
wedde *n.* in *to* ~ as a surety 36.65
wede *n.* clothing 5.74, 13.49, 15.87, piece
of clothing 33.159; weden *pl.* clothes
48.13
weep *see* wep(e)
weepin *n.* weapon 36.32
wei *n.* journey 48.50, wai 5.83
weilawai *see* wailowai
wel *n.* corpse 20.152n
wel *adj.* in ~ *is him* he is fortunate 2.44
weld *v.* possess 43.7
wel(le) *n.* prosperity 2.4, well-being
21.60, happiness 22.21, 15.16, 39.4,
goods 15.108, *worldis* ~ worldly goods
13.53
wel(le) *adv.* well 2.109, 4.14 (1), very
2.51, 13.16, 33.5, greatly 13.7, much
4.72, entirely 13.139, satisfactorily
13.190, properly 33.52, skilfully 4.17,
29, 95, fully 13.202, indeed 4.14 (2), *as*
~ also 36.15, *ful* ~ very well 4.5
wench *n.* girl 2.141
wend *v.* go 15.132, 20.78, 21.26, turn
48.30, ~ *of* leave 2.184, ~ *into* change
into 13.12; went *pr. 3 sg.* goes 15.152,
wend moves 39.67n; wendiþ *pl.* go
2.144, ~ *bifor* depart from 48.41n;
wend *imp. sg.* go 5.83, turn 19.21; *pa.
3 sg.* came 20.87, went 20.153, 36.126;
wend *p.p.* gone 5.39, iwent 39.56
iwend turned 44.1, *was* ~ came 20.96
wene *v.* believe 14.123; wen(e) *pr. 1 sg.*
think, believe 4.21, 33.12, 39.25;
wenist *2 sg.* expect to 5.65; weniþ *3
sg.* intends 15.135, 138, expects 15.139;
weniþ *pl.* think, suppose 5.17, wene
realize 48.50; wend *pa. 3 sg.* thought
33.65, 68; wend(e) *pl.* imagined 5.23,
36.55

wep(e) *v.* weep 13.140, 20.171, 22.2;
wepistou *pr. 2 sg. + pron.* are you
weeping 22.1; weep *imp. sg.* 19.2; wep
pa. 3 sg. 20.165

weping *n.* weeping 14.59

wer(e) *see* be

were *n.* doubt 2.21, apprehension 13.239

werist *pr. 2 sg.* wear 15.83; weriþ *3 sg.*
48.51

werk *n.* composition 4.60, 102; workis *pl.*
works 21.3, actions 13.3

werne *pr. 1 sg.* waste away 39.55

werrure *n.* warrior 36.25

west *n.* west 5.69, 33.139, *bi* ∼ to the
west of 2.1n

wet *pr. 3 sg.* is wet, drips 39.11

wexit *pr. 3 sg.* grows, becomes 39.35;
waxiþ *pr. pl.* 39.38

whan *conj.* when 2.113, 4.58, 5.129, given
that 33.87, ∼ *þat* when 20.175, wan
14.86, 135, 19.34

whannin *adv.* from where? 15.80

whar(e) *adv. and conj.* (in a place) where
2.16, where 2.150, 19.1, where (is he)?
13.38, wherever 20.58, in whatever
place that 36.123, war where 4.32

wharfor *adv.* on account of which 15.56,
72, warfor 20.130

wharmid *prep.* with which 15.158

wharof *adv.* made of what? 13.33, about
what 13.51, 169; *conj.* of which 15.24,
from where 48.73, of what 33.165

what *adj.* whatever 36.101

what *adv.* (introducing question) in ∼
weniþ þai do they really suppose? 5.17,
why 36.94n

whate *pron.* what 2.7, 5.48,13.41, ∼ *euir*
whoever 33.26, *mid* ∼ with which
15.81, wat(e) 5.52, 14.81, 14.132

what(e) *conj.* in ∼ *and* both . . . and
33.144; ∼ . . . ∼ whether . . . whether
33.28

whele *n.* wheel 22.23

whi *adv.* why 5.22, 13.28, 20.53, wy 39.8

while *n.* time 4.70, *bot a* ∼ more than a
short time 13.59, *þe* ∼ while 15.27

whil(e) *conj.* while 5.76, 13.61, 22.4,
wil(e) as long as 14.76, 164

white *n.* white flour 4.93

white *adj.* white 2.136, 142, 4.31, ∼
monkes Cistercians 2.52n

who *pron.* whoever 5.123, 36.32, anyone

who 20.173, wo who 13.212, ho
48.16*n; whom *dat.* 15.20

whoch *see* woch

whoder *adv.* whither 14.48, 15.134,
48.74, which way 22.24, whichever way
22.33

whos(e), whoso *pron.* anyone who 5.46,
4.80, whoever, if anyone 15.15, 44.11,
21.32, the one who 2.177; whose-euer
whoever 21.17

wy *see* whi

wichcraft *n.* witchcraft 21.47

wide *adj.* wide 13.213

wid(e) *adv.* widely 19.6, 36.129, 33.142

wid(e)whar(e) *adv.* far and wide 36.130,
wel ∼ far and wide 13.176, 36.51

wif *n.* wife 4.108, 13.219, 21.72, wiue
woman 15.30; wiues *pl.* 2.170

wiȝte *n.* person 5.72, creature 15.66

wikidnis *n.* wickedness 22.25, wikidnes
22.30

wik(k)id *adj.* wicked 20.145, 33.71,
wretched 13.49, 163

wil *adj.* pleasant 39.58n

wil *see* wol; wil(e) *see* whil(e)

wild *n.* wildness 22.12

wild *adj.* wild 4.27, 21.14

wildirnis *n.* wild places 4.38, wildernis
wild country 36.56

wil(le) *n.* will 13.187, 20.12, authority
20.63, desire 20.178, 39.17, *þi* ∼ if you
please 33.78

wille *n.* well 5.116; willis *pl.* springs 2.83

willing *n.* desire 39.62

wilniþ *pr. pl.* wish 39.8

wind(e) *n.* wind 2.41, 13.125; windis *pl.*
14.169

wine *n.* wine 2.46, 4.44, wyn 5.98

winges *n. pl.* wings 4.2

winne *n.* joy 33.4, happiness 43.7

win(ne) *v.* earn, gain 13.78,15.174, 20.70,
reach 2.182, succeed 36.32, attain 5.10;
wonne *pa. 2 sg.* gained 48.30; *3 sg.*
13.178, 20.112; iwonne *p.p.* 48.1

winter *pl.* (after num.) years 20.106

wirch(e) *v.* perform 13.3, 21.3, carry out
13.187, 20.136, 33.195; wrochte *pa. 3
sg.* made, composed 4.60, wrowȝte
4.71, wroȝt(e) 4.102, 5.141, *þe* ∼
prepared for you 22.35; iwroȝt *p.p.*
made 4.5, committed (sin) 14.82,
created 14.121, 15.109, iwrowȝte made
4.95

wirssip *n.* honour, veneration 21.36,
  worsip 20.6
wis *adv.* truly 21.51
wise *n.* manner, in *in none* ~ by no
  means 14.48, *in alle* ~ in all respects
  15.149
wist *see* wit(te); wit *see* witi
wiþ *prep.* with 2.110, 4.1, 21.79, among
  33.141, among, by 36.92, against 15.39
wiþal *adv.* then 14.75, 137
wiþin(ne) *adv.* inside 4.39n, 14.23, 19.40
wiþir *adj.* wicked 5.91
wiþoute *adv.* outside 4.39n, on the
  outside 13.26, 30, wiþvte 5.55, 19.39
wiþoute(n) *prep.* without 2.169, 5.98,
  apart from 15.67, without 43.11,
  wiþvt(e) 2.18, 20.203, 36.88
wiþstond *v.* hold firm 14.106
witi *v.* guard, watch over 15.120, 135;
  witiþ *pr. 3 sg.* 15.112; wit *imp. sg.*
  guard 21.67
witles *adj.* foolish 3.4
witnes *n.* witness, testimony 21.73
witte *n.* mind, intelligence 4.12, 5.91,
  14.56
wit(te) *v.* know, find out 5.33, 20.119;
  wost *pr. 2 sg.* 33.174; wot(e) *3 sg.* 2.34,
  103, 4.23; witte *pl.* 36.16; wist *pa. 3
  sg.* 20.89
witti *adj.* wise ; *be* ~ have wisdom 20.62
wiue(s) *see* wif; wl *see* wol
wlaseþ *pr. 3 sg.* mumbles 39.67n
wnde *see* wonde; wo *see* who
wo *n.* woe, misery 5.119, 14.166 13.131,
  19.14, ~ *is him* he is sorry 4.80, 33.156
woch *adj.* which 15.166, 20.120, whoch
  33.197
wodde *n.* wood 36.29
wode *n.* fury 13.122n
wode *adj.* mad 14.49, 21.14
wodwale *n.* woodwall (songbird) 2.97n
woȝ *n.* sin 20.203n, *wiþ* ~ sinfully 2.62,
  wouȝ state of sin 33.156, wow(e)
  wretchedness 15.16, wowȝ injustice,
  wrongful power 48.1, 41
woke *see* wak
wol *pr. 1 sg.* will, shall 15.50, 19.22, wl
  13.127; ichul (with pron.) 14.9, 20.55;
  wolt 2. *sg.* 20.62; wol *3. sg.* wishes to
  2.167, will 15.117, 21.8, wl 2.177; wol
  pl. 2.180, 5.22, will 14.159; wol *2. sg.
  subj.* 20.167; wil *imp. sg.* desire 21.66;
  wold *pa. 1 sg.* I would like 39.58;

wold *3 sg.* would, wanted to 5.46,
  15.15, was accustomed to 36.22, 58,
  wol 20.164; woldist *2 sg.* would wish
  to 13.118; wold *pl.* would wish 33.80,
  were accustomed to 36.60; wold *pa. sg.
  subj.* wanted to 5.50; ~ *he* if he would
  13.157, 33.17; *pl. subj.* would, should
  (expressing condit. future) 13.14, 14.19
wolf *n.* wolf 2.31, 33.52, 54
wolle *n.* wool 4.109
wollin *n.* wool clothing 15.92
wolny nulni *adv.* willingly or unwillingly
  14.173n
wol-sackes *n. pl.* bales of wool 4.62
wom(e) *n.* womb 14.23, 25
wom(m)an *n.* woman 2.30, 3.5, 14.5
won *n.* distress 20.75
wonde *n.* wound 5.110, wnde 19.4;
  wondis *pl.* 5.28, 13.116, wondes
  19.36, wound 21.15
wonder *n.* strange thing 20.165, 21.9, (it
  is a) wonder 21.55; wondres *pl.* awful
  events 14.7, wond(e)ris 14.99,130
wonder *adj.* extraordinary 14.101
wone *n.* custom, habitual practice 4.14,
  abode (of life) 14.164
woni *v.* dwell 5.115, live 13.208, 216,
  remain 15.77; woniþ *pr. pl.* live 2.16,
  4.117; woned *p.p.* accustomed 4.16
woningis *n. pl.* dwellings 13.209
wonne *see* win(ne)
word(e) *n.* word 4.78, 13.211, 15.52;
  wordes *pl.* 13.5, wordis 13.147
wore *see* be; workis *see* werk
world *n.* the world 2.184, 13.163, 14.30;
  worldis *gen.* 5.11,14.6, 15.16
worldlich *adj.* worldly 15.96
worme *n.* worm 2.40; wormis *pl.*
  worms, maggots 13.29, 42, 59, wormes
  48.14; wormeis *gen.* 13.27
worp *pr. 3 sg.* in *þe* ~ destined for you
  22.29
wors *adj. comp.* worse 14.35, 21.13
worsip *see* wirssip
worþ *adj.* fitting 4.83
worþe *pr. 2 sg.* (as fut.) will be 13.104,
  131; worþ *3 sg.* (aux. of fut.) will be
  5.36, 14.66, 70, 112, wurþ in *hit* ~
  ibroȝt it will be brought about 14.87;
  worþ *impers.* in *þe* ~ you will be
  20.63n; *pr. pl.* 14.42, 130
worþi *v.* reverence 21.36
worþi *adj.* fit 5.29, precious 21.15

worþing *n.* reverence 20.9, *to* ~ in honouring 15.5

wost, wote *see* wit(te); wouȝ, wow(e), wowȝ *see* woȝ; wound *see* wonde; wouw *see* hou

wowel *n.* vowel 4.18

wowes *n. pl.* town-walls 4.111

wrake *n.* retribution 5.119

wrec(c)h *n.* wretched person, miser 13.73, unfortunate person 21.60, wicked person 5.130, brute 33.183, villain 36.121; wrec(c)his *pl.* wretches 13.81n, 21.40, 43

wrec(c)h(e) *adj.* wretched 4.64, 15.17, 22.10

wrech(e) *n.* vengeance 13.120, retribution 14.156, destruction 13.132, misery, misfortune 21.10, wreech retribution 21.55

wreiiþ *pr. pl.* accuse 33.79; wreiid *pa. pl.* denounced 33.107; iwreiid *p.p.* accused 33.54, 59, 116, denounced 33.101

wrekke *n.* avenge 13.123

wreþ *n.* anger 14.100, 33.5

wrikkend *pr. p.* moving 48.13n

wringer *n.* squeezer, (fig.) miser 13.85

wringit *pr. pl.* wring out, squeeze 13.81n

writ(te) *n.* written document 4.66; in *Holi* ~ the Bible 4.11, 5.91, 20.107

wrochte, wrowȝte, wroȝt(e) *see* wirch(e)

wronge *adj.* bent, badly shaped 4.68

wrot *n.* snout, nose 39.11n

wroten *v.* wriggle 48.18

wroþ *adj.* angry 2.30

wurþ *see* worþe

ANGLO-NORMAN

Line references are to 'The Walling of New Ross' (text 40), unless prefaced by F or S, referring to text 11, 'Folie fet' and 'Soule su', respectively.

A

a *prep.* at 184, at (time) 24, to 18, 34; al *prep.* + *art.* to the 57, at the 69; au 49

a, ai *see* auer

acez *adv.* enough 168

ad *see* auer

afie *pr. 3 sg. refl.* put one's trust in F1

aillie *n.* clove of garlic 4n

aketun *n.* acton, padded jerkin 170

aler *v.* go 26, 205; vete *pr. 3 sg.* 70; vont *3 pl.* 31, 204, vount 61; alerent *pret. 3 pl.* 18, 25, 32; aleint *imperf. (for pret.) 3 pl.* 27; irrunt *fut. 3 pl.* would go 45

amdeus *adj.* both 12

an *n.* year (in final rubric)

apeint *pr. 3 sg.* befits 91

apeler *v.* call 15

aporter *v.* carry 127; aportee *p.p.* 140

apres *adv.* afterwards 78; *prep.* after 72, 106

arblasters *n. pl.* cross-bow men 172, 182

arblestes *n. pl.* crossbows 176

arc *n.* in ~ *de main* hand-bow 173

archers *n. pl.* bowmen 173, 186

armes *n. pl.* arms 204

armés *p.p.* armed 191

arollez *p.p.* inscribed 185

as *prep.* + *art.* to the 204

asailler *v.* attack 201

auberk *n.* hauberk, plate armour 169

aubersuns *n. pl.* habergeons, coats of mail 169

aucer *v.* speak? 6

ausi *adv.* also 104, ~ *com* just as 95, ~ *tost cum* as soon as 56

autre *pron.* the other 148; *adj.* other 65, 188, another 87; autres *n. pl.* others 106

autresi *adv.* likewise 117

auant *prep.* in ~ *qe* before 143

auer *v.* have 163; ai *pr. 1 sg.* 134, 174; a *3 sg.* 205, *i* ~ there are 89, ~ *en confort* encourages 148, n'ad there is not 200; ont *3 pl.* have 62, 140; auoint *imperf. (for pret.) pl.* had 10, 23, 28; auera *fut. 3 sg.* 150, 153; auereit *cond. 3 sg.* there would be 76

B

bachelers *n. pl.* apprentices 89n

baner *n.* banner 70, 90; *pl.* baners 54, 58

barouns *n. pl.* barons 11

bataile *n.* battle 193

bateus *n. pl.* boats 75

beiuent *pr. 3 pl.* drink 146

bel(es) *adj.* good 51, fine 73, lovely 8, 129; **beus** *pl.* fine 89

ben *adv.* well 6, 41, **bien** 132, at least, fully 73, 84, 100

blame *n.* accusation 154

blamer *v.* blame 196

blank *adj.* fair 133, **blanc** shining 169

ble *n.* corn 98

bon(e) *adj.* good 123, 136; **bons** *pl.* 147

bonement *adv.* well 50

burgeis *n. pl.* burgesses, townspeople 32

burnet *n.* dark cloth 130

C

carpenters *n. pl.* carpenters 115

ce *pron.* that which, what 17, this 121, c'est it is 16

cel *adj.* that 23

celers *n. pl.* saddlers 80

cent *n.* a hundred 30; **cenz** *pl.*73, **cens** 76, 84, 101

cert *adj.* in *de* ~ for sure 124

certein *n.* firm ground 213

Chandeler *n.* Candlemass (2nd February) 24

chanter *v.* sing 142; **chantant** *pr. p.* 59; **chantent** *pr. 3 pl.* 102; **chanté** *p.p.* sung (mass) 62

charité *n.* in *amen pur* ~ 211n

chater *v.* buy 216

chescun *pron.* everyone 148, 205; *adj.* each 30, every 53, 178

chiual *n.* horse, *a* ~ on horseback 190

choiser *v.* look 137

cil *pron.* that one 136

clos *p.p.* enclosed 17

colouree *p.p.* as *adj.* complexioned 133

com *prep.* like 103

combater *v.* fight 191

coment *adv.* how 26

command *pr. 1 sg.* commend 217

commencerent *pret. 3 pl.* began 24

commune *n.* people, community 19, 39, 41

conseil *n.* deliberation 18, 34, decision 20

conter *v.* count 125; **contez** *p.p.* 184

corage *n.* spirit 120

coraius *adj.* courageous 206

corant *pr. p.* running 204

cordiwaners *n. pl.* cobblers 88

corne *n.* horn 202

cornee *p.p.* sounded (horn) 202

crier *v.* made an announcement 38

cum *conj.* as 82

D

dame *n.* lady 129; **dames** *pl.* 122, 150

de, d' *prep.* of 7, 121, from 195, to (with infin.) 1, 2, 5

deboner *adj.* noble 156

dedens *adv.* within 71, 167, 219; *par* ~ therein 108

defendre *v.* in ~ *de* resist 181

deit *p. 3. sg.* ought to S4; **deuez** *pr. 2 pl.* should 15; **dut** *pret. 3 sg.* ought to 26, 196; **dussent** *imperf. subj. 3 pl.* would have to 49

deke *prep.* until 48

demainge *n.* Sunday 122

demandra *fut. 3 sg.* will demand 217

demy *n.* half 113, 118

depoint *p.p.* depicted 71, **depeint** 90, **depeins** 109

derer *adv.* behind 106

desirent *pr. 3 pl.* want 193

despendre *v.* use 177

Deu *n.* God 208, 218, **Deus** 210

deus *num.* two 11, 111*, 202*

deuant *adv.* before 82, ahead, in front 58, 114, **deuont** 70; *par* ~ earlier, above 103, ahead 107

die *pr. 1 sg.* say 52, **di** 154, 182; **dient** *3 pl.* 149; **diez** *2 pl. subj.* 211; **dit** *p.p.* 82

diuers *adj.* various 99

doint *pr. subj. 3 sg.* give, grant 208

dormir *v.* sleep 164

drapers *n. pl.* cloth sellers 46

durement *adv.* hard 64

dussent, dut *see* deit

duze *num.* twelve 186*

E

e *conj.* and 19, 97, 216

en *adv.* about it 38, in this regard 121, from there 70

en *prep.* in 7, 9, F1, on 105, by F4, (with *pr. p.*) 115

endemain *n.* next day 38

enemi *n.* enemy 207; **enemis** *pl.* 181

enparler *v.* speak of 159

ensemblement *adv.* together 47

ensembler *v.* assemble 39; **ensemblerent** *pret. 3 pl.* 19*; **ensemblés** *p.p.* gathered 145, 203

entrer *v.* go inside 143; **entrunt** *fut. 3 pl.*
   enter 167; *p.p.* **entré(s)** 144, 152
enture *prep.* around 22, 32, **entur** 142
enueisurus *n. pl.* jokes 147
envie *n.* in *a* ~ *pur* is keen to 205
envuysés *p.p. as adj.* dashing 66
escarlet *n.* fine wool material 130n
escoteir *v.* listen 2; **escoter** 5
escrit *p.p.* written 12
escuz *n. pl.* shields 179
esgarder *v.* watch 128
espleiterent *pret. 3 pl.* achieved 33
esquele *n.* bowl 108
estant *pr. p.* standing 115
estrange *adj.* in *hom* ~ outsider 214n
estre *v.* be 155, S6; **su** *pr. 1 sg.* S1; **est** *3
   sg.* is 3, 71, S7; **sunt** *3 pl.* are 66, 68,
   90; **sei** *pr. 1 sg. subj.* S3; **seit** *3 sg. subj.*
   may be 210; **fu** *pret. 3 sg.* was 11, 17,
   37, **fut** 128; **furent** *3 pl.* 7, 184, 188;
   fusent *imperf. subj. 3 pl.* 74; **serra** *fut.
   3 sg.* will be 162, 198; **serreit** *cond. 3
   sg.* would be 155; **esté** *p.p.* been 134,
   174
eus *see* il

F

failire *v.* fail F2
faille *n.* in *tot sanz* ~ without any doubt
   192
fameler *v.* go hungry F6
fausyne *n.* deceit F7, F8
faux *see* fiaux
fauelons *pr. p.* sweet talking F4
feble *adj. as n.* weak person F6, F7
feez *n. pl.* times 202
feie *n.* faith, trust F8
feire *v.* make 22, **fere** act as 157n, cause,
   bring about F4; **fet** *pr. 3 sg.* makes F2,
   fest F5, F7; **funt** *3 pl.* do, act 50, 65,
   make F3, **fount** F6; **firent** *pret. 3 pl.*
   caused to be 38; **fra** *fut. 3 sg.* will
   cause F8; **ferunt** *3 pl.* will make 149,
   151; **fet** *p.p.* composed (in final rubric)
fem *n.* woman 133
fere *adj.* violent F5, **fiers** F6
ferme *adj.* firm F8
fermer *v.* enclose 197; **fermé** *p.p.* 198
fest, fet *see* feire
feuers *n. pl.* smiths 117
fiaux *adj. as n. pl.* falsehoods F3,
   deceivers F5, **faux** F6

fie *pr. 3 sg. refl.* in *sa* ~ relies on F1
firent *see* feire
flatire *v.* flatter F4
floites *n. pl.* flutes 55
folie *n.* foolishness F3; *fet* ~ acts
   foolishly F1
force *n.* force, strength F1, F2, F5
forts *adj.* strong 67, **fort** in *funt* ~ make
   strong F3
fortune *n.* fortune F2
fosse, fossee *n.* ditch 25, 32, 49
fount *see* feire
franch *adj.* free, enfranchised 212
fremir *v.* tremble F7
fuir *v.* flee F5
fulrurs *n. pl.* fullers (of cloth) 80
fundre *v.* founder, collapse F8
funt *see* feire

G

gard *n.* in *n'auerunt* ~ *de* will not be
   worried about 165
garder *v.* protect 194, 209
garnesuns *n. pl.* armaments 168
garnis *p.p.* provisioned 180
garsun *n.* lad 171
gayte *n.* watchman 163
gent *n.* people 33, 51, 59
gerre *n.* war 10, **geere** 23
glenné *n. pl.* sheaves of arrows 175
gonfanuns *n. pl.* pennants 99
grand *n.* size 8
grand *adj.* great, large 31, 93, 101, **grant**
   61, 215 **grans** *pl.* 67, **grantz** noble 54

H

habitand *pr. p.* living 219
haches *n. pl.* axes 189
hardi *adj.* brave 200, 206
haut *adv.* loudly 59, 102
hautement *adv.* loudly 94
hom(e) *n.* man 125, 196, 217
honur *n.* distinction 31, 101, *a* ~
   honourably 209; **honurs** *pl.* emblems 54
hors *adv.* outside 127

I

i, y *adv.* there 31, 51, 53
i *see* il
icel *adj.* this 100, 105

il *pron. nom.* he 129; **li** *acc.* him 217, **le** it
15; **eus** *pl. nom.* they 50, 168, 193, **i**
66; **les** *acc.* them 196; **i** *dat.* to them 43
yle *n.* island 213
incarnation *n.* incarnation (in final
rubric)
Ires *n.* Irishman 200
irrunt *see* **aler**
issi *adv.* thus 110

J

ia *adv.* (in neg.) never 157, 163
ie *pron.* I 9, 92, 118, **me** 6
ieter *v.* throw out 126
ieuene *adj.* young 59, **ieuenz** 66
ioi *n.* joy 61, 215
iour(e) *n.* day 18, 30, **iure** day 100
Iudi *n.* Thursday 96, 105
iuent *pr. 3 pl.* play 146

K

kant *see* **quant**
kar *conj.* because 3, 66
karoler *v.* dance and sing 60, 94;
karolent *pr. 3 pl.* 102,146
ke *see* **qe**
kiqe *pron.* whoever 128

L

la *adv.* there 129, 151
laborer *v.* work 61
lances *n. pl.* lances 189
le *def. art.* the; *masc. nom. sg.* 16, 26; *acc.*
15, 28; **la** *fem. nom sg.* 19, 41; *acc.* 14,
25; **le** *pl.* 45, 75, **li** 57, **les** 62, 122, **lez**
47, 97, 196, **liz** 27
le, **les** *see* **il**
leireit *cond. 3 sg.* be fitting 157
lesser *v.* in **me** ∼ stop 158
li *see* **il**, **le**
lowis *adj.* hired 33
lue *n.* league (distance) 161
lundi *n.* Monday 44, 53
lung *n.* length 161
lur *pron.* in ∼ **deuant** ahead of them 138;
lur(e) *poss. adj.* their 18, 34, 81, **loure**
185

M

macecrers *n. pl.* butchers 88
maces *n. pl.* maces, spiked clubs 178

male *adj.* bad 165
mandé *p.p.* in ∼ **pur** sent for 29
maner *n.* manner, way 20, 69, kind,
group 87
mantel *n.* mantle 130
marchans *n. pl.* merchants 46
mardi *n.* Tuesday 78
mariners *n. pl.* mariners 68
masuns *n. pl.* masons 117
maueis *adj.* wicked 195
me *see* **ie**, **mes**
meimes *adj.* the same 105, 189*
meint *adj.* many a 129, 130, 133
mekirdi *n.* Wednesday 86
mercers *n. pl.* textile dealers 46
mercher *v.* mark out 25, 27; **merché**
p.p. 28
mes *conj.* but 10, 83, 164, **me** 192; ∼ **ke**
even if 166
mester *n.*[1] need, in **n'auera** ∼ there will
be no need 163
mester *n.*[2] trade 91; **mesters** *pl.* 81
mile *num.* thousand 52, 166, 188
morter *n.* mortar 21
mostresun *n.* muster 184
moune *poss. adj.* my S3
mult, **mut** *adj.* many 173, 89, 118; *adv.*
very 50, 64, greatly136
mure *n.* wall 21, 26, 28
mustra *pret. 3 sg.* presented 43; **mustré**
p.p. 40

N

ne *adv.* not 124, **n'** 3; **ne** . . . **pas** 4, 154;
conj. nor 37(2)
nee *p.p.* born 136
nef *n.* ship 71; **nefs** *pl.* 75
nombre *n.* number 124
nomer *v.* name 14, count 124
noun *n.* name 14; **auera a** ∼ will be
called 150; **nuns** *pl.* 12
nouel *adj.* new 16
nule *adj.* any 9, 193, no 125, 154
nune *n.* nones, i.e. about 3 p.m. 48,
noune 56

O

od *prep.* with 31, 101, 189, **o** 54
oiés *pr. 2 pl.* hear 6; **oie** *p.p.* heard 3
ont *see* **auer**
ore *adv.* now 158
orle *n.* edge 115

oserent *cond. 3 pl.* would dare 201
ostel *n.* house, home 57, 68, **oustel** 178;
  outeus *pl.* in *a l'* $\sim$ at home 74n
ou *adv.* where 134, 174
ou *conj.* or 30
oue *prep.* with 61; in *qe* $\sim$ . . . $\sim$ both
  . . . and 93
oure, vre *n.* hour 48, 136, time 162
outeus *see* ostel
ouere *n.* work 123
ouerer *v.* work 31, 49, **ouerir** 51, 53
ouerors *n. pl.* workmen 29

P

paié *p.p.* satisfied 41, 210
par *prep.* through 60; **par entre** *prep.*
  between 11
pareis *n. pl.* walls 176
parfeit *adj.* completed 162
parfunt *adj.* deep 160
parmenters *n. pl.* furriers 79*
parole *n.* word 3
parolent *pr. 3 pl.* speak 147
parpunt *n.* doublet 170
part *n.* in *de autre* $\sim$ in addition 188
pees *n. pl.* feet (measure) 160
peissun *n.* fish 108; *pl.* 98
pendre *v.* hang 176
pere *n.* stone 21, 126, 139
pesturs *n. pl.* bakers 96
petit *adj.* small, little 93, S6
plein *adj.* full 178
plest *pr. 3 sg.* it pleases 141, **plet** in *s'il*
  vous $\sim$ if you wish 2
pleui *pr. 1 sg.* promise 118, **pleuis** 180
plus *n.* more 30, 52; $\sim$ *de* more than 76
plus *adv.* most 8, 212; $\sim$ *qe* more than 65
poi *adv.* little 33
pont *n.* bridge 16
port *n.* gate 140, 150
portant *pr. p.* carrying 139*
porturs *n. pl.* porters, bearers 112*
poure *n.* fear 10, 17, 23
pouer *n.* in *a lur* $\sim$ with all their might
  195
prent *pr. 3 sg.* takes 1; **pristerent** *pret. 3
  pl.* 20
prestres *n. pl.* priests 62
prie *pr. 1 sg.* ask 5
prime *n.* prime, daybreak 48
primer *n. pl.* first ones 95, **primers** 103
primers *adv.* in *tot* $\sim$ at the beginning 44

prisune *n.* prison 151, 152
prochein *adj.* next 78, 86
prodome *n.* freeholder 42; **prodome(s)**
  pl. 27n, 57
puit *pr. 3 sg.* can 125, **put(e)** 216, might
  129; **puunt** *3 pl.* can 164; **purreit**
  cond. 3 sg. could 137
pur *prep.* for 154; (with infin.) in order to
  128; $\sim$ *ce* for this reason 5
purparlerent *pret. 3 pl.* discussed 35
purueans *n.* arrangement 35, **purueance**
  36, 40

Q

qe *pron.* which 3, that 9, 11, that which
  (is) 121, who 98, 184, whoever 152, the
  one who F1, S8
qe, ke *conj.* that 17, 21, 149, because 23,
  182
quan *conj.* when 62, **quant** 140, 144
quarant *num.* forty 166*
quarels *n. pl.* crossbow bolts 177
quatre *num.* four 84*, 101*, 190
quit *pr. 3 sg.* think 92

R

realerent *pret. 3 pl.* returned 34
reen *n.* anything 217
regraturs *n. pl.* retailers 97n
rescev *p.p.* received 215
richez *adj.* rich, great 145
ridee *adj.* pleated 132
rimaunceir *v.* write poetry in French 1
roket *n.* gown 132
rol *n.* muster roll 185

S

sa *poss. adj.* its 8, his 153
sache *pr. subj. 1 sg.* know 9; **sachez** *imp.*
  pl. 77, 85, 121*
sage *adj.* sensible 121
sagesse *n.* wisdom S4
sai *pr. 1 sg.* know how to, can 124
samadi *n.* Saturday 116
saunz *prep.* without S1, S8
sauage *adj.* wild 171
se *pron. indef.* (= *ce*) it S7(1)
se *pron. refl.* itself S4, oneself S7(2)
sei *see* estre
Seignur *n.* in *Nostre* $\sim$ Our Lord (in
  final rubric)
seignury *n.* noble rank S2

seissant *num.* sixty 183*
seit, serra, serreit *see* **estre**
sent *pr. 3 sg.* in *se* ~ considers her/
himself to be S8
si *adv.* and 5, thus 50, then 63, so 200, in
such a way 208
si *conj.* if 74, S3; ~ *com, cum* as 91, 92
simple *adj.* single, unmarried S1
sis *num.* six 73*
soiorner *v.* remain, stay S2, S5; **soiornés**
p.p. rested 67
solacer *v.* bring comfort S4; *refl.* S7
solai *imperf. 1 sg.* I was accustomed S5
solas *n.* comfort S1, S3, S6, S8
solein *adj.* solitary S6
somount *pr. 3 sg.* urges, instructs S2
souereyn *adj.* most important S7
soule *adj.* alone S1, S5, S8; **soul** *adv.*
alone S4
soune *pr. 3 sg.* strikes 56, **sonee** *p.p.*
sounded, was rung 48
su, sunt *see* **estre**
suent *pr. p.* following 72, 78, **suant** 86
suppris *p.p.* struck down S3
surement *adv.* soundly 164
susleua *pret. 3 sg.* got up 42

T

taburs *n. pl.* tabors 55
taillurs *n. pl.* tailors 79
talent *n.* wish, in ~ *me prent* I feel like 1
tannors *n. pl.* tanners 88
tant, tantz *adj. & adv.* so 206, so many
83, 135, 175; in ~ *cum* while 139, as
much as 141
tantost *adv.* at once 203
teint *pr. 3 sg.* in ~ *de vei* extends 161
tele *adj.* this 20, such 36
tenturers *n. pl.* dyers 80
tere *n.* land 9, 134
tolfaces *n. pl.* wooden bucklers 179n
tost *adv.* quickly 29, 204
tot, totz, tut, tuz *n. and adj.* all 19, 39,
75,126, every 214, everything 153; **tous**
n. pl. everyone 219; *de* ~ entirely 210
tot *adv.* fully 162, 199
trauellent *pr. 3 pl.* work 64
treis *num.* three 92*, 113*, 118*

trent *num.* thirty 111*
trestuz *adj.* all 97
tut, tuz *see* **tot**

U

vn, vne *indef. art* a 4, 7, 149
vnkes *adv.* ever 36, never 134, 174
vnt *pr. 3 pl.* have 29, 168, 202
vnze *num.* eleven 76*
vre *see* **oure**

V

uaut *pr. 3 sg.* is worth 4
ueir, veir, voir *n.* truth, in *pur* ~ truly
52, 77, 85, 187; **ueires** in *de* ~ truly
123
uendredi *n.* Friday 112
uenissent *imperf. subj. 3 pl.* should come
166
veer *v.* see 129; **vi** *pret. 1 sg.* 135, 175;
vei *imp.* in ~ *ci* see here are 12
vendre *v.* sell 216; **uendunt** *pr. 3 pl.* 98
venger *v.* in *en* ~ take vengeance 208; in
~ *de* avenge on 207
venu *p.p.* in *ben* ~ welcomed 214
verd *n.* green 131
verité *n.* in *pur* ~ truly 111
vers *n.* truth, in *pur* ~ truly 182
vete *see* **aler**; **vi** *see* **veer**
vile *n.* town 7, 14, 22
vilein *n.* villein, low-born person 157n
vineters *n. pl.* wine-merchants 45, 47
vint *num.* twenty 160*
vironé *p.p.* encircled 199
viuant *pr. p.* as *adj.* living 125
voil *pr. 1 sg.* wish 14, 158; **voilent** *pret. 3
pl.* 22
voir *see* **ueir**
volen *pr. 3 pl.* wish 143, **voleint** 194
uolunté *n.* desire 137, 141, 153
vont *see* **aler**
vous *pron. acc. pl.* you 5, 52, 118, **vus**
182

W

waynpayns *n. pl.* labourers 104n

INDEX OF PROPER NAMES

MIDDLE ENGLISH

ANGLO-NORMAN